UNDER THE BIG STICK

UNDER THE BIG STICK

*Nicaragua
and the
United States
Since
1848*

by Karl Bermann

South End Press
Boston

Manufactured in the USA
Production at South End Press, Boston

Library of Congress Cataloging-in-Publication Data

Bermann, Karl.
   Under the big stick.

   Includes index.
   1. United States—Foreign relations—Nicaragua.
2. Nicaragua—Foreign relations—United States.
I. Title.
E183.8.N5B46   1986   327.7285073   86-1767

ISBN: 0-89608-324-1   cloth
ISBN: 0-89608-323-3   paper

SOUTH END PRESS • 116 St. Botolph Street • Boston MA   02115

CONTENTS

ACKNOWLEDGMENTS

I would like to thank those people whose critiques, suggestions, encouragement, and other assistance at various stages have helped make this book possible: the members of the Tidewater Nicaragua Project Foundation, Holly Sklar at South End Press, Eugenia Monroy and Roberto Cajinas of the Instituto de Estudio de Sandinismo in Managua, Dick McCleary, and Carl Griffler.

I also wish to express my gratitude to the helpful personnel of the Interlibrary Loan Department at the Charles Taylor Memorial Library, Hampton, Virginia, and the Government Documents Department of the Old Dominion University Library, Norfolk, Virginia.

WHY THIS BOOK?

It was remarked by a participant at a conference I attended that in the United States we have tunnel vision, and the tunnel is a short one. Nowhere does this comment ring more true than in our country's relationship with Nicaragua.

Though the media spotlight has been on that nation since the Sandinista National Liberation Front overthrew the Somoza dynasty in 1979, the news commentators rarely hint that Nicaragua has been the object of public attention in the United States many times before. Few people in the US are aware that we have intervened more persistently in Nicaragua than in any other country in the hemisphere except Mexico and Cuba, whose geographic proximity to the United States has historically put them in a special category. Today's confrontation between the US and Nicaragua did not begin in 1979; it is but the latest chapter in a story that began more than 130 years ago.

As part of our nation's armed forces, as members of privately-organized groups, or as mercenaries, North Americans in large numbers fought in two full-scale wars in Nicaragua and joined—or helped to suppress— uprisings, rebellions, and civil disturbances. US Marines and sailors have landed there at least eleven times since 1853. In this century they occupied the country for two decades, during which it became a virtual colony of the United States. When they pulled out they left behind many ties of dependency, not the least of which was a US-organized and -trained National Guard headed by Anastasio Somoza.

Alone, these particulars might evoke little interest among North Americans. Teddy Roosevelt's "big stick" and intervention are implicit in our image of "banana republics." (Perhaps that partly explains why this history has been so easily forgotten.) But while the "big stick" phrase may have originated with Roosevelt, the policy certainly did not, nor did it end with him. And US involvement in Nicaragua has had little to do with bananas.

Before embarking on this project I was acquainted with many of the Marine landings and other dramatic incidents of our involvement in Nicaragua. But uncovering the reasons for the intervention became a detective work of more than two years' duration. What emerged was more intricate and more extensive than I ever imagined. The Marines, the gunboats, the carnage—all had their place. But the truly momentous intervention, that which disfigured a small nation, was often conducted in back rooms by men in pin-stripe suits.

The "Colossus of the North," as the US was long known in Latin America, has intervened repeatedly in many countries of Central America and the Caribbean, with motives and results similar to those in Nicaragua. But Nicaragua, perhaps more than any other country in the region, is a case study in intervention. It is a country whose political, economic, and social outlines have been formed by intervention.

What is more, the occupation of Nicaragua early in this century, and Sandino's rebellion against it, galvanized opposition to "Yankee imperialism" throughout the hemisphere. The repercussions from that intervention were largely responsible for a rethinking of US policy toward Latin America during the 1920s and '30s that resulted in a shelving of the rhetoric of the Monroe Doctrine and a retreat from overt military interventionism. Though the United States never renounced its "right" to intervene unilaterally, Latin opposition to *El Gran Garrote*—The Big Stick—did lead to creation of the Organization of American States (OAS) and other agencies through which the US hoped to avert criticism by giving its actions a multinational coloring.

With the 1983 invasion of Grenada and the growing United States military involvement in Central America the question of intervention seems to have come full circle, and Nicaragua is again at the center. While the backlash from its earlier actions there prompted the US to seek lower-profile, less politically-costly means of controlling events in Latin America, more recent developments in Nicaragua have gone hand in hand with what seems to be a return to the methods of the past. When, in 1979, the Carter Administration sought to repeat the 1965 OAS-sponsored intervention in the Dominican Republic, proposing that the OAS send a "peacekeeping" force to Nicaragua to prevent a Sandinista victory, the unanimous opposition it encountered made clear that that organization was not content to be a mere instrument of US policy. At the annual OAS meeting in Cartagena, Colombia, in December 1985, a blowup occurred over the US posture toward Central America, particularly Nicaragua. Afterward, Secretary of State Shultz told journalists he had "had enough of the Sandinistas." He might have added that Washington has had enough of the OAS: the US is no longer willing to endure the restraint that the quest for Latin approval imposes on its actions in the hemisphere.

But the clock cannot be turned back to 1900. For Latin Americans history is a lingering affliction; it is not as easily forgotten as it is with us. The efforts of the Contadora Group—Colombia, Venezuela, Mexico, and Panama—to find a peaceful solution in Central America without asking Washington's permission, whether successful or not, are an important sign of the changed reality. Though the US has publicly blessed the Contadora process (it could hardly do otherwise), it has not been able to conceal its chagrin at the unwelcome intrusion.

The long US involvement in Nicaragua raises larger questions. Is intervening in the affairs of the weak one of the prerogatives of the powerful? Throughout history the Great Powers have found pretexts to assert their dominance over weaker nations. The justifications have sometimes been blatant, as with the Master Race ideology of Nazi Germany or the White Man's Burden of pre-World War I imperialism. On other occasions the rich and powerful have veiled their hegemonic pretensions in hypocrisy. Our own intervention in Nicaragua has often been portrayed as philanthropic.

It is curious that most of us in the United States accept meddling by our government in the affairs of other nations. We would never tolerate anyone intervening to arrange things for us here in this country, nor as a rule, would we ourselves think of interfering in the business of our next-door neighbors.

Nowhere, in fact, is the idea that some nations have more rights than others as ingrained—to the point of being largely unconscious—as in the relations between our country and that portion of the hemisphere that lies to the south of us. That this is especially true in regard to Central America and the Caribbean is expressed by the habit of referring to the area as "our backyard." Even among critics of current US policy in the region there are few who question the assumption that the United States has some "right" to involve itself there.

Today, we are being asked by our government to view the Sandinista revolution in Nicaragua as a threat to our security. We are being called upon to become ever more heavily, and expensively, involved in Central America in order to quarantine that revolution, and to sponsor the *contras,* a group of so-called freedom fighters who are trying to destroy it. It behooves us to know that the Sandinista revolution is itself in large measure a product of the past involvement of our own country, and to the extent that the effects of more than a century of intervention are one of the chief causes of the Nicaraguan revolution, the very thing we are supposed to fear and hate bears the label "Made in USA." It behooves us to know, too, that the policies, the justifications, and even the stirring phrases are all retreads from the past. We are being taken down a road we have been down before, one whose pitfalls are well marked.

Karl Bermann
Hampton Roads, Virginia
March 1986

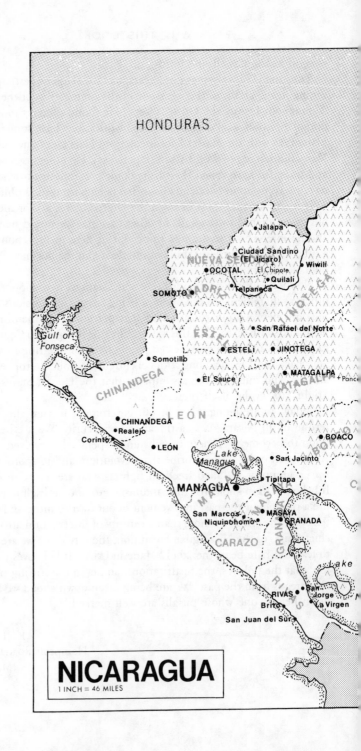

HONDURAS

Jalapa

Ciudad Sandino
(El Jicaro)

NUEVA SEG

OCOTAL El Chipote Wiwili

Quilali

SOMOTO Telpaneca

MADRIZ

JINOTEGA

ESTELI

San Rafael del Norte

Gulf of
Fonseca

Somotillo

ESTELI JINOTEGA

El Sauce

MATAGALPA

MATAGALPA + Panc

CHINANDEGA

LEÓN

BOACO

CHINANDEGA

Realejo

BOACO

Corinto

LEÓN

Lake
Managua

San Jacinto

MANAGUA Tipitapa

MASAYA

San Marcos MASAYA

Niquinohomo GRANADA

CARAZO

GRAN

Lake

RIVAS

San
Jorge

RIVAS La Virgen

Brito

San Juan del Sur

NICARAGUA
1 INCH = 46 MILES

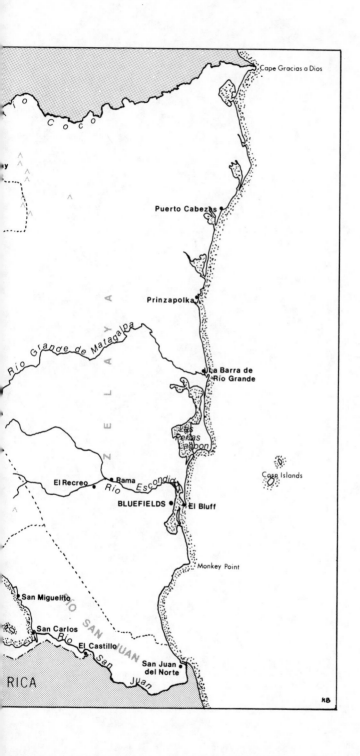

Cape Gracias a Dios

Puerto Cabezas

Prinzapolka

La Barra de
Río Grande

Las
Perlas
Lagoon

Corn Islands

El Recreo   Rama   Río Escondida

BLUEFIELDS   El Bluff

Monkey Point

San Miguelito

San Carlos

El Castillo

San Juan
del Norte

RICA

TWO AMERICAS

THE Spanish colonization of Nicaragua began with the exploration of the country by Gil González de Avila in 1523. At the time of González's arrival, the fertile valleys of the Pacific coast were occupied by the Nicaraos and Chorotegans, Aztec tribes whose ancestors migrated south from Mexico long before. The principal inhabitants of the thinly populated central highlands and Atlantic coast rainforests were the Bawiksas, a people of the same lineage as the Chibchas of present-day Colombia. [1]

The chronicler of the Spanish conquest, Gonzalo Fernández de Oviedo y Valdés, wrote enthusiastically about this new possession of the Spanish crown:

Nicaragua is a grand kingdom, of many and fine provinces, the plains of Nicaragua being among the most lovely and gentle lands to be found in the Indies; they are extremely fertile of cornfields and vegetables; of beans of diverse kinds; of many and varied fruits; of much cacao, which is that fruit resembling the almond that passes among the people as coin and with which all other things are purchased. There is much gathering of honey and wax, much hunting of wild boar and deer, of rabbits and other wild animals, and many good fisheries, in the sea as well as in the rivers and lakes; an abundance of cotton and much fine clothing which the Indians of the land make from it by spinning and weaving.²

Under Spanish colonial rule, Nicaragua, along with the provinces of San Salvador, Guatemala, Chiapas, Honduras, and Costa Rica, comprised the Captaincy-General of Guatemala, part of the Viceroyalty of New Spain. The conquistadors looted what gold was readily at hand. In their wake came the recipients of the royal land grants and the "civilizers" like Friar Bobadilla, who burned the books of the Nicaraos in the plaza of Managua in 1524.³ Under the *encomienda* system, the natives were parceled out to the conquistadors along with the land—their labor was supposed to constitute payment for the blessings of civilization and Christianity. With their culture suppressed and their numbers decimated, the indigenous populations were reduced to peonage on the plantations that exported cocoa, indigo, cattle, hides, and tallow to Spain and to the other provinces of Spanish America. So Nicaragua remained for nearly three hundred years—a stagnant tributary of the Spanish mercantile system. Wrote Nicaraguan historian José Dolores Gámez, "We arrived on the eve of our emancipation speaking bad Castillian, with our heads full of theological and metaphysical questions, but in everything else as destitute and backward as when Nicarao went out to receive Gil González."⁴

TAKING advantage of the brief Liberal interlude that followed the Spanish revolution of 1820,* the provinces of Central America declared their independence from Spain in 1821. But the Conservative aristocracy feared that republicanism would loosen the traditional bonds of the caste system and bring on an Indian-mestizo† uprising like that led by Father Hidalgo in Mexico in 1810-1811. Together with the clergy, therefore, in January 1822 they engineered the annexation of the Central American provinces to the reactionary clericalist regime of Emperor Augustin de Iturbide of Mexico.

But shortly thereafter a Liberal revolt throughout Central America and Mexico brought down Iturbide's empire. In 1823 a congress convened in

---

* The term "Liberal," as it is used here, refers to 19th century Liberals, who idealized the free market economy, individual merit, and the unrestricted pursuit of self-interest. They were generally anti-authoritarian and anti-clericalist, and—at least verbally—championed democratic liberties.

† *Mestizos* are people of mixed Spanish and Indian descent. In colonial times they formed a class of social outcasts whose lot was little better than that of the Indians.

Guatemala City to create the United Provinces of Central America—a republican federation of five of the six original provinces (Chiapas decided to remain part of Mexico). The new federal constitution borrowed heavily from that of the United States.

Unfortunately, it was a union without unity. Though a section of the dominant landowning class was influenced by progressive ideas, arrayed against it was the power of the Catholic Church, in which the spirit of the Inquisition was still very much alive. Arm in arm with the clergy were the former Spanish nobles, principally those in the capital, Guatemala City. Guarding their privileges against the corrosive effects of the new democratic environment, these powerful reactionary forces encouraged opposition among the propertied classes throughout the federation.

Typical of the latter was José Manuel de la Cerda, a landowner from Rivas, Nicaragua. De la Cerda had spent several years in a Spanish prison for revolutionary activity and had been a delegate to the Constituent Assembly that proclaimed the federal republic. Nonetheless, as Nicaragua's first chief of state under the federation, he decreed a series of reactionary and unpopular laws and prohibitions that inaugurated a long era of bloodshed in that province. De la Cerda was compared to "the feudal lords of the Middle Ages . . . He was incapable of stealing a penny; yet he smiled with pleasure when they presented him with the ears of his enemies, impaled on a sword."[5] De la Cerda fell before a firing squad in 1828.

The reactionaries always aimed at the reestablishment of one or another form of strong, paternalistic regime with which to enforce social "order." Owing to the difficulties of achieving this goal in Central America as a whole and to conflicting interests among themselves, they sought to break the federation into its constituent provinces, taking power in those where they were strongest. They often enjoyed support from the masses—people, in the words of a contemporary, "accustomed to hear no other voice than that of [religious] fanaticism, which fed their credulity with grotesque nonsense, entertained their curiosity with fake miracles and viewed with horror anything that tended to lead them out of their servility and ignorance."[6]

The congenital afflictions of the newborn nation of Central America proved fatal: torn apart by civil war from its inception, the federal republic ended its ephemeral existence in 1838, and Nicaragua became an independent state.

The frailty of the federation is no mystery. Communication between the provinces barely existed, much less anything like a national market, the foundation of the modern state. The large, self-sustaining haciendas of the aristocracy on the one hand, and the subsistence plots of the mestizo and the Indian on the other, resembled more than anything a collection of feudal principalities. The *hacendados* did not exchange the commodities they produced in local or regional markets, they exported them to England and France in return for luxury goods. What roads there were didn't link the provinces with each other, but led from the principal towns to the ports and thence to Europe. Internal commerce, if it may properly be called such, consisted only in the occasional exchange of small surpluses. To the extent that manufacturing existed at all, it was confined to the domestic production of the Indians and the marginalized layers in the towns, who, moreover, carried out these activities only as a sideline. The development of a market economy had not even reached a stage capable of sustaining artisan production on a full-time basis. Nowhere was this more true than in Nicaragua, where as late as 1870 even the most specialized of the haciendas had to depend in large measure on its own production of basic necessities.[7] Under the circumstances Central American union could have been nothing but a utopian dream.

Conditions such as these fettered not only the intercourse between provinces, but commerce within them as well. This was particularly so in Nicaragua, where the two principal cities organized their economic life independently of and, what is more, in rivalry with each other. Granada, on the shore of the Great Lake, was an agricultural and trading center with an outlet on the Atlantic via the Rio San Juan, while León to the north had its face to the Pacific through the port of El Realejo. Each was the urban center of a class of wealthy landowner-merchants who exercised control over the surrounding domains. Each presented itself as the substitute for a nonexistent national state.[8]

It would be a gross oversimplification to view the struggles between Granada and León in terms of emerging capitalists confronting the holdovers of a feudal aristocracy. In Nicaragua, as in all of Central America, both Liberals and Conservatives had one foot on the feudal estate and the other tentatively in the world market. It is true that León, the larger of the two cities, contained a number of middle-sized landholders and a more developed professional class owing to its position as the provincial capital; these groups were naturally attracted to Liberal ideas. But adherence to the Liberal or Conservative banner often had more to do with kinship ties and competition between the two urban centers than it did with progressive or reactionary class interests. This competition blurred the distinctions between Liberals and Conservatives more than anywhere else in Central America.

While Granada had been the more prosperous of the two cities under Spanish rule, and revolutionary ideas had made correspondingly less headway there, the city nevertheless had its share of Liberals. León, on the other hand, had a reputation as the center of Liberalism despite its being the seat of the diocese of the Catholic Church—the most conservative institution in society. In the recurring civil wars that plagued Nicaragua to an even greater degree than the rest of Central America, questions of principle soon became lost; the conflict degenerated into a blood feud between the two cities, each allied with its respective hinterlands. One group—a hodgepodge of Liberals and Conservatives—marched out under the red banner of León to slaughter and be slaughtered by a like party marching under the white flag of Granada.

To a limited extent Central American Liberalism did represent democratic ideas, but it had another face as well. Its advocacy of free trade in an already-developed world market, dominated by British manufacture, was not progressive: the resulting competition from cheap foreign goods undercut any possibility for development of local manufacture and alienated sections of the people that should have been the Liberals' natural allies. Though their promotion of public education and restriction of church privilege was laudable, the Liberals' encouragement of colonization by foreigners as the impetus to development was naive at best, disastrous at worst, and helped to undercut whatever support from the masses they might have otherwise had. The existence of the Liberals at all, indeed the acceptance of—or lip-service paid to—the ideas of republicanism and federalism by both Liberals and Conservatives, owed more to the hegemony that Liberal-democratic thought had attained in all corners of the globe since the North American and French revolutions than to the development of modern economic relations in Central America itself.

WHILE Central Americans were launching their ill-fated project of union, French intervention in Spain had restored the throne to Ferdinand VII, and it was rumored that the "Holy Alliance" of continental European reaction was planning to raise an armada to resubjugate Spain's lost American colonies.

Early in 1823 British Foreign Secretary George Canning called in Richard Rush, the US minister in London, to discuss with him the project of a joint British-US declaration against any such scheme for restoration of Spain's former possessions. Britain, the world's leading industrial and trading power, was already conducting a highly lucrative commerce with the newly-independent states of Latin America and opposed any reversion to colonial arrangements that might interfere with free trade. Discussion on Canning's proposal took place throughout 1823. But the United States ultimately decided to steal a jump on the English, issuing its own unilateral declaration. This was contained in President James Monroe's annual message to Congress delivered on December 2, 1823. Decades later, the statement would be resurrected from virtual oblivion and proclaimed as the

"Monroe Doctrine." The United States would present itself in the guise of a shepherd protecting Latin Americans from the European wolves, the so-called Monroe Doctrine its magical staff.

The fate of Nicaragua would be closely tied to both the metamorphosis of Monroe's statement and to the underlying evolution of Yankee objectives. In fact, the very phrase "Monroe Doctrine" was first heard in 1853 during congressional debates on the Clayton-Bulwer Treaty, a pact between the United States and Britain dealing primarily with Nicaragua.[9]

The statements that ultimately became known as the Monroe Doctrine really came from two separate parts of President Monroe's 1823 message to Congress. Both, however, derived from the same considerations. Discussing the progress of negotiations with Russia over control of the Pacific Northwest, Monroe had stated, rather offhandedly:

> the occasion has been judged proper for asserting a principle in which the rights and interests of the United States are involved, that the American Continents, by the free and independent condition which they had assumed and maintain, are henceforth not to be considered as subjects for future colonization by any European powers.

In a later part of his message, Monroe referred directly to the prospect of intervention by the Holy Alliance on behalf of Spain. What he had to say on that subject was based on the argument that the Old World and the New were two distinctly separate worlds with "essentially different" political systems, the one monarchical, the other republican. It was likewise based on the offer of a *quid pro quo:* "In the wars of the European powers in matters relating to themselves we have never taken any part, nor does it comport with our policy to do so." The United States would keep out of Old World affairs and the Europeans would be expected to do the same with respect to the Americas, at least those parts that were now independent. Said Monroe:

> We owe it . . . to candor and to the amicable relations existing between the United States and those powers [of the Holy Alliance] to declare that we should consider any attempt on their part to extend their system to any portion of this hemisphere as dangerous to our peace and safety. With the existing colonies or dependencies of any European power we have not interfered and shall not interfere. But with the Governments who have declared their independence and maintained it . . . we could not view any interposition for the purpose of oppressing them, or controlling in any other manner their destiny, by any European power in any other light than as the manifestation of an unfriendly disposition toward the United States . . . It is impossible that the allied powers should extend their political system to any portion of [North or South

America] without endangering our peace and happiness; nor can anyone believe that our southern brethren, if left to themselves, would adopt it of their own accord.[10]

The effect of the message was hardly earthshaking. Dexter Perkins, the noted authority on the Monroe Doctrine, wrote:

The Monroe declaration produced a very slight practical effect in the Old World, except in alienating [British Foreign Secretary] George Canning and arousing his jealousies. Its contemporary importance has been grossly exaggerated by historians of American foreign policy. It did not prevent intervention; it did not alter the views of the continental powers; it did not awaken any particular respect for the United States.

Perkins went on to say that "Bolivar, the most important figure of his day in South America, clearly regarded the message as of minor importance."[11]

In fact, though Bolivar admired the level of development of democratic political institutions in the United States, he distrusted the northern giant, which he believed to be pursuing its own selfish motives in regard to Latin America. In August 1829 he wrote that the United States "seem destined to plague America to misery in the name of liberty." A biographer of Bolivar noted that in the ensuing period, far from any view of the United States as a protector, "There was a universal feeling in South America that this first-born republic, which ought to have helped the younger ones, was, on the contrary, only trying to encourage discord and to foment difficulties so as to intervene at the appropriate moment."[12]

Owing to their close commercial ties with Britain and to her powerful navy, it was that country, not the United States, to which most newly-independent Latin nations looked for aid against any counterrevolutionary onslaught. Those that did seek the United States' protection as a consequence of Monroe's declaration were destined to be disappointed. This would be the experience of Nicaragua some years later. In 1824, just months afterward, both Brazil and Colombia perceived threats to their independence from the Holy Alliance and approached the United States seeking to formalize through treaties the guarantees implied by Monroe. Both were rebuffed, and what is more, with the explanation that the United States could not possibly undertake such guarantees except in conjunction with Britain.[13]

The Monroe Doctrine's mystique as a talisman for safeguarding the hemisphere from foreign influences is quickly dispelled by a knowledge of the discussions among North American leaders that attended formulation of the original statement. After Secretary of State John Quincy Adams had communicated the concerns of British Foreign Secretary Canning to the president, Monroe solicited the opinion of Thomas Jefferson, then in retirement from public life at Monticello. Monroe told Jefferson:

> My own impression is that we ought to . . . make it known, that we would
> view an interference on the part of the European powers, and especially
> an attack on the Colonies, by them, as an attack on ourselves, presum-
> ing that, if they succeeded with them, they would extend it to us.[14]

In reply to Monroe's letter, the author of the Declaration of Independence wrote:

> We have first to ask ourselves a question. Do we wish to acquire to our
> own confederacy any one or more of the Spanish provinces? I candidly
> confess, that I have ever looked on Cuba as the most interesting addi-
> tion which could ever be made to our system of States . . . Yet, I am
> sensible that this can never be obtained, even with her own consent,
> but by war; and its independence which is our second interest, (and es-
> pecially its independence of England) can be secured without it. I have
> no hesitation in abandoning my first wish to future chances, and ac-
> cepting its independence, with peace and the friendship of England,
> rather than its association, at the expense of war and her enmity.
>   I could honestly, therefore, join in the declaration proposed, that we
> aim not at the acquisition of any of those possessions.[15]

As to the question of the desirability of a joint declaration, as requested by England, Secretary of State Adams wrote the following entry in his
diary on November 7, 1823:

> By joining with her . . . in her proposed declaration, we give her a sub-
> stantial and perhaps inconvenient pledge against ourselves, and really
> obtain nothing in return. Without entering now into the enquiry of the
> expediency of our annexing Texas or Cuba to our Union, we should at
> least keep ourselves free to act as emergencies may arise, and not tie our-
> selves down to any principle which might immediately afterwards be
> brought against ourselves.[16]

For his part, Monroe justified the unilateral declaration saying, "By taking the step here, it is done in a manner more conciliatory with and respect-
ful to Russia [and] the other powers, than if taken in England, and it is
thought with more credit to our [government]."[17]

The Monroe message is generally attributed as much, if not more, to
the influence of Secretary Adams as to that of Monroe himself. Succeeding Monroe in the White House, Adams sent a message to the House of
Representatives in March 1826 in which he explained the intention of the
"doctrine" in these terms:

> It rested upon a course of reasoning equally simple and conclusive. With
> the exception of the existing European colonies, which it was nowise in-

tended to disturb, the two continents [North and South America] consisted of several sovereign and independent nations, whose territories covered their whole surface. By this their independent condition the United States enjoyed the right of commercial intercourse with every part of their possessions. To attempt the establishment of a colony in those possessions would be to usurp to the exclusion of others a commercial intercourse which was the common possession of all. It could not be done without encroaching upon the existing rights of the United States.[18]

Thus the "founding fathers" perceived a threat to their "commercial intercourse" and possibly to their security—though it's hard to imagine they really feared that the Holy Alliance would try to recolonize the United States. They calculated their statement so as not to unduly offend "Russia and the other powers"; far from seeing themselves as asserting some sublime universal precept, they worried about tying themselves down with "any principle which might immediately afterwards be brought against ourselves." Their rather prosaic discourse evokes more the image of a municipal chamber of commerce deliberating over real estate dealings than it does the fashioning of a "doctrine" of world-historical import. But however much it was motivated by self-interest, the original Monroe Doctrine was nevertheless reasonably benign, and to whatever modest extent it did help stay the hand of monarchical reaction it was objectively progressive.*

John Quincy Adams, with an eye to the future, apparently thought that by issuing a unilateral declaration the United States would leave itself free for future territorial expansion. But it is important to note that, like Thomas Jefferson, the North Americans who declared against further European colonization in the Western Hemisphere generally believed that by so doing they were themselves bound to forgo new conquests.

The specter of the Holy Alliance and colonial restoration soon evaporated: a feeble attempt by Spain to reconquer Mexico in 1829 turned into a fiasco. Meanwhile the Yankee pronouncement of 1823 was all but forgotten. The menace to the independence of the former Spanish colonies did not lie across the Atlantic.

A S THE provinces of the Central American isthmus were just beginning to stir from the torpor of three centuries of medieval hacienda life, the North American leviathan continually enlarged its domain. Fur merchants, land speculators, slave barons, and landless immigrants quick-

---

* Though the original Monroe Doctrine was self-interested in its motivation and cautious in its enunciation, nevertheless, in the words of Dexter Perkins, "the language of the message itself must have worn much the same aspect to a Metternich or a Chateaubriand that the manifestoes of Moscow wore to the conservative statesmen of 1919 or 1920."[19]

ly fanned out across the Louisiana Purchase, which stretched from New Orleans to Oregon. Spain was compelled to yield Florida in 1819 under the pressure of squatters from the Southern slave states. Andrew Jackson waged war on the Creeks and the Seminoles, and then pushed the Removal Bill through Congress, deporting to Oklahoma whatever Indian survivors remained in the way of Jacksonian Democracy; four thousand Cherokees died on the forced march that became known as the Trail of Tears.[20]

The land-hungry and the land-greedy next fixed their gaze on Texas, with its virgin lands waiting to receive the cotton planter. While "degenerate" Mexico impudently refused to sell Texas to Jackson for $5 million, private enterprise pressed ahead in a "creeping occupation."[21] First legally, with colonization grants, then disregarding Mexican law, Anglo settlers streamed across the border, soon outnumbering the Mexicans in the sparsely-populated territory. Taking advantage of the weakness and instability of Mexico, they consolidated their grip. They ignored Mexican customs regulations and anti-slavery laws; they disarmed and forcibly expelled Mexican officials who sought to uphold the laws. Finally, in 1836, when Mexican President Santa Anna tried to restore control, the Anglo Texans declared their "independence."

Opposition within the United States to the extension of slave territory stalled the annexation of Texas, and it was not until 1845 that President Tyler finally managed to push the measure through Congress—one of the last acts of his administration.

But with the inauguration of Democrat James Polk as president in 1845, the locomotive of empire was once again ready to roll. Polk's election brought with it an unparalleled expansionist fever. John L. O'Sullivan complained in the *United States Magazine and Democratic Review* that European powers had tried to prevent the annexation of Texas "in a spirit of hostile interference against us, for the avowed object of thwarting our policy and hampering our power, limiting our greatness and checking the fulfillment of our manifest destiny to overspread the continent allotted by Providence for the free development of our yearly multiplying millions."[22]

O'Sullivan's phrase "manifest destiny" became the war cry of the empire builders, whose appetites were exceeded only by their bombast. The New York *Herald* wrote:

> The final annexation of Texas, effected by this Congress, and the reoccupation of the whole of Oregon, now under animated debate, comprehending also a movement looking North towards the whole of British North America—looking South towards Cuba, San Domingo, California, nay the whole of Mexico—all point to the accomplishment of a destiny which is dazzling while it is terrible.[23]

While some envisioned the conquest of the continent and others, the hemisphere, many more would have no boundaries at all. John Reynolds of Illinois* told a rally:

> Let that western spirit continue to act, let the American people spread themselves over the continent of North America, carrying with them the principle of freedom and Democratic institutions, and ultimately extend the blessing of civil and religious liberty over the whole earth, beginning with the island of Cuba.[25]

In fact, the *Herald* reported, Americans were "puzzling their brains to find out new countries to annex," and it was the "stepping stone to popularity, now to invent some annexation scheme."[26]

The quest of Eastern shipping moguls for Pacific ports, a consequence of the opening up of the China trade, and the desire of Southern slaveocrats for a western outlet now spurred the acquisition of California. The fact that Texas had been annexed without a precise boundary gave these "apostles of empire" the opportunity they needed.[27]

When Mexico refused to receive US envoy John Slidell, who carried with him an offer to purchase New Mexico and California for $10 million, Polk ordered troops commanded by General Zachary Taylor to cross the Nueces River and occupy the banks of the Rio Grande. Officially, Mexico had never recognized the independence of Texas or its annexation by the United States, but seeing little choice, it had tacitly accepted the Nueces as the US boundary. By refusing Mexico's demand to vacate territory that had never been considered a part of Texas under either Spanish or Mexican ownership, the United States engineered the "Gulf of Tonkin" incident of an earlier era. The clash between US and Mexican troops that inevitably resulted furnished the pretext that Polk needed to secure a congressional declaration of war.[28]

Although the war brought numerous demands for annexation of the whole of Mexico, even expectations that such would be the inevitable outcome, the Mexicans proved to be a more formidable foe than anticipated.[29] Despite defeat after defeat, they doggedly fought on, confounding the United States for two years by their stubborn refusal to acquiesce to the demands to yield their territory. Mexican resistance in the face of an enemy vastly superior in resources, combined with the growing opposition to the war within the United States, compelled a settlement that did not measure up to the imperial fantasies of many.

Nonetheless, between 1844 and 1848, with the annexation of Texas, California, and the New Mexico Territory—which included the present states

---

* Reynolds, an avidly pro-slavery Democrat, had been a US congressman and governor of Illinois. As Illinois chief executive he had tried unsuccessfully to legalize slavery in the state.[24]

of New Mexico, Arizona, Nevada, Utah, and most of Colorado—the national territory of the United States increased from 1.8 million to 3 million square miles.[30]

Expansion westward was now contained by the Pacific Ocean, at least for the time being. Pressures from the Southern slave oligarchy, from land speculators, mining interests, and merchants, to annex even more of Mexico would continue. But for the moment the conquests of the Mexican War caused attention to turn even farther to the south.

II

THE PATH OF DESTINY

I suppose the right of a manifest destiny to spread will not be admitted to exist in any nation except the universal Yankee nation!

—Rep. Robert C. Winthrop of Massachusetts in a speech to the House of Representatives, January 3, 1846.

DURING the war, Commodore Perry wrote Secretary of the Navy Mason from Mexico:

Destiny has doubtless decided that the vast continent of North America from Davis' Strait to the Isthmus of Darien [Panama] shall in the course of time fall under the influence of the Laws and institutions of the United States, hence, the impolicy of permitting any European Power or interest to obtain a footing within the prescribed Latitudes.[1]

Perry's assertion was not new in 1847. This "destiny" of all North America to fall within the boundaries of the United States "manifested" itself to numerous expansionists in the 1840s and earlier. The notion that the actions of the Anglo-Saxon society of the United States represented the workings of some higher law took root shortly after independence from England, although its seeds had doubtless been planted long before. Variously known as "Providence," "destiny," "natural racial superiority," or later, "social Darwinism," the doctrine of Yankee exceptionalism came to full flower in the second quarter of the nineteenth century. Thus, in July 1848, J.D.B. De-Bow, a leading spokesman for the Southern cotton aristocracy, could proclaim:

With equal advantages of soil and climate, the inferiority of the Spanish and Creole character tend to place the countries inhabited and administered by them, even under the best possible systems, far, very far behind those in which the Anglo-Saxon element is allowed to operate . . . The Anglo-Saxons have been sweeping everything before them on the North American continent, and establishing an empire which is felt, respected and feared, in every quarter of the globe . . . Will the love of enterprise, and the desire of a more extended territory, already so plainly manifested among us, lead to excursions upon the impotent neighbors that surround us upon every hand? Have not results in Mexico taught the *invincibility* of American arms? What power on this continent is there that can arrest their progress? What army that would not be shattered to pieces in the encounter? . . . The North Americans *will* spread out far beyond their present bounds. They *will* encroach again and again upon their neighbors. New territories *will* be planted, declare their independence, and be annexed! We have New Mexico and California! We *will* have Old Mexico and Cuba! The isthmus cannot arrest— nor even the Saint Lawrence!! Time has all of this in her womb. *A hundred states* will grow up where now exists but thirty.[2] [Emphasis in original.]

Though Yankees took it for granted that Destiny had set Central America and Mexico aside for their eventual use, it was Chance that awakened an immediate interest in Nicaragua. The ink had barely dried on the Treaty of Guadalupe Hidalgo that ended the war against Mexico when the discovery of gold at Sutter's sawmill on the American River in California became known. News of the bonanza in the newly-conquered territory caused the United States to be swept by get-rich-quick fever. Seekers of Eldorado had little stomach for an arduous and dangerous journey across the trackless plains, mountains, and deserts. The long and costly voyage around Cape Horn was hardly more appealing. So attention naturally focused on the narrow waist of the Americas.

THE IDEA of a shortcut from Atlantic to Pacific across the isthmus of Central America was even then a very old one. Christopher Columbus, as we know, set out from Spain not to discover a new world, but to find a shorter trade route to Asia. On his last voyage he conducted his search along the Atlantic coast of Central America; for three weeks in the fall of 1502 the great navigator explored the shoreline of what was to become eastern Nicaragua. Landing at the mouth of a river near present-day Monkey Point, he encountered natives, reportedly kidnapped two of them for use as guides, and thus got relations between Spain and the inhabitants of Nicaragua's Atlantic coast off to a bad start.[3]

Despite Columbus' failure to attain his original object, others continued the search for a shortcut through the Americas by water. Lured by the natives' stories of a "South Sea" and an empire of gold (Peru), Balboa crossed the Isthmus of Panama in 1513 and "discovered" the Pacific Ocean. Knowledge of the proximity of the two oceans at the Central American isthmus intensified the search for the elusive channel. Gil González, the first Spanish explorer of western Nicaragua, interrogated the chief Nicarao about a water passage, and was directed to follow the outlet of the great lake, Cocibolca.*

When Pedro Arias Dávila, better known as Pedrarias, was appointed governor of Nicaragua in 1529, he received special instructions to explore the lake's outlet.[5] After several unsuccessful expeditions—including one by Hernando de Soto, who later became the first European explorer of the Mississippi River—in 1539 Diego Machuca and Alonso Calero successfully followed the San Juan River, outlet of Lake Nicaragua, to its mouth on the Atlantic. A natural water passage did not exist, but for the next 350 years—until the end of the 19th century—the San Juan River and Lake Nicaragua, separated from the Pacific by a mere twelve miles of land, would be the principal choice for a canal between the two oceans.

In 1551, Spanish historian Lópes de Gómara urged King Charles I of Spain to undertake construction of a canal by way of the Nicaraguan route, or at Panama, or farther north across Mexico at the Isthmus of Tehuántepec. For one reason or another nothing was done until 1781. In that year the Spanish government commissioned Don Manuel Galisteo to conduct a survey of the land between Lake Nicaragua and the Pacific. No steps were taken to follow up the survey, however, until 1813, when the Spanish *Cortes*, assembled after the expulsion of Napoleon, passed a decree providing for the construction of a canal.[6] But the ambitious plan dissolved in the smoke of revolution then rising from Spain's American colonies.

In 1823 the question of a trans-Nicaragua canal was raised in the Federal Congress of the newly-formed United Provinces of Central America by José Manuel de la Cerda, soon-to-be provincial chief executive of Nicaragua. The federation received several proposals for canal construction from British and North American capitalists. It seems, however, that none were considered to be serious, because in 1825 the Central American minister to the United States, Antonio José Cañas, wrote President Adams requesting United States government assistance for the project.[7] In response, Secretary of State Clay instructed the US chargé d'affaires in Central America, Colonel John Williams, to communicate United States interest and to undertake an investigation of the feasibility of the work. Apparently Wil-

---

* Those who came after González, establishing the city of Granada on the shore of the lake in 1524, referred to it as "Nicarao-agua"—the water of Nicarao. Later shortened to Nicaragua, the new name of the lake became also the name of the province.[4]

liams never carried out the latter portion of the instruction.

The Federal Congress of Central America nevertheless did pass a bill that allowed the granting of a canal concession, and a contract bearing the date of June 14, 1826 was signed with the "Central American and United States Atlantic and Pacific Canal Company." The chief shareholder in the concern was Aaron H. Palmer, a New York capitalist. DeWitt Clinton, the prime mover behind the Erie Canal and then governor of New York, was to be one of the directors of the project. But the undertaking was abandoned the following year when Palmer failed to obtain the backing he sought from British financiers.

The Dutch were next in line to try their hand: in 1828 a group supported by the King of Holland proposed to undertake canal construction. Negotiations were well underway in 1830 when another revolution—that which separated Belgium from Holland—scuttled the effort once more.

In 1835 the United States Senate passed a resolution requesting President Jackson to open negotiations with the governments of Central America and New Granada (present-day Colombia) on the subject of a canal. In response, Jackson dispatched Charles Biddle to examine the possible routes, but Biddle died before completing his survey.

Francisco Morazán, the last president of the Central American Federation, then commissioned John Baily, an English engineer, to survey the proposed routes across Nicaragua. Morazán tried to raise a loan in Europe, but both his hopes for a canal and his hopes for a strong, united Central America were casualties in the renewed outbreak of civil war that cut the feeble bonds of federation.

Unsettled conditions on the isthmus prevented any further consideration of a canal until 1844. In that year the fledgling Nicaraguan republic signed a contract with the King of Belgium, that for reasons now obscure, was no more fortunate than its predecessors.

Two years later, Francisco Castellón visited Louis Napoleon Bonaparte, then imprisoned in the French fortress of Ham. So successful was the Nicaraguan diplomat in interesting the future Emperor Napoleon III in the canal project, that when the latter escaped shortly thereafter he published a pamphlet on the subject. Nicaragua was to the New World what Constantinople was to the Old, wrote Napoleon: "The State of Nicaragua can become, better than Constantinople, the necessary route of the great commerce of the world, and is destined to attain an extraordinary degree of prosperity and grandeur."[8] Then exiled in England, his apparent aim was to interest the capitalists and government of Britain in the great enterprise. Failing this, the "Canal Napoleon" became but one more footnote to the tale of great power designs on Central America.

For the United States, however, the taking of California and the gold rush that followed invested the question of a Central American canal with an urgency it had previously lacked, and the route across Nicaragua was found to be the most attractive. It seemed that the interoceanic passage—a tantalizing vision for 350 years—was finally about to materialize.

T HE BRITISH had watched the march of events closely, anticipating their North American rival's next move. They fully understood the object of the United States' war against Mexico; the only doubts they entertained as to its outcome concerned the extent of the territory to be seized. They knew the next target of Yankee expansion would be Central America, and they feared their ungrateful offspring would seek to gain exclusive control of a canal across Nicaragua, or would annex all or part of the region to the detriment of their own trading interests. As early as 1840, with California still in Mexican hands, Alexander MacDonald, superintendent of the British colony at Belize, wrote Foreign Secretary Lord John Russell:

> The Americans are anxious above all things to possess that part of the shore [of Nicaragua] where the St. Juan flows into the sea, which if they acquired and created a communication by the Lake Nicaragua to the Pacific we might bid farewell to the high commercial footing we at present enjoy, and allow a power not indisposed to cripple our energies a fair stage for the execution of their hostile designs.[9]

Before the US-Mexican war came to its conclusion, the British decided to take preventive action.

Since 1740 they had claimed a protectorate over an ill-defined and sparsely-populated area along the Atlantic coast of Nicaragua and Honduras, whose most numerous inhabitants were the Miskito ethnic group. They installed a "king" of the Miskitos and variously referred to the area as the "Mosquito Shore" or "Kingdom of Mosquito."* These claims were never recognized by the Central American Federation or by the independent states of Nicaragua and Honduras. But Central Americans lacked the

---

* "Miskito" is the spelling in general present-day usage; it will be used throughout except in quotations or period references.

The Miskito ethnic group originated from a mixture of several hundred survivors of a wrecked slave ship with a part of the Bawiksas Indians during the early colonial period. The origin of the name is disputed. One theory holds that it derives from "Musketo" or "Musqueto"—from "musket"—and was conferred in the late 17th or early 18th century by the British, who supplied the people of Nicaragua's Atlantic littoral with weapons, which they used to attack Spanish settlements and to exact tribute from smaller tribes. The British relationship with the Miskitos began in the 17th century, when English pirates frequented the area, using it as a base for attacks on Spanish shipping during wars between the two countries. Britain relinquished its claim in a 1786 treaty with Spain, only to reassert it early in the 19th century as Spanish control in the Americas disintegrated. Britain resumed the crowning of a Miskito "king" at Belize in 1816.[10]

power to dislodge the British, and the geographical isolation of the region rendered the territories of little or no immediate practical value to them.

In 1848 British troops occupied Nicaragua's only Atlantic port, San Juan del Norte, also known as San Juan de Nicaragua. They expelled the Nicaraguan authorities, claiming the port belonged to the Miskito "king." England now controlled the Atlantic terminus of the proposed canal.*

Nicaragua, naturally, was not pleased with the loss of its only door on the Atlantic. The question of its sovereignty was not merely abstract: the Nicaraguan government had realized $100,000 annually in customs duties at the port, one of its few sources of revenue. Too weak to confront the British aggression alone, Nicaragua turned to the United States for help.

Two months before the actual seizure of San Juan, a British warship had delivered a note to the commandant of the port. Signed by a British subject named George Hodgson, who claimed to be acting on behalf of the Miskito king, it contained an ultimatum giving the Nicaraguans until January 1, 1848 to vacate the town. On November 12, 1847, Pablo Buitrago, the Nicaraguan minister of foreign affairs, wrote James Buchanan, then US secretary of state under President James Polk. Referring to the United States as "the natural protector of all the States of the Continent," Buitrago called Buchanan's attention to the British aim of controlling the prospective canal route and solicited United States mediation on behalf of Nicaragua. He assured the secretary of state that "any measure that [President Polk] may take to prevent interference by any foreign power in this part of the Continent, will be well received and highly valued by the Sovereign State of Nicaragua."[11] José Guerrero, the supreme director of Nicaragua (as the chief of state was then known), wrote directly to Polk in mid-December. Guerrero reiterated the desire expressed by his foreign minister for a treaty with the United States, and in the matter of the impending British occupation of San Juan, referred to Polk's 1845 reassertion of the Monroe Doctrine.[12]

The United States chargé d'affaires in Central America, Henry Savage, had by this time advised the Nicaraguans "not to undertake war, because the English may repulse the forces of [Nicaragua] and then allege the right of conquest," taking possession of the entire country. Savage assured them that "the United States will in no manner permit England to take posses-

---

* The British occupied San Juan briefly in August 1841, but soon departed, and the Nicaraguans resumed control. The English had not relinquished the claim that the port fell within their Miskito protectorate, however. Their action in 1841 was consistent with the concern about United States expansion expressed in MacDonald's message to Russell quoted above: they were content to let de facto control revert to Nicaragua while retaining the option of reoccupying the port at such time as they deemed necessary to block United States' designs in the area. In 1848 they apparently felt the time for such action had arrived.

sion of the territory, or even a part of the territory, of Nicaragua, and so the matter should be called to the attention of the President of the United States immediately in order that he may lend his aid."[13] The US chargé went so far as to send the Nicaraguans a copy of Polk's Monroe Doctrine speech in case they hadn't already read it.

In February 1848, when the occupation of San Juan was already an accomplished fact, the US chargé ingenuously asserted to the Nicaraguan foreign minister, "I can scarcely persuade myself that the British Government would wish to take possession of any part of the recognized territory of the State of Nicaragua, the President of the United States having publicly proclaimed to the world that he would not consent to such usurpation."[14]

But in spite of the Nicaraguans' repeated entreaties, no assistance was forthcoming. In fact, neither Polk nor Buchanan, nor anyone else in Washington, even bothered to acknowledge receipt of the appeals. This perplexing circumstance led Foreign Minister Salinas to delicately inquire of Savage whether he would "be so kind as to inform the Government [of Nicaragua] of the result of its appeal to the illustrious Government of Washington." But the Yankee diplomat was in the dark himself. A full year after the initial request for US assistance, Nicaragua was still "anxiously awaiting the answers."[15]

A satisfactory explanation for the lack of responsiveness seems to have eluded historians of United States foreign policy. Monroe Doctrine expert Dexter Perkins, who acknowledged that "extreme caution hardly seems characteristic of the Polk administration," asked:

> Why was there, then, not even the most casual public allusion to the British encroachments in Mosquitia? Why was there not the slightest notice paid to the entreaties of the Nicaraguan government? Why this complete inertia in a concrete case, the only concrete case, in which the Monroe Doctrine was directly and flatly violated during the whole Polk adminstration?

Attempting to answer his own questions, Perkins surmised that the answer lay "in the complete torpor of American public opinion at the time," "the distraction of the pending presidential election," and "the probable ignorance of Polk with regard to the whole matter."[16]

But it was Polk who had retrieved Monroe's original statement from twenty-two years of obscurity; more than any other president, it was he that transformed the original message of Monroe into the dogma of later years. Lack of information on Polk's part must immediately be discounted as an explanation for the inaction. The record of the diplomatic correspondence of that time shows that Nicaragua, Honduras, and the US representatives in the region did a creditable job of furnishing the State Department with background information on British activities on the Miskito Coast.[17]

The solution to the seeming paradox can be found in the context in which James Polk revived the 1823 Monroe declaration. He had been elected as the avowedly expansionist candidate of the Democratic Party, the party representing the most expansionist elements in United States society: the Southern slaveholders allied with Northern and Western merchants and land speculators. Against the backdrop of "manifest destiny" jingoism orchestrated by these interests, Polk's statement, contained in his first annual message to Congress in December 1845, was aimed not at blocking European colonization—then not a real threat—but at quashing the notion under discussion in Europe of a balance of power in the Americas to check the expansion of the United States. Polk was candid about this in the preface to his restatement of Monroe's ideas:

> The rapid extension of our settlements over our territories heretofore unoccupied, the addition of new States to our Confederacy, the expansion of free principles, and our rising greatness as a nation are attracting the attention of the powers of Europe, and lately the doctrine has been broached in some of them of a "balance of power" on this continent to check our advancement.[18]

The "advancement" that Polk had in mind was into Texas, New Mexico, California, and Oregon. European powers were not trying to establish new colonies in those territories. Rather, they were engaged in diplomatic efforts to prevent the United States from taking them, though it may be true, as Perkins said, that "Polk's own eager appetite for California made him ready to believe in the expansionist designs of others."[19]

In Monroe's original statement the message had been defensive in character. Its purpose was to protect against the recolonization of the Americas by European powers to the exclusion, or at least the detriment, of United States commercial interests. In the hands of Polk, however, the "doctrine" became an offensive weapon—wielded against European nations that now sought to protect their own commerce from United States expansion. The original intent, directed against European designs on the territories of the new American republics, had been benign; if the motives were selfish, at least they were in harmony with the self-interest of the other states in the hemisphere. But in the hands of the expansionists the Monroe Doctrine held a threat to the sovereignty of those same states, particularly those in North and Central America. The words were the same, but the meaning had been stood on its head.

Monroe and his advisors felt that the United States was itself bound

by the non-colonization principle, and they weighed this as a consideration in whether the declaration should be made at all. That is why both
Polk and Buchanan, along with other expansionist politicians, opposed
James Monroe's "doctrine" in 1823. But now they discovered that it could
be made to serve their own ends. Another historian of the Monroe Doctrine wrote that "the annexation of Texas, and of other Mexican Territory
by the treaty of Guadalupe Hidalgo, had ended a misconception that the
United States itself was bound by the Doctrine to refrain from the acquisition of territory on the American continent."[20] Remarkable though it
may be that this writer considered it to be a "misconception" that the
United States should itself be bound by the rules it sought to establish
for others, he had nevertheless come to the heart of the matter.

With the Monroe Doctrine being advanced against those who would
interfere with the expansion of the United States, it is not surprising that
it was not being employed in an area where the United States had no immediate territorial designs: when Nicaragua first appealed for help the
California gold rush was still a year away. In fact, under the circumstances
Nicaragua's attempt to invoke the Monroe Doctrine could have been quite
embarrassing. For even if Polk and his backers appreciated the potential
value of Nicaragua at that moment, their hands were tied.

The Treaty of Guadalupe Hidalgo ending the war against Mexico was
signed on February 2, 1848—one month after the British occupation of
San Juan. But there was some doubt as to whether the Senate would ratify
it and, when it finally did, it was far from certain that Mexico would accept the amendments that were added. Meanwhile, the unexpectedly high
cost of the war in both lives and dollars had stirred up strong domestic
opposition to its continuance. War-weariness and the anti-war stance adopted by the Abolitionists threatened Polk's administration with disaster: if
the treaty was not ratified, there was a distinct possibility that Congress
would cut off funds for further prosecution of the war.* The expansionists
stood to lose the cherished spoils that were finally within their reach. Sabre-
rattling over British actions in Nicaragua would further inflame domestic
debate and further jeopardize their position.

By the time the treaty ratifications were finally exchanged on May 30,
1848, attention was turning to the coming November elections, and the
Democrats' foreign policy was already a big liability. That is why Washington
made no reply to Nicaragua's appeals for aid, much less any public statement. As it turned out the Democratic Party lost the presidency in 1848

---

* The Abolitionists understood that any new acquisition of territory—particularly land suited to plantation agriculture—would give slavery a new lease on life. They believed—and they
were, at least in part, correct—that expansion of slave territory was the aim of the war.

even without any new foreign adventures.

The United States was to introduce the Monroe Doctrine again and again over the course of its relations with Nicaragua. But in this, the solitary instance in which Nicaraguans themselves saw their sovereignty jeopardized by a European nation and appealed to their northern neighbor to invoke the vaunted Doctrine, their plea fell on deaf ears.

T HE POLK Administration appointed Elijah Hise chargé d'affaires for Central America at the end of March 1848, but he didn't arrive on the isthmus till the end of October, just days before the presidential election. His instructions from Secretary Buchanan contained the usual generalities about cultivating friendly relations with the states of Central America, along with a generous dose of moralizing in which the political turmoil of the region was deplored. Hise was enjoined to impress upon the locals "our example, where all political controversies are decided at the ballot box." [21]

The new chargé was empowered to conclude treaties with Guatemala and San Salvador but not with Nicaragua, Honduras, or Costa Rica "until you shall have communicated to the Department more full and authentic statistical information in regard to those States." Buchanan's letter also contained a ritual condemnation of the British and some background history on the Miskito question, but it advised Hise that "the Government of the United States has not yet determined what course it will pursue in regard to the encroachments of the British Government" in the territory of the Miskitos. These Buchanan described as "a miserable, degraded and insignificant tribe of Indians." [22]

Chargé Hise could hardly contain his enthusiasm for Central America. He described Honduras, where he got off the boat, as

a most magnificent Country unsurpassed in Scenes of Granduer and Sublimity of Aspect, and unrivalled in Respect to its Agricultural and mineral resources. Gold Silver and Copper are or rather might be its Mineral productions; Sugar, Coffee, Rice, Indian Corn, Cotten, Cochineal and Indigo Die woods of Various Kinds, Valuable timber of several kinds, all kinds of Tropical Fruits, are or might become its productions from the Soil [which] as I am Informed, is of Great and Exhaustless fertility— Yet the Very best Portion of this Valuable Country has been Appropriated by Great Brittain to herself."* [23]

Regarding the British Miskito protectorate, Hise complained, "I have

---

* Unless otherwise noted, the original spelling and punctuation has been retained in quoted passages throughout this book.

not been charged with this Subject nor instructed particularly to take any action upon it. Indeed I could do nothing more than Say to these States of Central America be firm Do not Yield, Protest &c." Of his chief he inquired:

> Now will the U.S. Suffer Great Brittain to Enact on the Stage of North America the Same Bloody Tragedy which she has allready performed In Hindostan & Elsewhere and Stand by and Endure that She Shall have a Commercial Monopoly in all these fertile regions on this very Continent of North America where in our days of Weakness we Shook her dominion and where in our Strength our Commerce dominion & Influence should predominate?[24]

Notwithstanding his instructions to the contrary, the bilious but enterprising Kentucky lawyer proceeded forthwith to negotiate a "Special Convention between the United States of America and the State of Nicaragua," which he modestly described as

> the most advantageous treaty in its terms and provisions that human ingenuity can devise for the promotion of the views and Interest of the United States, and of the State of Nicaragua, and also for the promotion of the Grand Design intended, of opening an Oceanic Communication [that] if it should be approved and ratified by the two Govts, will, without doubt, in my judgement . . . produce the most important results, favorable to the future prosperity, wealth and Grandeur of the North American Confederacy, as well as to the perpetuation of the American Union, and the preservation of the integrity of the territories of the U.S.*[25]

The treaty gave the United States the complete and absolute right to establish any kind of transit through the territory of Nicaragua, whether by water, road, rail, or a combination thereof; the US could obtain any materials desired for the construction of these works free of charge from the state property of that country. Nicaragua was to cede "absolutely all the lands that may be required" for the location of canals, roads, buildings, or whatever. The US alone would have the right to grant a charter for the construction and operation of the transit facilities, and the company so chartered would become the sole owner of the works. The agreement also gave the United States the right to erect fortifications "at the ends and along the lines of said works" and to occupy them with as many troops

---

* Hise's phrase "the perpetuation of the American Union" was significant because in the decades preceding the Civil War such phrases evoked the ever-present threat of the Southern slaveholders to secede if their demands for new territory were not met. In other words, Hise saw his treaty as facilitating slavery expansion into Central America.

as it saw fit, plus the Yankees were to have perpetual right of free passage through any or all of Nicaragua. In exchange for these concessions Hise's treaty pledged the United States to defend Nicaragua's territorial integrity.[26]

Just as remarkable as the fact that Hise had no instructions to negotiate such a treaty was the circumstance that it was signed in June 1849, three months after the Polk Administration that appointed him had left office. Zachary Taylor, a Whig, had moved into the White House in March, and Hise had been recalled by the new secretary of state, John Clayton.

When, on June 20, Hise wrote Joseph Livingston, the United States consul in León, to acknowledge receipt of the dispatch that informed him of the impending arrival of his replacement, he claimed that his treaty had already been completed.[27] But in fact the document bore the date of June 21, the day following: Hise had signed the "most advantageous treaty that human ingenuity can devise" under false pretenses.

Upon his return to the US, the ex-diplomat wrote to Secretary of State Clayton, trying to justify his highly irregular actions:

> When I took my departure from the U.S. on the Mission to Central America the treaty of peace with Mexico had not been ratified by that power, and the Countries of Upper California and New Mexico had not yet been ceded to the U.S. Nor was it then known that the Mountains, plains and rivers of those Countries, contained the immense stores of mineral wealth which has since been discovered, nor was it forseen that such an immense impulse would, in so short a time be given to the commerce with, and the emmigration to those countries as hath since astonished the World . . . The vast importance which subsequent events has given to the subject [of interoceanic communication] does not seem to have occured to the existing administration of our Govt.

Despite his repeated requests for instructions, he had received no reply, he said, leading him to conclude that

> as the Republic of Guatemala was constantly in a revolutionary state, the country involved in civil strife and the paths to the coast infested with banditti . . . all letters public and private directed to me must be either detained at Balize or intercepted and destroyed . . . under these circumstances . . . I conceived it my duty . . . to seize the opportunity which offered.

Hise urged Clayton to accept the treaty, gloating over the fact that "Nicaragua is not allowed any part of the pecuniary proffits arising from the enterprise nor is she allowed to take or have at any future time, any right to, or property in the whole or any part thereof." He assured the secretary that "if terms more favorable are not offered," Nicaragua would ratify the treaty "in order to have the benefit of the protection [from Britain]."[28]

The Hise-Selva Treaty proved to be something of an embarrassment. It put the United States on a direct collision course with England, and for that reason, if no other, it was disavowed by the government in Washington and never submitted to the Senate for ratification. It is doubtful whether Nicaragua would have approved the treaty in any case, although the Liberals then in power were particularly naive about North American intentions. Though the Taylor Administration loudly repudiated its unequal terms, the treaty was not really very different from the one that gained the Panama Canal Zone for the United States a half-century later.

Hise was replaced as chargé d'affaires by Ephraim G. Squier, an individual who stands out among the cast of characters sent to represent the Yankee nation in Central America.* Only twenty-eight years old at the time of his appointment, Squier was an amateur archeologist who had already made a name for himself through his studies of the Mound Builders of the Ohio River Valley. But it was his training as a civil engineer that seems to have recommended him in Washington for a mission to Central America, for chief among the objects of that mission was the negotiation of another canal treaty with Nicaragua. As Secretary of State John Clayton explained the matter in his instructions to Squier, "a passage across the isthmus may be indispensable to maintain the relations between the United States and their new territories on the Pacific, and a Canal from Ocean to Ocean might and probably would empty the treasures of the Pacific into the lap of this country." While negotiating a treaty, Squier was instructed to use his "personal good offices with the Government of Nicaragua" to aid US citizens who were then in the country for the purpose of obtaining a contract to build the canal.[29]

The US citizens that Secretary Clayton referred to were representatives of a company just formed by Cornelius Vanderbilt, Daniel B. Allen, and Joseph L. White. White, a former congressman, was very influential in the Whig Party. Clayton himself, while a US senator from Delaware, had in 1835 introduced a resolution in the Senate calling on the president to negotiate treaties with Central America that would favor the interests of North American capitalists wishing to undertake canal construction.[30]

When Squier arrived at San Juan del Norte in June 1849, North Americans were already passing up the river in large numbers on their way to San Francisco. The previous year Gordon's Passenger Line of New York had begun service to San Juan; there passengers were transferred to large ca-

---

* Hise went on to become an elector for James Buchanan in the presidential race of 1856 and was afterward himself elected to the US Congress from Kentucky.

Ephraim G. Squier

noes for the 122-mile trip up the San Juan River to Lake Nicaragua. They then sailed to Granada, 120 miles across the lake, and were conveyed on horse- or muleback to the Pacific port of Realejo near present-day Corinto. At Realejo they hoped and waited for a vessel to carry them on to San Francisco. Gordon's offered a refund of seventy-five dollars plus sixty days provisions for anyone failing to secure passage from Realejo.[31]

Hundreds, however, were deciding not to continue the journey to California—there were fortunes to be made right there in Nicaragua. The climate was perfect, the soil rich, and the gold that lured the Spanish Conquistador to the land of the Nicaraos and Chorotegans was still to be found in unknown quantities. Enterprising individuals from the North built Nicaragua's first hotels in Granada and Realejo; their bonanza would be dollars panned from the expected inundation of fellow countrymen.

Squier found that not all Nicaraguans welcomed the coming of the gringos. For as North Americans passed up the lush San Juan River, he reported, they wantonly shot at Indians along its banks for target practice.[32]

Nevertheless, there is no reason to doubt his statement concerning the signing of the coveted canal treaty two months later: "The news of the event was everywhere received with extraordinary demonstrations of satisfaction and joy." For Squier, whose faith in the good intentions of his countrymen was not total, joy in the accomplishment of his mission was tempered with caution. "It is most earnestly to be desired," he wrote, "that the hopes which it created may not, from the mistaken policy of Government, or the bad faith of companies, owing their very existence to Nicaraguan generosity, give place to despair, and respect [be] changed into contempt, and friendship into hate."[33]

As Squier looked out over León one evening, the concerns of the diplomat gave way to the archeologist's detached musings on the clash of two societies, so different and so unequal:

> I sat on my horse for a quarter of an hour, listening to the music and the merriment, and speculated whether, after all, spite of unstable governments, and destitute of all those accessories which, according to our utilitarian ideas, are necessary to the popular welfare,—whether the people of Leon were not on the whole happier and more contented than those of any city of equal size in our own country? Here were no crowded workshops, where youth and age toil on, on, during the long day and by the pale gas light, amidst foul vapors, or in a corrupted atmosphere, that trade may thrive, and arrogant commerce strut in the Exchange! No thundering machines to disturb the calm of evening, to drown the murmers of the night winds and the gentle melody of the falling dews, with their hoarse, unearthly clangor![34]

Nicaragua's small merchants and embryonic capitalists, represented by the Liberal party then in control of government, thought that the new treaty and the contract simultaneously negotiated with Vanderbilt's company would usher in a bright future of development and trade. They also expected to receive US help in expelling the British from Miskitia. On the occasion of Nicaragua's ratification of the agreements, September 20, 1849, Don Toribio Terán, president of the Nicaraguan Senate, proclaimed:

> To foreign pretensions and the territorial aggressions with which we have been persecuted, and which are now the only sources of disquiet to the State, let us hope for the early interposition of that nation to which we have always been accustomed to look as a model for ourselves—a nation powerful, enlightened, and naturally called to defend our territory, in conformity with the great and glorious principle which it was the first to proclaim, and which finds a response in every American heart, viz.: that "the American Continent belongs to Americans, and is sacred to Republican Institutions."[35]

Don Toribio might not have been so sanguine had he been able to read the Yankee envoy's instructions from Secretary Clayton. For while the orders contained a lengthy refutation of the British claims to the Miskito Coast and the Port of San Juan, which controlled the Atlantic terminus of the prospective canal, Squier had been explicitly instructed that "it is not deemed expedient to give as compensation for the grant of the right of way any guaranty of the independence of the country through which the canal or rail road might pass. Such a guaranty is entirely inadmissible in the proposed treaty."[36] There is no doubt, however, that the British claim was an obstacle to the canal plans, and the United States now undertook to resolve the problem in a way that was not exactly what Nicaragua (or Squier) had in mind.

I T DIDN'T take a great deal of imagination to see that the US and Britain were headed for a collision over Nicaragua, and powerful interests in both countries were soon bringing pressure to bear to avoid such a contingency. As the New York *Herald* phrased it, "an influence of common sense arose from . . . the London Exchange on the one side and Wall Street on the other."[37]

On Christmas Eve, 1849, Sir Henry Lytton Bulwer presented his credentials in Washington as special envoy from Great Britain to the United States. Over the course of the next several months Bulwer and Secretary of State Clayton looked for a resolution to the Nicaragua situation that would serve the interests of both great powers.

Without doubt the paramount concern of the Whig administration that Clayton represented was to obtain an agreement that would remove any British obstacles in the way of Vanderbilt and his canal company; other considerations were strictly secondary. Squier's treaty, which had aroused such enthusiasm in Nicaragua, was now found to be inconvenient to an accommodation with Bulwer and was shelved. When it did go to the Senate in March it was solely for the purpose of exerting leverage in the talks with Britain.[38]

Though the US interest as interpreted by the Whigs lay chiefly, in Clayton's words, in "the treasures" that would empty "into the lap of this country" from a canal across the isthmus, the secretary of state didn't hesitate to employ a thinly-veiled threat to unleash the expansionists (represented by the Democrats) as a means to extract concessions from the British negotiator. Thus on February 15 Clayton wrote Bulwer:

> There is not one of these five Central American states that would not annex themselves to us tomorrow, if they could, and if it is any secret worth knowing you are welcome to it—*Some of them have offered and asked to be annexed to the United States already.** Your government

---

* Although the idea of annexation to the United States may have been, and probably was, considered at different times by various Central Americans, there was in fact only one instance in which a formal representation had been made. That was the case of San Salvador, which requested annexation to the United States in 1822 in order to avoid annexation to

could not annex one of them, with its own consent, and, in the face of these facts, we offer to agree with you, that we will not occupy (nor interpose to exercise any dominion over) any one of them, if you will only consent to give up your alliance with your Mosquito King . . . If you refuse to extinguish that Indian title or to abandon the protectorate, we shall hold ourselves at liberty to annex any part of the Central American states or to make any other contract with them, which our interests may dictate. The President thinks that we make, by far, the greatest concessions.[40] [Emphasis in original.]

The Clayton-Bulwer Treaty was signed on April 19, 1850. The first and most significant article provided that neither Britain nor the United States

will ever obtain or maintain for itself any exclusive control over the said Ship Canal; agreeing, that neither will ever erect or maintain any fortifications commanding the same, or in the vicinity thereof, or occupy, fortify, or colonize, or assume or exercise any dominion over Nicaragua, Costa Rica, the Mosquito Coast, or any part of Central America; nor will either make use of any protection which either affords or may afford, or any alliance which either has or may have, to or with any State or People for the purpose of erecting or maintaining any such fortifications, or of occupying, fortifying or colonizing Nicaragua, Costa Rica, the Mosquito Coast, or any part of Central America, or of assuming or exercising dominion over the same; nor will the United States or Great Britain take advantage of any intimacy, or use any alliance, connection or influence that either may possess with any State or Government through whose territory the said Canal may pass, for the purpose of acquiring or holding, directly or indirectly, for the citizens or subjects of the one, any rights or advantages in regard to commerce or navigation through the said Canal, which shall not be offered on the same terms to the citizens or subjects of the other.[41]

The most striking feature of the Clayton-Bulwer Treaty was that the United States and Britain negotiated it without troubling to consult Nicaragua or the other Central American states whose interests it vitally affected. Nevertheless, Secretary Clayton held out the promise of great blessings for the natives. He wrote Squier:

By kindness and conciliation on the part of Nicaragua, with the aid of the good offices of this government, Central America, capable as she

---

the Mexican Empire. Before the commissioners appointed by San Salvador could reach the US to negotiate the union, however, Emperor Iturbide was overthrown, Mexico withdrew its claim to Central America, and San Salvador changed its mind.[39] In short, Clayton's assertion was essentially false.

is of sustaining the population of a great empire, united in herself and exerting her best energies for the development of her great resources, may date the commencement of a career of unexampled prosperity from the date of the ratification of the Treaty.[42]

Any Nicaraguans who trusted in Secretary Clayton's balmy forecast were soon to be disappointed. Nicaragua had been assured that the US would defend its sovereignty over the Miskito Coast, but that is not what happened. The treaty, it is true, did bar colonies. But the British later argued, with considerable justification, that the understanding had been that it was a prospective, not a retrospective, ban. Moreover, the treaty's use of the term "Mosquito Coast" as distinct from "Nicaragua," and of "alliances" and "protection"—clearly referring to the British relationship with the Miskitos—did nothing to establish Nicaraguan sovereignty; indeed, it had the opposite effect. In any case, the British retained de facto control over Nicaragua's Atlantic coast for some time to come, and when they finally did return the territory to Nicaragua it was for reasons that had little or nothing to do with pressure from their American cousins, claims to the contrary notwithstanding.

The Whigs cannot be censured for failing to force the British out of Nicaragua, even though Monroe Doctrine drum-beaters repeatedly laid this charge at their door. The United States did not yet have the power to force the British out of Central America—or anywhere else—even if it wanted to. It can be said, however, that the Taylor-Fillmore Administration was guilty of bad faith and duplicity: it failed to live up to the pledge of President Zachary Taylor to José Guerrero, Nicaragua's supreme director, "that our efforts . . . will be animated by the desire which we sincerely cherish that the just territorial rights of Nicaragua may be respected by all nations."[43] Notwithstanding this and numerous like declarations by spokesmen for the Yankee republic, the signing of the Clayton-Bulwer Treaty gave the United States what it wanted—a green light for the canal project and for "Commodore" Vanderbilt. Nicaraguan sovereignty over the canal route suddenly lost the value the US had formerly placed on it.

Many historians of US foreign policy have said that though the Clayton-Bulwer Treaty did not immediately exorcise the British presence in Central America, it did nevertheless block further colonization of the area. They view the treaty, therefore, as an application of the Monroe Doctrine. Dexter Perkins wrote that the pledges contained in the first article "present the first, and indeed the only formal, treaty assurance in history by a European state with regard to colonizing activities in the New World."[44] If real, this achievement would merit approbation. But it rests on the postulate that it was the intent of Britain to acquire more colonies in the New World, while the United States was animated by a selfless desire to curb such depredations. The image of Uncle Sam as benevolent policeman has been so laboriously cultivated that the chastity of Yankee foreign policy in a world of loose morals is unquestioned. But if the Clayton-Bulwer Treaty was indeed a barrier to British ambition in Central America it would be logical to assume that if anyone tried to remove it, it would be they. But for the next half-century it was North Americans who would declaim against the treaty's restrictions. This leads to the inescapable conclusion that the British could—with greater justice—assert that the Clayton-Bulwer provisions "present the first, and only formal, treaty assurance in history by the *United States* with regard to colonizing activities in the New World."

The treaty had little difficulty gaining passage in the US Senate. Cornelius Vanderbilt, already one of the richest men in the United States, launched an intense lobbying effort on its behalf. In a preview of things to come, however, Stephen Douglas, a leader of the Democrats, opposed ratification on grounds that the treaty blocked US expansion.[45]

An interesting footnote to the treaty is the attitude the United States manifested toward the Miskitos. Secretary Clayton wrote Squier:

> We have never acknowledged, and never can acknowledge, the existence of any claim of sovereignty in the Mosquito King or any other Indian in America. To do so would be to deny the title of the United States to our own territory. Having always regarded an Indian title as a mere right of occupancy, we can never agree that such a title should be treated otherwise than as a thing to be extinguished at the will of the discoverer of the country.[46]

A CCORDING to the terms of the concession granted by Nicaragua, Vanderbilt's American Atlantic and Pacific Ship Canal Company acquired the exclusive right, pending completion of the canal, to steam navigation of the San Juan River and Lake Nicaragua, and to conveyance on land via rail or carriage. The company lost no time in taking advantage of these provisions to begin a highly lucrative passenger service from New York and New Orleans to San Francisco.

New ocean-going passenger steamships were put in service for both the Atlantic and Pacific legs of the journey, and special shallow-draft steamers were built for navigation of Nicaragua's inland waters. Vanderbilt expressed his gratitude to the British by naming one of these the *Sir Henry Bulwer.* Engineering works were undertaken to make the San Juan's rapids passable, and a road was marked out from La Virgen on the western shore of Lake Nicaragua to the Pacific port of San Juan del Sur, only twelve miles distant.

On July 14, 1851 the new steamer *Prometheus* sailed from New York with the first load of passengers for the route; Vanderbilt himself was on board. The first passages were difficult, and there were numerous complaints from passengers about poor food, crowded and unhealthy conditions on the vessels, and the discomforts of the twelve mile ride from Lake Nicaragua to the Pacific. A *New York Times* correspondent described a journey to California over the Nicaragua route: "Poor accommodations, poor attendance, poor fare, general confusion and universal discomfort were the order of the day," he reported. "The Company, in selling more tickets for the trip in question than their accommodations would warrant, did most grossly violate the rights of the travelling public, by forcing passengers to go like cattle, in a promiscuous jam, and that, too, through a hot and unhealthy climate."[47]

Gradually improvements were made, however. A mini-railroad, 1,500 feet long, was built to carry passengers and baggage around the San Juan rapids at Castillo Viejo. The mule path from La Virgen to San Juan del Sur was improved and paved with gravel. Fancy carriages—painted up in blue and white, the Nicaraguan colors, no less—were imported from the United States to carry gringos in style over the newly-surfaced road.

The war of the "Steamboat Commodores" was on: Vanderbilt was in hot competition with George Law's United States Mail Steamship Line, which operated a transit route across Panama. During 1849 Law's steamers had made the run from New York to Panama thirty times, with the profits estimated at $100,000 per trip. But now Vanderbilt's line across Nicaragua shaved several days off the journey to California, and to Yankees afflicted with gold fever those few days meant everything. The very first year of operations the Commodore's enterprise grossed $5 million with the net profit estimated between 20 and 40 percent.[48]

The advantages to the Nicaraguans were not so obvious. In fact, Nicaragua, which had expected so much in trickle-down benefits from the operation of Yankee-style free enterprise, soon began to collect some unexpected dividends.

At the beginning of August 1851, the factional squabbling that characterized Nicaraguan politics at the time boiled over when Leonese army officers arrested several Granadino members of the government. According to John Bozman Kerr, who replaced Squier as US chargé d'affaires, the action had no popular support; it seemed that the matter could be resolved peacefully and renewed civil war averted.[49] But there existed a state of nominal civil war in which governmental authority was claimed by both rival parties. Joseph L. White, Vanderbilt's partner in the Canal Company, took this opportunity to secure from the Grandinos a modification of the original Canal Company charter, creating the Accessory Transit Company as a separate entity, exclusively authorized to operate a transit route across the country.

Vanderbilt's operations had already created a great deal of suspicion in Nicaragua, Kerr reported, suspicion that "the Canal was only the stalking-horse for the transit"—a means for the company to gain admittance to Nicaragua and reap quick profits from the relatively low capital outlay involved in the mere shuttling of passengers across the isthmus. Himself concerned that the Nicaraguans' worries were justified, Kerr wrote:

> I fear from the excited state of the public mind in Leon this morning that an imprudent step has been taken by Mr. J. L. White, in his zeal to bring about a modification of the terms of the Charter and act of incorporation of the Canal Company, more favorable to those interested in the mere transit route . . . Mr. White seems very naturally to have regarded these people, as mere children, who could be led or driven any way, he might be disposed; but I fear, he may have carried his contempt for their intellect somewhat too far.

Nevertheless, he continued, "commended to me by the [State] Department, I will make it a point, however much I may differ with him . . . to sustain him as far as I can."[50]

The separation of the Canal Company charter to the detriment of Nicaraguan interests was highly unpopular, and coming as it did at a time when governmental authority was in dispute, it helped to sabotage the efforts at reconciliation. The result was the renewal of actual civil war.

In their weakness, the Leonese enlisted the aid of a group of North Americans then in Realejo, an ominous harbinger of things to come. One John Maclaine of Louisiana was commissioned a colonel, and he, along with some twenty-five other North Americans, attempted to capture a Granadino stronghold. They boasted publicly of their prospective feat, however, and the Granadinos had little difficulty in apprehending them and putting them on the next ship for California. This outbreak of the on-again, off-again war between León and Granada ended three months later when Honduran and Salvadoran mediators arranged a Leonese surrender.[51]

B Y 1852, prices for the new Accessory Transit Company shares had risen from $18 to $50. The Canal Company stock was being quoted at $3,600 a share, up from $800.[52]

Under the terms of its contract, the Canal Company was bound to begin a survey within one year. The subsequent report projected a canal that did not satisfy the contractual requirement that it be able to handle ships of the largest draft. When the proposal was submitted to the British, whose approval was needed under the Clayton-Bulwer Treaty and whose capital was necessary in any case, they turned it down. Britain was not interested in a canal that could not accommodate the larger ships used in the trade with Asia, and the greater costs of a deeper canal could only be repaid by charging prohibitively high tolls. As projected, the canal would mainly benefit the east-west coast trade of the United States.

In the spirit of free enterprise, Vanderbilt unloaded his Nicaragua Canal Company stock at $3,600 a share before announcing England's decision to disapprove the plan. Almost overnight the stock became worthless. The British rejection of the canal scheme helped make the Clayton-Bulwer Treaty an important issue in the 1852 election campaign, as the Democrats charged the Taylor-Fillmore Administration with betrayal of US interests.

Meanwhile the operations of the Transit Company, carrying the gold-seekers to California and the gold-finders back East, continued to be a windfall for the Commodore and his associates. US Chargé Kerr voiced his suspicions about the intentions of the Transit Company on several occasions, but the State Department continued to promote Vanderbilt's Nicaragua operations, owing to, in the words of Secretary of State Daniel Webster, "the magnitude of the interests, both public and private, at stake."[53] During the Fillmore Administration these became the chief, if not the sole, concern of United States policy in Central America.

One of the fruits of this policy was an attempt to negotiate a settlement to an old Nicaragua-Costa Rica border dispute and to the outstanding differences between Britain and Nicaragua over the Miskito question—issues that still clouded the prospects for a canal. The negotiations were held in Washington between the United States and Britain with the participation of Costa Rica. Amazing as it may seem, Secretary Webster did not invite the Nicaraguan minister to the United States, José de Marcoleta. The reason given was that Nicaragua, Honduras, and San Salvador were then engaged in an effort to revive the federation; the real reason was what Webster considered to be Marcoleta's irritating unwillingness to compromise Nicaraguan sovereignty.

The result of the negotiation was the "Webster-Crampton Agreement," signed by the United States and Britain on April 30, 1852. The Costa Rican representative, Felipe Molina, refused to sign, although his government later capitulated to pressure and ratified the accord anyway. Nicaragua rejected it, however, and a decree of its legislative assembly protested "all foreign interference in matters of her administration, and against the use of force to restrain her will and rights." At the same time it indicated a willingness to submit the issues to impartial arbitration.[54]

For Nicaragua to have ratified the Webster-Crampton agreement would have meant recognition of the separate existence of a "Mosquito Kingdom" comprising approximately one-third of what it had always claimed as its national territory. Although San Juan would have been returned to their jurisdiction, the Nicaraguans, in essence, were required to buy it back! On top of that, the agreement obligated them to make territorial cessions to Costa Rica.[55]

In a note to Acting Secretary of State Charles Conrad explaining his country's rejection (Webster had died in office), Nicaraguan Minister Marcoleta commented:

> The [Nicaraguan] Assembly could not help wondering . . . at the kind of imperative manner, in which the Government was asked to give [immediate approval of the treaty], knowing that the first despatch, which its plenipotentiary in Washington, had the honor of addressing to the Department of State, on the 24th of February of 1851, a despatch containing, and treating of a question of vital interest to Nicaragua, had remained unanswered, and that a reply to the same had always been evaded, under various pretexts, for a period of seventeen months, and that this reply, was still waited for, at the present day.[56]

The "despatch" to which Marcoleta referred had requested a clear statement from Webster as to whether the language of the Clayton-Bulwer Treaty implied US recognition of the British Miskito protectorate.

The Nicaraguan minister charged also that Robert Walsh, a US special agent then in Nicaragua to promote the treaty, had, "without being previously announced," gone to the residence of Nicaragua's supreme director. There he had failed to show, "either in his language or his deportment, the respect due to the representative of the Supreme Magistracy, breaking out into threats unbecoming the place where he was, and to his own self respect, & the decorum due to the government which had sent him there."[57]

Referring to Nicaragua's rejection of the agreement, Chargé Kerr had written Webster, "Strong motives may be found for this decided course in the sneers & insinuations of the other States, conveyed in the oft repeated sentiment, that Nicaragua was already lost to Central America, having been passed over into the hands of Americans." By attributing Nicaragua's recalcitrance to the attitudes of other states, the Yankee diplomat displayed a lack of appreciation for the value Nicaragua placed on its own territory. But his analysis did show that apprehensions were afoot even at that early epoch of US involvement in the region. And, as he pointed out in the same dispatch, those apprehensions were not without foundation:

> I have had occasion in a previous communication to deprecate the evils likely to result from the loose & unguarded conversations of Mr. White even during his short stay. It is this same imprudent talking among Americans, that has caused an immense amount of injury to the commercial interests . . . There are two or three Americans only in the in-

terior & some few others settled at Punta Arenas, yet this sentiment of vague apprehension has become a settled conviction, altogether traceable to blurting words about conquest & possession in due course of time.[58]

Further evidence that anxiety about the visitors from the North was well-founded came from the aforementioned Robert Walsh. Arriving at San Juan/Greytown in May 1852, Walsh wrote Secretary Webster that there were a number of North Americans then in the port who had designs on Nicaraguan territory.[59]

A letter from Joseph L. White of the Transit Company, addressed to Kerr, furnishes an interesting sidelight to the Webster-Crampton affair. In it he proposed to cheat the Miskitos out of the monetary compensation to which they would have been entitled under the agreement, and to bribe Nicaraguan officials into signing. For all this he claimed the authority of President Fillmore, while presuming to give instructions to the US representative:

Joseph L. White, Esq. to John Bozman Kerr, United States Chargé d'Affaires in Nicaragua

(CONFIDENTIAL)

My Dr. Sir: Enclosed I send to you the letter of Mr. Webster. The treaty I have of course seen.

The part about the *three years duty* to be paid to the Mosquitoes I wrote & caused to be inserted in lieu of the sum of $100.000, which was agreed on & put in the treaty. This I knew would deter Nica. from signing. Whereas the *nett proceeds* of a ten per cent duty will be *nett nothing*. Indeed nearly all the duty collected will be from those persons living at San Juan del Norte, & the State may still collect duties at San Carlos for her own benefit.

The Company have requested me to go to Nica. in obedience to the request of the President [of the US] as contained in the letter. I am obliged however to go first to Europe (the 15th inst.) & cannot reach Nicaragua before August. Long ere then however, you will I hope have procured the signature of Nica. to the treaty— If she proves obstinate & refuses to sign, *dont send the treaty back before I come, but protract the negotiations* until I come *with the means which never fail of success among Spaniards*—

These the Govt. will not of course furnish, but my *associates & myself will*.

Please present my regards to Mrs. Kerr, & remember me kindly when you see them to Señors Don Alfaro & Chamorro.

Very truly Yours.[60] [Emphasis in original.]

To his credit, Kerr sent the letter to the State Department with an indignant repudiation of White's presumptions. But the incident neverthe-less suggests the close relations that existed between the US administra-tion and the Transit Company.

T HE GOVERNMENT of Millard Fillmore, who became president when
   Zachary Taylor died in office, was principally noted for assiduous perse-cution of runaway slaves and for the employment of gunboat diplomacy to force open the markets of Japan to Yankee trade. It had no concern for what Nicaragua perceived as its vital interests. Instead, it forged ahead in promotion of "American Enterprise" as personified by Vanderbilt and his associates. There ensued an increasingly acrimonious interchange over the Webster-Crampton affair and relations between the two countries grew steadily worse.

Alleging that Marcoleta had leaked the contents of the Webster-Crampton Agreement to its opponents in the US Senate, the administra-tion demanded his recall. When Nicaragua failed to comply, Chargé Kerr was instructed to demand his own passport. During the final months of Fillmore's term of office, therefore, diplomatic relations were, in effect, broken off.

This symbolic first crossing of swords between superpower and ministate was anything but trivial, for through Nicaragua lay the chosen path of Manifest Destiny.

III

ADVENTURES ON
THE MISKITO COAST

> *[The Central American states] have
> yet a great deal to learn, and it will
> be for their advantage, if, in the result
> of the recent connection with other
> powers more advanced than them-
> selves, they shall derive some impor-
> tant lessons.*
>
> —*Edward Everett, US Senator
> from Massachusetts, March 1853.*

I F NICARAGUANS rejoiced at the Whigs' defeat at the polls and the
inauguration of Democrat Franklin Pierce in March 1853, their
hopes were ill-placed. Just eight days after the new president took office
there occurred an incident that, while insignificant measured against the
events that would follow, held great portent. Coming as it did so soon after the transfer of power (communication was slow at that time) it surely
bore the stamp of approval of both the incoming and outgoing administrations.

In accord with the Clayton-Bulwer Treaty, San Juan del Norte—renamed
"Greytown" after the governor of Jamaica—had been turned into a free
port. It functioned independently of the fictitious Kingdom of Mosquitia,
though remaining under a British protectorate.

Vanderbilt's Accessory Transit Company had obtained a spit of land across
the harbor from San Juan/Greytown, called Punta Arenas, for use as a coal-
ing station. It held this on lease from the "agent of the Mosquito King"
at a nominal rent of sixpence per month. Exceeding the terms of the lease,
the company erected other facilities on the site, which it used to transfer
passengers between ocean steamers and riverboats rather than unloading
them in town across the bay. The practice angered San Juan's residents,

who were thus denied any income from commerce with the travelers.

In February 1853 the municipal authorities decided to avail themselves of a clause in the company's lease that required it to vacate the property on demand. The company ignored the order even though the town offered—gratis—an alternative site on the south side of the bay and volunteered to pay moving expenses.

The municipal council then passed an ordinance giving the company thirty days to move and five days to take down the illegal structures, which were really no more than sheds. The company appealed to Henry Stevenson, the US commercial agent, and Stevenson, in turn, referred the matter to Washington. When the five days had elapsed, officers of the town proceeded to demolish the unauthorized buildings. Thomas Baldwin, a company agent who tried to interfere, was arrested for "threatening and seditious language," but immediately released on bond.

On March 10, deadline for the Transit Company to vacate, the US sloop-of-war *Cyane* sailed into San Juan harbor and landed a detachment of Marines at Punta Arenas. The next morning, when the town marshal and two workmen arrived to execute the writ of ejection, the Marines ordered them off.[1] The *New York Times* commented:

> We see no reason why the great and weighty interests of a Corporation like [the Transit Company] should be placed at the mercy of a gang of vagrants mustered from all quarters of the globe . . . In this prompt action of the commander of the *Cyane* we have an omen of the energy with which American interests are hereafter to be cared for abroad.[2]

A public meeting called by the municipal government of San Juan/Greytown approved a formal protest, which read in part:

> The occupancy of a portion of this city, by an armed force from the United States ship-of-war *Cyane,* for the purpose of resisting the execution of a legal process . . . and the actual resistance by force and arms presented to the officer charged with the execution of said process, cannot be viewed in any other light than as a direct invasion of the territory of this city.

Therefore, "being unable to repel force by force," the officers of the municipality registered their "solemn protest" and surrendered the town to the United States, charging Captain Hollins of the *Cyane* with "responsibility for any losses or damages the city or its inhabitants may sustain in the absence of lawful authority."[3]

Although the United States did not accept the symbolic surrender with its attendant responsibilities, the landing of Marines for the explicit purpose of protecting the Transit Company from due process of law was the first of many military interventions carried out by the US on Nicaraguan territory. The Nicaraguan government made no protest, however, owing to its hostility toward the local authorities at San Juan/Greytown.

Nicaragua did not recognize the town's government, a creature of the British Miskito protectorate. Moreover, since the beginning of the cross-country transit, an assortment of foreigners had made San Juan a center for land speculation schemes menacing to Nicaragua, some of which involved members of the municipal administration. Despite its own difficulties with the Transit Company, Nicaragua's main objective was to restore its uncontested control over the Atlantic Coast, especially San Juan. Up to that time its friction with the United States resulted from the latter's failure to live up to its promises, real or implied, to help restore Nicaraguan sovereignty. Mistakenly, the Nicaraguans took the landing of Marines as a sign that, under Pierce, the US was finally going to enforce the Monroe Doctrine and expel the British.

P RESIDENT Pierce appointed Solon Borland, a US senator from Arkansas, to be his minister to Nicaragua. The previous year Borland had created quite a stir when, in the Senate, he punched the superintendent of the census, breaking his nose. The *Times* had written on that occasion:

> It gives one such a pleasant impression of the character of an American Senator:- it holds up to admiration so beautifully Mr. Borland's personal accomplishments and official dignity:- it reflects such distinguished honor upon him and the country, that the world ought not willingly to let its memory die . . . It is a pity . . . that while a drunken vagabond about our wharves for a similar offence would be sent to Blackwell's Island, Mr. Borland should still waste his sweetness upon the Senate Chamber.[4]

As unlikely a candidate as he might have seemed for the job of diplomat, it was no accident that Pierce selected Borland, a representative of the slave states. It was generally understood in the United States at the time that the South wanted Central America for the expansion of slavery. And as Franklin Pierce launched his administration, Stephen Douglas and other leading Democrats in Congress were loudly denouncing the Clayton-Bulwer Treaty, which prevented the US from acquiring territory in the region.

Among other things, Secretary of State Marcy instructed Borland to seek from Nicaragua a treaty provision "allowing citizens of the United States to purchase and hold real estate for any purpose whatever."[5] Such colonizing had paved the way for the annexation of Florida, Texas, and California.

After his arrival in Nicaragua, Borland sent Marcy lengthy treatises denouncing Clayton-Bulwer:

To bind any nation indefinitely, thus, is not merely to place her at a disadvantage in the world's career, but absolutely, to enslave her, to the will or interests of another. To one, with character, position, wants and necessities, like ours, it would end in convulsions, paralysis, or death. To bind us, young, vigorous, growing, as we are, endowed with capabilities of indefinite expansion, and conscious of a necessity of existence which impels us to keep those capabilities forever on the stretch, to a time-worn, decaying, effete old monarchy, were, indeed, to tether the lithe, strong, progressive limits of youth, to the tottering, retrograde decrepitude of age.[6]

When flights of sexual imagery failed him, Borland came straight to the point: the Clayton-Bulwer Treaty would bring "serious and irretrievable injury to a government like ours, the necessity as well as the law of whose very existence, is *rapid enlargement—in this direction*."[7] [Emphasis in original.]

While expressing such sentiments to Marcy, Borland made an ostentatious pronouncement on the Monroe Doctrine in his introductory address to Nicaragua's supreme director. He followed this up with a lengthy defense of US territorial acquisitions, going so far as to announce that the Mexican War had "left [Mexico] richer and in better condition, every way, than when the war began."[8] These assurances to the Nicaraguans were necessary, he felt, because they were "a people ignorant, undiscriminating, conscious of their feebleness, jealous of their rights, and proverbially suspicious and excitable."[9]

But Minister Borland got carried away with his obsession to have the Clayton-Bulwer Treaty abrogated, inundating the State Department with dispatches recounting all kinds of fantastic intrigues by the British. The administration in Washington had its hands full elsewhere, and Secretary Marcy rebuked his minister to Nicaragua for this annoying activity. The huffy Borland took offense and tendered his resignation.

Solon Borland was on duty in Nicaragua less than a year. The career of this namesake of the ancient Greek lawmaker would be entirely forgettable had it not been for an incident that occured as he made his way home. On May 16, 1854, while Borland traveled down the San Juan River on board the Transit Company steamer, *Routh*, the boat rammed a bongo, one of the large canoes engaged in transporting freight between San Juan and Granada. The owner of the vessel, Antonio Paladino, proceeded to berate the steamer's captain in Spanish. The latter, a Captain Smith, grabbed a rifle and shot the Nicaraguan dead.[10]

When the *Routh* docked at Punta Arenas, the town marshal from San Juan/Greytown, a Black man, rowed across the bay with a party of deputies, intending to arrest Captain Smith for murder. Borland intervened and, at gunpoint, ordered the marshal and his men to depart.

That night the US minister went into town to see Joseph W. Fabens, the new US commercial agent. While he was at Fabens' house, the mayor—an old French merchant named Sigaud—came with some other municipal officers to discuss the Captain Smith affair. Borland became abusive, and one of the gathered bystanders threw a bottle, lightly grazing the minister's face. The blow caused a minor cut—less serious damage than the pugilistic diplomat had himself inflicted on the superintendent of the census two years earlier.

The crowd was then dispersed and the US minister spent the night in Fabens' house; the next morning he departed for the United States. Borland later charged that he had been held in the house under arrest.

The Pierce Administration turned the alleged insult to Borland into a major international incident with strong racial overtones. The warship *Cyane*, the same that had landed Marines a year earlier, was dispatched to San Juan to demand reparations or inflict punishment as Captain Hollins, its commander, saw fit.

Ephraim Squier had described San Juan in his book *Nicaragua*, first published in 1852:

> The town of San Juan consists of fifty or sixty palm thatched houses, or rather huts, arranged with some degree of regularity, upon the southwestern shore of the harbor . . . The dwellings . . . are of the rudest and most primitive description . . . They are, in fact, mere thatched sheds, roughly boarded up and floored, or made of a kind of wicker work of canes, sometimes plastered over with mud. The furniture, which seldom consists of more than a hammock, a high table, a few chairs, and a bed, is entirely in keeping with the edifices. Yet mean and uninviting as these structures are, they answer a very good purpose in a climate where anything beyond a roof to keep off the sun and the rain may almost be regarded as a superfluity.[11]

In 1854 San Juan was much the same as Squier had described it, with the addition of a few clapboard structures of a more imposing sort, the growth stimulated by the increased traffic up the river.

Finding no local authority willing to recognize the claim for reparations, on the morning of July 13, 1854 the *Cyane* began bombarding the town. Earlier, a shore party had seized the two ancient brass cannons and some small arms from the police station—apparently a precaution against any chance that the municipality might try to defend itself. Between 9:00 A.M. and 4:00 P.M. the ship's guns fired more than 200 rounds at point-blank range. When the shelling ended, few of San Juan's simple structures remained intact. Nonetheless, another party of forty or fifty sailors and Marines went ashore; torch in hand, they passed from house to house and burned all that remained. Witnesses testified that before setting fire to the town the sailors and Marines looted the wreckage, including warehouses containing liquor. They became so drunk that many had to be carried back aboard ship, that task being accomplished only with great difficulty.

Fortunately, the town's inhabitants had warning, and were able to evacuate before the bombardment began. No lives were lost. But the destruction of San Juan left the local population without food or shelter, which caused most to suffer severe hardships.

Claims against the United States on behalf of the merchants whose goods were destroyed—English, French, German, Spanish, Nicaraguan, and even US—amounted to $2 million. A number of hapless individuals were totally ruined. Though some of them, or their descendants, pursued the claims for the next half-century, successive United States' governments steadfastly refused to make reparation.

Spain's minister in Washington, Don Leopoldo Augusto de Cueto, in a dispatch to Madrid, characterized the destruction of San Juan as "a sort of biblical punishment, which, being exercised by mortals and inspired by the designs of an inhumane and egotistical policy, can produce only scandal and indignation."[12] Indeed, the destruction of San Juan del Norte was condemned by the world, even by many in the United States, causing President Pierce to devote a large portion of his second annual message to Congress to defense of his action.

San Juan, said Ephraim Squier, was a place where "Whites, Indians, negroes, mestizos, and sambos— black, brown, yellow and fair,—all mingle together with the utmost freedom, and in total disregard of those conventionalities which are founded on caste."*[13]

Race relations as lax as these must have been galling to most, if not all, of the two thousand or so North Americans transiting through San Juan each month. The United States was then the most race-conscious nation on earth, slavery being the contemporary national preoccupation. The fact that some runaway slaves from the US had apparently found their way to San Juan only added to the irritation. To John Wheeler, Borland's replacement as US minister to Nicaragua and himself a North Carolina slave owner, San Juan was "the refuge of runaways, renegades, & rascals."[14]

Race mixing was not in itself sufficient reason for the United States to obliterate the town, but it did allow the Pierce Administration to appeal

---

* "Sambo" is a corruption of the Spanish *zambo*, the term for a mixture of African and indigenous blood, as *mestizo* is a mixture of European with indigenous. The Miskitos are *zambos*.

to rampant racism for support of its action. Pierce himself described San Juan/Greytown as a "pretended community, a heterogeneous assemblage gathered from various countries, and composed for the most part of blacks and persons of mixed blood, [who] had previously given other indications of mischievous and dangerous propensities." They had followed "a course of insolence and plunder," he said, "tending directly to the insecurity of the lives of numerous travelers and of the rich treasure belonging to our citizens passing over this transit way." They were "incapable of being treated in any other way than as a piratical resort of outlaws or a camp of savages." If the action had not been taken, Pierce claimed, "it would have encouraged in these lawless men a spirit of insolence and rapine most dangerous to the lives and property of our citizens at Punta Arenas, and probably emboldened them to grasp at the treasures and valuable merchandise continually passing over the Nicaragua route."[15]

But while Pierce exploited racism, the actual motives for the destruction of San Juan del Norte were political. The claimed British protectorate over the port allowed him to appear to be taking strong action against Britain, and to show contempt for the Clayton-Bulwer Treaty. More meaningful moves on behalf of his constituency in the Southern slave states were then stalled by growing resistance in the United States to slavery expansion. Moreover, the attack on San Juan was virtually risk-free. Britain, then bogged down in the Crimean War, was not in a position to respond even if it had wanted to.

Also prompting the action was the Transit Company, which desired to demonstrate, once and for all, who was boss on the isthmus. From New York, the ubiquitous, letter-writing Vanderbilt partner, Joseph L. White, wrote Joseph Fabens, the US commercial agent at San Juan:

Captain Hollins, commanding the corvette, *Cyane*, leaves on Monday. You will see by his instructions, which I have written on the margin, that it is intended his authority would not be so exercised as to show any mercy to the town or people.

If the scoundrels are soundly punished, we can take possession, and build it up as a business place, put in our own officers, transfer the jurisdiction, and you know the rest.

It is of the last importance that the people of the town should be taught to fear us. Punishment will teach them. After which you must agree with them as to the organization of a new government, and the officers of it. Everything now depends on you and Hollins. The latter is all right. He fully understands the outrage, and will not hesitate in enforcing reparation.

I hope to hear from you that all has been properly executed.[16]

Departing from the policy of silent acquiescence that it followed during the Marine landing a year earlier, the Nicaraguan government condemned the destruction of San Juan, notwithstanding that its continued animosity toward the town's authorities led it to accept the US version of events, which cast Borland as the innocent victim of an outrage. Through its minister in Washington, José de Marcoleta, Nicaragua demanded reparations for the losses sustained by its citizens. Secretary Marcy rejected the Nicaraguan claim, telling Marcoleta, "Nicaragua may think herself kindly treated if she is not held responsible for the acts of those who were permitted by her to occupy her territory and perpetrate deeds injurious to friendly powers." Marcy went on to berate the Nicaraguans for failing to drive out the British.[17] In reply, Marcoleta reminded Marcy that

> the government of Nicaragua has always been ready to take possession of that port, and to reestablish its authority and Jurisdiction there, if the government of the American Union had thought it prudent to sustain Nicaragua in this undertaking . . . [but if] the American Union, with 26 millions of inhabitants, with its navy, its militia, its revenues, its power and immense influence, has shrunk before the responsibility and the contingencies of this enterprise, can Nicaragua be justly censured?[18]

Lacking warships with which to raze New York or San Francisco, however, Nicaragua could not enforce its demand for reparations, and there the matter ended.

N EW concerns soon began to occupy the attention of the assiduous Señor de Marcoleta. In the autumn of 1854, advertisements for the "Central America Land and Mining Company" began to appear in newspapers throughout the United States. Prime mover behind the enterprise was "Colonel" Henry L. Kinney.

Kinney was an important citizen of early Texas, one of the founders of the town of Corpus Christi, where he amassed a fortune trading in livestock and speculating in real estate. He served in the Mexican War as quartermaster of the Texas Volunteers and got himself elected for several terms to the Texas legislature. But the most promising of Kinney's land dealings was the acquisition of a title to 22.5 million acres of Nicaragua's Miskito Coast.

In December 1854 Kinney was in Washington promoting a colonization scheme for the territory among friends in the Pierce Administration. The *New York Times* Washington correspondent wrote:

> Col. H. L. Kinney, the celebrated founder of the Texan Rangers, is still

in town . . . The latter gentleman has been here now a week or more, has had interviews with the President and other members of the Government, and has satisfied them entirely that the enterprise is not a filibustering one in any sense,* and contemplates neither a violation nor an evasion of our neutrality laws . . . The territory covered by the Company's grants . . . lies just north of the latitude of Greytown, and extends from the Caribbean sea to the mountain ridge which divides the Atlantic and Pacific slopes . . . If this enterprise is carried forward in a spirit of justice, and with the promised energy, its political results will necessarily be very important. Central America is destined to occupy an influential position in the family of nations, if her advantages of location, climate and soil are availed of by a race of "Northmen," who shall supplant the tainted, mongrel and decaying race which now curses it so fearfully. The success of Col. Kinney and his friends will settle our Mosquito question with Great Britain most effectually. That power is estopped from murmuring when she sees her long coveted power in Central America receding at the advances of the white man; for these colonists hold their lands by undoubted, undisputed grants from the Mosquito King of Britain's own making. That the influence of the new Republic will speedily spread itself all over Nicaragua, and absorb the whole of that State with its inefficient Government, there can be little doubt; humanity will be the gainer by the event, and the commercial world will reap great benefit from the settlement of an enterprising, energetic people, and the establishment of a strong Government at a point where promptness and security in interoceanic communication is of primary importance.[19]

Kinney had bought his title to 70 percent of Nicaragua's land area from Samuel H. Shepherd, a trader living in San Juan, for an estimated one-half million dollars. Shepherd, in turn, had received it in 1839 as a grant from Robert Charles Frederick, "king" of the Miskitos. The claim had been declared null and void in 1841 by the late "king's" son, for whom Alexander MacDonald, the British superintendent of Belize, was then acting as "regent," the "prince" not yet having reached majority.

The Nicaraguans were obviously not going to recognize such a claim emanating from the Miskito "kingdom." Kinney apparently hoped to be sustained by the United States, and he seems to have had good reason to think that he would be. His company issued 225,000 shares of stock, each of which was supposedly convertible into one hundred acres of land

---

* The word "filibuster" comes from Spanish, French, and Dutch roots meaning "freebooter" or "pirate." At the time, filibustering did not refer to long-winded speechmaking in Congress, but to privately organized military expeditions for the conquest of foreign territory. It was a common phenomenon in the epoch of Manifest Destiny, although when successfully employed, as it was, in part, in the acquisition of Florida and Texas, it was no longer referred to as filibustering.

in Nicaragua. Thomas Rusk, a US senator from Texas, reportedly bought 5,000 shares. Caleb Cushing, President Pierce's attorney general, was also said to be a stockholder. Kinney's partners and associates included Sidney Webster, Franklin Pierce's private secretary; Fletcher Webster, son of the late Secretary of State Daniel Webster; and Joseph Warren Fabens, United States commercial agent at San Juan and confidant of the Transit Company's Joseph White.[20]

Pierce had appointed Fabens to the post of commercial agent the previous year. Originally from Massachusetts, the latter went to Texas after a brief stint in the foreign service; there he became a colonel in the army of the Texas Republic and made friends with Kinney and with General William L. Cazneau. All three would become intimately involved in schemes to annex prospective slave territory to the United States. While sending Fabens to San Juan del Norte, Pierce dispatched Cazneau to Santo Domingo, where he would sniff out the prospects for US acquisition of that island.*

When the Central American Land and Mining Company began purchasing arms it became clear that it was not looking toward the peaceful litigation of its dubious claim. Opening offices in several major US cities, it advertised extensively for colonists and chartered a steamship. W. B. Phillips, a Central American Land and Mining Company representative, wrote a prospective colonist:

> The distracted, decaying state of society in the countries of Central America leads us to suppose that the day is not far distant when the whole of that interesting and important part of the world must be controlled by a more vigorous and enterprizing race, such as we contemplate transporting there.[22]

Marcoleta bombarded the State Department with protests. He called on Marcy to enforce the US neutrality laws against the planned expedition and backed up his demands with the evidence from his latest detective work on the company's activities. Not resting there, he took out newspaper advertisements that warned the gullible against Kinney's schemes.

Marcy at first brushed off the protests, claiming the company was simply "an association for business purposes . . . having a peaceful pursuit in

---

* General William Cazneau was one of the early Anglo settlers in Texas; he had been closely connected with its separation from Mexico and annexation to the United States. After Pierce appointed him special agent to Santo Domingo, he became involved in efforts to annex the island. Both he and his wife, Jane Maria Cazneau—an eminent pro-slavery publicist—participated in numerous schemes to expand slave territory. Mrs. Cazneau was said to be a cousin of James Buchanan, who succeeded Pierce in the presidency and again dispatched Cazneau as "special agent" to Santo Domingo.[21]

view," with which the United States "has no authority to prohibit or interpose."[23] But by the spring of 1855, something of a change in attitude had come about. The ruckus raised by Marcoleta, who was joined by Costa Rican minister Felipe Molina, apparently had some effect.

Perhaps more efficacious in producing results, however, was a proverbial falling out among thieves: the various participants and backers of the scheme began intriguing against each other.[24] The Transit Company, which had at first looked with favor on the enterprise, became suspicious that, once established at San Juan, Kinney might interfere with their operations. It now brought its considerable influence to bear against the planned invasion.

Kinney and Fabens were indicted by a Federal Grand Jury in April 1855 for organizing a military expedition against Nicaragua. They were subsequently arrested, but released on bond. Secretary Marcy fired Fabens from his position as US commercial agent, though not till a week after his arrest.[25] Nevertheless, despite the legal action pending against them and the fact that the Coast Guard had been ordered to prevent the sailing of their chartered steamer, the pair were able to proceed with their plans.

In one of his many protest notes to Secretary Marcy, Marcoleta noted the lack of enthusiasm with which the scheme was being hindered by the United States:

> The facility with which Col. Kinney and his associates abandon one vessel and one port of departure and secure another vessel at another port has induced a belief in the mind of the undersigned that the numbers and ramifications of this Expedition are far greater and more extended than has hitherto been supposed.[26]

Kinney finally succeeded in setting out for Nicaragua, but owing to the various obstacles placed in his path, the number of his "colonists" had dwindled to thirteen. Arriving in San Juan, now largely rebuilt after the destruction of 1854, he gained control of the municipal administration and proclaimed himself "governor." He began publishing a newspaper called *The Central American*, whose purpose was to attract North Americans. The British refused to recognize his claim, however, and Kinney failed to obtain further support in the US. He abandoned his "governorship" in 1856 and returned, broke, to the United States. Not one to give up easily, he managed to interest a group of English Mormons in his claim and went back to San Juan in 1858. He again tried to gain control of the local government, but this time he was placed under arrest. The US Navy intervened on his behalf, securing his release after he promised never to return.

Colonel Henry L. Kinney was killed in a gunfight in Matamoros, Mexico, in 1861. The State of Texas has seen fit to name one of its counties in his honor.[27]

SLAVERY, WAR, AND WILLIAM WALKER

*Slavery and war have thus been the
two great forerunners of civilization.*

—*The* Richmond Enquirer, *1854.*

H ENRY Kinney's filibustering expedition to Nicaragua had been
set to depart on May 7, 1855. It was delayed by legal challenges until
June 6. On May 4, 1855, while the attention of Nicaraguans and
the North American press was focused on Kinney, William Walker set sail
from San Francisco.

Over the years a small number of books about Walker have appeared
in his homeland. Some were personal reminiscences; others were written
in the vein of adventure stories—Walker's "adventures" were quite unusual;
at least one took the form of a novel. The rest are found among the dusty
historical treatises that occupy the sparse shelf of Yankee knowledge reserved
for doings "south of the border."

Most North Americans are ignorant of Walker. His name doesn't appear in school books. Even in Nashville, Tennessee, his birthplace, no doubt
but few have stopped to read the small plaque at 4th Avenue North and
Commerce Street that tersely commemorates his career. Yet in Central
America almost every child lucky enough to go to school has heard of William Walker, because Walker was, as it says in *Ripley's Believe It Or Not,*
the "American who became president of Nicaragua."[1]

Walker has not always been the victim of his country's ignominious
neglect. In fact, during the 1850s his name was a household word; he frequently made the newspaper headlines, receiving more attention from the
press than the president of the United States. On four occasions during
1857 the *New York Times* devoted its entire front page to him.[2]

But Walker has not found favor with the writers of history. He was, after all, a failure. For the socializers—those who look to the past for role

models, for confirmation of the prevailing institutions, ideology, and political practice of the present—Walker is a skeleton in the closet; he doesn't fit in the pantheon of Founding Fathers, Pioneers, and Captains of Industry who "made America what it is today." He is part of an unpleasant chapter in the history of the United States they would rather forget—or rewrite.

WALKER was born in 1824 in Nashville, where his father ran a mercantile and insurance business. He graduated from the University of Tennessee and went on to medical school at the University of Pennsylvania, receiving an M.D. After pursuing further medical studies in Paris, he returned to Nashville, but apparently decided that medicine was not his true calling. He moved to New Orleans, studied law, and passed the Louisiana bar exam, only to discover that lawyering was not his vocation either. Turning next to journalism, he became editor and co-owner of the New Orleans *Crescent,* a short-lived enterprise whose main claim to fame, aside from Walker himself, was that Walt Whitman worked there as a printer for a few months in 1848.[3]

Though destined to quit the bar, there was a lawyerly cautiousness about William Walker that manifested itself even at his most prodigious moments. During his tenure as *Crescent* editor he advocated a low-key approach on the slavery issue, arguing that the "fire-eaters," who favored an aggressive policy by the slave states, would only radicalize the Abolitionists, thereby leading to the destruction of the slave system altogether. Such "conservatism" on the question had been in vogue in the Old South in balmy days gone by, but in the late 1840s the clock was running out for planter society. The knives were being sharpened for the coming showdown, and Walker's views were out of tune. The *Crescent* folded in late 1849. But for the ambitious Walker changing views would come as easily as changing professions. Soon he would do more than fall into step—he would move to the front rank.

There were great stirrings on the horizon. Vast new territories had been seized from Mexico; the California gold rush was on. It was the age of Manifest Destiny and Walker was not to be left out. He joined the California migration, but not to hunt gold with a pick and shovel, for at no time did this taciturn little man—who resembled more than anything a Calvinist preacher—fall prey to vulgar avarice.

In California he plied his trades of lawyer and journalist, even dabbled in Democratic politics while waiting to find his true life work. He did not have to wait long.

The California newspapers were filled with stories of rich gold and silver deposits in Sonora and of atrocities committed by the Apaches against the other inhabitants of the Mexican state. They urged North Americans to "save" the citizens of Sonora from the Indians and from the alleged incompetence of their own government. Their noble endeavors would be rewarded, naturally, with the gold and silver.

Through his own journalistic efforts, Walker gained some notoriety in San Francisco, then still a small town, and became associated with the mining and commercial interests who were eager to grab more of Mexico. In June 1853 the lawyer-journalist represented a group of Californians trying to gain Mexican government approval for a colonizing scheme in Sonora, one of many such attempts made in those days. However "incompetent" the Mexicans may have appeared to the gringos, they had learned their lesson from the experience of Texas, and weren't about to repeat it in Sonora if they could help it. William Walker, the lawyer, was rebuffed.

But opportunity knocked, and if it required him to adopt yet another profession, Walker was ready to oblige. Filibustering was the profession that now suggested itself.

Walker purchased a brig and collected forty-five disappointed gold diggers and miscellaneous fortune hunters whom he dubbed the "First Independence Battalion." He appointed himself to the rank of colonel, and the troupe set sail for Mexico. Thus outfitted, Manifest Destiny landed at La Paz, Baja California, on November 3, 1853. The filibusters immediately proclaimed the "Republic of Lower California," and Colonel William Walker became President William Walker. They moved the "capital" north to Ensenada, near the US border, where supplies and reinforcements could reach them more easily. *Alta California*, a San Francisco newspaper, hailed Walker for "releasing Lower California from the tyrannous yoke of declining Mexico."[4]

After two months in Ensenada, the "president" was joined by his law partner, Henry Watkins, with 230 recruits. Thus far Walker had encountered only light resistance, owing to the sparse population and the weakness of Mexico. On January 18, 1854, therefore, he expanded his domain by proclaiming the "Republic of Sonora," which included both Baja California and Sonora, even though he had yet to set foot in the latter Mexican state.

While Walker was thus occupying part of northern Mexico, James Gadsden, the United States minister to that country, succeeded in gaining Mexican assent to the sale of nearly 30,000 square miles of northern Sonora for $10 million. Mexico had previously refused to sell the territory, which included valuable mineral deposits. The Gadsden Purchase agreement was signed in Mexico City on December 30, 1853.

The US government then decided the time had come for one of its selective enforcements of the neutrality laws against filibustering. Walker's recruiting office in San Francisco was closed, and the supply of recruits and provisions dried up. Their morale declining, Walker's followers began to desert. An attempted crossing of the Colorado River to occupy Sonora turned into a disaster; the party lost all its horses as well as the cattle it had stolen. Chased by Mexican irregulars, Walker and thirty-three bedraggled followers fled north to the California border. There they ignominiously surrendered to US military authorities on May 8, 1854, six months and five days after beginning their escapade.

Standing trial in October 1854, Walker was acquitted of violating the neutrality laws. Although his partner, Watkins, and his "secretary of state," a man named Emory, had been tried earlier and fined $1,500 each, the sums were never paid. Emphasizing the federal government's lack of seriousness about neutrality law enforcement, Secretary of War Jefferson Davis wrote the commander of the Department of the Pacific, Major General Wool, whose troops had acted against Walker, "In instructing you to aid the civil authorities it was not intended that you should originate arrests and prosecutions for civil misdemeanors."[5]

More was at stake in Sonora than the designs of commercial and mining interests. The Southern Pacific Railroad had become one of the pet projects by which the South hoped to revive its stagnant slave economy, and the most practicable route for the line passed through the territory acquired in the Gadsden Purchase. The slaveholders saw the railroad as a means "to bind California to the South with hooks of steel," as well as to facilitate the expansion of slavery into the Southwest. James Gadsden, a South Carolina planter and railroad promoter, was not only a prime mover behind the Southern Pacific plan, but is said to have personally chosen the route through northern Sonora.[6]

Historians have treated Walker's exploits in Mexico as a comic opera affair. Yet the same interests spurred both Gadsden's mission to the Mexican capital and the filibuster expedition. Until Walker's invasion, which for Mexico bore an uncomfortable resemblance to the opening gambits in the seizure of Texas and California, the Mexican government showed no inclination to part with more of its territory. Explicit or implicit, the threat was clear: if Mexico failed to cede the real estate for the price offered, it risked losing even more with no compensation whatever.

It was not just coincidence that linked Gadsden's carrot to Walker's stick. Perhaps the filibuster was an unwitting cat's paw; perhaps these merely represented separate efforts toward the same end. In any case, having winked at Walker's filibustering, the Pierce Administration made use of his presence in Northern Mexico to lubricate the course of negotiations in Mexico City.

U NDAUNTED by the turn of events that prevented him from becoming the Sam Houston of Sonora, Walker returned to law practice in the northern California town of Marysville. He supplemented this with editorship of the Sacramento daily *Democratic State Journal* and participation in the internal politics of the California Democratic Party. Shortly afterward he returned to San Francisco to edit a new paper, the *Commercial Advertiser.*

One of the paper's proprietors was an entrepreneur named Byron Cole, who was also part owner of the Honduras Mining and Trading Company. Like many others, Cole had become interested in the potential wealth of Central America as a passenger of Vanderbilt's Nicaragua Transit Company. On a recent trip to Honduras he had passed through Nicaragua, where civil war had broken out once again. Stopping in León, headquarters of the "Democrats," as the Liberals then called themselves, Cole met Liberal leader Francisco Castellón, whose side was not faring well. Foolishly, Castellón solicited Cole to recruit a force of 300 North American mercenaries to help turn the tide against the Granada-based "Legitimists"— Conservatives who held that their control of the government was "legitimately" derived from the constitution of 1854.

Cole took the proposal to Walker. The latter, satisfying his lawyer's circumspection with a signed contract, was only too happy to oblige.

Though the doctor-lawyer-journalist and ex-"president" of Sonora agreed to provide 300 mercenaries to the Nicaraguan Liberals, when he set sail from San Francisco on May 4, 1855, his party numbered only 58. These Walker anointed with the title "The Fifty-Six Immortals"—apparently someone couldn't count.

Docking at Realejo on June 16, the Immortals were greeted by Castellón, who gave them a second christening: "El Falange Americano," the American Phalanx.[7] The Liberal leader restored Walker to his former rank of "colonel," the seeming favorite of Southern aristocrats, Latin dictators, and freebooters alike.

With the formalities ended, Walker at once became embroiled in a conflict with his employers. They counseled an immediate advance on Granada, but the colonel of the American Phalanx wanted to sail south and secure the "Vanderbilt Trail," to recruit from the transit passengers and—though he didn't tell the Nicaraguans—build up a purely North American force. The Liberals were desperate, so they let Walker have his way.

The filibuster landed his men near Brito on the Pacific coast during the night of June 28, intending to stage a surprise attack on Rivas, only a few miles inland. The town lay just north of the transit road, and the strong Legitimist force there posed a serious obstacle to Walker's plan. As it was, the garrison had been warned of his impending arrival on the coast by Thomas Manning, the British vice-consul in León.

Walker was in luck that night. A detachment sent to ambush his landing party failed to arrive in time, its commander having sustained an eye injury from an overhanging branch. Nevertheless, when the American Phalanx arrived on the outskirts of Rivas at noon the following day, after stumbling around in the woods all night, the garrison was waiting.

Military strategy was not William Walker's long suit. His battle plan consisted of a frontal assault into the center of town to capture the main plaza. Once there, the Fifty-Six Immortals found themselves surrounded and had to fight their way back out, at the cost of twelve dead and ten wounded. The Nicaraguan Liberal troops who accompanied the filibusters, seeing nothing in it for themselves, had faded away as the battle commenced. That Walker's career did not end that day, or at least much sooner than it did, was due in large part to the fact that the North Americans were armed with rifles and Colt revolvers, while the Central American armies, made up of conscripted peasants, carried antiquated, inaccurate, flintlock muskets. And, in most cases, the landed gentry and merchants who comprised the general staffs of the native armies were no more competent militarily than Walker.

The filibusters retreated to León, where they blamed their defeat on treachery by the Liberal commander-in-chief, General Muñoz. After a period of recuperation, Walker, insubordinately refusing to integrate his American Phalanx into the Liberal army, coerced Castellón into providing him with support for another attempt to establish control over the transit route. The Liberals, who had looked on the United States as the beacon of democracy, were beginning to repent their credulity, yet the very weakness that induced them to place their hopes in foreign mercenaries in the first place now rendered them incapable of taking timely action to check the threat.

Meanwhile, the first group of reinforcements had arrived from the United States, including a former Prussian military officer named Bruno von Natzmer. The new arrivals more than compensated for the earlier filibuster losses.

Walker now landed at San Juan del Sur, western terminal of the Transit. He was not yet ready to chance another attack on Rivas, however. Instead he marched his men over the transit road to La Virgen, western disembarkation point for Vanderbilt's Lake Nicaragua steamers, there to await reinforcements from among the California-bound passengers.

To Santos Guardiola, the Honduran general who had recently arrived to take command of the Legitimist forces at Rivas, it looked as though Walker were trying to commit suicide. The wooden Transit Company warehouses on the lakefront that the filibusters occupied were no fortification against cannon, and the lake cut off all retreat. Guardiola's plan for a three-pronged assault to do away with the northern interlopers was an able one. But the cannon broke its carriage on the rough mule path from Rivas and was consequently useless. Then, during the attack, when a flanking movement had fought its way close enough to storm the filibuster positions, the needed reserves failed to arrive and the advance was pinned down and cut to pieces by the superior range and accuracy of Walker's rifles. The vicissitudes of warfare turned certain victory into disaster. More important, from the battle at La Virgen there began to spread among the natives a terror of the Yankees' weaponry and a belief that their diminutive leader in his black frock coat was some sort of reincarnated Napoleon.

Walker was having a run of luck. After his success at La Virgen, the Legitimists sent the bulk of their army to reinforce Rivas. Colonel Fernando Chamorro, commander of the garrison at Granada, committed the indiscretion of sending a dispatch to Rivas via the captain of a Transit Company steamer warning that the Legitimist capital had been left virtually undefended. Captain Scott immediately handed the dispatch over to Walker, who now devised the single clever piece of strategy in his self-made military career. Taking possession of one of the lake steamers, he sailed around Granada and disembarked his men three miles to the north. They attacked the city on the morning of October 13, 1855; the only defenders, a detachment of convalescents, were overcome in a matter of minutes.

The "Grey-Eyed Man of Destiny," as Walker dubbed himself, now controlled the Conservative capital. Holding the leading families hostage, he forced the surrender of General Ponciano Corral, the Legitimist military commander. As a demonstrative measure, Walker ordered Nicaraguan Minister of Foreign Affairs Don Mateo Mayorga shot. He had General Corral himself killed a few weeks later. Although José Maria Estrada, the Legitimist president, took refuge in Masaya and called for resistance to the death against the filibusters, his resolve was not shared by those whose relatives were in Walker's clutches.[8]

The head filibuster compelled the warring parties to sign a truce, creating a puppet government in which he pitted the rival factions against each other. For president he selected an aging former customs official, Patricio Rivas, who, for his lack of mettle, was known as "Patas Arriba" ("feet up"), a pun on his name meaning "topsy-turvy." Walker promoted himself to "general-in-chief" of the "Nicaraguan" army. But he and his adventurers became the real power in the state as they effectively disbanded the native armed forces of both sides. Walker accomplished this by the stratagem of declaring an all-volunteer army, knowing that the peasants conscripted as cannon-fodder for Nicaragua's civil wars were anxious to get back to cultivating their little plots. Here and elsewhere the lawyer-filibuster showed a definite talent for achieving his ends through legalistic dissimulation. In this he was the prototype of the briefcase-carrying freebooters of a later era.

Acquiescence to Walker's imposed regime was not total, however. Estrada, the Legitimist president, Colonel Tomás Martinez, the able commander of the Masaya garrison, and a number of loyal government officials and troops went into exile in Honduras. They denounced as traitors those who had signed the agreement with Walker, and a few months later they returned to Nicaragua to establish a provisional government at Ocotal. The

José María Estrada

indefatigable Don José de Marcoleta refused to abandon his post as Nicaraguan minister to the United States; instead he carried on an international diplomatic struggle against the filibuster regime, and made himself once again the nemesis of the State Department.

Yet a question remains, one that long plagued the psyche of Nicaragua: how could a small handful of North American adventurers, virtually overnight, take control of an independent nation? Luck, superior armaments, the shortage of professional officers among the native troops—all these played a role, but were not decisive. The most important part of the answer lay in the condition of Nicaraguan politics. Factionalism had reached such a pitch that both sides, Democrat and Legitimist—or more appropriately, Leonese and Granadino—were oblivious to the tiger at the gates.

D ON FRUTO CHAMORRO, godfather of the Conservative Granadino aristocracy, had been elected supreme director in 1853. He believed that Nicaragua's troubles would be solved by strengthening the executive—transforming the two-year, relatively ineffectual supreme directorate into a four-year presidency with greater powers. There was little opposition to these reforms in theory. But in practice a very uneasy truce reigned, and the Leonese were less than elated about the prospect of a strong central power under the control of their archrivals. Don Fruto did nothing to calm their fears when he pledged in his inaugural address, "I will pay special attention to the maintenance of peace; like a good father, I will, with a lump in my throat, wield the lash to chastise the errant son who disturbs it."[9]

He called a Constituent Assembly to effect the necessary changes to the 1838 constitution. A large number of Liberals were elected. But before the Assembly could convene, Chamorro declared that three of the leading León delegates—Francisco Castellón, Máximo Jerez, and José Guerrero—were convicted of conspiracy by "secret documents," and exiled them from the country. Now under the control of Chamorro's Conservative circle, the Assembly proceeded to draft a new constitution that contained not only the desirable changes in the executive, but also a series of oligarchic measures that restricted the franchise and created a number of property qualifications for officeholding. Chamorro's heavy-handed policies were unpopular even in supposedly Conservative Granada, where they provoked a heated debate. But most influential citizens resolved to back Chamorro for reasons of factional discipline. For their part, the Leonese declared the new consititution illegal on account of their delegates' expulsion. Civil war was once again the order of the day.

At first the combat went well for the Leonese. Championing the democratic cause against the oligarchic pretensions of Chamorro and his clique, they enjoyed popular support. But then, committing a number of atrocities and politico-military blunders, they lost the moral high ground. The pendulum swung back to the government in Granada, where José Maria Estrada had assumed the presidency on Fruto Chamorro's death.

General José Trinidad Muñoz had just returned from exile in El Salvador to take command of the Leonese troops when news arrived that William Walker, the invader of Sonora, was on his way to Nicaragua in fulfillment of the contract signed by Francisco Castellón and Byron Cole. Muñoz at once saw the danger to the nation and did his best to avert it by seeking an end to the conflict. Others, like Dr. Rosalio Cortés in Granada, were moved by similar sentiments. But the few farsighted individuals in each camp were unable to prevail: the peace talks foundered on the question of whether the Chamorro-Estrada government and its 1854 constitution would be recognized as the "legitimate" authority.

There matters stood when Walker and his Fifty-Six Immortals landed. Muñoz soon earned Walker's enmity as he continued trying to convince Castellón to expel the filibusters before it was too late. But Castellón was unwilling or unable to act.

A few days after Walker returned from his defeat at Rivas, Muñoz was killed at the Battle of El Sauce under suspicious circumstances: his troops had defeated a column of Hondurans on their way to join the Legitimists, and with the battle already over, Muñoz received a fatal bullet wound in the back.

Most Liberal leaders simply refused to take the filibuster threat serious-ly. Dazzled by the prospect of factional gain, they deluded themselves into thinking they could use Walker to attain their own objectives. As for the Legitimists, their emblem bore the motto "Legitimacy or Death": they were prepared to follow that absurd prescription wherever it led, even to the death of the nation. Nor was Walker's capture of Granada sufficient to awaken many leading citizens to the peril. Máximo Jerez, who enjoyed a reputation as Nicaragua's greatest Liberal, joined Walker's puppet regime as a cabinet member for a time, thinking to use the position to the advan-tage of his party.[10]

ONCE the North Americans established themselves in Granada, aid from the Accessory Transit Company began to arrive. With a yearly salary of $60,000, Cornelius K. Garrison, the West Coast agent for the com-pany, was easily one of the highest paid men in the United States. A ship-ping, banking, and railroad magnate, some years later Garrison was listed as the country's sixteenth wealthiest capitalist.[11] Garrison's fortunes, as well as those of the Transit Company, would soon become closely entwined with filibustering in Nicaragua.

There is no evidence that the Transit Company provided backing for Walker before he had established a foothold in Nicaragua. But Garrison, who was also mayor of San Francisco, was apparently aware of and approved Walker's plans before he sailed. Though the successful businessman was not yet ready to invest money or reputation in such a speculative enter-prise, it is said that he used his position as mayor to see that the neutrality laws were not invoked to block the expedition.[12]

When the attempt to seize control of Nicaragua appeared to be suc-cessful, company agents presented themselves in Granada with a $20,000 "loan" for Walker, to be deducted from royalties owed to Nicaragua un-der the Transit charter. The money came in the form of gold bullion taken from a shipment then in transit from San Francisco to New York. The owner had been compensated with a draft on the company's New York office, which was honored there without question.[13] Because of the time involved in communicating the necessary arrangements between the company's San Francisco and New York offices, contingency planning to support the filibusters must have begun months before Walker's capture of Granada.

Besides the "loan," the company agreed to transport an unlimited num-ber of Walker recruits to Nicaragua at $20 per head, that sum also to come from monies owed to Nicaragua. The Transit Company thus became Walk-er's umbilical cord to the United States—an umbilical cord with which the Man of Destiny would soon choke himself.

In 1853, while Cornelius Vanderbilt was on a much-publicized trans-Atlantic cruise, his cohorts Charles Morgan and Cornelius Garrison manipulated the company stock and caused him considerable losses. Vanderbilt had relinquished direction of the company to Morgan before beginning his European holiday, and returned vowing revenge. A drawn out battle for control of the company ensued. Shortly after Walker's conquest of Granada, Morgan and Garrison saw that Vanderbilt was gaining the upper hand, and decided to enlist the filibuster in their intracorporate struggle, capitalizing on his gratitude to them for company support. They sent Edmund Randolph—the grandson of George Washington's attorney general, then a prominent San Francisco lawyer and close friend of Walker—along with Cornelius Garrison's son William, to persuade the filibuster leader to have the transit charter revoked. A new one could then be issued to a rival company that Vanderbilt's erstwhile partners would set up. Nicaragua's long-standing claim against the Transit Company for nonpayment of royalties would furnish the pretext for the revocation.*

Vanderbilt completed his coup on January 30, 1856, forcing Morgan's resignation from the presidency of the Accessory Transit Company. Morgan immediately gave the go-ahead for the charter revocation plan.[15]

"PATAS Arriba" was well-pleased on February 18, 1856 when Walker handed him a proclamation revoking the Transit Company charter. By signing it, Rivas was doing more than complying with the filibuster's wishes: he was taking a popular action as well, for the transit had meant nothing but trouble for Nicaragua from the beginning. So much the greater, then, was the old man's dismay, when on the following day Walker presented him with a new charter to sign; this one, made out to Morgan and Garrison, was even more a giveaway of the country's resources and sovereignty than the first had been. It was so bad, in fact, that even the normally pliant Rivas balked at signing it until some of its worst clauses were modified.

Unaware of the conspirators' plans, Vanderbilt resumed day to day direction of the Transit Company. Just two weeks before the bad news arrived, he personally signed drafts giving free passage to 250 Walker recruits shipping on a company steamer out of New Orleans.[16]

But when word came on March 13 that Walker had revoked the Transit

---

* Under the terms of its charter, the company was supposed to pay Nicaragua an annual operating fee of $10,000, plus a 10 percent royalty on its profits. It had never paid the royalties, however, juggling its books to make it appear that it lost money on the isthmus crossing. The Nicaraguans were not taken in by this ploy, and at the time of Walker's arrival representatives of the Legitimist government were in the United States demanding payment. A commission set up by Walker, which had the benefit of inside information, charged that the company had cheated Nicaragua out of $412,589.

Over 104,000 passengers used the transit between 1851 and 1856. The company had reported a net profit of $1,149,235 for the fifteen months of July 1854 to September 1855 alone.[14]

charter, the "commodore" took immediate action to divert the ships then en route to Nicaragua. Thereafter Cornelius Vanderbilt, perhaps the wealthiest capitalist in the Western Hemisphere, did everything in his considerable power to prevent supplies and men from reaching the filibusters.

Morgan and Garrison were unable to restore service to Nicaragua for six weeks, and even then Vanderbilt made their operations difficult. Walker's North American sympathizers thought him a fool for antagonizing Vanderbilt and thus losing an important source of support. But matters were not so obvious to the Grey-Eyed Man of Destiny, who lacked the benefit of hindsight. Morgan and Garrison were no small fry themselves; moreover, they were said to be better managers, having reportedly improved the transit line after they took over day to day operations from Vanderbilt in 1853.[17]

Meanwhile, resistance to filibuster control in Nicaragua was finally beginning to coalesce. In December 1855, two months after the fall of Granada, José Trinidad Cabañas, the recently-overthrown Liberal president of Honduras, came to the city seeking the help of the Walker-Rivas government for a return to power in his own country. Cabañas had been in exile in El Salvador, the only Central American country where Liberals were still in control, and the only one that had recognized the filibuster regime— under the mistaken notion that it represented the triumph of Liberalism. Meeting Walker, Cabañas at once took the true measure of the Yankee interloper and his intentions.

In a dispatch to Washington, US Minister to Nicaragua John H. Wheeler, an ardent Walker admirer, recounted an interview with Cabañas that took place on December 15, 1855. The former Honduran president, wrote Wheeler, asked him whether the US "approved of citizens of the U.S. coming to Central America; and if these persons attempted to destroy the nationality of Central America, would the Government of the U.S. prevent it?" Further, "if Guatemala, joined by other govts made war on Walker to drive him from the country, would the Govt. of U.S. use any efforts to protect him?" According to Wheeler, Cabañas "was dissatisfied with the condition of things now in Nicaragua. The belief was current that all the [offices] and emoluments of office would be absorbed by North Americans."[18]

Thus, two months after Walker seized control in Nicaragua, the more far-sighted of the Liberals had begun to set aside their factional preoccupations, and to view the dispatch of Walker by the combined Conservative governments—Guatemala, Honduras, and Costa Rica—as a lesser evil. What made Cabañas' suggestion of an anti-Walker Central American alliance even more significant was that it came before Walker had turned down his request for aid in regaining the Honduran presidency from Guardiola. Central American nationalism was beginning to supplant factional squabbling, with an unintended boost from the gringos.[19]

After Cabañas returned to El Salvador that country withdrew its recognition from the Rivas puppet government; on February 16, 1856, the filibuster newspaper *El Nicaraguense* reported that "a league" of the other Central American states had been formed against (Walker's) Nicaragua.[20]

Costa Rica, where many Nicaraguan Conservatives had taken refuge, was the first to act. Costa Rican President Juan Rafael Mora declared war on the Yankees on March 1. When the news reached Walker he immediately resolved on a pre-emptive strike at Costa Rica. His army had by then risen to a strength of 850, and there were another 600 North Americans in the country whom the filibuster felt he could call on if needed. With great bravado and fanfare, four companies totaling 350 men, mounted on "fine caparisoned horses," rode off to invade Nicaragua's southern neighbor. Commanding the outfit was Colonel Louis Schlessinger, a Hungarian who had seen action in his own country during the revolutionary events of 1848, and, after emigrating to the United States, participated in filibustering expeditions against Cuba. Two of the companies under Schlessinger's command were North American; the others consisted of German and French immigrants to the US who, having failed to find the streets of New York paved with gold, turned to Nicaragua as a more fertile ground for self-aggrandizement.[21]

Boldly marching across the Costa Rican border, the filibuster legion camped at the Santa Rosa hacienda in the province of Guanacaste. Surprised there by Costa Rican troops, the invaders indecorously took to their heels. The myth of Yankee invincibility had suffered a severe setback.[22]

According to Walker, one of the officers commanding the Costa Rican advance guard was Manuel Argüello, a Nicaraguan Legitimist, and the troops wore red ribbons "with the view both of deceiving the Americans and of conciliating the Nicaraguan Democrats."*[23]

Continuing north into Nicaragua, the Costa Rican forces captured La Virgen, where they killed a number of North Americans working for the Transit Company. The United States later demanded reparation from Costa Rica for the deaths of its citizens, claiming they were innocent, neutral civilians. But Walker regarded all North Americans in Nicaragua as his reserves, and the Transit Company employees were probably armed; moreover, the company's support for the filibusters was well-known. Costa Rica neither apologized nor paid the reparations demanded.

The Costa Ricans next occupied Rivas, and Walker, now in personal command, counterattacked them there on April 11. The Second Battle of Rivas, as it became known, was in many respects a reinactment of the first. Walker again led a charge into the main plaza and again found himself

---

* The Nicaraguan Conservatives (Legitimists) traditionally wore white ribbons and the Liberals (Democrats), red. The "Americans" were then still pretending to be part of the Democrats.

surrounded. This time the filibusters slipped out of town under cover of darkness and retreated back to Granada. The battle gave Costa Rica its national hero, Juan Santamaria, who was killed while braving a hail of bullets to torch a house that served as a Yankee redoubt.

Despite the victory, the Costa Ricans were not in position to exploit their advantage because a cholera epidemic immediately struck at Rivas. The disease was aggravated by the general lack of sanitation and by contamination of the town's water supply by putrefying corpses from the battle. Decimated by cholera, the Costa Ricans were forced to withdraw; the spread of the plague to Costa Rica delayed their reentry into the war against the filibusters for nearly a year.

With the outbreak of cholera among the Costa Ricans and with the transit service, restored by Morgan and Garrison, now furnishing recruits and supplies once again, the Man of Destiny had a new lease on life. So buoyed was Walker by the turn of events that he decided to dispense with the fig leaf of a native president. Besides, his Nicaraguan "allies" were growing less reliable as the anti-filibuster coalition ripened.

He arranged an election for June 29, 1856. Immediately after signing the election decree, Patricio Rivas, with his entire cabinet but one, fled to Chinandega; there he denounced Walker and seconded President Estrada's call for help from Guatemala, Honduras, and El Salvador to evict the North American usurpers.[24]

After the June 29 election, the filibuster paper, *El Nicaraguense,* reported that an enormous turnout had given Walker the presidency by a large margin. It went so far as to publish a vote breakdown by city for the various candidates. In truth, few Nicaraguans voted; those who did were in Granada, Walker's capital. The Yankees, on the other hand, were so inured to democratic processes that they voted many times. The filibusters simply "estimated" the vote count for parts of the country outside Granada, owing to the difficulty of collecting ballots in areas not under their control. Nevertheless, newspapers in the United States eagerly swallowed this medicine show concoction. On July 11, 1856, the Pygmy Colossus, as a contemporary detractor styled him, was inaugurated as "president of Nicaragua," undaunted by the fact that the Nicaraguan constitution specifically excluded from that office all who were not native-born.

It is for the series of decrees following shortly after his inauguration that the tenure of "President" Walker is chiefly noted. The first, dated September 5, provided for sentences of forced labor of one to six months for anyone without visible means of support or not actively seeking employment. Another, the following day, legalized labor contracts of unlimited duration—indentured servitude—with the penalty of forced labor for workers who failed to fulfill their obligations.

Other decrees made land registration a legal requirement, and established English as an official language co-equal with Spanish. Until that time Nicaraguans had had no system of land registration. They would now have to compete with gringos for whom the process was familiar; moreover, they would have to do it in a foreign language. The properties of enemies of the state—anyone opposing Walker—were declared forfeit and sold at auction, where filibuster military scrip was accepted as payment.

Walker himself wrote:

> The general tendency of these several decrees was the same. They were intended to place a large portion of the land in the hands of the white race. The military force of the State might, for a time, secure the Republic, but in order that their possession might be permanent, it was requisite for them to hold the land.

Such action was justified, he explained, because

> the natives who had held the lands for more than a generation admitted that the cultivated fields had diminished in number and extent every year since independence, for want of a proper system of labor . . . The reorganization of labor was necessary for the development of the resources of the country.[25]

Most important of all, however, was a decree of September 22, annulling legislation inherited from the defunct Central American Federation. The operative result of this decree—and its avowed purpose—was to rescind the abolition of slavery. It was characteristic of Walker to accomplish the reintroduction of slavery through a lawyer's maneuver.

Walker's followers made the most of the decrees. They dashed off letters to the southern United States appealing for support to this new outpost of slavery expansion. Typical of those published in most Southern newspapers was what the *Richmond Enquirer* billed on its front page as "extracts from the private correspondence of a very intelligent citizen of Nicaragua," which read in part:

> The lands are rich, and the productions those most adapted to slave labor . . . This magnificent country Gen. Walker has taken possession of in the name of the white race, and now offers to you, to you and your slaves, at a time when you have not a friend on the face of the earth . . . Here is a new State soon to be added to the South, in or out of the Union—here is the first piece of Mexico in fact, the whole of which in a short life time, will fall into the hands of the white men of North America, and it behooves you to begin in time to secure your portion of the prize.[26]

Though the open proclamation of Nicaragua as slave territory aided fundraising efforts in the South, Walker's white planter utopia was not to be. For while his inauguration band played "Yankee Doodle" in the plaza of Granada, the clatter of muskets reverberated through the streets of León where the armies of El Salvador, Honduras, Guatemala, and Nicaragua were mustering.

The usurpation of government by aliens and their theft of landed property had made enemies of Central America's propertied classes, both Liberal and Conservative. The filibusters' increasingly frequent predatory raids on the countryside were the scourge of small subsistence farmers. The slavery and other forced labor decrees mobilized the artisans and day laborers of the towns, as well as the indigenous tribes who lived on the fringes of Nicaraguan society. The latter had only recently thrown off Spanish slavery of one kind or another and stood to lose their communal *ejido* lands besides. The intrusion of North American Manifest Destiny had produced a national unity never before seen: more than the hostility of Vanderbilt, it was this that sealed the filibusters' fate.

A S THE Grey-Eyed Man in Granada played to the gallery of slaveocrats back home, the Central American armies began their southward march. Getting started had not been easy. In April, commissioners of the Estrada government in Ocotal had succeeded in convincing Guatemala to dispatch a division of troops to their aid. But in June, El Salvador extended recognition to Patricio Rivas after he defected from Walker. Honduras and Guatemala, though Conservative, now withheld support from Estrada, and pressured him to reach an accord with the Leonese that would present a united front to the North Americans. At first Estrada resisted ("legitimacy or death"), but was apparently about to give in when he was brutally murdered. The killers were known to be "Democrats," perhaps renegades, from nearby Somoto Grande. The involvement of Rivas supporters, then working for accommodation with Estrada, was improbable, as the result of the murder was the near-collapse of peace talks. The act may have been no more than the working out of the old blood feud, but the perpetrators had recently been in Granada, suggesting Walker's hand behind the killing.[27]

Estrada's successor, Senator Nicasio del Castillo, signed a treaty on September 12 that dissolved the Legitimist government. As an expedient, Rivas was to be recognized as president until the termination of the war against Walker, at which time new elections would be held. Del Castillo became minister of state in the new coalition government.

Tomás Martínez, who had been named general-in-chief of the Legitimist army by President Estrada, ordered Colonel José Dolores Estrada to lead a detachment south from Matagalpa to interdict the supply of cattle to Walker's men from Chontales and Boaco. Estrada's force, consisting of one hundred Legitimist troops and sixty Matagalpa Indian archers, occupied a hacienda on San Jacinto hill near Tipitapa. On September 14, 1856, the day before the thirty-fifth anniversary of independence from Spain, 300 Walkerites led by Byron Cole, now a filibuster lieutenant colonel, assaulted San Jacinto in an effort to dislodge them. The Nicaraguans put up a fierce resistance. Andrés Castro, a sergeant, killed a filibuster with a rock when his carbine misfired and achieved immortality as one of Nicaragua's national heroes. The North Americans fled from the field in disarray. Byron Cole, who had brought Walker to Nicaragua, was caught by a group of peasants and hanged.[28]

The victory by an all-Nicaraguan force at San Jacinto was as great a boost to the confidence of the Central Americans as it was a blow to the invaders. Until then Central American victories had been accomplished only with superior numbers and fearful losses. San Jacinto proved that, ably led and motivated, Central Americans could stand toe to toe with Yankees.

The allied armies encamped at León now began to advance. On September 24 the Nicaraguan western—formerly Leonese—army, commanded by Máximo Jerez, entered Managua, followed by the forces of the other Central American states. They were joined there by the vanguard of the northern—formerly Legitimist—army, led by Estrada. The filibusters abandoned the town without resistance.

A week later Walker withdrew his troops from Masaya, which the Cen-

The Battle of San Jacinto, as painted by a Nicaraguan artist

tral Americans immediately occupied and fortified. But then the filibuster leader changed his mind. On October 11 he attacked Masaya with 800 men, trying to retake the town so recently abandoned. Heavy fighting continued for two days with many losses on both sides. But while Walker, with most of his effective force, fought to recapture Masaya, Estrada and his Nicaraguans launched an attack on his base at Granada. The filibusters broke off the engagement at Masaya to relieve their Granada garrison.

There followed a respite of nearly a month as the Central Americans regrouped. But the situation had become desperate for the Walkerites; the cholera epidemic that ravaged the Costa Ricans earlier in the year had spread to Granada. An estimated 25 percent of Walker's force was hospitalized at a given time from cholera or other infirmities. By the start of the Central American offensive the Yankees were sustaining a *daily* mortality rate of 2 to 3 percent from disease alone.[29]

Walker, a puritanical martinet, strove to maintain military discipline, but morale was at such a low that his men had sunk to outright banditry. In August a company of Walker's cavalry, which he dubbed "rangers," was sent north on patrol. Happening upon a French prospector, they tied him up and whipped him when he refused to tell where he had cached his gold. Other French miners in the area banded together and fought the marauders till the latter ran out of ammunition and surrendered. Not inclined to stand on ceremony, the Frenchmen executed all but two.

Walker sent his officers the following message:

The commander-in-chief sees with regret that one of the chief military virtues—temperance—is not as much esteemed as it should be in the Army. He earnestly exhorts the officers of the Army to furnish in this respect an example of self-restraint and control to the men and to see properly punished socially as well as legally the intemperance which is calculated to bring the Army into contempt and disgrace.[30]

The memorandum, written in Walker's characteristic moralizing monotone, grossly understated the actual condition of "contempt and disgrace" to which the filibuster army had long since fallen; Walker himself retained but a feeble grip on reality. The degeneration of the "regenerators" testified that the Anglos in Nicaragua had met the fate of would-be master races throughout history.

By the beginning of November, Costa Rica had sufficiently recuperated from the cholera epidemic to reenter the war, and again threatened the transit route—Walker's lifeline—in the south.

The filibusters made another attempt to retake Masaya in mid-November but were once more repulsed with heavy losses. On November 15, 1856, during a lull in the fighting, Walker wrote (as always, in the third person):

As the general-in-chief passed from one point to another, in order to see his commands executed, he found so many of the officers in such a state of languor and exhaustion, that they were incapable of controlling their men. Some of them during the long march had taken a great deal of liquor, and this, as well as the excitement of the conflict dying out, left them utterly deprived of moral strength. It was only by his personal exertions that Walker obtained any security for the camp; and never, during the whole time he was in Nicaragua, did he find it so difficult, as on that night to have his orders executed. The will of the force seemed to be momentarily paralyzed by the fierce fight through which it had passed.[31]

The collapsing morale observed by Walker at Masaya manifested itself in another way: the retreating filibusters burned the Indian neighborhood of Monimbó and the church of San Sebastian—acts entirely without military rationale.

The "general-in-chief" resolved to abandon Granada and make a strategic retreat to Rivas. From there he hoped to keep his supply lines—and escape route—open. What followed was the most disgraceful episode of the Yankee occupation. On November 19 Walker embarked the bulk of his forces on a lake steamer for La Virgen. He left behind 300 in Granada, commanded by Charles Frederick Henningsen, with orders to destroy the 332-year-old city.

Breaking into wine cellars, the filibusters who remained in Granada looted and burned in an alcoholic orgy. Realizing what was happening, the Central Americans launched a three-pronged attack on the city. The Battle of Granada began on November 24 and lasted into the second week of December when the surviving filibusters escaped on a lake steamer, which Walker brought from La Virgen to effect their rescue. As they retreated, Henningsen, an English soldier of fortune married to a Georgia plantation heiress, erected a sign in the smoking rubble that read, "Aquí Fué Granada"—here was Granada.

The Central American armies would in all likelihood have made short work of Henningsen. But the appointment of Salvadoran General Belloso—a Liberal—as commander-in-chief of the allied forces caused friction with the Conservative Hondurans and Guatemalans, paralyzing the command structure. The still-smoldering rivalries and animosities from so many years of intestine warfare were not easily extinguished.[32]

The destruction of the ancient city made it difficult for Walker promoters in the United States to explain his "civilizing" mission. But the author of the deed wrote:

As to the justice of the act, few can question it; for its inhabitants owed life and property to the Americans in the service of Nicaragua, and yet they joined the enemies who strove to drive their protectors from Central America. They served the enemies of Nicaragua in the most criminal manner; for they acted as spies on the Americans, who had defended their interests, and sent notice of all their movements to the Allies. By the laws of war, the town had forfeited its existence; and the policy of destroying it was as manifest as the justice of the measure.[33]

Meanwhile, Cornelius Vanderbilt, seeking revenge on those who had double-crossed him as well as to regain the highway for himself, sent Sylvanus Spencer to help the Costa Ricans close the transit. Spencer, a company engineer familiar with the operations and personnel of the system, had reportedly lost a fortune on Transit Company stock as a result of the charter revocation.[34] With Spencer's aid, the Costa Ricans captured Hipps Point on the Rio San Juan on December 24. Thereafter they took Castillo Viejo and Fort San Carlos, effectively controlling the artery and blocking reinforcement of Walker from the east. Following the victories, Costa Rican General José Joaquin Mora was named commander-in-chief of the Central American armies, replacing General Belloso. Although a Conservative, his appointment resolved the problem of the command structure, because Costa Ricans had always tried to remain neutral in the infighting between the other Central American states.

The noose tightened around the filibusters, who now held only a small area at the western end of the transit route. On January 28, Central American troops occupied the town of San Jorge, just east of Rivas. Efforts by the filibusters to dislodge them were turned back with heavy casualties on the 29th, and again on February 4 and March 16. On March 5, Costa Ricans mauled a troop of Walker "rangers" trying to secure the transit road south of Rivas.

The siege of Rivas began in earnest on March 27. General Mora, who earlier had vowed execution for all filibusters, changed his tactics, promising good treatment and safe conduct out of the country for all who would desert.

To his starving, demoralized, and fever-ridden followers, Walker exhorted, "The destiny of this region and the interests of humanity are confided to our care. We have come here as the advance guard of American civilization."[35] But for those who had come seeking adventure, glory, and plunder—now reduced to eating their horses and mules—General Mora's offer of safe passage had greater effect. Each night more and more slipped through the lines to surrender.

The fighting continued sporadically until May 1, 1857, when Commander Charles E. Davis of the US sloop-of-war *St. Mary* negotiated safe conduct out of the country for Walker and his remaining followers.

Ostensibly, Davis had been sent to San Juan del Sur to see to the protection of US citizens. But when asked by the Central Americans to prevent the landing of filibuster reinforcements at the port, he refused, giving the excuse that the United States government recognized a state of civil war in Nicaragua and would not take sides.[36] Davis' equivocation—claiming neutrality in a Nicaraguan "civil war" and simultaneously asserting the right to protect the US citizens who were one of the parties to it—was characteristic of United States policy toward the filibusters.

Nicaraguan General Martinez and Honduran General Xatruch considered the accord ignominious and refused to sign. They demanded the surrender of Walker to Central Americans, not to Davis, or at least some guarantees against further filibustering from the United States. But the majority of Central American commanders acquiesced to the rescue, not wishing to prolong the war or provide a pretext for direct US intervention.[37]

FOUR hundred and sixty-three North Americans surrendered to Davis. During the final four months of the war alone, Walker is said to have lost 566, either killed, died of disease, or deserted—more than half his force at Rivas. In his memoirs, Henningsen estimated that between the time of Walker's arrival in June 1855 and the surrender to Davis in May 1857, a total of 2,518 had joined the filibuster army. He put the number of those killed in combat or died of disease at 1,000; 700 had deserted, 250 were discharged, 80 taken prisoner, and the remainder surrendered at Rivas.[38] But a *New York Times* correspondent reported, two months before Walker's rescue, that as of then 5,400 filibusters had been killed.[39] The anonymous writer, though identifying himself as "The Voice of Nicaragua," was apparently not a Nicaraguan at all, but a North American—hostile to Walker—who had lived in the country for a number of years. He contributed several detailed exposés of filibuster depredations in Nicaragua to the *Times* between December 1856 and April 1857. Though a number of letters to the paper from Walker supporters tried to undermine the writer's credibility, disputing various of his facts and figures, none attacked the accuracy of his casualty estimate.*

Joseph N. Scott, Transit Company agent at San Juan del Norte between 1855 and 1857, testified under oath before the New York Supreme Court in April 1861 that 11,000 North Americans had traveled to Nicaragua on "emigrant tickets" during the Walker period.[40] Not all those necessarily

---

* The only comment on the casualty figures of "The Voice of Nicaragua" came from a Costa Rican who criticized the writer for failing to report the casualties among Central Americans. "The Voice" responded that he could not compile statistics for them because they did not report their dead and wounded, but he supposed that Central American casualties were three to four times those of the Yankees, which was probably an accurate estimate.

joined Walker and many were wives and children. Part of the discrepancy may also stem from the fact that Henningsen's totals count only the "army," not those serving the Walker regime at one time or another in a "civil" capacity, though Walker considered all to be combatants in time of need. The real number of filibusters, therefore, probably lies somewhere in-between. What can be said with certainty is that several times more North Americans were killed in the "Filibuster War" in Nicaragua than in the Spanish-American War four decades later.

Returning to the United States, Walker was greeted by many as a con-quering hero. He made several unsuccessful attempts to launch new inva-sions in the years that followed, finally landing with about seventy followers at Trujillo on the Atlantic coast of Honduras in 1860. Ordered to surrender by the British, who had imposed a customs receivership on the port, Walker and his men fled into the jungle where they were pursued by Honduran troops. Ultimately surrendering to the British navy, they were turned over to Honduras. Walker was tried and executed by a Honduran firing squad on September 12, 1860. His second in command, a Colonel Rudler, was briefly imprisoned and then pardoned. The remainder of the filibusters were repatriated to the United States.

Two months later Lincoln was elected to the presidency of the United States. Five months after that many of the veterans of Walker's filibuster-ing expeditions found a new home in the Confederate army.

V

IRREPRESSIBLE
CONFLICT

> *They are but drivellers who speak of establishing fixed relations between the pure white American race, as it exists in the United States, and the mixed, Hispano-Indian race, as it exists in Mexico and Central America, without the employment of force. The history of the world presents no such Utopian vision as that of an inferior race yielding meekly and peacefully to the controlling influence of a superior people. Whenever barbarism and civilization, or two distinct forms of civilization, meet face to face, the result must be war. Therefore, the struggle between the old and the new elements in Nicaraguan society was not passing or accidental, but natural and inevitable. The war in Nicaragua was the first clear and distinct issue made between the races inhabiting the northern and the central portions of the continent.*
>
> —*William Walker,* The War in Nicaragua.

I N THE more sophisticated and discreet world of today, William Walker's ideas would place him in the fanatic fringe of neo-Nazis and Ku Klux Klansmen. He might easily be dismissed as a misfit. But in his own day Walker was no oddity, and his filibuster invasion of Nicaragua was not merely an isolated episode, an obscure footnote to the history of the Western Hemisphere. Both were natural outgrowths of the slave-labor system of plantation agriculture in the southern United States, as much its products as cotton or tobacco.

Despite Walker's actions and pronouncements on slavery, his biographers, apparently desiring to cast him in a good light, have tried to dissociate him from the slavery question, the paramount political issue in the United States of his time. They argue that the supreme filibuster promulgated his slavery decrees in Nicaragua merely as a strategem to gain Southern support after alienating Vanderbilt. Some have gone so far as to assert that he was really an opponent of slavery![1] As evidence, they cite articles he wrote as editor of the New Orleans *Crescent* and argue that while in California he was affiliated with what they term the "anti-slavery wing" of the Democratic Party.

William Walker

As *Crescent* editor, Walker had taken the "conservative," position, once common in the South, that pro-slavery agitation would only serve to provoke the Abolitionists and lead to new anti-slavery legislation. Later, he himself characterized those who held such views as "the shallowest of thinkers."[2] J. D. B. DeBow, the influential New Orleans publisher of *DeBow's Review,* theoretical journal of the slave power, was in his own words, "familiarly associated with General Walker, and enjoyed his close and intimate friendship," during the latter's tenure as editor of the *Crescent.*[3] Such friendship would have been impossible in the highly-charged decades preceding the Civil War had Walker been opposed to slavery.

When Walker dabbled in California politics the Democratic Party had no "anti-slavery wing"—opponents of slavery were found in the abolition organizations, the Free Soil Party, in the Whig Party before its demise, or later, in the Republican Party. The factions of the California Democratic Party reflected varying degrees of *support* for slavery, but the issues animating them were predominantly local; California had by then joined the Union as a free state, removing much of the immediacy from the slavery issue.[4]

In any event, the relationship between the question of slavery and the filibuster invasion of Nicaragua does not depend on Walker's personal history, however interesting or erratic—politicians' views often change with the color of the foliage in which they find themselves.

WALKER was, without doubt, propelled by strong personal ambition. Illuminated by the expiring candle of the slave order, he cast a big shadow and imagined himself the Man of Destiny. On his arrival in New York after his ouster from Nicaragua in 1857, he proclaimed to a crowd from his hotel balcony:

> I feel not ashamed to say that I am favored by the gods, for I feel that an overriding Providence, which has carried us so far, has not permitted us to do so much for naught. I feel that luck—as my enemies call it—or Providence as I term it—will carry us successfully yet, and enable us to accomplish yet more for the greatness and glory of the American people.[5]

But the currents of history were running against, not with, William Walker. Charles Doubleday, who accompanied him in Nicaragua, described Walker as being

> bold and capable, but not sagacious, inasmuch as he took no account of a factor in modern politics all powerful now, however insignificant it may have been anterior to the first French Revolution,—that of popular ideas.
>
> As his scheme included the re-establishment of slavery in a population the majority of which were of mixed African blood, and an affiliation of power with the Church in a time when freedom of thought had made progress, it came at too late a day in the world's history.[6]

Nevertheless, the filibuster viewed his own efforts as an expression of the values, ideas, and politics of mid-19th century North America. This consciousness was strikingly revealed in his remark that "The Americans, with that faith in themselves which has carried them in a wonderfully short period from one ocean to another, regarded their establishment in Nicaragua as fixed beyond the control of casualties."[7] His vision of himself as the agent of Manifest Destiny was, moreover, widely shared by contemporaries. *Blackwood's Magazine* commented:

> When they first landed in Nicaragua, not ten months ago, they num-

bered only fifty-six men; but in as far as they had the good-will of the majority of the American People, they represented the nation as truly as General Pierce and his Cabinet. Colonel Walker was merely the practical exponent of a popular theory, and his success has been so rapid and decisive, and such is the position he now holds . . . that the Americanisation of Nicaragua may almost be considered an established fact.[8]

At a Walker fund-raising rally in New York in December 1856, General Thomas Green of Texas, a veteran of the War of Texas Independence and of the US-Mexican War, spoke on the historical continuity of filibustering. He complained that the term "fillibuster" was coming into disrepute. A reporter attending the event summarized his message:

> He was, he said . . . an old fossil specimen of fillibustering of many years standing. He had gone to Texas with his friend Gen. Cazneau twenty-five years ago. Fillibustering was then an honorable trade, but then Jackson was in the Presidential Chair.[9]

While Walker was carrying out his depredations in Nicaragua, at home he was toasted at banquets, hailed at mass meetings, and idolized by much of the press. A "Broadway" musical opened at Purdy's National Theatre in New York on July 21, 1856, titled "Nicaragua, or General Walker's Victories." Its cast of characters included "General Walker, the Hope of Freedom," and "Ivory Black, a superior nigger." The supernumeraries were listed as "Nicaraguans, Costa Ricans, Niggers, Etc." Among its musical numbers was a medley entitled the "Filibuster Overture" that included such tunes as "The Star Spangled Banner," "Columbia the Pride of the Ocean," and "Yankee Doodle."[10]

The vast majority of Walker's contemporaries embraced the unabashedly racist doctrine he espoused. The presumption of white superiority was, after all, the philosophical underpinning of the slave society that, until the Civil War, dominated every aspect of life in a large part of the United States and profoundly influenced the remainder. The "peculiar institution" of slavery—implicitly sanctioned by the framers of the Constitution—and the bigotry fostered by it formed an inseparable part of the fabric of North American life and profoundly disfigured the world's first modern republic.

I N THE decades before the Civil War it was generally acknowledged that slave production required constant accretions of new territory for its survival. Karl Marx, keenly interested in the slavery problem in the United States, contributed articles on the subject to a number of contemporary newspapers and magazines, including Horace Greeley's New York *Tribune*. In 1861 Marx wrote:

Continual expansion of territory and continual spread of slavery beyond its old limits is a law of life for the slave states of the Union.

The cultivation of the southern export articles, cotton, tobacco, sugar, etc., carried on by slaves, is only remunerative as long as it is conducted with large gangs of slaves, on a mass scale and on wide expanses of naturally fertile soil, which requires only simple labor. Intensive cultivation, which depends less on fertility of the soil than on investment of capital, intelligence and energy of labor, is contrary to the nature of slavery. Hence the rapid transformation of states like Maryland and Virginia, which formerly employed slaves on the production of export articles, into states which raise slaves to export them into the deep South. Even in South Carolina, where the slaves form four-sevenths of the population, the cultivation of cotton has been almost completely stationary for years due to the exhaustion of the soil. Indeed, by force of circumstances South Carolina has already been transformed in part into a slave-raising state, since it already sells slaves to the sum of four million dollars yearly to the states of the extreme South and South-west. As soon as this point is reached, the acquisition of new Territories becomes necessary, so that one section of the slaveholders with their slaves may occupy new fertile lands and that a new market for slave-raising, therefore for the sale of slaves, may be created for the remaining section.[11]

On the opposite end of the political spectrum, Congressman Hiram Warner of Georgia defended the extension of slavery in a major speech to the House of Representatives on April 1, 1856, declaring:

There is not a slaveholder in this House or out of it, but who knows perfectly well that, whenever slavery is confined within certain specified limits, its future existence is doomed; it is only a question of time as to its final destruction. You may take any single slaveholding county in the southern States, in which the great staples of cotton and sugar are cultivated to any extent, and confine the present slave population within the limits of that county. Such is the rapid, natural increase of the slaves, and the rapid exhaustion of the soil . . . that in a few years it would be impossible to support them within the limits of such county. Both master and slave would be *starved out;* and what would be the practical effect in any one county, the same result would happen to all the slaveholding States. Slavery cannot be confined within certain specified limits without producing the destruction of both master and slave; it requires fresh lands, plenty of wood and water, not only for the comfort and happiness of the slave, but for the benefit of the owner.[12] [Emphasis in original.]

The issue of slavery extension formed the axis of the political struggle between the retrograde plantation system and its opponents—the ascendant industrial capitalism based on free labor, the "free soil" farmers, and the objectors of conscience, the Abolitionists. Understanding the need of slavery to expand, its enemies had from the earliest days of the republic sought to kill it by confinement.

The "Ordinance of 1787" had banned slavery from all territories north and west of the Ohio River. Subsequent concessions to the slave owners, however, progressively eroded the restrictions on its geographical extension. First, the Missouri Compromise of 1820 allowed the admission of that state into the Union as a slave state, while the remainder of the Louisiana Purchase north of parallel 36°30' was to be free. The effect of this legislation was to extend slavery not only to Missouri, but westward, south of 36°30', as well. That limitation was abandoned in turn by the Compromise of 1850, in which the slave power agreed to the admission of California as a free state in return for the application of the "doctrine of popular sovereignty" to Utah and New Mexico. Under this formula, the states to be created from those territories would make their own decision on the question of slavery. The Compromise of 1850 also included the notorious Fugitive Slave Law, which reduced the federal government to the role of bloodhound for the cotton barons.

The last geographical barriers to slavery expansion were finally erased in the Kansas-Nebraska Bill of 1854, which repealed the Missouri Compromise and extended the "doctrine of popular sovereignty" to all the territories. Once the geographical restrictions had been thrown out, the only remaining obstacles were political. In the 1857 Dred Scott Decision the Supreme Court removed even these.*

But each new victory for the Southern oligarchy, registering its increasing hold on the federal government, also served to intensify the resistance. The tide began to turn in 1854 with the Kansas-Nebraska Bill. Immediately after its passage gangs of thugs organized by the slaveholders began making raids in Kansas. Known as the "Border Ruffians," they committed numerous atrocities in an effort to drive out the small farmers who constituted the opposition to slavery.

Kansas residents took up arms for self-protection. Throughout the North, aid organizations sprang up to support the opponents of slavery in Kansas. During the Kansas Civil War that raged from 1854 till 1858, the attempt to spread slavery to Kansas was effectively thwarted. From the movement supporting the Kansas free-staters emerged the Republican Party.

Prior to the Kansas Civil War the slave power had shown considerable

---

* In the Dred Scott Decision the court maintained that since slaves were recognized as property by the Constitution, slave owners had a "right" to take their slaves anywhere, regardless of the will of the majority in the territory, and that the federal government was bound to protect this "right."

interest in various potential conquests, most notably Cuba, Mexico, and Central America. In an 1854 article entitled "The Destiny of the Slave States," the *Richmond Enquirer* waxed eloquent over the possibilities:

> The black man loves to breathe the humid air of his native swamps, while the white man exults and bounds in the elastic air of his native hills. Where you can combine the administrative governing qualities of the one race with the patient endurance and physical capacities of the other, you have that perfect system by which the vast tropical regions of the earth are to be developed.[13]

There were numerous plans to acquire these lands through filibustering expeditions, purchases, or outright war. But as long as the planters enjoyed success in their efforts to extend slavery to the existing territories of the United States, it was there that they chose to devote most of their energies. When they saw that direct action by slavery opponents was converting the passage of the Kansas-Nebraska Bill into a Pyrrhic victory, however, they turned their attention in earnest to the conquest of new territories.

Walker, aware that his fortunes were linked to those of the slave power, wrote:

> The Southern States, satisfied with their inability to carry slavery into Kansas, were then prepared [in 1857] to concentrate their labors on Central America; and not only were the men who went to the San Juan [after its capture by the Costa Ricans] of good quality, but they were also furnished with excellent supplies and equipments. Had the same effort and expenditure been made three months earlier, the establishment of the Americans in Nicaragua would have been fixed beyond peradventure.[14]

Rallying support for the filibusters in Nicaragua after the failure in Kansas, the New Orleans *Delta* declared:

> The fate of Cuba depends upon the fate of Nicaragua, and the fate of the South depends upon that of Cuba. This is the hour of destiny. We must live now or have no life. We must do or die.[15]

For the slaveholders, there were decided advantages to acquiring territory by filibustering rather than the "official" means of government purchase or seizure. Direct annexation by the United States would involve incorporating the new territories with large, free, non-white populations. Conquest by private enterprise, on the other hand, would allow for the "reorganization"—enslavement—of those populations prior to formal association with the United States. It would also prevent Abolitionists from contesting slave status as they had done in Kansas.[16]

Filibustering served another purpose as well—that of diverting the unemployed who might otherwise pose dangerous social problems. Wrote Marx:

> The number of actual slaveholders in the South of the Union does not amount to more than three hundred thousand,* a narrow oligarchy that is confronted with many millions of so-called poor whites, whose numbers have been constantly growing through concentration of landed property and whose condition is only to be compared with that of the Roman plebeians in the period of Rome's extreme decline. Only by acquisition and the prospect of acquisition of new Territories, as well as by filibustering expeditions, is it possible to square the interests of these "poor whites" with those of the slaveholders, to give their restless thirst for action a harmless direction and to tame them with the prospect of one day becoming slaveholders themselves.[18]

Illustrating the phenomena described by Marx, J. A. W. Brennan, an employee of a grain merchant in New Orleans wrote in a letter to his father in 1855:

> This is a City in which I would dread being idle, as it is a kind of rendezvous for all reckless characters and men of desperate fortunes—whose acquaintance I should judge it would be hard to shun were a person out of Employment—for they are always looking for young men without prospects for various filibustering and piratical expeditions. There are at present numbers of such men in town recruiting for Col. Walker's forces in Nicaragua and they find but little difficulty in procuring young men for their purposes.[19]

The appeal of filibustering wasn't confined to the poor whites of the South, however. As Walker did in San Francisco, the filibusters were able to attract the unemployed from the other parts of the country, including many recently-arrived immigrants, whose quest for a plot of land was thwarted by the opposition of the slave power to free soil legislation.†

The primacy of Walker's connection with the cause of slavery expansion was not diminished by his association with Vanderbilt or his rivals, Morgan and Garrison. On the contrary, the interests of slaveholders and shipping magnates were closely intertwined. The vast bulk of Southern export articles were shipped through Northern ports on Northern ships. The financiers, merchants, and shipping tycoons of Philadelphia, New York, Boston, and other mercantile centers had close economic ties to the South, and

---

* The number of slaveholders in 1850 was 347,525. Of that number half owned four slaves or less, and could not be considered planters. The oligarchy, however, was much smaller: fewer than 1,800 persons owned more than one hundred slaves.[17]

† The Homestead Act was finally passed by the Republicans, in fulfillment of a campaign promise, on May 20, 1862, during the Civil War.

up till the eve of the Civil War supported its cause.[20] They were, so to speak, the camp followers of slavery expansion. It was its alliance with Northern "merchant capital" that enabled the slave power to exercise a dominant influence over the government of the United States in the years before the Civil War; together they formed the mainspring of Manifest Destiny. In the political arena this convergence of interests took the form of the Democratic Party.

The Northern Democrats who were allied with the Southern planter aristocracy were known as "doughfaces." Franklin Pierce, fourteenth president of the United States, was a doughface from New Hampshire. In his inaugural address on March 4, 1853 he asserted:

> I believe that involuntary servitude, as it exists in different States of this Confederacy, is recognized by the Constitution. I believe that it stands like any other admitted right, and that the States where it exists are entitled to efficient remedies to enforce the constitutional provisions. I hold that the laws of 1850, commonly called the "compromise measures," are strictly constitutional and to be unhesitatingly carried into effect. I believe that the constituted authorities of this Republic are bound to regard the rights of the South in this respect as they would view any other legal and constitutional right, and that the laws to enforce them should be respected and obeyed, not with a reluctance encouraged by abstract opinions as to their propriety in a different state of society, but cheerfully and according to the decisions of the [Supreme Court]. Such have been, and are, my convictions and upon them I shall act.[21]

It was no accident that Pierce, who looked forward to "cheerfully" enforcing the Fugitive Slave Law, said in the same address, "It is not to be disguised that our attitude as a nation and our position on the globe render the acquisition of certain possessions not within our jurisdiction eminently important for our protection, if not in the future essential for the preservation of the rights of commerce and the peace of the world." Where "acquisition" of foreign territory was not contemplated, he assured merchants that "upon every sea and every soil where our enterprise may rightfully seek the protection of our flag American citizenship is an inviolable panoply for the security of American rights."[22] Pierce carried out this pledge by destroying San Juan del Norte, providing an "inviolable panoply" for the Accessory Transit Company.

Under Pierce's presidency the expansionist union of Southern planters and Northern commercial capitalists bore fruit in the Gadsden Purchase and the passage of the Kansas-Nebraska Bill. Pierce was also deeply involved in schemes to obtain Cuba, long coveted by the slaveholders. When Spain appeared ready to emancipate the Cuban slaves, the Pierce Administration tried to block the move, making it known in diplomatic circles that the United States would not tolerate Black rule there—such a development might have had the effect of agitating slaves in the United States.[23] Moreover, emancipation in Cuba would have made its acquisition by the US as a slave territory virtually impossible: the US Constitution would not permit the re-enslavement of Cuba's Blacks, once freed.

James Buchanan, John Mason, and Pierre Soulé, Pierce's ministers to England, France, and Spain respectively, produced the "Ostend Manifesto," a document recommending that if Spain refused to sell Cuba to the United States, it should be taken by force. Made public, the Ostend Manifesto provoked a storm of protest in Europe and among slavery opponents in the United States; the uproar put a stop, for the time being, to the plans to obtain the Pearl of the Antilles.

Thwarted in Cuba, Pierce did what he could to aid William Walker in Nicaragua.

VI

THE DOCTRINE OF THE HIGHWAYMAN

*We northern Democrats believe that
the Government should, by conquest,
do certain things; but that this business of Walker was committing petty
larceny. We northern Democrats are
rather in favor of national grand
larceny.*

—*Rep. John B. Haskin of New
York in a speech to Congress,
January 6, 1858.*

PRESIDENT Pierce appointed John Hill Wheeler to replace Solon
Borland as his minister to Nicaragua. Like Borland, Wheeler came
from a slave state—North Carolina. He would later write in
his memoirs that "the race of Central Americans have conclusively proved
to all observant minds that they are incapable of self-government." It was
said that he helped write Walker's slavery decrees.[1]

Wheeler arrived in Granada, Nicaragua, in early 1855, several months
before William Walker. With him were three other North Americans, Thomas F. Fisher, Julius De Brissot, and Captain C.C. Hornsby, a Mexican War
veteran. The country was then in the midst of civil war and the Democrats
had laid siege to Granada, seat of the Legitimist government. Wheeler's
companions visited both camps, seeking opportunities for the introduction of filibusters. The new US envoy and his party then returned to Rivas,
and Fisher, De Brissot, and Hornsby continued their journey to California; all three later joined Walker's invasion.[2] John Hill Wheeler became
known in Central America as the "filibuster minister."

As soon as Walker gained control of Granada, Minister Wheeler extended
recognition to his puppet president, Patricio Rivas, without waiting for instructions from Washington. He was chastised for this hasty action by Secre-

tary of State Marcy, but not recalled. Costa Rica's consul general in London wrote of the incident:

> I send to the Government a copy of the *Times,* in which is found a letter from Mr. Marcy to the American Minister to Nicaragua. Though this letter appears to censure the Minister, and holds out a threat to Walker, the true sense is, that in a short time the government of the United States will recognize Walker's government. May God help us."[3]

Luis Molina, Costa Rican chargé d'affaires in Washington, protested Walker's usurpation to Secretary Marcy. He characterized the filibuster undertaking as "a great crime, complex and multiform . . . hatched and set on foot within the territory of the United States and continued without interruption in a foreign land, by North American citizens, with means and assistance and, to a certain extent with the moral force of the nation." If the filibusters, he continued, "are disowned by the government to-day, they hope, not without cause, to be received with open arms to-morrow, arrayed in holiday attire for annexation, and to be exalted, their booty being legitimized."[4]

Diplomatic circles expected the Pierce Administration to quickly recognize Walker's takeover of Nicaragua. British minister John Crampton advised the Foreign Office that José de Marcoleta, still the accredited representative of Nicaragua, was being treated with "meanness and vulgarity" by the North Americans.[5]

The State Department would not accredit Parker French, the Walker regime's first envoy-designate to the United States. It would have been difficult to admit French, a notorious scoundrel, to the diplomatic corps under any circumstances.* But the filibusters had better luck with their second try, a Nicaraguan lawyer-turned-priest, Father Augustin Vigil, the curate of Granada.

Even then, the polarization of politics in the US had become so acute that President Pierce felt obliged to defend his recognition of the Walker-Rivas government in a lengthy message delivered to Congress on May 15, 1856. Seeking to rebut the charge that his administration was in collusion with the filibusters, Pierce asserted, "The American Government has uniformly and steadily resisted all attempts of individuals in the United States to undertake armed aggression against Spanish American Republics." He acknowledged that "our laws in this respect are sometimes violated or successfully evaded," but did not view the present case in that light. This was a question, he said, of a "small body of citizens of the United States from the State of California, whose presence, as it appears, put an end at once

---

* French was accused, among other things, of highway robbery and of defrauding and abandoning the members of a wagon train that he had contracted to lead to California.[6]

to civil war and restored apparent order throughout the territory of Nicaragua."[7]

Despite his best efforts on their behalf, under difficult circumstances, the slaveholders were dissatisfied with Franklin Pierce. They blamed him for failing to prevent their defeat in Kansas, for not seizing Cuba, and for hedging on support to Walker. His recognition of the filibuster regime in Nicaragua was therefore timed for maximum effect on the Democratic Party convention, then just a few weeks away.

But even with the recognition of the Walker regime, Pierce was not renominated by his party. On the seventeenth ballot the convention chose James Buchanan, the candidate most favored by the slave power. Buchanan was widely recognized as the actual author of the Ostend Manifesto. "The position assumed by Mr. BUCHANAN in the Ostend Manifesto, in regard to the acquisition of Cuba, ought certainly to decide every Southern man to cast his vote cheerfully for him," declared the Montgomery, Alabama *Advertiser.* "Every Southern man," no doubt, also took heart in the party platform's proclamation of "Non-interference by Congress with slavery in state and territory, or in the District of Columbia."[8]

Though unable to attend in person, William Walker loomed large at the Cincinnati Democratic convention of 1856; the local Democratic organ, the *Enquirer,* had given him a buildup for months beforehand. Walker lobbyists were everywhere during the convention sessions, and Parker French gave a talk on Walker at Masonic Hall.[9]

The platform adopted by the party included a plank that resolved:

> the great highway which nature . . . has marked out for free communi-
> cation between the Atlantic and Pacific oceans . . . should be secured
> by a timely and efficient exercise of the control which we have the right
> to claim over it, and no power on earth should be suffered to impede
> or clog its progress by any interference with the relations it may suit our
> policy to establish between our government and the governments of the
> states within whose dominions it lies. We can, under no circumstances,
> surrender our preponderance in the adjustment of all questions arising
> out of it.

The following plank asserted, "In view of so commanding an interest, the people of the United States cannot but sympathize with the efforts which are being made by the people of Central America to regenerate that portion of the continent which covers the passage across the interoceanic isthmus"—a reference to Walker's activities in Nicaragua.[10]

Prime responsibility for drafting the Central American planks at the Democratic Convention is said to have rested with Pierre Soulé, head of the Louisiana delegation. Soulé was a former US senator, lately a signer of the Ostend Manifesto as Pierce's minister to Spain, and one of slavery's leading spokesmen. He was also one of Walker's most prominent supporters. Just two months after the convention Walker feted Soulé in Nicaragua, where the latter had gone to buy land, help with the slavery decrees, and plan an ambitious bond sale for the filibusters' benefit. Soulé reportedly bought "Las Mercedes," a cacao hacienda near Granada belonging to the Chamorro family, which the invaders had expropriated.[11]

Father Vigil lasted only six weeks in Washington. Repudiated by other Latin ministers and spurned by US churchmen, he resigned his post and returned to Nicaragua. By then "Patas Arriba" Rivas had defected also, and Walker was hard put to find trustworthy natives to do his bidding in the Yankee capital. His next emissary was Appleton Oaksmith, a fellow filibuster. At a private meeting on the night of August 4, 1856, Mississippi Congressman John Quitman, himself the organizer of filibustering expeditions against Cuba, tried to persuade President Pierce to recognize Oaksmith, who was also in attendance.[12] Lame duck Pierce declined, but the meeting was, nevertheless, evidence of the filibusters' ready access to the White House.

The fact that Walker had by that time proclaimed himself president of Nicaragua made it much more difficult for the administration to accredit his representatives. Perhaps, too, Pierce was bitter at not being renominated by his party, and took this opportunity to get even. More likely, however, the issue had simply become too hot to handle in an election year that saw the new anti-slavery Republican Party field its first presidential candidate.

Believers in the immaculate conception of United States foreign policy cite the anti-filibustering proclamations of the Pierce and Buchanan Administrations as proof of their innocence of complicity with Walker. But presidents are bound to uphold the law—in this case the neutrality statutes—and are therefore obligated to make such statements whatever their real policy may be. Of more importance than the pronouncements themselves are the context in which they are made and other actions that may negate their effect.

Frequently mentioned is a proclamation signed by Pierce on December 8, 1855, warning United States citizens against undertaking military operations in Nicaragua.[13] The most striking thing about the "warning," however, was that it came nearly two months after Walker had captured Granada—when the filibusters seemed to be securely in control. It appears that Pierce timed the statement not to affect the course of events in Nicaragua, but to deflect attacks at home and avoid international censure. Open association with the seizure and colonization of Nicaragua was a patent violation of the Clayton-Bulwer Treaty and certain to be viewed as such by Britain.

The aforementioned message from Jefferson Davis—secretary of war, Mississippi plantation owner, and future president of the Confederacy—cautioning Major General Wool against too rigorous enforcement of the neutrality laws after Walker's Mexican escapade manifested the Pierce Administration's real attitude. So well had Wool understood the policy that when Walker informed him of his plans to go to Nicaragua, "the old man, shaking him heartily by the hand, said he not only would not interfere with the enterprise, but wished it success."[14] The avowal of a law was one thing, its implementation quite another.

Shortly after being rescued from Rivas by Commander Davis, Walker traveled to Washington. There he met privately with President Buchanan on June 12, 1857. The filibuster later asserted that the president had encouraged him to return to Nicaragua.[15] Whether Walker's claim was true or not, his reception at the White House could hardly be construed as a sign of determined opposition to filibustering.

Undaunted by the ritual neutrality law proclamations, Walker recruiters had a free hand in the US; the thousands who joined the invasions of Nicaragua did so virtually without impediment. In the few cases where some perfunctory enforcement measures were taken, no convictions were obtained, no fines paid, no jail terms served.

There was only one instance when decisive action was taken against filibustering, the exception that proved the rule. Immediately after his meeting with Buchanan, the Grey-Eyed Man of Destiny made a whirlwind tour of major US cities, drumming up support for a new invasion. Knowledge of the planning was so widespread that the ministers from Central America protested, compelling Secretary of State Lewis Cass to issue instructions for federal agencies to be on the lookout for filibustering expeditions.

Cass himself made no secret of his sympathy for Walker. A year earlier, as a candidate for the Democratic presidental nomination, he had declared:

> I am free to confess that the heroic effort of our countrymen in Nicaragua excites my admiration, while it engages all my solicitude. I am not to be deterred from the expression of these feelings by sneers, or reproaches, or hard words. He who does not sympathise with such an enterprise has little in common with me. The difficulties which General Walker has encountered and overcome will place his name high on the roll of the distinguished men of his age . . . That magnificent region, for which God has done so much and man so little, needs some renovating process, some transfusion by which new life may be imparted to it. Our countrymen will plant there the seeds of our institutions, and God grant that they may grow up into an abundant harvest of industry, enterprise, and

prosperity. A new day, I hope, is opening upon the States of Central America.[16]

But Commodore Hiram Paulding, the distinguished naval officer who commanded the United States Home Squadron, took the order to apprehend filibusters seriously. Receiving news that Walker had landed a force at Punta Arenas for a new attempt on Nicaragua, Paulding sailed from Aspinwall, Nueva Granada, (now Colón, Panama) on the steam frigate *Wabash,* put ashore a detachment of 300 Marines and sailors, arrested Walker and 150 followers, and hauled them back to the United States. There Walker was placed in the custody of the US marshal. Secretary Cass promptly ordered the Man of Destiny released.

"General" Cass was a man who, in the words of the *New York Times,* had a "gay and expansive way of alluding . . . to the development of the American idea and the extension of our star-spangled empire." Referring to Cass' earlier statements on enforcement of the neutrality laws, the *Times* wrote:

> [Cass] had no hesitation in laughing heartily at the thought of the official solemnities with which he had been attempting to delude the American public. It is reported that he received in an unofficial, friendly and sympathizing manner that very William Walker whom he had denounced to the officers of the national justice as a "lawless person,"—that he "shook hands" with him most cordially, and even underwent a compliment from Captain Rynders, the companion of the ex-fillibuster, to the amiability of his demeanor and the statesmanlike justice of his views.*[17]

Commodore Paulding's action, spoiling the filibusters' invasion plan, stirred up a hornets' nest in Congress and the press. Manifest Destiny partisans railed against Paulding for aborting Walker's "Americanization" of Nicaragua. Alexander H. Stephens of Georgia was a leader of this group in the House of Representatives. Taking the floor during debate on the "Paulding Affair," as it became known, Stephens demanded to know how anyone could oppose a pastime as American as filibustering: "General [Andrew] Jackson himself took possession of Florida," he protested, "He was, if you please, a grand filibuster himself."[18]

All charges against Walker arising from the incident were dropped. The ship that carried the invasion force, having been seized by federal authorities for sailing with a forged port clearance, was now sold for $200—to the "Mobile and Nicaragua Steamship Company," a Walker front.[19] Walker

---

* "Captain" Isaiah Rynders was the US marshal for New York in whose custody the filibuster had been placed. A leader of the Tammany Hall Democrats, he was one of Walker's main New York boosters. Rynders accompanied Walker to Washington for a meeting with Cass at which the filibuster was ordered released.

immediately set about preparing yet another expedition.

On January 7, 1858 Buchanan sent Congress a message announcing, "In capturing General Walker and his command after they had landed on the soil of Nicaragua Commodore Paulding has, in my opinion, committed a grave error." Paulding's error, said Buchanan, consisted in "exceeding his instructions" by "leading his sailors and marines in Nicaragua, whether with or without her consent." The president wished it to be clear, however, that "no inference must be drawn that I am less determined than I have ever been to execute the neutrality laws of the United States."[20]

It soon became apparent just how determined Buchanan really was: the hapless Commodore Paulding was relieved from duty for, of all things, violating Nicaraguan sovereignty. Paulding's action was heartily applauded by the Nicaraguans themselves. The Nicaraguan Congress memorialized the commodore and presented him with a jewelled sword.*

The sacking of Commodore Paulding and the "Catch 22" instructions issued to his successor, Commodore McIntosh, sent a much clearer signal than all the presidential proclamations against freebooting combined. US warships were now ordered to station themselves in the harbor of San Juan del Norte, but only permitted to arrest filibusters on the high seas—three nautical miles off shore. As if those mutually exclusive strictures were not enough to guarantee inaction, naval commanders were forbidden to make arrests without proof of filibustering intent. Moreover, they were told not to interfere with commerce! Attempts by naval officers to get these orders clarified were fruitless. It is little wonder that British Foreign Secretary Lord Clarendon, who was personally acquainted with James Buchanan when he was US minister to England, characterized him as an "artful dodger."[22]

But even many of those who favored "Americanization" of Nicaragua were beginning to see filibustering as counterproductive. Though the *New York Times* had been sympathetic to Walker, after the disastrous defeat of his first attempt it had declared:

---

* Paulding was subsequently harassed by lawsuits from members of Walker's expedition, and the Buchanan Administration refused to provide for his defense. Paulding had his revenge, however. He was restored to service during Lincoln's term, when Congress voted to reimburse his legal expenses. Promoted to rear admiral, he played an important part in building the Union navy, personally overseeing construction of the first ironclads.

In June 1862, at the ceremony in which he was presented with the sword, Paulding credited the Nicaraguan government with "a sense of justice that I did not find in my own." "I remember," he declared, "the bitter denunciation of the prominent scoundrels who had partioned among themselves the homes of an unoffending people, how they deplored with imbecile rage the loss of a new empire for the institution of slavery, to be established on the ruin of a free people.

"My proceeding was approved by every good citizen, yet such were the influences then controlling the administration of the Government that the course of justice due to a friendly nation was set aside."[21]

No set of men ever proved themselves more absolutely incompetent to accomplish what they had undertaken than did he and his friends . . . The interests of Commerce demand not less imperatively than the honor of our national character that a definite and determined stop should be put to everything that bears the semblance of "Walkerism." So long as another *avatar* of this detestable kind of free-booting shall seem to be possible, so long will the trade of the Isthmus be liable to interruptions and annoyances of all sorts.[23]

During the Paulding Affair the *Times* wrote:

Nothing can be more fatal to the hopes of those who desire to see these fertile regions redeemed by American energy and enterprise than the bloody and lawless invasions . . . The first step towards bringing Nicaragua under American influence will have been taken when an end is put to these piratical invasions of her soil.[24]

President Buchanan himself denounced private military expeditions as "a usurpation of the war-making power, which belongs alone to Congress." He declared that "it would be far better and more in accordance with the bold and manly character of our countrymen for the Government itself to get up such expeditions than to allow them to proceed under the command of irresponsible adventurers."[25] On several occasions the Artful

James Buchanan

Dodger sought congressional authority to "get up such expeditions," but failing this he continued to wink at filibustering—both as a sop to the South and because it was the "covert operations" of the day.

James Buchanan was one of the era's leading expansionists. Though a Pennsylvanian, his interest was never far from any enterprise likely to result in territorial aggrandizement for the benefit of his political allies and backers, the Southern slaveholders. As Polk's secretary of state, he played an important part in the seizure of half the territory of Mexico. As Pierce's minister to England, he produced the Ostend Manifesto, seeking to acquire Cuba. As president, he sent federal troops to intervene in the Kansas Civil War on the side of the slavery faction, describing the anti-slavery element as "revolutionaries" who were "subverting the territorial government."[26]

Buchanan also devoted considerable attention to finding ways of taking more of Mexico. Those included schemes for a railroad or canal across the Isthmus of Tehuántepec and a recommendation to Congress that the US "assume a temporary protectorate over the northern portions of Chihuahua and Sonora" and "establish military posts within the same."[27] Finally, he demonstrated an untiring interest in the republics of the isthmus, particularly Nicaragua.

The lure of Nicaragua was not simply its location as a potential hub of commerce and its suitability for plantation agriculture. With a foot in the door via the transit route—the "filibuster highway"—Nicaragua was the key to Central America. Once North Americans got control there, the other Central American countries would drop into their laps like so many plums. Then, as Walker associate Charles Doubleday put it, "the old [Guatemala-Chiapas] boundary question—were any necessary—would furnish pretexts for adding Mexico to the Central American Empire."[28] Later, Cuba and Santo Domingo would fall into place.

The slave power had for a long time toyed with the idea of secession, but after reaching the turning point of its fortunes in Kansas, it began serious contingency planning. If new slave territories in Central America, Mexico, and the Caribbean could be brought into the Union to help restore the dominant political position of the South, so be it. If not, control of those countries would make the seceded Southern states not only a viable entity, but a powerful empire—or so they thought.

The nature of the designs on Central America was apparent to participants in the congressional debate during the Paulding Affair. Representative Francis P. Blair, Jr. of Missouri* declared on that occasion:

---

* Francis Preston Blair, Jr. was elected to the House from St. Louis on the Free Soil Party ticket. In May 1861, while the new Lincoln Administration hesitated, Blair, without authorization or direction from the federal government, organized a virtual insurrection of the citizenry

There is a party in this country who go for the extension of slavery; and these predatory incursions on our neighbors are the means by which territory is to be seized, planted with slavery, annexed to this Union, and, in combination with the present slaveholding States, made to dominate this Government and the entire continent; or, failing in the policy of annexation, to unite with the slave States in a southern slaveholding Republic.[30]

Reporting on the extent of support for Walker in the South, the *Philadelphia Press* wrote:

The fillibuster feeling is a very prevalent one among the warlike Southrons, and this feeling has received a new and powerful impulse from the failure of the South to secure Kansas as a Slave State. Southern expansion is now the great idea, as essential to maintain, at least, an approach to equilibrium of the North and South, to preserve the Union, and to draw the South off from the unwise policy of seeking to extend slavery into the northern latitudes. The Democratic Party throughout the Union will acquiesce in this policy. The acquisition of Cuba or some adjacent southern country, is the very best step to calm and extinguish the discord which has for some time disturbed the quiet of these States. It was wisely said to Mr. Buchanan a few days ago, by a gentleman whose opinion he asked as to the best remedy for the Kansas troubles: "change the programme: substitute *Cuba* for *Kansas* and the *Ostend Manifesto* for the *Lecompton Convention*."* The President smiled and brightened up at the idea which went home to one of his warmest feelings and aspirations.[31] [Emphasis in original.]

The paper might have added that "Nicaragua" could just as easily have been substituted for "Kansas" in the new "programme."

Seeing the Clayton-Bulwer Treaty as an obstacle to US expansion into Central America, Buchanan had been one of its chief opponents from the outset. On April 2, 1850, trying to rally opposition to ratification of the treaty, he wrote to John A. McClernand, editor of the *Democratic Journal* in New York, telling him that Clayton-Bulwer constituted

---

of St. Louis against the Missouri state government, then controlled by the slave power. With Blair's decisive leadership, the St. Louisians took the state troops prisoner, saved the large federal arsenal at St. Louis from capture by the South, and prevented the secession of Missouri. Shortly thereafter Blair resigned from the House to join the war effort, rising to the rank of major general. While militantly anti-slavery, Blair did not believe in racial equality, and later authored a plan to resettle freed slaves in Central America. Lincoln pursued Blair's plan through diplomatic channels, but was rebuffed by the Central Americans. Blair ran for vice president on the unsuccessful Democratic slate of 1868.[29]

* The "Lecompton Convention" was the slavery constitution that the Buchanan Administration tried to impose on Kansas with the help of federal troops.

a solemn stipulation on the part of the United States to Great Britain, that at no future period, shall we ever annex to our country, under any circumstances, any portion of the vast country of Central America . . . It is a stipulation by which Great Britain, in fact guarantees, as against the United States, the integrity of the different States of Central America: and if we had just cause of war against these States at the present moment, and should conquer any portion of their territory, Great Britain, under the Treaty, might and would require us to abandon it . . . Let us then enter into a similar stipulation with Great Britain in regard to Mexico, and our limits are forever bounded by the Rio Grande, for such would be the true purport and meaning of our engagement with that overreaching power . . . The treaty altogether reverses the Monroe Doctrine, and establishes it against ourselves rather than European Governments.[32]

Buchanan tried during his presidency to get England to agree to abrogate the treaty, but failing this, Clayton-Bulwer remained in force and continued to bar the United States from seizing Central American territory or establishing protectorates.

The Clayton-Bulwer Treaty and congressional recalcitrance prevented Buchanan from taking direct action, while Walker's failures called into question the efficacy of private enterprise military adventures. As a Buchanan biographer expressed it, "The procedure would have to be more subtle. Buchanan thought that the canny use of claims and the peaceful migration of North Americans to the region might accomplish the desired result without raising the issue with England."[33] A large emigration to Nicaragua would provide the necessary base of support for whatever action might follow, as had been the case in Texas. Buchanan explained the scenario to Congress:

It is beyond question the destiny of our race to spread themselves over the continent of North America, and this at no distant day should events be permitted to take their natural course. The tide of emigrants will flow to the south, and nothing can eventually arrest its progress. If permitted to go there peacefully, Central America will soon contain an American population which will confer blessings and benefits as well upon the natives as their respective Governments. Liberty under the restraint of law will preserve domestic peace, whilst the different transit routes across the Isthmus, in which we are so deeply interested, will have assured protection.[34]

But polarization over the slavery issue was causing many, inside as well as outside the United States, to question the purported benefits of "Americanization." The radicalization was strikingly evident in a speech

to Congress by Republican Representative Emory B. Pottle of New York
on January 13, 1858:

> It seems to be taken for granted, upon all sides of the House, that we
> are to proceed with this process of Americanizing Central America . . . I
> wish to know, in the first place, by what right we propose to render this
> service to our southern neighbors? Have they invited us to Americanize
> their institutions?
>
> .   .   .
>
> And then, sir, I desire to know distinctly, from gentlemen advocat-
> ing these projects, precisely what this Americanization is to be. Sir, if
> the Americanization of this or any territory is to be to give it the insti-
> tutions manifestly existing already in fifteen of the States of this Un-
> ion . . . then I have to say . . . I trust in God the last foot of this
> continent has been Americanized that ever will be!
>
> Sir, before we induce any other country or people to accept this sort
> of Americanization, it may be well to inform them of the difference be-
> tween our institutions, theoretically, as contained in the Declaration of
> Independence and in the Constitution of the United States, and as they
> are at this time practically illustrated. It would be well to inform them
> that with us freedom means human bondage; the right of the majority
> to rule means the right of a conservative minority to control and take
> care of "factious" majorities, and make for them unalterable constitu-
> tions; that guarding the ballot box means simply to surround it with
> ruffians and bayonets, driving from it honest and legal votes, and fill-
> ing the poll-list with names copied from old directories in their stead.*
>
> .   .   .
>
> Then, sir, you should go further than this, and inform them that the
> practical workings of this Americanization in the States where it has been
> adopted has not only been a curse to the very soil . . . it has exhausted
> and rendered the most fertile region of the earth almost a barren waste;
> that its effects have been to degrade labor, to prevent the development
> of the resources of the country, to deny intelligence not only to the slaves,
> but, as a necessary consequence, to the laboring whites . . . Inform them
> that the practical operation of this peculiar Americanization which gen-
> tlemen are seeking, has been to reduce millions, not of slaves, but white
> men, to a degradation upon which even the slaves look down with
> contempt.[35]

BUCHANAN'S colonizing strategy would require two things: the reopening of the transit to encourage emigrants, and a treaty with
Nicaragua that would permit emigration from the United States and al-

---

* These are references to the attempts to forcibly impose the Lecompton slavery constitution
in Kansas.

low for the employment of force to back up the emigrants' claims. While Buchanan vigorously pursued these objectives through diplomatic channels, he simultaneously accommodated the impatient by leaving the door open to filibustering.

After Walker's surrender at Rivas, William Carey Jones, a Washington lawyer, was sent as special agent to Central America. One of his assignments was to arrange for repatriation of the numerous vagrant North Americans—remnants of the filibuster invasion—who were stranded, penniless, in Central America. The other was to assess the possibilities open to the US in the aftermath of the fiasco.

Special Agent Jones made no secret of his sympathy for the filibusters' cause. Writing from Costa Rica, he described that country's entry into the war against Walker as having been motivated by "jealousy of the ingress & consequent dominancy, of a superior race." More important, his letters strongly suggested the direct involvement of the US government in filibustering plans. He wrote Secretary Cass:

> I shall have the hope that until I have an opportunity to communicate with the [State] Department from Nicaragua direct, no "expedition" will have left for Isthmian America, and that the government will not, on the other hand, have entered into any arrangement for the "security" (which means the non-occupation by Americans) of the Nicaraguan route.[36]

The end of the Filibuster War confronted the victorious Nicaraguans with the task of rebuilding their ruined country. A compromise accord signed in June 1857 established a provisional government in which Con-

Tomás Martínez

servative General Tomás Martinez and Liberal General Máximo Jerez served as co-presidents until November, when a Constituent Assembly elected Martinez to continue alone as chief executive.

Arriving in Nicaragua, Special Agent Jones reported, not surprisingly, "a settled dislike to the American government and people." He found these sentiments to "apply especially to the members of the existing Administration, with, perhaps a single exception—the Minister of Foreign Relations" (Gregorio Juárez). Juárez, Special Agent Jones believed, "is disposed to take a philosophic, sensible and practical view, of the destiny of his country,—recognizing as certain, the ultimate dominancy here of our race."[37]

Antonio José de Irisarri had been designated as Nicaragua's minister in Washington. A Guatemalan national, he also represented both his own country and El Salvador. Apparently acting without instructions, Irisarri signed a draft treaty of "amity, commerce and navigation" with Cass in November 1857. The Cass-Irisarri Treaty provided that the United States would "extend their protection" to all transit routes across Nicaragua, being permitted to use force for the "security and protection" of the transit and the "lives or property" of US citizens. It also granted North Americans the right to own real estate in Nicaragua.[38] With perhaps unintended symbolism, the Buchanan Administration dispatched Mirabeau Buonaparte Lamar—former "president" of the "Republic of Texas"—to Nicaragua with instructions to press for the treaty's ratification and the reopening of the transit.

That sector of the Nicaraguan elite that had favored opening the country to foreign immigration was thoroughly discredited by the Walker experience. The transit had brought the country only trouble; the last thing Nicaraguans wanted was to restore the filibuster highway—especially in the hands of a Yankee company—or to sign any treaty that would facilitate the same object. But their leaders found themselves in a bind: the nation was hardly able to fight off another filibuster invasion, which threatened constantly, much less directly confront the power of the United States. So they resolved to play cat and mouse with the northern giant while trying to secure protection from Europe.

José de Marcoleta, Nicaragua's former minister to Washington, went to Paris in an effort to arrange for France to take over the transit/canal project. Now that Louis Bonaparte, author of the pamphlet on the Nicaragua canal, was Emperor Napoleon III, France seemed the logical place to go for help. Marcoleta's mission stimulated the interest of a French promoter named Felix Belly, who visited Nicaragua early in 1858.

President Martinez and Costa Rican President Juan Rafael Mora met at Rivas to consider Belly's proposals and to resolve their border disputes. Their summit resulted in a tentative contract with Belly and in a declaration by the two presidents that became known as the "Rivas Manifesto."

Signed on May 1, 1858, the anniversary of the Walkerites' capitulation, the Rivas Manifesto denounced the threat of new aggression, charging that "this invasion, officially reproved by the Govt. of the U.S., is in reality preparing itself under its patronage, as the means of definitively taking possession of Central America if Central America refuses to surrender herself to the United States" (through the Cass-Irisarri Treaty). It called on France, England, and Sardinia—the powers that had intervened in the Crimean War on behalf of the Ottoman Empire—to guarantee the sovereignty of Central America, a sort of Monroe Doctrine of Europe against the United States.[39] While the document expressed the well-grounded fears of the two countries, it was ill-advised from a diplomatic standpoint and misguided in its belief that European powers were ready to make a formal commitment to protect Central American independence.

The United States was furious. Minister Lamar wrote of his

> indignation and disgust towards this perfidious and profligate people . . . I feel constrained to express the sincere desire and hope, that some prompt, energetic and decisive measures may be taken to convince them that they are responsible for their conduct, and that if they are determined to be enemies, they will be treated as enemies . . . The Central American question has to be settled some day; and I know of no better time than now . . . England's false interpretation of the Clayton-Bulwer Treaty [retaining its Miskito protectorate], furnishes good ground for abrogating that Convention; and I think our government ought to avail itself of this opportunity of getting rid of it *before Great Britain recedes from her interpretation, and throws the responsibility of violating it, upon the United States.* If that Treaty is to continue under either of the interpretations given to it, we may abandon all hopes of progress in this direction.[40] [Emphasis added.]

Convinced by cooler heads that the Rivas Manifesto merely served the interests of those in the United States who sought to drum up support for direct intervention, Martinez and Mora repudiated it. For better or worse, the Belly contract fell through when financing arrangements failed.

Nicaragua's efforts to secure European protection were more successful, however, and this was particularly galling to Yankee expansionists. Lamar warned that Nicaraguans were allowing Europeans to get control of the country, "and if we would arrest the work, there is but one way to do it, and that is to unfurl the Monroe Banner at once, and defy the foe to strike it down."[41]

Lamar did "unfurl the Monroe Banner." He labored to make the recalcitrant Nicaraguans see that "the doctrine not only saved this country from a resubjugation to Spain, but that it had secured it against the aggressive

power of Great Britain." But despite his best efforts, the US minister reported, Nicaraguan Interior Minister Rosalio Cortés

> seemed to think that Nicaragua ought not to forego the advantages of
> British protection against the Filibusters—I answered that I did not think
> the United States would consent for Great Britain to land troops on this
> soil under the pretext of expelling filibusters from it; for any attempt
> of that kind would not be for the good of Nicaragua; but in hostility
> to the United States.[42]

Whatever the shortcomings or weaknesses of General Martinez and his cabinet, suicidal tendencies were not among them. They opted not to "forego
the advantages" of European protection, despite the Buchanan Administration's lack of "consent."

Though unwilling to sign treaties incorporating formal guarantees, Britain and France did send warships with orders to land troops if necessary
to apprehend any filibustering attempt. The US protested in November
1858, but to no avail.[43] The presence of British and French forces played
no small part in bringing Walker's career to its conclusion two years later.
With British and French ships guarding Nicaraguan ports, Walker landed
his final expedition in Honduras. He did not anticipate the intervention
of the British navy there, intending to make his way overland to Nicaragua.

The Nicaraguans gave the Buchanan Administration a run-around on
the Cass-Irisarri Treaty for six months. The Constituent Assembly finally
ratified it on June 28, 1858, but with a number of amendments. Chief
among these was the following article:

> The government of the United States shall prevent the preparation, with-
> in said States, of expeditions and armaments against Nicaragua, even
> under the pretext of assisting any of the parties that may exist in that
> country.[44]

The administration was apoplectic at what Secretary Cass called the
"offensive doubt whether this Government will continue to execute in good
faith the neutrality laws." With this and other amendments limiting the
power of the United States, the treaty was unacceptable to Washington.
Cass wrote his representative in Managua, "I need not inform you that
these proceedings, on the part of Nicaragua, have been viewed with serious dissatisfaction by the President, and that, if this course of conduct
towards the United States continues to be pursued, it cannot fail to lead
to the most painful consequences."[45]

In light of the Paulding Affair, the Manifest Destiny pronouncements
of Buchanan and others, and the continual threat of new filibuster invasions, diplomacy was proving insufficient to persuade the Nicaraguans that
their northern neighbor was sincere in its professed determination to

safeguard their sovereignty. So the administration resolved to employ more expeditious methods.

In the course of the frequent alarms prompted by the activities of Walker and others in the United States, Nicaragua had taken a number of defensive measures. It had deported some North Americans who had been associated with the filibuster occupation. In December 1857, at the time of Walker's landing at Punta Arenas, it ordered all foreigners in the department of Rivas to present themselves to the military governor. During a subsequent alert the garrison at Fort San Carlos impounded the river steamers—owned by US citizens—to prevent their use by invaders. The boats were not then in service, as the owners had defaulted on a contract to reopen the transit route; nevertheless, company agent Louis Schlessinger—the one-time leader of Walker's ill-fated invasion of Costa Rica—complained to the State Department about the seizure of US property.

The Buchanan Administration availed itself of these purported injustices to US citizens as a pretext for threatening action. This, it hoped, would pressure Nicaragua into signing the Cass-Irisarri Treaty without amendments. "I think it will suffice for the present," wrote Lamar, "if our Government would make a rigorous collection of our reclamations against her. I do not know to what extent the President is authorized to make reprisals; but if a Man of War could appear at Realejo, demanding immediate indemnity for the murder, robbery, and persecution of our citizens, there would be no further difficulty with this blind, infatuated people." Secretary Cass replied that "preparatory to such action as may be necessary," warships would be stationed on Nicaragua's coasts "with orders to afford all necessary protection to the persons and property of American citizens."[46]

Regarding the transit route, Minister Lamar urged "our Government to take measures of its own for opening this Route; and to plant the necessary force in the country to protect it, without any reference to [Nicaragua's] government. It will come to this at last; for I am satisfied that this country does not desire the Transit."[47]

A week later, the former president of Texas wrote with a sense of urgency from Managua, "The soldiers destined for Castillo Viejo are now parading before me." He advised prompt action by the United States to seize the old fortress, which occupied a commanding position on the San Juan River, because

to capture the place, when once repaired and properly garrisoned would cost much blood and treasure. This naturally suggests the importance of not allowing any power to hold possession of it, except our own government; for I consider it as a settled matter that the United States are bound to have a transit across this Isthmus at all hazard.[48]

Lamar subsequently recommended the seizure of several other strongpoints as well.

Gunboat diplomacy was one thing, but an actual invasion was quite another. Unlike later US presidents, James Buchanan lacked the power to take military action without congressional approval. And as the "irrepressible conflict" drew nearer, it became ever more difficult to get congressional approval for anything.

Endeavoring to convince Congress to grant him the power he sought, Buchanan, the Artful Dodger, adduced a remarkable thesis:

> If an arm of the sea connecting the two oceans penetrated through Nicaragua and Costa Rica, it could not be pretended that these States would have the right to arrest or retard its navigation to the injury of other nations. The transit by land over this narrow isthmus occupies nearly the same position.

But Nicaragua had refused to accede to this view by ratifying the Cass-Irisarri Treaty in the form demanded by the United States. Buchanan continued:

> The Executive of this country in its intercourse with foreign nations is limited to the employment of diplomacy alone . . . It cannot legitimately resort to force without the direct authority of Congress, except in resisting and repelling hostile attacks. It would have no authority to enter the territories of Nicaragua even to protect the lives and property of our citizens on their passage . . . Under these circumstances I earnestly recommend to Congress the passage of an act authorizing the President, under such restrictions as they may deem proper, to employ the land and naval forces of the United States in preventing the transit from being obstructed or closed by lawless violence, and in protecting the lives and property of American citizens travelling thereupon, requiring at the same time that these forces shall be withdrawn the moment the danger shall have passed away."[49]

The president's requests for congressional authority to send troops into Nicaragua and Mexico, though repeated the following year, were ignored. In a book written to answer the many charges leveled against him during the Civil War, Buchanan lamented, "These recommendations of the President were wholly disregarded by Congress during the session of 1859-1860 . . . The members of both parties were too exclusively occupied in discussing the slavery question, and in giving their attention to the approaching Presidential election."[50]

Nevertheless, the threats and verbal bullying continued, succeeding, finally, in gaining Nicaragua's assent to drop the anti-filibustering provision from the treaty. But it was a hollow victory—the Civil War intervened to prevent the agreement's ratification by the US Senate. Lamar's successor, Alexander Dimitry of Louisiana, expressed his frustration in a dispatch to Cass: Nicaragua, he said, "in the inexhaustible treasury of her subterfuges, had discovered reasons, one more flimsy than the other, to suit her day to day purposes and stave off the directions of the President of the United States."[51]

Marx wrote, "Under the presidency of Buchanan the sway that the South had gradually usurped over the Union through its alliance with the Northern Democrats attained its zenith."[52] The South and its policies had undeniably gained control of the executive branch of government, but an ever larger majority in the rapidly growing nation were unwilling to have their interests subordinated to the rule of the slave-owning oligarchy and its "doughface" allies. Pressure on Northern Democrats in Congress to distance themselves from the slave power became increasingly intense, ultimately resulting in the split of the party in the 1860 election that permitted Lincoln's victory.

Jared V. Peck personified the political changes taking place in the United States. A former Democratic congressman from New York, Peck enumerated the reasons why he had quit the party in a letter read to a mass rally against slavery extension: "For the first time in the History of this Country, there is an attempt made to establish Slavery as a National Institution," he said. He recounted how the Pierce Administration "came forward as the special advocate" of the Missouri Compromise, "and with a liberal distribution of government patronage, succeeded in forcing it through Congress," only to turn around and push for its repeal "the very moment the act ceased to promote the extension of Slavery." The ex-Democrat then called the attention of his hearers to

> the state of affairs in the Territory of Kansas—men strung up by the neck on the first tree for expressing sentiments favorable to freedom— the actual settlers driven from the Territory by a band of ruffians from a neighboring State—outrages of the most aggravated character committed daily, and all done with the knowledge and countenance of [President Pierce].

He concluded by pledging to join forces with others

> who do not believe that this Government was established for the express purpose of fostering and extending Slavery; or that we should sacrifice our National honor and degrade ourselves in the eyes of the whole world, merely to acquire new possessions where Slavery already exists, or where it could be easily established. The doctrine of the Highwayman, that

might makes right, is not the sentiment of the American people, although it may be adopted by a party and its candidate [James Buchanan].*[54]

On October 2, 1860, the eve of Lincoln's election, Luis Molina, Nicaragua's chargé d'affaires in the US, charged that "in the Southern States of this Republic there exists a conspiracy . . . whose object is to destroy the nationality and independence of the States of Central America, to subdue them by fire and sword, and introduce slavery." Walker had been brought to justice in Honduras just three weeks earlier, but, continued Molina, "there is a probability that these criminal acts may be repeated, whilst their authors can reckon, in the Southern States, upon the sympathies and complete impunity they enjoy." He cited the "notorious malevolence, gratuitous injustice, and irritating tone, which even at this day, are prominent in the generality of the organs of the press of the United States, whenever they treat of Central Americans," and called upon Buchanan to "devise a radical remedy for evils so transcendently serious."[55]

It was not for Buchanan, however, himself a symptom of the disease, to devise its cure. That remedy came as the denouement to the "irrepressible conflict" between the antagonistic social organisms within the United States. It was a radical remedy, indeed—one that made the bloodletting that for so long had characterized Central America, and drawn self-righteous Yankee ridicule, seem moderate. But the North American Civil War did allow Nicaragua and the rest of Central America—for the moment, at least—a breathing space.

---

* The phrase "the highwayman's plea, that 'might makes right,' " referring to the Democrats' foreign policy, appeared in the first Republican Party platform, adopted in Philadelphia the previous month.[53]

VII

FROM SEA TO SHINING SEA

It is a real misfortune to the world that the narrow neck of land connecting the two continents should be in the possession of weak and ill-governed States.

—New York Times *editorial, 1877.*

S EVERAL half-hearted efforts were made to reopen the Nicaragua transit in the dozen years following the Filibuster War, but compared to the flow of passengers before Walker's arrival, the traffic across the isthmus was reduced to an erratic trickle. The silting of the harbor at San Juan del Norte and other problems on the route demanded major capital improvements; without these the line could not hope to compete with the trans-Panama railroad. Completion of the first transcontinental railway across the US in 1869 ended the interest of North Americans in a Nicaragua passenger transit once and for all.

The result of the Civil War was to turn the attention of the United States inward for a long time after the dead were buried. The defeat of the slave power, the rapid extension of the railroads, and the homesteading of the West opened vast new markets and enormous untapped resources for exploitation.

Latin America and the Caribbean were not completely forgotten, however. The war, so propitious for the expansion of capitalism in the long run, had a negative short-term impact on foreign commerce. It enabled European nations, especially Britain, to expand their already dominant share of Latin American trade at the expense of Yankee merchants. The latter didn't take kindly to the inroads, believing that, as natives of the Western Hemisphere, they were entitled to consider Latin America and the Caribbean as their exclusive preserve.

Concern over the trade situation prompted the Senate, in 1870, to request President Grant to prepare a report on the condition of commercial relations with Latin America. In remarks motivating the resolution, Senator Fenton of New York reported that for the year ending June 30, 1869, trade with "Spanish America" accounted for only $75 million, out of a total US foreign trade of $876 million.[1]

The reply drawn up by Secretary of State Hamilton Fish noted that the "necessity . . . of preserving the great interest of the Southern States in African slavery" had handicapped relations with Latin America, causing "their trade to pass into hands unfriendly to the United States." But prospects for the future looked brighter, he said:

> The abolition of slavery in the United States . . . has caused us to be regarded there with more sympathetic as well as more respectful consideration. It has relieved those Republics from the fear of filibusterism which had been formerly incited against Central America and Mexico in the interest of slave extension.*[2]

Though the secretary's statements contained much truth, the trumpets of Manifest Destiny were not completely silenced by the Civil War. The end of the slave system did indeed remove the chief propellant of prewar expansionism. But the results of the "irrepressible conflict"—the abolition of property in humans, the extension of free market relations to the entire country, the crushing of the political power of the slave system—did not mean that the cotton barons were extinct. They had merely been compelled to adjust to new economic and social realities. In fact, the transition from slavery to Jim Crow, from lashing to lynching, proved easier than the plantation owners could have imagined. With the aid of the Ku Klux Klan and friends in Washington, they soon reharnessed the former slaves to a form of peonage that harmonized nicely with the needs of agrarian, export-oriented capitalism.

Not only did the reborn planters of the Old South resume their former friendship with Northern merchants, they now found new allies among the up-and-coming wheat and timber exporters of the West. Unlike the prewar predators, this new expansionist league sought territory not so much for its own sake. While there were among them, certainly, prospective investors in the lucrative productions of the tropics, their main interest lay in the competitive advantage for US commerce that a base in the Caribbe-

---

* In the same report Fish gave the following figures for US-Latin America trade for the year ended June 30, 1869: imports from Latin America, less than $25,000,000; exports to Latin America, $17,850,313. Great Britain (estimated): imports from Latin America, $42,820,942; exports to Latin America, $40,682,104. These figures did not include Brazil, Cuba, or Puerto Rico.

an would provide. Along with this, they sought to break down the trade barriers in the remaining Spanish colonies—Cuba and Puerto Rico. In fact, even as Secretary Fish made his report to the Senate, an effort was underway to take possession of Santo Domingo, as the Dominican Republic was then known.

The attempted annexation of the Dominican Republic revealed a great deal about the evolving United States policy toward Latin America and the Caribbean—in which Nicaragua was destined once again to play a principal part. It highlighted, too, the rapid transformation of the Republican Party. Initially a vehicle for the democratic aspirations of millions of small farmers, laborers, and immigrants, now, just fifteen years later, it had become the home of wealthy merchants, industrialists, and speculators.

The Dominican oligarchy was then torn by factional warfare. Fearing his own downfall, President Buenaventura Báez sought to save his position through annexation of the island to the United States. He was encouraged by North American speculators living in Santo Domingo, including General William Cazneau and former Henry Kinney partner and ex-US commercial agent in Nicaragua, Joseph W. Fabens. Fabens reappeared here in the guise of President Báez's "special commissioner" to the US.[3]

A draft annexation treaty, negotiated under suspicious circumstances by General Orville E. Babcock, special agent of President Grant, was submitted to the Senate for ratification early in 1870. The *New York Times* hailed the agreement: "The Administration . . . actuated solely by a desire permanently to serve the commercial interests of the country, has pushed the negotiation vigorously and successfully."[4]

On May 12, 1870, a "large and enthusiastic meeting" gathered at New York's Cooper Institute "for the purpose of giving expression to the views of our commercial community in favor of the ratification of the treaty for the annexation of San Domingo," reported the *Times*. "The large hall of the Union was filled to overflowing, mainly with substantial business men." Shipping tycoon Moses H. Grinnell called the meeting to order, reading a list of honorary vice-presidents and secretaries that included such prominent citizens as Moses Taylor and John Jacob Astor.* Congressman Thomas Fitch of Nevada, one of the main speakers, delighted the audience with a depiction of the windfall that annexation would bring, then added: "If we can gain a foothold in the islands of the Caribbean by the annexation of San Domingo, every other island will speedily follow."[6]

Zachariah Chandler of Michigan was a leading spokesman for annexa-

---

* Moses Taylor was president of the City Bank of New York and the principal stockholder in the Delaware, Lackawanna, and Western Railroad. Astor, the inheritor of a vast commercial and financial empire, sat on the boards of many banks and other enterprises. At his death in 1890 his personal fortune was estimated at between $75 and $100 million.[5]

tion supporters on the floor of the Senate. On May 28, 1870, in the midst of a debate on subsidies for US shipbuilders, Senator Chandler interjected, "There is one other way in which we might increase our commerce—one that is simple—and that is by enlarging it." This could be accomplished, he said, by

> enlarging our borders. Take in the islands of the Gulf; take in the Sandwich Islands; in process of time take in the Dominion of Canada; take in Colombia; and you will enlarge your commerce immeasurably.

But Chandler was content to take "one thing at a time." He would start with "San Domingo [which] stands rapping at the door for admission."[7] For the next hour he reviewed for his fellow senators the commercial history of Santo Domingo since the time of Columbus.

Three days later, in a message to the Senate, President Grant declared:

> The acquisition of San Domingo is desirable because . . . it commands the entrance to the Caribbean Sea and the Isthmus transit of commerce . . . Its possession by us will in a few years build up a coastwise commerce of immense magnitude, which will go far toward restoring to us our lost merchant marine . . . It is asserting our just claim to a controlling influence over the great commercial traffic soon to flow from east to west by way of the Isthmus of Darien.[8]

The New York *Star* was typical of those voices ever ready to renew the familiar refrain. The Santo Domingo annexation scheme, it blustered,

> implies the recognition by this government and people of their inevitable destiny—the eventual control and absorption of this continent and its adjacent territory. It implies the immediate control of the commerce of the Caribbean seas in peace, and of the seas themselves in war.[9]

Leading the opposition to annexation were two radical Republican senators, Charles Sumner of Massachusetts, chairman of the Senate Foreign Relations Committee, and Carl Schurz of Missouri. Before the Civil War Sumner had been one of the foremost anti-slavery voices in Congress and the nation. He survived two attempts by slavery partisans to assassinate him, one by Congressman Preston Brooks of South Carolina. But, unlike many, Sumner did not just favor ending the South's "peculiar institution"; he fought a valiant but losing battle to gain full equality for Blacks after the Civil War.

Carl Schurz was a revolutionary democrat transplanted from Germany. Having gained military experience in the ill-fated German revolution of 1848, he served capably as a Union general in the Civil War, continually urging the emancipation and arming of the slaves as a means to undermine the war-making power of the Confederacy.[10]

Senator Sumner charged that Báez was "sustained in power by the presence of our naval force . . . that he may betray his country." "Are we not now treating Baez in some measure as England treated the Mosquito king?" he asked. He appealed to President Grant "not to follow the example of Franklin Pierce, James Buchanan and Andrew Johnson." He protested, he said, "in the name of the weak trodden down; in the name of Peace imperiled, and in the name of the African race, whose first effort at Independence [in Santo Domingo] is rudely assailed."[11]

Schurz, meanwhile, aggressively unraveled the plot in the Senate "Davis Hatch" hearings. He exposed the collusion of General Babcock—one of Grant's closest friends—with Fabens and Cazneau, as well as the means by which the supporters of annexation had conspired to keep Báez in power till the scheme could be consummated.[12]

Most opponents of annexation were not as principled as Sumner and Schurz, however. Some expressed a racially motivated reluctance to bring more Blacks into the United States. Among these was Senator Thomas Bayard of Delaware—later to become secretary of state. Bayard argued that the people of the Dominican Republic

> can never be governed by a constitutional government like ours . . . We are unable to elevate such a race as inhabit that island to the level of our own. If a level is to be achieved at all it will only be by dragging us down, and not by bringing them up.[13]

Others manifested a widespread concern about the potential costs, both financial and military, of a Caribbean empire. Senator Morrill of Vermont argued for annexation of Canada instead!

The treaty failed ratification for lack of a two-thirds majority. Neither subsequent maneuvering by the administration nor the removal of Sumner from his longtime Foreign Relations Committee chairmanship sufficed to carry the measure.

The clash over annexation of the Dominican Republic began a foreign policy struggle that would grow in intensity until the Spanish-American War, closely paralleling the debate over protectionism versus free trade. Export-oriented producers, largely in the South and West, were joined by merchants in promoting an aggressive, expansionist foreign policy, whose centerpiece would be the project of an isthmian canal. Ranged against them were the emergent industrial trusts, nourished by protectionism and wary of dangerous foreign adventures that might jeopardize domestic economic development. Allied with these were the transcontinental railroad interests who feared competition from a canal.

What the railroad could do for travelers—eliminating the need for a transit across the Central American isthmus—it could not do for freight.

California, Oregon, and Washington were already exporting significant quantities of wheat and timber. These commodities had to be carried around Cape Horn to reach markets in the Caribbean and Europe. Trade from the East and South had to take the same route to reach Asia or the west coast of South America. The cost of transcontinental rail transport was prohibitive. Thus the post-Civil War development that made the Nicaragua passenger transit obsolete simultaneously gave rise to increasing demands that the government become actively involved in construction of an isthmian canal. The clamor took on added urgency with the opening of the Suez Canal in December 1869, which gave Europe a decided advantage in the East Asia trade. The growing preoccupation with a canal as the lever to elevate US commerce insured that Nicaragua would once again become a prime object of Yankee interest.

In 1850 the task of constructing the waterway had exceeded the aggregate financial capacity of government and private enterprise in the United States. Despite the aggressive expansionism of that era, the assertion of exclusive control would have exceeded also the nation's military capabilities. The Clayton-Bulwer Treaty, under which the canal was to be jointly constructed and operated by the United States and Britain, had therefore been a necessary compromise. But by 1870 the matter had begun to assume a different aspect. The United States was desirous of asserting what Grant had called during the Santo Domingo affair "our just claim to a controlling influence over the great commercial traffic soon to flow from east to west." This translated into a canal controlled exclusively by the US.

Several serious obstacles, however, would humbug the grand design for the next thirty years; among these were Colombian and Nicaraguan nationalism, domestic political questions, and the Clayton-Bulwer Treaty. Then, too, the United States was still not strong enough to risk a direct test of military strength with Europe—particularly not with the British navy, which at that time truly did rule the waves. These obstacles required the United States to make a number of policy zig-zags before the goal of a Yankee-owned and -operated canal could become a reality.

In the post-Civil War period, canal interest centered first on Panama, largely as a result of a private survey commissioned by financier Frederick M. Kelley of New York in 1864. In 1867 Congress appropriated funds for another survey of the Panama route; this was begun in 1869. But negotiations with Colombia, of which Panama was then a part, failed during 1869 and '70. The Colombians refused to accede to demands that the canal be under the exclusive protection of the United States or that the US Navy be permitted passage during wartime. With the military value of the canal thus nullified, the draft treaty was unacceptable to the United States.[14]

Congress voted money for surveys of the Tehuántepec (Mexico) and

Nicaragua routes in 1870. A United States naval expedition began the Nicaragua survey in April 1872. The expedition's report, presented to Secretary of State Fish on January 31, 1874, concluded that the Nicaragua route "presents by far a better combination of favorable conditions than any other route which has yet been examined."[15]

The Interoceanic Canal Commission, established by President Grant to compare the reports of the various surveying expeditions, made its recommendation on February 9, 1876. It affirmed

> that the route known as the "Nicaragua route" . . . possesses, both for the construction and maintenance of a canal, greater advantage, and offers fewer difficulties from engineering, commercial, and economic points of view, than any one of the other routes.[16]

A Nicaragua canal was now the settled policy of the United States. But before it could become a reality, it would be necessary to modify an 1867 treaty under which Nicaragua retained sovereignty over all transit routes through its territory.* Late in 1876 Secretary Fish began negotiations with Dr. Adán Cárdenas, special emissary of Nicaragua to the United States.

During its final months in office the Grant Administration appeared willing to back down from the demand for a US-controlled canal, at least in regard to the Nicaragua route, which was explicitly covered by the provisions of the Clayton-Bulwer Treaty. Fish presented Cárdenas with a draft treaty containing provisions similar to those the US had rejected in the Panama negotiations. According to its terms, the United States and Nicaragua would seek to obtain the guarantee of the "principal maritime powers" that none "will ever obtain or maintain for itself any exclusive control over the said ship-canal, or will ever erect or maintain any fortifications commanding the same." Vessels of all types belonging to the signatory powers would "at all times, whether in peace or war" have equal access to the waterway. The work was to be undertaken by private capital, with the US reserving the right to approve the contractor. Upon completion, an international "board of control," having two members each from the US, Nicaragua, and the other guarantor nations, would approve tolls and operating regulations. Nicaragua was to retain a purely nominal sovereignty over the canal and adjacent territory.[18]

Dr. Cárdenas notified Secretary Fish that the draft was "inadmissible on account of its incompatibility . . . with the sovereign rights of Nicaragua . . . as well as with the interests of the commerce of the world,

---

* Among other things, the Dickinson-Ayón Treaty of 1867 granted the US transit privileges across Nicaragua. Although it was virtually identical to the unratified Cass-Irisarri Treaty, after the North American Civil War the Nicaraguan government was willing to give the language a different construction.[17]

and particularly with those of the republics of Central America." Nicaragua was ready, he said, to grant a company building and operating a canal "with some modifications, all that is asked . . . and much more," but would not consent to any infringement of its sovereignty over the territory. Cárdenas also objected to favoring the guarantor nations with toll rates one-half those of other states. Such a provision, he said, would mean that "the canal, instead of being, as was to be hoped . . . a universal highway, open to the world, on conditions of perfect equality, would be converted into a monopoly for the benefit of a few maritime powers." Cárdenas was particularly concerned that all American states—not just the United States—should enjoy most-favored-nation status. He also proposed that, in conformity with the Clayton-Bulwer Treaty, a clause be added providing that none of the guarantor powers "shall occupy, fortify, colonize, assume, or exercise any dominion whatever over Nicaragua or over any part of Central America."[19]

Fish replied that the United States was willing to admit all the Central American states, and possibly Colombia, to equal status, but not the other American nations who were, he said, "without the power to make their guarantee practically, and, if need be, physically efficient." Nor would the United States agree, he added, to include the pledge made to Britain in the Clayton-Bulwer Treaty, because "that still being in force, its repetition in a treaty with Nicaragua might imply a doubt of the good faith of the United States on the subject."* Fish terminated the negotiation by informing Cárdenas that "your views . . . continue to be so contrary to those entertained on the part of the United States, that I can see no hope for the construction of the canal." Nicaragua was, he said, unwilling to make concessions

> such as would be sufficient to tempt the cupidity and inspire the confidence of capital. It is feared that because this great natural pathway happens to lie within the jurisdiction of Nicaragua, she may be disposed to be somewhat unduly sensitive in regard to her sovereignty, and to assert her technical rights in the matter in a way not only inconsistent with her own interests, but with those of commercial nations generally . . . I am forced to think that her counter-draft of the treaty is unconsciously framed upon the theory that the world desires a transit through her territory and must make all exacted submission to obtain it.[20]

---

* Nicaragua was not signatory to the Clayton-Bulwer Treaty and the pledges were therefore of no value to it: they could be withdrawn at the pleasure of the United States and Britain.

I T WAS during the Grant Administration's consideration of a Nicaragua canal that Secretary Fish articulated what, in justice, should probably be called the Fish Corollary to the Monroe Doctrine. In an 1871 instruction to Charles Riotte, the US minister to Nicaragua, Fish wrote:

> The United States have an obvious interest that in any such undertaking their own citizens should have a predominating interest or control. While, therefore, it is not expected that you will incur any risk of giving offence by undue forwardness or importunity, you will endeavor by all proper means, to prevent that government from irrecoverably committing itself to the citizens or subjects of any other country for the construction of the Canal, until citizens of the United States and their government shall have had a full opportunity to decide upon the practicability and expediency of the enterprize.[21]

Though the instruction was expressed in the circumspect language of the early post-Civil War period, and made no mention of the Monroe Doctrine as such, its intent was clear. Claiming its vital interests were at stake, the United States would henceforth assert the right to exercise veto power over all means of trans-isthmian communication.

The following year, 1872, Minister Riotte reported to Fish that a certain Mr. Carmichael, an "agent of one or more European houses," was in Nicaragua trying to negotiate a contract to construct a railroad from Monkey Point on the Caribbean to Corinto Bay on the Pacific. The proposal, said Riotte, was "one apt to seriously compromise the interests of our citizens and counteract the views of my Government as stated in your despatch No. 43 of Febr. 1st 1871."[22]

Describing the Monroe Doctrine as a "continental gospel," Riotte notified the Nicaraguan government:

> It was and is still held by the Govt. of the U.S. that, in the establishing of interoceanic thoroughfares be it by rail, by canalization or other means,—if not effected by the nation itself whose territory they are to cross—the citizens of the U.S. should have a predominating interest or control, since from them and their government no action contrary to the spirit of the American system need be apprehended . . . By the investment of large capital in an interoceanic transitline within the domain of the Republic by subjects of European Powers, as well as by the subsequent management thereof by them, both her institutions and independence and the fundamental premises of the American system may be imperiled . . . With the sole view of preventing possible later difficulties between the U.S. and this country . . . [I hope] the Govt. of the U.S. and its citizens may have ample opportunity to consider and decide upon the practicability and expediency of the enterprise.[23]

For whatever reason, the efforts of Mr. Carmichael produced no result.

O N MAY 15, 1879 an International Canal Congress convened in Paris. Ferdinand de Lesseps, the French promoter responsible for the Suez Canal, was elected its president. Rear Admiral Daniel Ammen, head of the US Bureau of Navigation, which had overseen the Nicaragua surveying expedition, and A.G. Menocal, its chief civil engineer, attended the congress representing the United States. Their recommendation of the Nicaragua route was ignored by the congress, which voted to support de Lesseps' scheme for a lockless, sea-level canal at Panama.

Reporting back to the secretary of state, Admiral Ammen charged that the Paris congress had been packed with delegates who held an interest in an already existing French concession in Panama. Moreover, according to Ammen, most delegates lacked the engineering background necessary to decide on the merits of the Panama project, which he declared to be hopelessly impractical.[24]

The efforts of a French company to build a canal across Panama, with an international guarantee of neutrality, conflicted with the US desire for a "controlling influence," and de Lesseps' undertaking created great consternation notwithstanding the US engineers' prediction that it would fail. President Rutherford Hayes, reasserting what was then the clearly established US attitude, declared, "The policy of this country is a canal under American control. The United States can not consent to the surrender of this control to any European power or to any combination of European powers."[25] The big question was what the US could do about it.

Throughout 1880 and '81, de Lesseps' canal, with its international neutrality guarantee, received considerable attention from the House Foreign Affairs Committee. A Committee report issued in April 1880 concluded that the Clayton-Bulwer Treaty, binding the United States to the policy of a canal jointly controlled by the US and Britain, was

> an obstacle and possible peril in the way of a complete and pacific assertion of the sound, necessary, and vigorous American policy laid down in the President's message of March 8, 1880 . . . [and] should now be finally and formally abrogated.*[26]

The congressmen lost no time calling into play the Monroe Doctrine, which would see regular service as the United States carved out its sphere of influence and control in the Americas. An 1881 report by the same committee, entitled "The Interoceanic Canal and the Monroe Doctrine," resolved:

---

* Hayes' message is quoted above.

That the construction of any public work, connecting the waters of the Atlantic and Pacific, by any European government or power, whether the same be constructed at Panama or elsewhere, would be in violation of the spirit and letter of the Monroe doctrine, and could not be sanctioned by the Government of the United States.

The report concluded with a recommendation that steps be taken by the president to abrogate "any existing treaties whose terms are in conflict with this declaration of principles."[27]

The only weapons the US administration could realistically employ were diplomatic and political. These it did use in a vain effort to thwart de Lesseps' project and to free itself from the Clayton-Bulwer restrictions. US diplomats in Europe were told to argue that any international neutrality guarantee for a canal was superfluous, since the US had already included such guarantees for the isthmus in its 1846 treaty with Nueva Granada (Colombia). Moreover, it was said, an international neutrality agreement "would partake of the nature of an alliance against the United States and would be regarded by this government as an indication of unfriendly feeling."[28]

Secretary of State Blaine informed James Lowell, US minister to England, that the United States "will not consent to perpetuate any treaty that impeaches our rightful and long-established claim to priority on the American continent." He instructed his minister that "Every part of the [Clayton-Bulwer] treaty which forbids the United States fortifying the canal and holding the political control of it in conjunction with the country in which it is located [is] to be cancelled." Not very convincingly, Blaine argued that only the US could assure the neutrality of the canal, the guarantee of European powers being worthless because of their mutual animosities. Though claiming that the United States wanted no exclusive advantage, what he in fact proposed was that US warships be permitted use of the canal at all times, while those of other nations could only pass during peacetime. Such a formula rendered the term "neutrality" meaningless.

Of greatest interest, however, was the rationale Blaine advanced to support the doctrine of US control. Great Britain, he argued, asserted control over the Suez Canal, "the interior and nearest route to India," by means of its "large military and naval establishments." Why then, "for the protection of the distant shores of her own domain, for the drawing together of the extremes of the Union" should the US not assert control over a waterway linking the Atlantic and Pacific, "which [waterway] the United States will always insist upon treating as part of her coast-line"?[29]

Blaine's "national security" argument, an extension of Buchanan's "arm of the sea" thesis, has been handed down as the principal justification for US control over the present Panama Canal, and for US hegemony over Central America and the Caribbean Basin. Even if it is accepted that the US desire to control the canal has had no other motivation than this, the doctrine is remarkable. It negates the rights of the nation through which the canal passes, and implies that any country with distant possessions has a right to control both the most convenient route to those possessions and the territory through which the route passes. Presumably, then, the more possessions a country acquires, the more routes—and subsequently, territories—it is justified in claiming. The only limit on the extension of the doctrine would be the power of a country to enforce its claims. Many nations throughout history have practiced such great power politics, but few have been so bold as to assert them as a doctrine.

The issue of neutrality versus US control became a topic of increasingly intense debate within the United States as the canal project came closer to realization. There were arguments even among confirmed imperialists. Neutrality, it was pointed out, would only have meaning if the canal were open to all ships of all nations at all times, while hostile acts were prohibited within the canal zone itself. Any attempt to exclude the warships of belligerents, even on the basis of equal treatment for all nations, would create insuperable obstacles: it was often difficult to determine when a state of belligerency actually existed; the problem would be compounded by the question of who would be able to make an impartial determination.

On the other hand, it was argued, the attempt of any one nation to control the canal would simply turn it into a military target that would be difficult and expensive to defend. Critics pointed out even then, long before the advent of aircraft or guided missiles—not to mention nuclear weapons—that a determined enemy could easily render the canal useless with nothing more than a few sticks of dynamite.

The advocates of US control replied that the Monroe Doctrine would not allow the participation of European powers in Western Hemisphere affairs to the degree required for an internationally-supervised neutrality guarantee. To this they added the military argument that unless the US controlled the canal, as Theodore Roosevelt put it, "it strengthens against us every nation whose fleet is larger than ours."[30]

In an influential essay dealing with questions raised by the canal, John Bassett Moore, a renowned US expert on international law, commented, "There seems to be an incongruity between that just confidence which we feel in our power and the extreme apprehensions sometimes expressed for our safety."[31] But, as it happened, logic had little to do with the final outcome.

The canal that was ultimately constructed in Panama—under US control—has never been seriously imperiled, notwithstanding that it was opened less than two weeks after the outbreak of World War I, and the

United States has been involved in military action of one sort or another almost continuously ever since. Nor has the US ever faced the kind of naval threat to its own shores that would have given meaning to the military argument advanced by Roosevelt and others. Still, the canal security question seems to have nine lives: the purported need to safeguard the waterway has paid off handsomely in both economic and political terms.

The demand for abrogation of the Clayton-Bulwer Treaty was not well received by England, which assumed that it had equal claim to a route that would link it with British Columbia and Australia. The London *Times* asked, "If the United States cannot trust England, why should England be required to trust the United States?"[32]

The British lion was still rampant. US objections to de Lesseps' Panama canal project were ignored, and the demand for abrogation of the Clayton-Bulwer Treaty was rejected. It was one thing to declare United States hegemony in the Americas, quite another to carry it into practice. But the US engineers' assessment as to the impracticability of the de Lesseps plan was soon validated. The French company went bankrupt in 1889, and the argument became moot.

Meanwhile, the US had decided to go ahead with its own canal. It brought heavy pressure to bear on Nicaragua, and a treaty was finally signed in Washington on December 1, 1884 by President Arthur's secretary of state, Frederick Frelinghuysen, and a Nicaraguan envoy, former President Joaquin Zavala. The Frelinghuysen-Zavala Treaty provided for a canal to be built entirely by the United States on a strip of land two-and-one-half miles wide that would be "owned by the two contracting parties." Nicaragua would exercise civil jurisdiction over the territory "in time of peace," but the canal would be administered by a joint board of directors controlled by the United States.

Significantly, there was no provision for neutrality of the canal, nor was there any mention of fortifications. Article II declared, however:

> There shall be perpetual alliance between the United States of America and the Republic of Nicaragua, and the former agree to protect the integrity of the territory of the latter.

In return for the concession Nicaragua was to receive one-third the net proceeds from the completed work. It also extracted a pledge that "The United States frankly disavow any intention . . . to impair the independent sovereignty of Nicaragua, or to aggrandize themselves at the expense of that State or of any of her sister republics in Central America."[33]

A *New York Times* correspondent commented:

> It is unquestionably true that the Nicaraguan Government did not desire to make the present treaty . . . [but] the will of a mighty nation of

55,000,000 of homogeneous, progressive, and patriotic people is of course irresistable when it runs counter to the wishes of feeble and unstable Governments like those of Central and South America . . . Nicaragua desires to have the canal built, but she wants the work to be done by a corporation rather than a Government, because she wants to yield the least possible control over it.[34]

But the United States had made some real concessions. The provision for a canal zone two-and-one-half miles wide represented a retreat from the ten mile width traditionally insisted upon. So did the provision for sharing revenues and the pledge to respect the territorial integrity of Central America, which the US had previously been unwilling to include in any treaty. But perhaps the chief inducement for Nicaragua to compromise its sovereignty was the situation on the Miskito Coast.

Under the terms of the Treaty of Managua of 1860, Britain had agreed to relinquish its claim to Miskitia in return for Miskito autonomy within the Nicaraguan state. But the British then proceeded to interpret the treaty in such a way as to block Nicaragua's genuine reincorporation of the area. They were upheld in an 1881 arbitration award by the Emperor of Austria, which went against Nicaragua. The US protectorate provided for in the Frelinghuysen-Zavala Treaty seemed to be the way out of Nicaragua's frustrating dilemma.

In his message to the Senate urging ratification, President Arthur did not mention that the treaty constituted a clear violation of the Clayton-Bulwer stipulations with Britain.[35] The omission was not overlooked by the legislators, however. Notwithstanding all the commercial advantages to be gained from a Nicaragua canal, the US, including powerful business sectors, was not yet willing to jeopardize domestic economic development in a showdown with Britain for which it was not prepared. The *Times'* Washington correspondent wrote:

A member of the Foreign Affairs Committee of the House . . . said that it must strike foreign nations as absurd that the United States should undertake to possess itself of a part of Nicaragua with a view to commanding control of a ship canal, yet with nothing more formidable than the beef boat Tallapoosa to enforce the attempt.[36]

Support for the treaty did bring out the torchbearers and flagwavers. The New Orleans *Daily Picayune* commented:

We must adopt a policy of acquisition, of territorial aggrandizement to the southward . . . The Nicaragua treaty is an opening wedge. Let us drive that home, and by investing $100,000,000 in a ship canal thus secure the country. American enterprise will soon annex the whole of Central America from that base line . . . Sectional discord has happily ceased, and the South is primarily and deeply interested in turning the tendency of enterprise and the march of empire *southward*.[37] [Emphasis in original.]

But the empire-builders were unable to carry the day. Though most senators voted for ratification, the treaty fell short of the two-thirds majority required. Before a motion to reconsider could be acted upon, it was withdrawn by the incoming Grover Cleveland Administration, inaugurated in March 1885. Cleveland was the first Democrat elected to the presidency since the Civil War. Demonstrating how far the two parties had gone in reversing their prewar roles, he declared himself opposed to "a policy of acquisition of new and distant territory or the incorporation of remote interests with our own." Duty, he said, "instructs us to address ourselves mainly to the development of the vast resources of the great area committed to our charge and to the cultivation of the arts of peace within our own borders."[38] Cleveland was willing to forgo the demand for exclusive US control and leave the waterway to private enterprise. By circumventing the obstacles presented by the Clayton-Bulwer Treaty, such an approach would actually bring the canal—and its attendant commercial benefits—closer to realization.

In fact, private enterprise had already been busy. In May 1880, Navy civil engineer A.G. Menocal and Commander Edward P. Lull, both of whom had been intimately involved with the US government canal surveys, signed a contract with Nicaragua on behalf of the Provisional Interoceanic Canal Society. Along with Menocal and Lull, the society counted among its members Rear Admiral Ammen, ex-President Grant, and General George McClellan. Having obtained the concession, the society changed its name to the Maritime Canal Company of Nicaragua.[39]

There was talk that Ulysses Grant would take charge of the project. Speaking before the American Geographical Society in December 1879, Ammen, a personal friend of Grant, told his audience that the former president was willing to head the project "under such conditions . . . as would enable it to be prosecuted vigorously and effectively." In June 1880 Grant turned down an offer to head the US subsidiary of de Lesseps' Panama Canal Company. In doing so he declared, "While I would like to have my name associated with the successful completion of a ship channel between the two oceans, I was not willing to connect it with a failure."[40] But Grant was willing to connect his name with the Maritime Canal Company of Nicaragua. Writing for the February 1881 issue of the *North American Review,* he appealed for support to the company's Nicaragua enterprise, claiming it represented an affirmation of the Monroe Doctrine. Concluded Grant:

I shall feel that I have added one more act of my life to those already recorded, if I shall succeed in impressing upon Congress and the people the high value, as a commercial and industrial enterprise, of this great work, which if not accomplished by Americans, will undoubtedly be accomplished by some one of our rivals in power and influence.[41]

Maritime Canal Company laying rails to service construction on the Nicaragua Canal, four miles west of San Juan del Norte, 1890

Bills to give the company a national charter were introduced in four consecutive sessions of Congress, but opposition from several sources prevented any from coming up for a vote. Opponents included partisans of rival canal schemes as well as ultra-expansionists who objected to features of the company's concession explicitly recognizing the Clayton-Bulwer Treaty and providing for international neutrality guarantees.[42] The Arthur Administration seems to have numbered among the latter.

Grant, who had gone into the investment banking business after he left the presidency, was trying to arrange financing for the Maritime Canal Company when his firm, Grant and Ward, went bankrupt in 1884. Unable to begin construction for lack of funds, the Maritime Canal Company defaulted on its contract with Nicaragua and the concession expired later that same year.

But Cleveland's withdrawal of the Frelinghuysen-Zavala Treaty in 1885 again opened the door for private enterprise. Menocal, Ammen, and others secured a new concession from Nicaragua in 1887. This time, with well-orchestrated pressure from commercial interests, they succeeded in getting a bill of incorporation passed by Congress. With the bill signed into law in February 1889, the new Maritime Canal Company of Nicaragua was able to issue stock and raise an initial capital of $6 million. Actual work on the canal began in October 1889, less than a year after the French Panama Canal Company declared bankruptcy.

The company dredged the silted harbor at San Juan del Norte, constructed a number of auxiliary facilities, including 11.5 miles of service railroad, and even began dredging operations for the canal channel itself. But funds ran out in 1893, and the financial panic of that year doomed efforts to obtain further private financing. Congressional attempts to secure a governmental loan guarantee or a purchase of company stock were consistently blocked by the same coalition that thwarted the company's earlier efforts.

In typical fashion, the legislators did appropriate funds for a commission to study the problem. The United States-Nicaragua Canal Board, also known as the Ludlow Commission, visited Nicaragua in 1895. It was the first of three consecutive survey commissions that would spend considerable time and money arriving at essentially the same conclusions reached by the Menocal survey more than twenty years before. The Ludlow Commission generally approved the plans and operations of the Maritime Canal Company but, apparently due to political pressure, recommended only further studies. While its successors, the first and second Walker Commissions, surveyed the potential routes again between 1897 and 1901, the deadline for completion of the canal (October 9, 1899) came and went. Once again the Maritime Canal Company defaulted on its contract.

THE END of the century saw big political changes in the United States, along with a shift in the world balance of power. US industry, carefully nurtured by protective tariffs since the Civil War, had outgrown its domestic markets. The time had come to break out of the protectionist incubator and join the scramble for world markets. Industrialist and merchant, financier and planter, Republican and Democrat—all now harmonized the same jingo tune. The Spanish-American War in 1898 finally afforded the opportunity to make the move into the Caribbean foreseen by Jefferson, Monroe, and Adams. The United States took Puerto Rico outright and made Cuba a US protectorate. In a single stroke it became the region's dominant power.

Britain, bogged down in the costly Boer War, diplomatically isolated, and desiring to cultivate the US as an ally, was ready to recognize the Caribbean as a Yankee lake. Following the victory over Spain, the stepped-up agitation for an exclusively US-controlled canal found the British ready to come to terms on modification of the Clayton-Bulwer Treaty.

Secretary of State John Hay and British Ambassador Sir Julian Pauncefote signed an agreement in Washington in 1900 to amend the treaty. The US would be allowed full power to construct and maintain the canal. Neutrality rules would be established similar to those in force for Suez: the waterway would be open equally to commercial and naval vessels both during war and peace, fortifications would be prohibited, and other powers invited to join the agreement.

But before ratifying the new treaty, the US Senate added amendments that completely changed its meaning: these declared the Clayton-Bulwer Treaty to be voided—not simply amended—by the new agreement, granted the United States the right to supersede the neutrality provisions whenever it thought necessary for its own defense, and dropped the provision inviting other powers to adhere.[43] As amended, the treaty was unacceptable— British Imperialism was willing to admit the United States into the club; it wasn't willing to be humiliated by it.

But in what was essentially a face-saving move, Hay and Pauncefote signed a new treaty in November 1901 that achieved the objectives of the earlier Senate amendments. This agreement was ratified by both governments. Article I specifically declared the Clayton-Bulwer Treaty superseded. Earlier language allowing equal access to commercial and war ships of all nations had been weakened and the provision barring fortification by the US was dropped. There was no mention of inviting other nations to join in the agreement. The Clayton-Bulwer ban on occupying, fortifying, colonizing, or exercising "any dominion over" any part of Central America was no longer in force. In fact, the new treaty foresaw the eventuality of the United States doing some of those very things by specifying, in Article IV, that its terms were not to be affected by any "change of territorial sovereignty or of the international relations of the country or countries traversed" by the canal.[44]

Meanwhile, mounting pro-canal pressure in Congress led to the introduction early in 1900 of the Nicaragua Canal Bill, or Hepburn Bill as it became known. The measure authorized the president to acquire territory from Nicaragua and Costa Rica for a US-owned and -controlled canal. Its sponsor, Representative William P. Hepburn of Iowa, Chairman of the House Committee on Interstate and Foreign Commerce, expressed the impatience of a growing number of congressmen, tired of Nicaragua surveys: "Mind you, every portion of this route has been investigated," he declared, certain that the US already had "almost . . . a photograph of every grasshopper and bug that could be found in all that 179 miles of tropical country."[45] Hepburn appealed for support to

those who want to see our coasts, now so distant and so difficult of access, brought in close proximity; those who want to see this nation go forward as it will with this great aid in the race for the commerce of the world; those who want to see that position of empire secured to us, commercially, politically, among the world powers that will come to us if we utilize our possibilities.[46]

Congressman DeAlva S. Alexander of New York spoke for the prevailing sentiment in favor of the bill when he proclaimed:

the breast of every patriotic American should swell with pride in contemplation of the magnificent results to our nation which are certain to flow through the waters of this canal. We are today the greatest force on earth for the higher civilization and improvement—moral, physical, and economical—of our race. We have a world mission before us, and the sphere of our influence is widening and deepening very rapidly as the years fleet onward. Let us prepare well for the task of our manifest destiny. Let us provide for the great commercial war whose clouds now faintly hover on our horizon. To accomplish these ends and be successful in the coming battles, no armor will be so valuable as an American canal, on American soil, owned, controlled, and protected by Americans. (Loud Applause)[47]

Barriers to the new march of "destiny" were giving way quickly. Just as the Hay-Pauncefote agreement removed the major legal obstacle, the Isthmian Canal Commission (the second Walker Commission) made its report. Its appraisal of the benefits of a canal gave foundation to the enthusiasm of the imperialists in Congress. The report concluded:

As soon as it has been opened, our trade with the west coast of South America will increase more rapidly, as will also the volume of our trade with the Orient. An Isthmian canal will strengthen the unity of the national and political interests of the United States, develop its Pacific territory, and promote the commerce and industries of the entire country. The benefits which Europe will derive from the canal will be commercial. In addition to this, ours will be political and industrial.[48]

The relative pluses and minuses of the Nicaragua and Panama routes were found to be about equally balanced. It was noted, however, that

a canal by the Nicaragua route would bring Nicaragua and a large portion of Costa Rica and other Central American States into close and easy communication with the United States and with Europe. The intimate business relations that would be established with the people of the United States during the period of construction by the expenditure of vast sums of money in these States and the use of American products and manufactures would be likely to continue after the completion of the work, to the benefit of our manufacturing, agricultural, and other interests.[49]

Because of the amount of work already accomplished in Panama by de Lesseps' company and its successor, the New Panama Canal Company, costs of completion on the Panama route were estimated to be $45 million lower. But the US would have to buy out the assets of the New Panama Canal Company; as the price being asked was exorbitant, the commission recommended that the canal be dug in Nicaragua.

But early in 1902, when the French company offered to sell out to the United States for $40 million (the actual value of its assets) the commission changed its recommendation in favor of Panama.[50]

Shortly afterward, the Hepburn Nicaragua Canal Bill, held up in the Senate to avoid embarrassment to the Hay-Pauncefote negotiations, passed both houses with little opposition. But intense lobbying efforts by agents of the Panama company caused the bill to be amended in the Senate. The Spooner Amendment—to the Nicaragua Canal Bill—authorized President Roosevelt to acquire the Panama company's assets and complete the canal through Panama, provided the US could obtain control of the canal zone from Colombia.[51]

The story of the machinations of Philippe Bunau-Varilla, president of the French Panama company, and the collusion of the United States in promoting Panama's breakaway from Colombia is beyond the scope of this narrative. It is enough to say that the result was attainment of the long sought-after US objective, on terms that could hardly have been more favorable.

VIII

THE RISE AND FALL OF JOSÉ SANTOS ZELAYA

> *Today, more than ever before, American capital is seeking investment in foreign countries, and American products are more and more generally seeking foreign markets . . . This Administration, through the Department of State and the foreign service, is lending all proper support to legitimate and beneficial American enterprise in foreign countries, the degree of such support being measured by the national advantages to be expected.*
>
> —*President William Howard Taft, 1909.*

THE EXPULSION of the filibusters in 1857 and the inauguration later that year of Tomás Martinez as president ushered in a period known to Nicaraguans as the Thirty Years. This interlude of relative peace and stability—actually lasting thirty-six years, until 1893—not only coincided with, but was in part due to, the Civil War in the United States.

Martinez and his seven successors, though nominally Conservative, represented the more progressive and farsighted wing of the Granada-based oligarchy. To a greater or lesser extent, they recognized the need to accommodate their Leonese rivals, put an end to the blood feud that had nearly destroyed the country, and chart a course of economic development and modernization. These goals were not achieved without opposition from the more reactionary elements of their own party, however. In 1863 José Dolores Estrada, the hero of San Jacinto, was exiled in disgrace to Costa Rica, having joined an abortive uprising by Conservative recalcitrants.[1]

Martinez, who held office until 1867, got the Thirty Years off to a good start. Under his administration, Managua—midway between León and Granada—became established as Nicaragua's capital. León had been the capital in colonial times, but during the years of civil war that followed independence the government shifted back and forth between León and Granada and occasionally rival governments existed simultaneously at both places. Managua was originally chosen as the seat of government in 1846, and served as the sometime meeting place of the Legislative Assembly. But the real establishment of the capital at Managua could not take place before attainment of the geographical harmony that the move was meant to symbolize. Even more significant for the future, the Martinez Administration introduced a system of government incentives to promote coffee cultivation in the sierras of Managua and nearby Masaya.*

The first commercial coffee plantation in Nicaragua had been established in 1845. But extensive cultivation of the bean was delayed by the chaos of domestic turmoil, British occupation of the Miskito territory, and the sundry invasions, interventions, and pressures from the United States. Nicaragua's economic development was retarded accordingly. By the 1860s, when coffee production was just getting underway in Nicaragua, it had already revolutionized the economic structure of Guatemala, El Salvador, and Costa Rica.[3]

With the introduction of coffee came a series of structural reforms and infrastructural improvements. Under President Martinez the port of Corinto was constructed. Granada, destroyed by the filibusters, was rebuilt. Roads were improved, enabling stage coach travel between the major towns of the Pacific region for the first time—a development that highlighted the extreme backwardness of the country. The *capellanias,* a form of Church lien on landholdings, were amortized. Martinez's successors built the first railroads and telegraph lines.[4]

Education was secularized and upgraded. A *New York Times* correspondent wrote in 1868 that there were thirty-four free schools giving primary education in the department of Rivas alone, compared with only eight fifteen years earlier.[5] A decade later a North American living in Granada wrote of the Nicaraguans:

> during the last 10 or 12 years a great change is coming [sic] over them, which is due in a great measure to the liberty of the press and to the establishment of an excellent college in this city, which is preparing the

---

* Francisco Ortega Arancibia, a contemporary, claimed that one of the aims of this policy was to promote the development of a group that could act as a counterbalance to the traditional rivals of León and Granada.[2]

youth of the principal families to take the place of the old fogies with the ideas of the past.[6]

The increasing world attention that Nicaragua received as the likely site of an interoceanic canal produced a sense of optimistic anticipation. The unhappy experience of Panama later demonstrated that there was little basis for such a sunny outlook. But at the time there seemed every reason to suppose that under the right conditions, given proper safeguards for Nicaraguan sovereignty, a canal would bring enormous benefits in commerce, immigration, and development. If, for better or worse, the waterway did not materialize, it was not for want of trying on the part of Nicaragua's statesmen of the Thirty Years.

T HE RAPID strides of coffee toward economic dominance, combined with the measured progress in transportation, communication, education, and law, signaled that the bases of modern capitalism were being established. As with the big neighbor to the north, much of the advancement was achieved at the expense of the Indian, who in Nicaragua occupied a good part of the hilly country best suited to coffee growing.

The old oligarchs had been content with the power and prestige derived from their vast haciendas. Production on their underutilized lands, however inefficient, provided them with a comfortable way of life, and profits from commerce or the export of surpluses furnished the luxuries they desired. They had no need to disturb the Indians or the mestizo squatters who lived on the margins of their estates, supplying such labor as the *señores* required.

But coffee radically altered the picture of feudal somnolence. With it came an economy organized and directed toward export for the world market. Competition, investment, and profit were the order of the day. If the communal lands of the Indians were the best ones for growing coffee, the Indians would have to go; if more than 80 percent of the sparse population eked out its living from subsistence farming, and was therefore unavailable to pick coffee, something would have to be done about that too.[7]

Through various means, legal and extralegal, the lands were taken and the former occupants compelled to hire out their labor for whatever pay was offered. In practice these measures began with the Agrarian Law promulgated in 1877 during the administration of Pedro Joaquin Chamorro. In 1881 they sparked a rebellion by the Matagalpa Indians, thousands of whom were killed in the fierce repression that followed.[8]

A S THE CENTURY entered its final decade, progress outpaced the ability of the "old fogies" to keep up. Coffee exports had increased nearly tenfold in fifteen years. Favorable prices on the world market were pushing the extension of coffee cultivation into Jinotega and Matagalpa at an accelerated rate.[9] Around Managua a new class of capitalists had come of age, and for them the pace of change was not quick enough. Raising the banner of a renovated Liberal Party, they anxiously awaited their turn to assume leadership of the nation.

The "old fogies" had accomplished a good deal during their Thirty Years, even taking into account the negative features of development: they brought a degree of peace and general prosperity unknown since the conquest, and to the extent their lights permitted, they defended Nicaragua's integrity against the ever-present menace of voracious superpowers. But in 1893 their political capital ran out.

President Evaristo Carazo had died in office in 1889, and the succession of events over the next four years conclusively demonstrated the decomposition of the Conservative club that held power since 1857. The National Assembly chose Conservative Senator Roberto Sacasa to serve the remainder of Carazo's term. But Sacasa, a native of León, was not trusted by many of the Granada Conservatives, and his renomination in 1891 provoked a split in the party. The dissenting faction charged that the constitution had been violated and, feeling they had sufficient pretext to return the country to the chaos of the past, in 1893 they launched an armed uprising and called on other disgruntled groups to join them.

In the resulting economic paralysis, businessmen invited US Minister Lewis Baker to mediate the dispute. A settlement was quickly reached: Sacasa resigned, to be followed by the calling of a Constituent Assembly. But the coalition that forced his ouster was inherently unstable, composed of conflicting elements whose only basis of agreement was aversion to the incumbent. In a second uprising that soon followed, the Liberals swept the interim government aside, Conservative resistance disintegrating before their advance. The controversial figure who led this "July Revolution," named by the Constituent Assembly a few months later to the country's presidency, was General José Santos Zelaya.[10]

Just forty years old in 1893, Zelaya was the son of a Managua coffee planter. He had attended the Instituto de Oriente in Granada—the very institution the North American had in mind when he wrote of the youth who were preparing to replace the old fogies. After further studies in France, Zelaya served as a municipal official in Managua, establishing, it is said, the first lending library there, which he stocked with the works of the French philosophers.[11]

To the rest of the world, the forceful personality of José Santos Zelaya would soon become synonymous with Nicaragua; he would be denounced by enemies at home and abroad as a ruthless tyrant and dictator. But during the next sixteen years, under Zelaya's leadership, a Nicaragua began to emerge that might almost be called dynamic. Public education was greatly expanded. Society was democratized, at least to the extent that members of the lower classes had opportunities for advancement as never before. Clericalism was curbed sharply, and there were substantial improvements in services, transportation, and commerce. Public administration and the military were modernized and professionalized.

José Santos Zelaya

ZELAYA had barely begun his term as president when events thrust his administration onto the world stage. War broke out with Honduras over alleged support by Nicaragua for Liberal opponents of the Honduran president, General Domingo Vázquez. Honduran troops invaded Nicaragua at Gracias a Dios on the Atlantic Coast, and in January 1894 Nicaraguan soldiers landed at Bluefields on their way to counterattack.

There should have been nothing remarkable about such an operation—Bluefields was supposed to be Nicaraguan territory. But, in fact, an anomalous situation existed on the whole of Nicaragua's Atlantic Coast, and the landing of troops, perhaps intentionally, perhaps not, precipitated a crisis. The Miskito authorities at Bluefields (Chief Robert Henry Clarence and his council) tried to interfere. In response, Zelaya's government disbanded Clarence's council and placed the region under martial law. The result was to involve Nicaragua in a complicated stew with Britain, the United States government, and US business interests.

When Nicaragua signed the Treaty of Managua with England in 1860, it thought the question of the Miskito "kingdom" had been resolved once and for all. Britain had agreed to recede from its protectorate in an arrangement that gave the Miskitos a large measure of autonomy in their traditional homelands, designated the Mosquito Reserve. The Reserve would, however, fall within the territorial sovereignty of the Nicaraguan state. The arrangement was similar, on the surface, to that of Indian reservations in the United States, with the Miskitos enjoying somewhat greater autonomy. But even though the treaty clearly stated that the British protectorate would end three months after the exchange of ratifications, over the following decades inhabitants of the Reserve continued to appeal their disputes with national authorities to England, and the British continued to interpose.[12]

This state of affairs induced Nicaragua to agree to submit the question of Britain's suppositious residual rights to the arbitration of the Emperor of Austria. Franz Josef's award, given in 1881, did not address itself to the question of Britain's continued protectorate at all, but created even greater confusion and frustration by declaring, "The sovereignty of the Republic of Nicaragua . . . is not full and unlimited . . . but is limited by the self-government conceded to the Mosquito Indians." Within the territory, Nicaragua had the right, he said, to hoist its flag and "to appoint a commissioner for the protection of its sovereign rights" whatever those may have been, limited as they were.[13]

In 1853 British Foreign Secretary Lord John Russell had conceded that "The Mosquito Indians, instead of governing their own tribe according to their own customs, furnish a name and a title to Europeans and Americans, who carry on trade at Greytown and along the coast of Mosquito according to the usages of civilized nations." In 1894 Miskito self-government—its figurehead hereditary "king" demoted to "chief" by the Treaty of Managua—was as much a fiction as ever. According to the testimony of one of its members, the Executive Council in 1894 consisted of sixteen persons, of whom only three were Miskitos.[14] The remainder were Jamaicans claiming British citizenship, North Americans, and Creoles (inhabitants of African descent).

Aside from San Juan del Norte, which had served as the chief outlet for commerce with Spain during colonial times, the extensive and thinly populated Atlantic Coast region had never been integrated into the economic life of Nicaragua. Natural geographic barriers and Nicaragua's own backwardness combined with the British influence to keep the regions east and west of the isthmian cordillera worlds apart. But the valuable natural resources on the Atlantic Coast, the ease of sea communication with Eastern and Gulf Coast ports of the United States, the predominance of the English language, and the political limbo of the zone all made it attractive to foreign investors, especially Yankees.

US investment on Nicaragua's Caribbean littoral, principally in banana plantations and mahogany export, had become such that in 1888 Secretary of State Bayard asserted, "By far the larger part of the foreign commerce of that region is at present carried on between the ports of Bluefields and New Orleans."[15] Robert N. Keely, a North American, decided to look into the investment opportunities for himself after receiving a letter from a friend working a one hundred-square-mile grant on the Mosquito Reserve. "The bottoms are rich in timber and the uplands abound with gold," his friend had written; "Native help is plentiful and can be hired for a song and sixpence, and the mahogany can be floated all the way to the coast."

After visiting the area in 1893, Keely wrote of the banana plantations that covered the banks of the Rio Escondido for a distance of more than forty miles, exporting, on average, 40,000 bunches a week. "Bluefields ships more of this fruit than any two other ports of the world," he noted.[16]

By the time the issue of the political status of the Mosquito Reserve came to a head, United States capital reportedly accounted for 90 to 95 percent of all investment there. The US consular agent in Bluefields, B.B. Seat, estimated the amount of that investment at $1.5 million, not a huge sum even in those days, but its importance was magnified by the fact that the highly profitable banana and mahogany operations required little capital investment.[17]

A letter from Sigmund Braida, United States consul at San Juan del Norte, to Baker, the US minister in Managua, conveys a picture of the cozy relationship between foreign investors and the Miskito authorities at Bluefields:

> The merchants in the reservation had been the beneficiaries of special privileges . . . For example, they had not been required to present certified invoices upon their importations; and consequently, the values of such importations were accepted upon the mere statements made by themselves or their agents, and these practices or privileges must have been allowed, either by agreement or through the ignorance of the former authorities.[18]

With such "privileges," freely granted concessions, and the lack of any taxes or governmental controls, it is no surprise that North Americans and other foreigners found the Miskito government—or rather, the government exercised in the name of the Miskitos—much to their liking. As for the Miskitos themselves, who did not live in Bluefields, but out in the hinterlands, Consular Agent Seat reported that they

> know but little of the Government as it exists; and according to well authenticated reports have become dissatisfied and have recently developed considerable opposition to this local régime. They claim that they are not the beneficiaries of anything that is done; that their country is being alienated and its wealth squandered for the enrichment of their rulers, while they as a people are left destitute and poor.[19]

The solicitude for the welfare of the Miskitos that President Zelaya expressed may be treated with a certain amount of skepticism.[20] But the wholesale giveaway of resources by those controlling the reserve was certainly a serious concern for Nicaragua. With the emergence of the country from the troubles that plagued it since independence and the progress in developing the Pacific zone, economic integration of the Atlantic Coast with the rest of the country had become a real prospect, particularly given the apparent certainty of an interoceanic canal.

For a number of years settlement by Hispanic Nicaraguans had pushed steadily eastward, and conflicts with holders of concessions from the Mosquito Reserve were becoming a regular occurrence. In 1892, Nicaraguan Foreign Minister Jorge Bravo wrote of the

> tendencies of the Mosquito council to go beyond the limits traced by the Republic for the Reserve, establishing a new boundary line by which they pretend to include our gold placers at Cuicuina, and posting notices threatening all those who construct buildings in the town . . . with the loss of their property.

Bravo complained that the authorities of the Reserve had repeatedly granted long-term concessions for exploitation of natural resources, "even in places not embraced within the limits established by the treaty of Managua."[21]

Conflicts soon developed between Nicaraguans and North Americans, the most frequent recipients of Mosquito Reserve concessions. The town of Rama, at the confluence of the Rama, Siquia, and Escondido rivers, lay just outside the boundary of the Mosquito Reserve in an area where the eastward flow of Nicaraguan settlers met the westward moving US-owned banana plantations. Rama was the scene of two incidents that exemplified the friction between North Americans and Nicaraguans. Both of these brought the intervention of the US State Department.

In 1888, a North American named N.P. Allen complained that his US-registered schooner, the *Merida,* had been illegally seized by Nicaraguan authorities. His complaint, transmitted to Washington by the US consular office at Bluefields, resulted in the usual preliminary diplomatic inquiries. In response, Nicaragua produced a police report showing that the *Merida* was not engaged in navigation at all; it was nothing more than an old hulk that Allen had towed to Rama and turned into a combination trading post, gambling house, and, in the words of the police commissioner's report, "general resort for men and women, who may be properly styled *professionals.*"[22] Nor had the Nicaraguans seized the *Merida;* they had merely searched it for proof that Allen was selling liquor without a license. The State Department dropped the case when no evidence to refute the Nicaraguan version was forthcoming.

An incident occurring a few years later was somewhat more serious. On the night of March 20, 1894, police at Rama attempted to arrest a drunk on the doorstep of a warehouse belonging to a US-owned company. William Wilson, a US citizen and company employee, was sleeping on the second story of the building. Disturbed by the commotion, he came downstairs and began pushing the Nicaraguans. Norberto Argüello, the police inspector, drew his revolver and shot Wilson, who died shortly afterward.

The Zelaya government ordered Argüello's arrest and trial. But Argüello twice escaped from jail, apparently with help from other police officials. Claiming that "the whole business is marked by such contempt for the most obvious dictates of justice, and such disregard of the simplest obligations of international duty," the United States presented Nicaragua with an ultimatum: Nicaragua must "adopt such measures as will leave no doubt of its sincere purpose and ability to protect the lives and interests of the peaceable citizens of the United States dwelling in the Mosquito Indian Reservation and to punish crimes committed against them." Minister Baker underlined the US demands by reading Nicaraguan Foreign Minister José Madriz a telegram from the captain of the USS San Francisco: "Ready to assist with all my force," it said.[23]

As the Zelaya government had already disciplined Argüello's superiors for suspected complicity in his escape, it "declined" the US ultimatum, though manifesting a conciliatory attitude.[24] Baker was not satisfied, but US President Grover Cleveland decided to let the matter rest.

With the tendency of Yankees to call for the intervention of their government on any pretext—real, exaggerated, or invented—and the inclination of the latter to respond, the United States soon became involved once again with the question of the political status of the Miskito Coast.

During the era of emerging 19th century imperialism the Great Powers routinely used their navies to enforce the claims of their citizens doing business abroad. If a small nation failed to show sufficient alacrity in paying its bills, or in making reparation for some real or imagined injury, or was not sufficiently cooperative in setting its tariff rates, a warship steaming into port would invariably produce the desired result by seizing control of the customs house or simply training its guns on the town.

But the ambiguous status of the Mosquito Reserve gave rise to special problems for the United States. Secretary of State Bayard described these in 1888:

> It is important that Nicaraguan sovereignty should exist in fact as well as in name within the Mosquito reservation. With the sovereign alone can we maintain diplomatic relations, and we have a right to look to that sovereign for redress in the event of wrongs being inflicted upon any of our citizens. If the Republic of Nicaragua is to be limited to the

mere formal right of hoisting a flag and maintaining a commissioner within the reservation, how can it be called upon to perform any of its international obligations?[25]

The projected canal with its Atlantic terminus at nearby San Juan del Norte made the need to support Nicaragua's clear title to the territory even more imperative. And, of course, the United States was anxious to remove the source of any British claim to share in controlling the destiny of the region. These larger objectives led the US to support Nicaragua's assertion of un-limited sovereignty over the Mosquito Reserve. But the policy conflicted with the immediate interests of US investors on the "banana coast," com-plicating the crisis that came to a head in January 1894.

WHEN Nicaraguan troops landed at Bluefields and imposed martial law in the Reserve, Consular Agent Seat and fifty US citizens in Bluefields telegraphed Washington, requesting that a warship be sent to protect their lives and millions of dollars in property. Though they professed to fear the Honduran invasion, it soon became clear that what really con-cerned them was the "oppressive" Nicaraguan authorities who tried to im-pose an export tax on bananas and enforce the customs regulations. Consul Braida wrote, "Mosquito under Spanish [sic] rule means the utter ruin of all that American capital and energy has accomplished and built up here in such a wonderfully successful manner in the past few years."[26]

The *USS Kearsarge,* dispatched to the scene, wrecked while en route and a ship summoned by the British consul, the *HMS Cleopatra,* arrived first and landed a force of fifty Royal Marines. General Lacayo, the Nicaraguan commissioner, reached an agreement with British officials to form a provisional council to govern the Reserve. It would include represen-tatives of the various nationalities, but the Nicaraguan commissioner would preside. Though the agreement also called for withdrawal of British troops, anti-Hispanic agitation, largely fomented by North American residents, resulted in civil disturbances and Lacayo asked the British to assume police duties until a local police force could be organized.

The Anglo-Nicaraguan protocol for governing the Reserve and the presence of Royal Marines greatly upset the State Department. Britain im-mediately assured Washington that the agreement was merely for the pro-tection of its citizens, not to uphold the regime of Clarence against Nicaragua. In the curious state of affairs that ensued, however, the United States government—presuming to be a better defender of Nicaragua's rights than the Nicaraguans themselves—protested that the arrangements vio-lated the Treaty of Managua, an agreement to which it was not a party.[27] Representatives of US corporations on the Coast, meanwhile, demanded that the United States uphold the arbitration award by the Emperor of

Austria and restore their friend Clarence to power. The latter were supported, to one extent or another, by the local US consular officials, Seat and Braida.

Under such circumstances it is not surprising that US Minister Baker, in Managua, became confused. Reluctant to make the journey to Bluefields to investigate matters for himself, he at one point wrote Secretary of State Gresham, "The powerful naval force of the United States now on the Mosquito coast is much more able to enforce any demands that should be made than I am."[28] Finally ordered to go, Baker got himself into trouble by trying to negotiate the withdrawal of Nicaraguan troops, counter to official US policy.

On July 5, after the British withdrew, part of the local populace rose in revolt, proclaiming as their goal the restoration of Clarence and the expulsion of the Nicaraguans. Seat requested that Marines be landed from the USS Marblehead, standing off the coast, for protection of life and property. General Cabezas, who commanded the small force of Nicaraguan troops then in town, gave his approval.

The insurrectionists surprised a squad of Nicaraguans at El Bluff, the entrance to Bluefields harbor, and captured a small field piece. Hauling the gun into town, they trained it on Government House, where General Cabezas and twenty-five soldiers were quartered. Commander Charles O'Neil, captain of the Marblehead, arranged for a cease-fire and for withdrawal of the Nicaraguans from their untenable position.

COMMANDER O'Neil's reports to the secretary of the navy on the state of affairs at Bluefields are noteworthy for their clarity and degree of objectivity. They contrasted markedly with the inflammatory allegations of the US businessmen, which were, in large measure, supported by the reports of Seat, Braida, and Baker.[29]

O'Neil's testimony contradicted the claims that North American residents were threatened by depredations from Nicaraguan troops. He reported that they were, in fact, in no danger—unless caught in a crossfire between the contending forces. Any harm to US business interests, he said, would likely result from the fact that "owing to the recent excitement the natives have many of them quit work."[30]

The commander described Clarence, then twenty-one years old, as "merely a puppet, and is neither bright, clever nor well-educated . . . an inexperienced boy [who] did not know what he was talking about, nor did he have the faintest idea as to the gravity of the situation." "Under Mosquito rule the planters hired or leased land at 3 cents an acre per annum for 50 years," reported O'Neil, "and at the present value of the local coin their rental is 1 1/2 cents per acre in United States currency. The Nicaraguans do not look with favor upon such leases."[31]

Robert Henry Clarence, last hereditary ruler of the Miskitos (seated center), with members of his Council, 1893

As evidence that Nicaraguans had acted with restraint toward US citizens, the commander cited the case of a North American employee of the Bluefields Banana Company, who just before the uprising "in a half intoxicated condition, went into General Cabezas's office and flourished a revolver, [declaring] himself 'governor of Bluefields.'"[32] Cabezas had laughed off the episode, O'Neil reported.

There were other, more serious incidents in which US citizens had compromised themselves. According to the North Americans' weekly newssheet, a public meeting had taken place at their clubhouse, presided over by "a prominent American citizen." The assemblage had denounced Nicaragua and proclaimed support for Clarence. Later, O'Neil found, the Yankees elected one of their own "governor" of Prinzapolka and hoisted up the US flag there. Moreover, at the start of the insurrection Clarence appointed a Texan "chief of police"; he and another US citizen had taken part in the raid at El Bluff in which two Nicaraguan soldiers were killed.[33]

I mention these matters [O'Neil wrote] to give the Department a correct idea of how Americans have mixed in local matters, and it will readily be seen how it complicates the situation. I think they are beginning to be thoroughly frightened however . . . The part of [the British vice-consul's] letter in which he says: "What have we as foreigners to do with this question?" is, to say the least, entertaining, as the foreigners seem to have been at the bottom of the whole business.[34]

O'Neil warned US citizens against the possible consequences of taking part in any civil administration issuing from the insurrection. His warning was given emphasis when the Nicaraguan-led Provisional Council declared that "all those who support and encourage or otherwise help and serve the present regime" would be treated as accomplices of rebellion.[35] Despite the warnings, however, several North Americans did join Clarence's council.

Notwithstanding O'Neil's belief that North Americans were largely responsible for creating the crisis, he took a boatload of Marines up the Escondido River and compelled the Nicaraguans to release impounded banana boats, threatening to force them to pay for any spoiled fruit.[36]

A contingent of 500 Nicaraguan troops arrived on August 3 to restore control at Bluefields. For a few tense hours a junior officer, temporarily in command of a US naval vessel, tried to block their landing, but the matter was resolved in Nicaragua's favor and no further incidents ensued.[37] Realizing that neither Britain nor the United States were inclined to sustain them, the supporters of Clarence ended their resistance to Nicaraguan authority.

In November, delegates from all the indigenous groups of the Mosquito Reserve met in convention at Bluefields. They voted for full reincorporation into Nicaragua, while retaining for themselves certain privileges such as exemption from taxation and military service. Also, henceforth only Miskitos would hold office in Miskito communities. "In token of gratitude to General J. Santos Zelaya," the convention decreed, "the district which has heretofore been known as the Mosquito Reservation shall henceforth be called the Department of Zelaya." Signing as witnesses to the document were "B.B. Seat, U.S. consular agent; J. Weinberger, alcalde of the city of Bluefields; Sam. Weill, mayor; A. Aubert, treasurer-general"[38] Since Weinberger and Weill were both North American businessmen— the former, manager of the Bluefields Banana Company—the Zelaya government was clearly willing to go to considerable lengths to accommodate US business interests on the Coast.

British warships blockaded Corinto for a few days the following year, exacting a small monetary reparation for the alleged insult of the arrest and expulsion of the English vice-consul at Bluefields for his role in the events there. But Britain did not object to Nicaragua's assertion of complete sovereignty over the Mosquito Reserve, and the Treaty of Managua was abrogated a few years later.

Some in the United States have credited the Monroe Doctrine with expelling British influence from the Miskito Coast, but the facts do not support such an interpretation. Continual remonstrances by US emissaries in London were certainly helpful, and Nicaragua expressed its gratitude. But Britain's conduct throughout the affair demonstrated that it simply did not desire any longer the burden of a protectorate in an area where US capital accounted for most foreign investment and where the British subjects were nearly all Jamaicans.

US Minister Thomas Bayard wrote Secretary of State Gresham from London:

> His lordship [British Foreign Secretary Lord Kimberly] repeated to me . . . that he had no other wish than to act in accord and with the approval of the United States in matters concerning political control in Central America."[39]

As 1894 came to a close, the United States had plainly become the supreme arbiter of the destiny of Central America and of Nicaragua in particular. Just a few months later, in July 1895, Secretary of State Olney would assert in a similar instance involving Britain, "To-day the United States is practically sovereign on this continent, and its fiat is law upon the subjects to which it confines its interposition."*[40]

THE EVENTS at Bluefields did not end Nicaragua's vexatious problems with the Atlantic Coast. Five years later, a sequel to the occurrences of 1894 showed that President Zelaya had not succeeded in conciliating Yankee businessmen. These had, nevertheless, continued to invest on the Atlantic Coast at such a rate that by 1899 Minister William L. Merry valued the properties of just five of the firms operating there at $2.5 million.[41]

In February 1899 General Juan Reyes, governor of Zelaya Department, declared against President Zelaya and launched an uprising, seizing control of Bluefields. Though nominally a Liberal, Reyes was aided by Conservative leaders who tried to open a second front in Chontales, on the eastern shore of Lake Nicaragua. Minister Merry wrote Washington that Reyes was "reported as having also the united support of all foreigners as well as native interests on the Mosquito coast" and that "a considerable number of parties claiming American citizenship are aiding the revolutionary movement."[42] US warships were again sent to Bluefields to "protect lives and property."

The revolt collapsed in less than a month. As Nicaraguan government troops reentered Bluefields, thirty-two US citizens surrendered to the captain of a US cruiser. The group, presumably employees of North Ameri-

---

* The occasion was a boundary dispute between Venezuela and British Guyana.

can companies, had joined Reyes' ranks styling themselves "Rough Riders."[43]

The United States government was not involved in the uprising. But the State Department, with help from the navy, did intervene to prevent Nicaragua from levying $6,000 in customs duties that US firms had paid to Reyes in defiance of instructions from the US consular agent. The companies claimed they had been coerced by Reyes, the de facto government. Nicaragua maintained, however, that they had merely taken advantage of circumstances to finance the rebellion. While the businessmen protested their innocence, Minister Merry confirmed that they "have many complaints of long standing against the Zelaya Government" and "desire aggressive action, aided by [US] military power, which is not permissible under present conditions."[44]

The anti-Zelaya uprising of 1899, short-lived though it was, served as a warning that the isolated Atlantic littoral was Nicaragua's Achilles' heel. Where foreign capital held sway it had the power to corrupt. But even with difficult logistical problems, the government had been able to crush the rebellion easily, a feat that could not have been accomplished had Zelaya not enjoyed overwhelming support from the population in the interior.[45]

The subsequent decision by the United States to dig the canal in Panama actuated Zelaya's most ambitious development project—the construction of a railroad through the jungle from western Nicaragua to Monkey Point on the Atlantic, where a deepwater port would be built. If completed, the line would end the historic separation of the country's Atlantic region and open a large, uninhabited territory with valuable natural resources to settlement and exploitation.

RISING tensions brought Central America to the flash point several times during the years 1906 and 1907. Plotting by exile groups in this country or that, competition for influence by Zelaya and Guatemalan President Manuel Estrada Cabrera, Liberal-Conservative differences, old political feuds, and long-standing border disputes piled one on top of another to produce a sort of spontaneous combustion. The administration of Theodore Roosevelt became very much involved in looking after growing Yankee investments, and in jealously guarding against any opening that might present European rivals with an opportunity to increase their influence. Nor was the US about to permit any development with a potential to adversely affect the Panama Canal. US warships were sent to patrol both coasts, with orders to land Marines whenever their captains or local consuls deemed necessary.* Such actions, though usually heavy-handed, were not meant

---

* Marines and/or sailors were landed at Amapala, Honduras—in the Gulf of Fonseca—and at Puerto Cortéz, La Ceiba, and Trujillo—all on Honduras' Atlantic coast—on different occasions during 1907.

to, nor did they, tip the scales in favor of any party—at least not any party of Central Americans.

Roosevelt complemented the "big stick" with continual efforts—frequently pressures—to bring about negotiated settlements. Understanding that US involvement was viewed with suspicion, Roosevelt and Secretary of State Elihu Root persuaded Mexican President Porfirio Diaz to join them in their pacification efforts.

Zelaya frequently played an influential part in peacemaking, also. In 1902 he hosted a peace conference at the Nicaraguan port of Corinto. The treaty signed there provided for an arbitration panel to settle disputes among Central American nations. The following year, when it seemed that one or more of the other states might intervene in an uprising by Nicaraguan Conservatives, Foreign Minister Fernando Sánchez cabled the Nicaraguan minister in Washington, instructing him to secretly urge Secretary of State Hay to suggest another peace conference, "which would guarantee the peace of these nations in such a way that the governments would neither attack each other nor in any way protect the disturbers of order."[46] Zelaya sometimes initiated and usually supported negotiations during the events of 1906-1907.

In January 1907 Honduras requested permission from President Zelaya for its troops to enter Nicaragua in pursuit of rebels. Zelaya refused, asserting that he had adequate forces to disarm and remove from sensitive border areas any Honduran insurgents that entered Nicaragua. The Honduran army crossed the border anyway. According to the Nicaraguan account, they attacked a small party of Nicaraguan soldiers, killed several, and committed various outrages before returning to Honduras. Honduran President Manuel Bonilla admitted his troops had violated Nicaraguan territory, but claimed they had done so accidentally. He denied they had attacked Nicaraguan forces, insisting they had encountered only anti-government Hondurans.[47]

Zelaya demanded reparations. The Central American arbitration panel established under the 1902 Corinto Pact was called into session, but its efforts to reach a solution broke down when both countries, accusing each other, refused to halt their military buildup.

The blame for the events that followed has never been clearly established—the facts were buried by the exigencies of politics. What is certain is that a proclamation by Nicaraguan exiles, dated at Choluteca, Honduras, February 13, 1907, called for President Zelaya's overthrow. A few days afterward Honduran troops reportedly attacked Nicaraguan border posts. Later press accounts said the Nicaraguans began the conflict.

Whatever the truth of the matter, President Zelaya asserted that the alleged attack constituted a declaration of war. He granted recognition to a provisional junta set up by Bonilla's opponents, and Nicaraguan troops invaded Honduras, joined by Honduran rebels. El Salvador, in turn, came to General Bonilla's aid, as did the Nicaraguan exiles; Nicaraguan Conservative General Emiliano Chamorro was named commander-in-chief of the Honduran army.[48]

At the Battle of Namasigue, fought between March 17 and 19, Zelaya's army decisively defeated the combined Honduran-Salvadoran-Nicaraguan exile forces. It was, perhaps, the largest military engagement in Central American history. The Honduran government and its army collapsed. Nicaraguan troops, supported by gunboats, took possession of Honduras' Atlantic ports, prompting the US to land Marines to protect the banana companies operating there. Tegucigalpa and Choluteca fell in rapid succession. By the second week in April, General Bonilla, with a handful of Honduran and Salvadoran troops, was reduced to the port of Amapala on Tigre Island, there besieged by the tiny Nicaraguan navy. Fearing the port would be shelled, the US consul called for the intervention of the cruiser *USS Chicago*, then in the Gulf of Fonseca. The ship's captain negotiated a cease fire. An accord signed on board the *Chicago* on April 12 provided for the surrender of Amapala, safe passage out of Central America for General Bonilla, and the withdrawal of Salvadoran troops. US Marines landed to police the town.[49]

Nicaragua had become a regional power to be reckoned with. President Zelaya, apparently, now sought to use the prestige gained by Nicaragua's decisive victory to bring about the ever-elusive reunification of Central America. Resisted by Salvadoran President Figueroa, he provided support for Salvadoran rebel forces who landed at Acajutla and La Libertad in June 1907. Though Salvadoran troops quickly crushed the invasion, Zelaya's action precipitated a new crisis.*

Salvadoran, Guatemalan, and Nicaraguan armies mobilized, as did the miscellaneous exile groups. El Salvador and Guatemala sought permission to cross Honduran territory to invade Nicaragua. Though Honduras refused, it looked as if the invasion would be launched anyway, plunging Central America into general war. By the end of July, however, President Zelaya realized his error and sent emissaries to Washington and Mexico City, joining Honduras' call for US-Mexican mediation.[51]

---

* US ships in the Gulf of Fonseca, with no equipment more sophisticated than electric searchlights, intercepted and turned back several attempts to supply the rebels by boat from Nicaragua.[50] Seventy-five years later, with far more sophisticated equipment, the US Navy would be unable to produce evidence to substantiate charges that similar arms trafficking was taking place.

The result was the Central American Peace Conference, held in Washington between November 14 and December 20, 1907. Neither the United States nor Mexico played a direct role, but Secretary Root and his Mexican counterpart, Ignacio Mariscal, acted as convenors, and both nations had special representatives present at the deliberations.

While the conference divided on the question of union, no less than nine treaties were signed. The most important of these were the General Treaty of Peace and Amity and the Convention for the Establishment of a Central American Court of Justice. The former, together with a supplementary agreement, barred intervention in each other's civil wars, recognition of any government arising out of a revolution or coup d'etat, or the settling of political exiles in border areas. In creating the Central American Court of Justice the five states pledged to submit to the court's arbitration all conflicts not resolvable through negotiation, and to respect its decisions.[52]

The United States was not a signer of the Washington Conference treaties, but its prestige was clearly behind them. Delivering the closing speech at the conference, Secretary Root congratulated the delegates on having "pursued the true method by which law, order, peace and justice are substituted for the unrestrained dominion of the strong over the weak."[53] The court was inaugurated in Cartago, Costa Rica, on May 25, 1908—thirteen years before establishment of the International Court of Justice at the Hague.

After the Washington Conference there came a period of relative peace in Central America. An unsuccessful attempt to overthrow the Honduran government did take place in 1908 and Honduras charged before the new court that El Salvador and Guatemala had aided the rebellion, in violation of the Washington accords. In its first decision, the court's majority voted to absolve the accused, and there the matter ended.[54]

FOR MANY YEARS William L. Merry had been accredited as minister to Nicaragua, serving out of the US legation in San José, Costa Rica. But in 1908 the Roosevelt Adminstration decided to reestablish a legation in Managua. John Gardner Coolidge, from the US legation staff in Mexico, was appointed minister.

Coolidge arrived in Managua in August 1908. In November, William Howard Taft, a conservative Republican, was elected to the presidency of the United States. Celebrating Taft's victory, Nicaraguan Conservatives staged a demonstration in Granada. Several North Americans took part, carrying US flags, and, it seems, speakers called for annexation of the country to the United States. Police broke up the demonstration. Several Nicaraguans were jailed briefly and some were fined for wearing US-flag lapel pins. The Granada flag incident became the principal subject of Coolidge's dispatches to Secretary Root.

The US minister portrayed the affair as a manifestation of Zelaya's "anti-Americanism." "Nothing effective . . . can be accomplished in accordance with our policy of friendly guidance of the Central American Republics," he wrote, "as long as Zelaya remains in absolute power." He suggested as a "palliative" that the US use the flag incident as a pretext to force Zelaya "to reaffirm solemnly the Constitution of Nicaragua of 1905, pledging himself to abide by it as long as it shall remain the law of the land."[55] Advised Coolidge:

> If we are to undertake some action in this case, it would be very hard to see how far it might lead us, which would be embarrassing unless we realized the possibilities at the outset and were fully decided to what lengths we were prepared to go.[56]

Significantly, Coolidge did not base his proposal of drastic action on any belief that affairs in Nicaragua were radically different from the rest of the region. On the contrary, "if it were done it would have a salutary effect," he said, "not only in Nicaragua, but in other Central American states as well where similar methods of government obtain."[57]

But nothing came of the affair; Secretary Root manifested no enthusiasm for intervening in Nicaraguan politics. After several notes had been exchanged Coolidge admitted that the assurances given by the Nicaraguan government after the repression of the pro-Taft demonstration were "fairly satisfactory."[58]

The following day Coolidge telegraphed his resignation to the State Department, "being no longer in accord with the views of our government." He said he had become convinced that the Zelaya government was "entirely false" in its dealings with the United States and the rest of Central America, and

> in internal affairs its rule is unconstitutional, despotic and very cruel. I feel that it is consistent with neither the dignity nor the interest of the United States to maintain a representative here of high rank whose duty is mainly to hold the Nicaraguan government to its international pledges, and who, as long as these are not openly violated, must maintain an official attitude of cordiality.[59]

What made these accusations by the US minister especially remarkable was that during his three-month tenure he had communicated little information to support them. Apart from the Granada demonstration, which the Nicaraguan Conservatives appear to have staged deliberately in order to provoke an incident, there were few clues to explain Coolidge's attitude.

He had expressed annoyance at plans by the Zelaya government to establish a chemical laboratory to analyze and regulate imported foodstuffs and medicines. This, he felt, would adversely affect the sale of US products. And he had reported the intention of Nicaragua to negotiate a loan in Europe, suggesting that this, too, would conflict with US interests.[60]

After Coolidge left, the legation chargé, J.H. Gregory, reiterated the urgings for intervention, without, however, furnishing any more justification than had Coolidge. Gregory wrote:

> It seems to me that some decisive and peremptory action by our government is necessary and would not only not hurt our prestige and commerce with these countries, but would have exactly the contrary effect; for there is nothing these people respect and follow like power, and our prestige would increase and commerce be stimulated.[61]

Later, the US consul—a Nicaraguan hostile to Zelaya—relayed a small newspaper clipping to the State Department, which reported that Luis Corea, the former Nicaraguan minister to the US, would visit Europe and then travel to Japan via the trans-Siberian railway. Consul de Olivares claimed that the article confirmed rumors that Nicaragua would try to interest Japan in a canal concession.[62]

The attitude of US representatives toward Zelaya had formerly been very different. In 1898, US minister Lewis Baker, having dealt with Zelaya for five years, judged that "he has given the people of Nicaragua as good a government as they will permit him," in view of the continual Conservative disruptions. Baker cited many improvements in the country, and affirmed that "foreigners who attend to their own business and do not meddle with the politics which does not concern them, are fully protected." In 1900 Secretary of State John Hay referred to the "respect already entertained by this Government for the ability, integrity, and high character of President Zelaya." The following year, William B. Sorsby, United States consul at San Juan del Norte, asserted that Zelaya was "the ablest and strongest man in Central America. He is very popular with the masses, and is giving them an excellent Government." As recently as 1908, President Roosevelt had addressed Zelaya as "Great and Good Friend."[63]

Coolidge and the other legation personnel had apparently been won over by the business interests on the Atlantic Coast. Several US companies had pending claims against the Zelaya government arising from contract cancellations and other grievances related to its nationalistic policies. They were anxious to get rid of Zelaya and replace him with the Nicaraguan Conservatives, who were closely tied to them.

William Howard Taft was inaugurated as president of the United States on March 4, 1909. To head the State Department, he appointed Philander

Chase Knox, a corporation lawyer who had served as Roosevelt's attorney general. With the new government in Washington came a decided shift in policy toward partisanship in Central America's internal conflicts.

Unlike Roosevelt and Root, Taft and Knox lent a sympathetic ear to the complaints against Zelaya, and to the suggestions for intervention that came from Coolidge and other legation personnel. Knox's law firm represented the Fletcher family of Pittsburgh, chief owners of the United States and Nicaragua Company and its subsidiary La Luz and Los Angeles Mining Company, one of the firms with a claim against Zelaya.[64] Knox himself is thought to have owned stock in the company.

For two years the George D. Emery Company had had a claim before the State Department. It had been engaged in logging a large tract of mahogany on Nicaragua's Atlantic Coast, but in January 1907 Nicaragua annulled the concession, charging that the company had failed to carry out a stipulation that it plant two new trees for every one cut, and had abused a privilege of duty-free importation, reselling goods it brought into the country.

The Taft Administration barely took time to settle into office before it began pressuring Nicaragua on the Emery claim. Simultaneously, anti-Zelaya articles and columns began to appear in the press, a number of them written or inspired by Frederick Palmer, a *Chicago Tribune* reporter who had visited Minister Coolidge during a trip to Nicaragua in 1908. One such story reported that the US had obtained a translation of "a fiery editorial in the official newspaper of the Nicaraguan Government condemning the United States and advocating an offensive and defensive alliance with Japan, aimed against this country."[65] Other articles reported warlike moves in Central America, implying that Zelaya was planning attacks on his neighbors. These were not substantiated by actual developments.

State Department spokesmen accused Zelaya of being the sole cause of Central America's troubles, though no charges to that effect were brought before the Central American Court of Justice either by the United States or by the supposed victims.*[67] Columnists embellished the theme with juicy tales of Zelaya's crimes and peculations. Selling monopolies and concessions for private gain, murdering his opponents, hatching Machiavellian plots against his country's neighbors, deflowering virgins—it seemed there was no sin Zelaya had overlooked. None of these articles backed up its allegations with evidence, or even contained the sort of details that would make it verifiable. It was, in short, yellow journalism.[68]

Nicaragua and the US reached an agreement in the Emery case in Sep-

---

* Article IV of the convention creating the court provided that nations outside Central America could submit complaints against Central American countries.[66]

tember. Nicaragua would pay the firm $600,000 to settle its claim and buy out its assets. Additional benefits to the company were valued at $200,000. The settlement, which Nicaragua regarded as extortionary, was considerably more than the company itself had originally asked. The windfall was a result of the pressure exerted on Nicaragua by the growing United States hostility.[69] Yet, despite settlement of the Emery claim, there was no softening of the Taft Administration's attitude.

On October 11, less than three weeks after the signing of the protocol in the Emery case, General Juan J. Estrada, governor-intendant for the Atlantic Coast, declared himself in revolt against President Zelaya, following the path taken by General Reyes ten years earlier. Estrada established a provisional government at Bluefields; joining him were Conservative leaders Emiliano Chamorro and Adolfo Diaz. As in 1894 and 1899, United States business interests on the Coast were "enthusiastic."[70] But this time they had the support of the US government.

Thomas P. Moffat, the US consul at Bluefields, reported plans for the revolt several days before it occurred. Given that consular officials normally maintain close contact with business interests, and are therefore privy to their activities, Moffat's foreknowledge was not remarkable. But José Joaquin Morales, a Conservative participant intimately acquainted with the rebellion's personalities, asserted that Salvador Castrillo, who became the provisional government's envoy to Washington, had, "after several conversations with high functionaries of the American Legation, departed for the Atlantic Coast for the ostensible purpose of handling some matters for his law practice, but with the real object of promoting a revolution." Years later, during Senate hearings, Consul Moffat implicated US naval officers and diplomatic personnel on the Atlantic Coast.[71] Regardless of what role Washington played in fomenting the rebellion, its support would quickly become apparent.

The La Luz and Los Angeles Mining Company, with which Secretary Knox was connected, had its headquarters in Bluefields. Adolfo Diaz was the company's corporate secretary there. Diaz became treasurer for the uprising, and later presented a bill for 750,000 pesos (about $63,000), money he claimed to have loaned the insurgents from his personal savings. Though Diaz was also an agent for the Nicaragua Sugar Estates Limited and a member of a prominent Conservative family, the $63,000—representing forty-two times his annual salary at La Luz—was beyond his means. It was thought that most, if not all, of whatever money Diaz had actually advanced came not from his own pocket, but from US companies operating on the Coast. Moffat testified that the La Luz manager at Bluefields urged him to use his influence to seat Diaz as president of Nicaragua, telling him his own future would be assured if he "put Adolfo over the line there."[72]

Other evidence of outside sponsorship for the uprising eventually came to light. President Estrada Cabrera of Guatemala, Zelaya's Conservative archrival, loaned $90,000 in gold. The *Puerto Perlas,* a US-owned (but Nicaraguan-registered) boat on its way to Guatemala to pick up arms for the rebels, was seized by Honduras for violating its neutrality; the US threatened to take the boat by force unless Honduras released it. The Hondurans had no alternative but to submit.[73]

New Orleans was the base of supply for Estrada's forces. From there they received arms and recruits furnished by, among others, the Emery Company, with whom Nicaragua had so recently reached a generous settlement. Other support came from the United Fruit Company manager at Bocas del Toro, Panama. Financial aid from US companies reportedly reached $1 million.[74]

North Americans by the dozens joined the rebellion, instructing the Estrada-Chamorro forces in the use of machine guns, frequently operating the modern weapons themselves. Others commanded bodies of rebel troops in combat. They included not only employees of US companies on the Coast, as in 1894 and 1899, but recruits direct from the States as well. Among the latter was Captain Godfrey Fowler of the Texas National Guard, an active-duty member of the Texas governor's staff.[75]

Another North American who joined the Conservative revolt was a Virginian named Lee Roy Cannon. A civil engineer by profession, Cannon had lived in Central America for several years. He was formerly a part owner of a mercantile business at Matiguás in the Matagalpa mountains, engaged in buying and selling rubber and other goods. In 1906, after a squabble with the local commandant, he left Nicaragua for Honduras. There he was connected with the Conservative Bonilla government and with Lee Christmas, a North American soldier-of-fortune who held the rank of general in the Honduran army. When Bonilla fell as a consequence of the disastrous war with Nicaragua in 1907, Cannon went to El Salvador, becoming a police official in San Miguel. Described as "brave, bold, intelligent and likeable . . . the Walker of our times, with even more ambition and greater talents than that ill-fated adventurer," Cannon returned to Honduras in 1908 to join the unsuccessful attempt to restore Bonilla to power.[76] Taken prisoner, he was pardoned and given money to leave Honduras on the pledge that he would never again take part in Central American conflicts. But when the Estrada revolt broke out, Cannon, then living in Guatemala, accepted an offer from Emiliano Chamorro and joined his staff with the rank of colonel.

Leonard Groce, a Texan, had also lived in Nicaragua for a number of years. He had a Nicaraguan wife and four children in Nandaime. Groce was residing in Bluefields when the Estrada rebellion began, working some mining claims. He, too, accepted a commission as colonel in the rebel forces.

On October 31 Cannon was taken prisoner by government troops operating on the San Juan River. Two days later Groce was captured also. Admitting their participation in the rebellion, both were tried before a court martial. Groce testified that his assignment had been to blow up the *Diamante,* a riverboat carrying 500 government troops on their way to recapture the lower San Juan. Cannon, who had been making a reconnaissance of the river, confessed to being present during the placing of the mine, a device consisting of seventy-five pounds of dynamite. The charge, detonated from the riverbank, had been carried out of the main channel by the current, and exploded harmlessly as the boat passed by.

Cannon and Groce, found guilty of the crime of rebellion, were sentenced to death. Citing the severity of the national emergency, Zelaya turned down their appeals for clemency. On the morning of November 16, 1909 they were passed before a firing squad.

Some of Zelaya's advisers reportedly counseled him to commute the sentences of Cannon and Groce. But Zelaya insisted the executions were just; moreover, he declared that "in the face of the enemy . . . this extreme means of bringing the two confessed and convicted criminals to justice was necessary to maintain the order and morale of the army."[77]

Just or not, the shooting of Cannon and Groce furnished the pretext for the famous December 1, 1909 letter from Secretary of State Knox to the Nicaraguan chargé d'affaires in Washington. The "Knox Note" declared:

> Since the Washington conventions of 1907, it is notorious that President Zelaya has almost continuously kept Central America in tension or turmoil . . . It is equally a matter of common knowledge that under the regime of President Zelaya republican institutions have ceased in Nicaragua to exist except in name, that public opinion and the press have been throttled, and that prison has been the reward of any tendency to real patriotism.

The secretary furnished no substantiation for these dramatic accusations, affirming that personal consideration for the Nicaraguan chargé "impels me to abstain from unnecessary discussion of the painful details of a regime which, unfortunately, has been a blot upon the history of Nicaragua."

"Appeal against this situation has long since been made to this Government by a majority of the Central American Republics," claimed Knox in the letter. To this "a great body of the Nicaraguan people" had supposedly added their appeal by means of revolution. Given such a state of affairs and the alleged condition of anarchy in Nicaragua, the United States, Knox said, was left with "no definite responsible source" to which it "could look for reparation for the killing of Messrs. Cannon and Groce, or indeed, for protection which must be assured American citizens and American interests in Nicaragua." He declared diplomatic relations with the Zelaya government to be at an end.[78]

The Knox Note was an amazing document on several counts. The allegation that Zelaya had engaged in wholesale violation of the Washington accords, frequently repeated later, was not supported then, or afterward, by any evidence.[79] Nor is it credible that aggrieved parties would have appealed to the United States as Knox claimed. The very conventions that the United States was purportedly interposing to uphold had established the Central American Court of Justice to handle just such contigencies; the court received no complaints about Zelaya. Moreover, the proclaimed purpose of the United States to promote peace in the region, especially the moral authority it had placed behind the Washington Peace Conference, demanded that if any Central American state did complain to the US, they be directed first to the arbitration court.

The extent to which republican institutions and what are now called "human rights" existed in Nicaragua is debatable. There were many charges of abuses, but these came mostly from the Conservative opposition, which was hardly an unbiased source. Zelaya, in turn, described the latter as

> that party that conceals the dagger and the poison of the Borgias behind a crucifix, that Jesuitical legion that thinks power is the divine right of its caste and aspires to erect the throne of privilege over the lowly . . . [that] has a hundred times seized the rifle and a hundred times had to put it down again in the bitter disappointment of its ineptitude and unpopularity.[80]

Though the hyperbole may have been overdone, the Conservatives, as they were then, were certainly a factious lot and probably provoked such repression as befell them. It is also true that their continual rebellions were, until they received substantial external support, ineffectual. The repression that did occur under Zelaya was surely no worse than in the other Central American countries, and conditions were good compared to the regimes that would follow, or to the wholesale political killings and state terrorism that has characterized Central America in recent years.* In any event, neither in the Washington agreements nor anywhere else was the United States

---

* In a history of the period written by a Conservative who was involved in many of the uprisings against Zelaya the complaints against him seem, on the whole, petty. The only convincing case in which Zelaya is accused of being responsible for the deaths of political opponents involved the execution of two army officers who were convicted, apparently on flimsy evidence, of blowing up a barracks in Managua in 1902. But at the same time, the author recounts how Conservative leaders like Emiliano Chamorro who continually organized armed uprisings were repeatedly pardoned after serving only short jail sentences.[81]

elected to pronounce judgement on what were, after all, the internal affairs of Nicaragua.

The position taken by the Taft Administration with respect to Cannon and Groce was a radical departure, both from past policy of the United States and from accepted international practice. Citizens who took up arms against friendly powers were regarded as having forfeited their right to the protection of their government. Andrew Jackson cited these criteria as justification for his execution of Robert Ambrister and Alexander Arbuthnot in 1818. He alleged that these two British subjects had aided Seminole Indians who were resisting his invasion of Florida, then a Spanish colony. Jackson was upheld by President Monroe, and the English government made no protest. Just such a hands-off view regarding filibusters with US citizenship had been reaffirmed by Presidents Zachary Taylor in 1849 and Millard Fillmore in 1851.[82]

The breaking of relations with Nicaragua, accomplished by the Knox Note, put the Nicaraguan government and rebels on the same footing in regard to US neutrality laws. Since the United States officially recognized neither belligerent, weapons and supplies could legally be shipped to both. In practice they went mainly to the anti-Zelaya forces in Bluefields.

Confronted with the implacable hostility of the US, Zelaya saw no alternative but to resign. The National Assembly unanimously accepted his recommendation of José Madriz as his successor. Madriz, a prominent jurist and former foreign minister, was well-known both in and outside Nicaragua. Having spent several years of Zelaya's administration in exile, he returned to the government on the eve of the 1907 war with Honduras, and served as Nicaragua's chief negotiator at the Washington Conference. When Zelaya resigned Madriz was the Nicaraguan member of the Central American Court of Justice in Cartago.

Madriz received an enthusiastic welcome on his arrival in Managua.[83] Honduras and Costa Rica recognized his government, and it was hoped that the rebels, confined to the Atlantic Coast, would come to terms. But convinced of United States support, Chamorro, Estrada, and Diaz remained obstinate.

Even with the flow of money and war materiel from North American companies, however, the rebellion soon began to founder. Government forces recaptured San Juan del Norte and won several other significant victories. In May 1910 they retook El Bluff, the entrance to Bluefields harbor and location of the customs house. With a newly acquired gunboat, the *Máximo Jerez,* they declared a blockade of the port and announced their intention to assault Bluefields, the last rebel stronghold. But US warships intervened, keeping the port open and preventing the government from collecting the customs, which therefore continued to furnish revenue to the rebels. The US Navy declared Bluefields a "neutral zone" and landed Marines commanded by Major Smedley Butler, who announced they would oppose any attempt by the Nicaraguan government to retake the town from the insurgents.[84]

Unable to act, with difficult supply lines, the pro-Madriz army was soon compelled to withdraw. With the rebellion having the support of the US and an inexhaustible base of supply in New Orleans, loyal troops became convinced that further sacrifices were futile. The government effort, on the verge of victory at the end of May, had collapsed by late August. Confronted with the seemingly invincible power of the United States, Madriz, like Zelaya, relinquished the presidency and fled.

WHAT, THEN, was the crime of Zelaya that made Washington turn thumbs down on Nicaraguan Liberalism? Zelaya himself cited the canal question, since, in his own words, he had "demanded above all that the sovereignty of Nicaragua be guaranteed" and that it receive monetary compensation "corresponding to the importance of the concession."[85] But that explanation, perhaps intended to appeal to nationalist sentiment, does not correspond to the facts.

In December 1900, Luis Corea, Nicaraguan minister to the United States, had signed a protocol with Secretary of State John Hay agreeing to open canal negotiations with the US as soon as Congress granted Roosevelt the necessary authorization. At the time, Hay submitted a draft canal treaty for the Zelaya government's consideration. It would have given the United States the perpetual right to construct, own, and operate a canal across a six-mile-wide strip of Nicaraguan territory. In return, the United States was to guarantee "in perpetuity the sovereignty, independence and territorial integrity" of Nicaragua, which would retain a merely nominal ownership of the canal zone. The Nicaraguans were to receive monetary compensation of $1.5 million on ratification and $100,000 per year thereafter.

At the end of 1901, as the canal question came to a head in Congress, Secretary Hay instructed Minister William Merry to press for Nicaragua's approval of the draft treaty. The Zelaya government initially raised several objections, but all the important ones were overcome within a few days. On December 6, 1901, Foreign Minister Fernando Sánchez signed a new protocol, agreeing to the main provisions of the draft treaty in return for a single lump sum payment of $6 million. All that remained to be worked out, after Roosevelt received congressional authorization to proceed, was a minor matter of court jurisdiction in the canal zone. Sánchez told Merry that President Zelaya was "very content" with this agreement. The failure of the United States to build a canal across Nicaragua resulted from maneuvering by the pro-Panama interest; it had nothing to do with any objection or obstacle raised by Zelaya.[86] The subject of a canal was never broached again during Zelaya's administration.

Another frequently alleged cause for US hostility was the connection of Secretary Knox with the Fletcher family and its Nicaraguan mining concession. This and other individual business interests may have played a role in helping call Nicaragua to the attention of the new administration. But the policy pursued by Taft and Knox appears to have been based primarily on larger considerations of US influence and strategic objectives.

Zelaya's tampering with the concessions of US companies and other nationalistic economic policies conflicted with the Taft Administration's plans to promote greater US investment in Central America and the Caribbean, while his prestige challenged US political hegemony in the area. There was no significant, credible evidence that he tried or intended to sell a rival canal concession to Japan, although it was certainly within Nicaragua's sovereign rights to do so. There was even less evidence to support a supposition that the Japanese, or anyone else, were inclined to waste enormous sums on a project as absurd as building a rival canal, or that Washington ever seriously believed they would. But Zelaya did negotiate a loan with a British-French syndicate, which the US tried unsuccessfully to block, and contracted with a German company to build the Atlantic railroad.[87] Such dealings with US competitors, signs of a dangerous degree of independence on the part of Zelaya, clearly violated the interpretation of the Monroe Doctrine that was then current.

Salvador Castrillo, the anti-Zelaya rebels' ambassador to the United States, averred that he, more than any other Nicaraguan, was responsible for the intervention, "understanding that only by turning a key in Washington could Zelaya be overthrown." Twenty years later, acknowledging "that which is plain as day," he wrote:

> The fall of Zelaya brought the disgrace of Nicaragua . . . The evils to be remedied were relative, and we could have washed that dirty laundry in the family . . . It was a paradise then compared with today. And the Atlantic Railroad, which he was building—which only he with his great strength and energy could have succeeded in completing—would have redounded to the grandeur of Nicaragua, which instead has retrogressed to the days of [18]55 and '56.[88]

THE BEST LAID PLANS

We, of America, have discovered that we, too, possess the supreme governing capacity, capacity not merely to govern ourselves at home, but that great power that in all ages has made the difference between the great and the small nations, the capacity to govern men wherever they are found.

—*Elihu Root, 1904.*

AFTER THE fall of the Madriz government, the victorious Conservatives named General Estrada to head their new regime. Estrada immediately telegraphed Washington requesting recognition. US government and business had given the Conservatives the boost that made their victory possible; Washington's blessing seemed to be a foregone conclusion. But the State Department intended to extract a price for its approval, which Conservative leaders knew they must have if they were to stay in power.[1]

Thomas C. Dawson, then US minister to Panama, was named United States special agent and sent to Managua. Dawson wasn't a casual choice: he had recently been promoted to head the State Department's Division of Latin American Affairs, and had a reputation as the leading US troubleshooter in the region. As minister to the Dominican Republic from 1904 to 1907 he negotiated the agreements that gave the United States control of that country's finances and made it a US protectorate.[2]

Working with Thomas P. Moffat, the former consul at Bluefields, Dawson dictated the terms for US recognition. On October 27, 1910, he obtained the Conservative leaders' signatures on a series of agreements that became known as the "Dawson Pact." Signed by Juan J. Estrada, Adolfo Diaz, Luis Mena, and Emiliano Chamorro, these agreements pledged the new regime to take a series of steps regarding the country's future. It would convoke a Constituent Assembly the following month to pick a president and vice president; Estrada and Diaz would be put forward as candidates for the respective offices. The Assembly, in turn, would schedule a presidential election to choose successors to Estrada and Diaz, and for that election the signers agreed to nominate only candidates who "represent the revolution and the Conservative party." To insure these would win, they agreed that "the Government to be established in Nicaragua must not permit, under any pretext, the Zelayista element in its administration." Likewise, the Constituent Assembly would adopt a constitution "tending to the abolition of monopolies [and] guaranteeing the legitimate rights of foreigners." A mixed commission would be established to resolve all outstanding claims arising from the annulment of contracts and concessions by the previous government; its makeup and the details of its operations had to have prior approval from the State Department.[3]

The linchpin of the Dawson Pact, however, was the Conservatives' pledge to solicit "the good offices of the American Government" to arrange for a loan to be guaranteed by Nicaragua's customs duties. These duties would then be collected "in accordance with the terms of an agreement satisfactory to both Governments."

That Washington's recognition for the Estrada-Diaz government should hinge on the latter's negotiation of a loan in the United States seems curious at first glance, especially since Madriz had left a surplus in the nation's treasury.[4] But the binding of Nicaragua to the United States by

Philander Chase Knox

means of a loan was the basic tenet of a policy that Theodore Roosevelt and Secretary of State Elihu Root had first employed in the Dominican Republic. In Nicaragua, under President Taft and Secretary Knox, it would become known as "dollar diplomacy."

In 1904 Roosevelt had declared that the United States, as a "civilized state," would henceforth assume the "duty" of policing the financial and political affairs of the other—presumably uncivilized—states in the Western Hemisphere. This, he explained, would forestall the possibility of European intervention.[5] Roosevelt's "corollary" to the Monroe Doctrine was put into practice the following year in the Dominican Republic. The agreements that Dawson negotiated there—with the backing of US naval vessels—gave the US control of Dominican customs collection and debt payment and made the country a US dependency.

From the standpoint of establishing United States dominance in the Caribbean, the policy was a tremendous success. Taft and his secretary of state were anxious to put it into practice in Nicaragua, and the loan was the means to that end. Unlike the Dominican Republic, however, in Nicaragua there was no threat of European powers intervening to collect debts that could be used to justify a US takeover of the country's finances. In fact, under President Zelaya, Nicaragua had one of the better debt payment records in Latin America. A new justification was needed. So Taft and Knox broadened the Roosevelt Corollary to encompass the argument that Roosevelt himself had used during the diplomatic intervention that led to the 1907 Washington Conference: political instability invited European intervention and threatened the as yet uncompleted Panama Canal. "Dollar diplomacy"—financial intervention by the United States—was the remedy. As Taft explained US actions in Nicaragua in a 1912 message to Congress:

> It is obvious that the Monroe doctrine is more vital in the neighborhood of the Panama Canal and the zone of the Caribbean than anywhere else . . . It is therefore essential that the countries within that sphere shall be removed from the jeopardy involved by heavy foreign debt and chaotic national finances and from the ever-present danger of international complications due to the disorder at home. Hence the United States has been glad to encourage and support American bankers who were willing to lend a helping hand to the financial rehabilitation of such countries because this financial rehabilitation and the protection of their customhouses from being the prey of would-be dictators would remove at one stroke the menace of foreign creditors and the menace of revolutionary disorder.[6]

Taft's aversion to "revolutionary disorder" was obviously selective, since

he had just supported the revolution that returned the Nicaraguan Conservatives to power. The revolutions the US sought to prevent were those
led by nationalists who might implement policies counter to Yankee economic and strategic objectives. In any case, US control of Nicaraguan
finances (and therefore the government) by means of a loan did not take
away the incentive to revolution; it created powerful new incentives. But
it did provide the means and the pretext by which the United States could
intervene to prevent revolutions from succeeding. And, as Taft pointed out,
there was a second advantage to the policy,

> one affecting chiefly all the southern and Gulf ports and the business
> and industry of the South. The Republics of Central America and the
> Caribbean possess great national wealth. They need only a measure of
> stability and the means of financial regeneration to enter upon an era
> of peace and prosperity, bringing profit and happiness to themselves and
> at the same time creating conditions sure to lead to a flourishing inter-
> change of trade with this country.[7]

A T FIRST all went according to Dawson's script. On December 31, a
newly-elected Constituent Assembly, presided over by Emiliano
Chamorro, ratified the Dawson Pact selection of Estrada and Diaz for president and vice president. The pair officially began their term of office the
following day, January 1, 1911, and with all in constitutional order, the
US granted its recognition. Taft sent Estrada a telegram congratulating him
"upon his assumption of the presidency by popular mandate, unanimously
expressed through the constituent assembly." In his instruction to Elliott
Northcott, the new US minister, Secretary Knox wrote:

> The Department is glad to bear witness to the favorable impression creat-
> ed by these officials in performing in such good faith certain of their
> promises and in renewing their determination to execute without un-
> necessary delay the undertakings which remain to be fulfilled.[8]

Northcott's job was to insure that those remaining "undertakings" were
fulfilled. He was aided by Ernest H. Wands, a monetary expert who would
advise the Nicaraguan government on restructuring its finances, and help
arrange for the loan.

But after its initial successes, the plan began to run into trouble. Once
the Conservative Party was restored to power, the same personal rivalries
and intra-party factionalism that had caused its demise two decades earlier immediately returned to the fore. Emiliano Chamorro, the leader of
one powerful faction, held sway in the Constituent Assembly. As its president, he labored for a constitution that would strip President Estrada of
real power and pave the way for his own ascendancy; until that happened he

was prepared to block authorization for the loan.[9] General Mena, the minister of war, controlled the army and led another important faction maneuvering against Estrada.

Popular indignation at the idea of the loan caused further trouble. On February 25, Minister Northcott reported that "the natural sentiment of an overwhelming majority of Nicaraguans is antagonistic to the United States, and even with some members of Estrada's cabinet I find a decided suspicion, if not distrust, of our motives." To make matters worse, according to Washington's man in Managua, the Zelayistas were "constantly scheming and plotting." The following month he reported that Estrada, who was determined to push through the loan agreement over all opposition, was being "sustained solely by the moral effect of our support and the belief that he would unquestionably have that support in case of trouble."[10]

On April 4, Chamorro's Constituent Assembly adopted a new constitution opposed by Estrada. The president responded by dissolving the Assembly and calling new elections in the hope that another Assembly would be more cooperative. Chamorro went into exile. Minister Northcott and Secretary Knox expressed their support for Estrada's high-handed action, for as Northcott put it, "Chamorro would never have allowed any ratification of the loan that did not give him control of its expenditure."[11]

But when the new Assembly convened at the end of April, General Mena's supporters had control, not Estrada. In a clumsy move to head off an alleged plot against him, Estrada ordered Mena arrested. The army, loyal to General Mena, prepared to move against the capital. Estrada turned to the US legation for help, but Northcott, who thought "Estrada's attack on Mena without advising with the [US] legation violates the agreement given Dawson," refused to support him. Estrada was left with no alternative but to resign in favor of Diaz, the vice president. Since a new constitution had not yet been adopted, and vice presidents did not traditionally succeed to the presidency in Nicaragua, the US had to instruct the Constitutent Assembly on the procedure to follow to confirm Diaz. But once that was done the crisis passed, for the moment.[12]

By the end of the month, however, Northcott reported that the Liberals were planning an uprising to defeat the loan. "It is difficult to estimate how serious a measure this might be if well organized and led," he wrote, "as the Liberals are in such a majority over the Conservatives. I therefore hasten to repeat my suggestion as to the advisability of stationing permanently, at least until the loan has been put through, a war vessel at Corinto." Washington granted Northcott's request for a warship for "moral effect."[13]

Thomas P. Moffat, the former US consul in Bluefields, did not think

Diaz was capable of holding an important office. "He is a delightful little fellow," he told Dawson, "and he speaks English, and I like him, but he is no executive, he is not an administrator . . . he has just been a sort of boy." Diaz himself didn't feel up to the job; unlike Mena and Chamorro, he had no personal following and believed himself to be merely a figurehead without authority. The US representatives had to coax and cajole him not to resign. Meanwhile, they had to put pressure on Mena to keep him from staging a coup. But at the end of July, US Chargé Franklin Gunther assured the State Department that Mena "is now fully awake to the need for preserving the status quo."[14]

Mena had his own ideas, however. He was willing to play ball with Diaz and the US only on condition that the Constituent Assembly be allowed to elect him president for the following term. For his part, Diaz was "heartily in favor of the plan, remarking that free elections are hopelessly impractical for several years in Nicaragua"—no doubt due to the unpopularity of the Conservative Party. Chargé Gunther also approved, advising that "the tacit consent of the Department to this plan would result in the immediate approval by Assembly of the loan and mixed commission matters." On the other hand, Gunther wrote, failure to approve Mena's succession could lead to a series of events "which would doubtless split the Conservatives, cause an anti-American uprising, and put an end to the Department's present program."[15] But the Department was not inclined to do any bargaining. It wanted action on the loan and the claims commission first; then there would be time to discuss how future Nicaraguan presidents would be chosen.

Ignoring the wishes of the United States, the Assembly proceeded to enact a law designating Mena president for the term beginning January 1, 1913. At the same time it approved several constitutional provisions that ran counter to the Dawson Pact, and therefore to the US "program" for the country. These provided that all government employees must be Nicaraguan except for the mixed claims commission, thus excluding North American customs collectors. They also required foreigners to present claims in accordance with Nicaraguan law, in the same manner as Nicaraguan citizens, negating the possibility of future mixed claims commissions. And they authorized only Congress to approve loans. Moreover, Article 2 provided that

> No compacts or treaties shall be concluded which are contrary to the independence and integrity of the Nation, or which in any wise affect its sovereignty, except such as may look toward union with one or more republics of Central America.[16]

For adopting these measures, Chargé Gunther characterized the Mena faction, which controlled the Assembly, as "uniformly anti-American." He tried to block promulgation of the constitution until January, when a new US minister would arrive. But when Gunther and Diaz called Constituent Assembly President Ignacio Suárez in for a conference, the Assembly made the new constitution official anyway, inserting a preamble that declared, "The interposition of the Chargé d'Affaires of the United States carries with it, in effect, an insult to the national autonomy and the honor of the Assembly."[17]

But plans for the loan were proceeding even without Assembly approval. The previous June, Salvador Castrillo, Diaz's representative in Washington, had signed an agreement with Secretary Knox providing for a $15 million loan from North American bankers and for US control of Nicaraguan customs. This loan was supposed to reform Nicaragua's currency, restructure its debt, pay the claims of foreigners, and create a new National Bank—all under United States supervision and control. The banking houses of Brown Brothers & Company and J. and W. Seligman & Company of New York obligingly agreed to float the loan.

Although the Knox-Castrillo Convention was never ratified by the US Senate, its provisions were carried into effect anyway. While awaiting Senate approval, the bankers negotiated an interim $1.5 million loan with the Diaz government. Modeled on the Knox-Castrillo agreement, it was secured by Nicaraguan customs receipts; the collector would be a US citizen picked by the bankers, approved by the secretary of state, and finally "appointed" by Nicaragua.[18] This loan was approved by the Constituent Assembly on October 9, reportedly without discussion.

Of the $1.5 million, $100,000 was to constitute the initial capital for a National Bank. The rest would go toward currency reform, retiring Nicaragua's inflated paper pesos. The rationale for obtaining a US loan in the first place had been, according to the Dawson Pact, the need to "rehabilitate the public finances." Perhaps the signers of the pact—Estrada, Diaz, Chamorro, and Mena—had foreseen that their regime would bring public finances to a state where they truly would need rehabilitation, because that is exactly what happened. The condition the monetary reform was supposed to correct resulted, by and large, not from the Zelaya-Madriz Administration, but from that which followed it—that is, from the very regime established by the US intervention.

At the time of Zelaya's demise the Nicaraguan peso—nominally worth a dollar—had been trading at nine to one. By the time the US monetary experts arrived at the end of 1911, however, it was being exchanged at the rate of twenty to the dollar. Of the more than 49 million paper pesos then in circulation, between 32 and 36 million had been issued since the Conservatives' return to power. Of that amount, 10 million was a secret printing ordered by Diaz in October of 1911—after the loan agreement had been signed. In other words, a large part of the $1.4 million—perhaps $600,000—would be used up in retiring 10 million in paper pesos that Diaz had printed after contracting the loan. Diaz was signing the loan agreement with one hand, as it were, and throwing the money away (so far as the nation was concerned) with the other.[19] And he gave away the customs and the National Bank in the bargain. Such were the doings of the "reformer" put in power by the United States to clean up the "mess" supposedly made by Zelaya.

The new emissions of paper money, along with the balance left in the treasury by Madriz, had gone to pay the claims of the victorious Conservative leaders—Diaz and his cronies—against the former Liberal government. Many of these monetary compensations were for "moral sufferings." Numerous allegedly fraudulent claims were presented and paid; Diaz personally got the equivalent of $63,000, the amount he claimed to have loaned the anti-Zelaya uprising. US citizens and business interests on the Atlantic Coast received at least $400,000 in secret payments from the Nicaraguan treasury, either to refund sums advanced to the "revolution" or as compensation for other services rendered. Some Conservative leaders made out even better than Diaz. General Mena and his relatives received upward of $100,000. Topping the list was the Chamorro family, which helped itself to 6,138,837 pesos—more than $500,000. All these payments, moreover, were made in violation of the Dawson agreements, which specified that all claims were to be adjudicated by the Mixed Claims Commission. Chargé Gunther obtained copies of treasury records documenting the sub rosa payments and forwarded these to the State Department early in 1912. But Washington confined itself to a perfunctory and unpublicized protest to Diaz, apparently disinclined to pursue the embarrassing issue with its Nicaraguan protégés.[20]

In March 1912, Charles Conant and Francis Harrison, financial experts appointed by the New York bankers, finished drafting a monetary law for Nicaragua. It established a new unit of currency, the *córdoba*, which would be backed by gold and valued at par with the US dollar. Since the $1.4 million provided by the loan was not sufficient for the conversion, they recommended a supplementary loan of $750,000.

As security for the first loan, the US bankers held a lien on Nicaragua's customs receipts. These were collected under the supervision of Colonel Clifford W. Ham, a retired US army officer who had served in the Philippine occupation administration. Ham's appointment by the bankers was officially approved by Secretary Knox. In addition, the first loan agreement created the National Bank of Nicaragua—as a US corporation, incorporated in Connecticut. Its initial $100,000 capital was furnished by

Nicaragua out of the first loan. Although Nicaragua was therefore the sole stockholder, all shares were retained by the US bankers as additional collateral for the loan, and the Diaz government agreed to vote the stock for the directors they selected. In short, Brown Brothers and Seligman had obtained control of the National Bank of Nicaragua without paying a cent for it. In addition, they got a preferential option to buy 51 percent of the Bank's shares whenever they wanted.[21]

In the supplementary loan agreement signed in March 1912 the bankers obtained, besides a second lien on the customs receipts, control of the Nicaraguan railroad and steamship company. The Pacific Railroad of Nicaragua was incorporated in Maine. As with the National Bank, Brown Brothers and Seligman had an option to buy; meanwhile they controlled the board of directors.* They were also named fiscal agents for the republic and authorized to renegotiate the Ethelburga loan, which Zelaya had contracted in 1909, shortly before his downfall. The Ethelburga Syndicate in London retained a credit of some $2 million that was intended for the purchase of equipment for the Atlantic railroad. These funds, too, were now pledged to Brown Brothers and Seligman against their outstanding loans to Nicaragua.[23]

To gain National Assembly approval for dealings that clearly violated the three-month-old constitution required some extraordinary—not to say astounding—measures. Orders were given to delay the train carrying deputies from the Liberal departments of the Northwest until the contracts were approved. This was done with the active collusion of General Mena, who controlled the railroad. Mena had been cooperating with Diaz in view of the latter's seeming support for the law passed the previous October that named him as Diaz's successor. But while the Mena faction backed the proposed new loan agreements in the preliminary Assembly discussion, at the eleventh hour they realized that the railroad scheme was part of a plan by Diaz and the Yankees to deprive their leader of the presidency. In a sudden about-face, General Mena's supporters blocked the legislation.

At Diaz's orders, the Assembly held a rump nighttime session without the presence of either its president or secretary. Since the secretary refused to hand over the keys to the archives where the national seal and the necessary documents were kept, the Diaz supporters simply broke in. The ses-

* The bankers contemplated using the railroad as the western leg of a new ocean-to-ocean shipping line that would include canalization of the San Juan River. Reiterating the "Fish Corollary," Acting Secretary of State Huntington Wilson told them they were free to make the necessary contracts with Nicaragua, provided that "no transisthmian route shall be established without the advice and consent" of the United States, and that there be no "alienation" of the line "to any foreign company or government," except with US approval.[22]

sion, which lasted only long enough to read aloud the laws in question and approve them, lacked even a statutory quorum.[24] The US advisers and diplomatic personnel who were so interested in these measures and carefully watched their progress made no protest however.

About this time Secretary of State Philander Knox visited Nicaragua. Considered by many the father of Dollar Diplomacy, Knox was then on an image-building tour of Latin America. The hostility that greeted this high US official was without precedent; it would not be equaled until Richard Nixon's disastrous tour in the 1950s, following the US-sponsored overthrow of the Arbenz government in Guatemala. In Nicaragua March 5-6, 1912, Knox was greeted by anti-US demonstrations despite the imposition of rigid press censorship and the imprisonment of the staffs of two Liberal newspapers. There were even rumors of a plot to blow up the train that carried Knox from Corinto to Managua.[25]

NICARAGUA began paying 6 percent interest on the first loan as of October 15, 1911, the nominal date of issue. But the monetary conversion didn't begin until April 1912, and therefore none of the money left New York until that time. In the interim, the funds were held by a "trustee," the United States Mortgage and Trust Company. The trustee paid no interest on the money held; instead, it charged Nicaragua for its services. Out of the funds it administered, the trustee also paid fees to Brown Brothers and Seligman for acting as fiscal agents for Nicaragua, and reimbursed the expenses they incurred contracting the loan and incorporating the National Bank and railroad. Meanwhile, Colonel Ham, the collector-general of customs appointed by the bankers, had begun his work in December 1911; during the ensuing six months he turned approximately $900,000 over to them. Since the first phase of the monetary conversion involved only $780,000, Brown Brothers and Seligman were, in effect, lending Nicaragua its own money.[26]

At the end of May 1912, Brown Brothers and Seligman, as fiscal agents for Nicaragua, signed an agreement with the Ethelburga bondholders. After deductions for the interest and principal payments suspended after Zelaya's fall, they received the remaining credit of $1,660,000 to be applied against Nicaragua's outstanding loans. Added to the $900,000 in customs receipts already collected, this money more than repaid the $2,225,000, including interest charges and expenses, that Nicaragua had borrowed—but not yet wholly received—from the New York bankers. It should then have been possible, therefore, for the republic to finance the monetary conversion with its own customs receipts, and without Brown Brothers, J. and W. Seligman, or Ham, the customs collector. But that is not what happened. For the bankers had arranged as part of the agreement with the Ethelburga

Syndicate that the collector-general of customs would continue his collections to pay off the 1909 bonds, while they themselves would remain as fiscal agents to manage the business. This, it seems, turned into another highly profitable operation for Brown Brothers and Seligman. According to US Senator William Alden Smith of Michigan, instead of retiring the Ethelburga bonds by buying them up on the open market, the bankers purchased an undetermined number for their own account at 25 percent of face value, and as fiscal agents redeemed them at par. In addition, they were accused of making a profit of several hundred thousand dollars by employing different exchange rates for the English pound in calculating the debits and credits of the country they supposedly represented.[27]

These new agreements signed in the spring of 1912 intensified Nicaraguans' outrage at the wholesale giveaway of the nation's resources and sovereignty. The growing mood of rebelliousness was fed by the Diaz clique's looting of the treasury, which not only produced moral indignation, but worsened the economic difficulties stemming from the 1909-1910 civil war. General Mena, who saw his own ambitions for the presidency being thwarted by the intrigues of Diaz and the North Americans, saw an opportunity to capitalize on the nationalist, anti-Diaz sentiment. He began to do some plotting of his own.

Matters came to a head at the end of July 1912. Diaz tried to wrest control of the army from Mena by naming Emiliano Chamorro, who had recently returned from exile, as commander-in-chief. Fighting broke out between troops loyal to the competing factions.[28] Retreating to Masaya, Mena reconvened the National Assembly and organized a rival government. His action was seconded by Liberal uprisings in other parts of the country, leaving the Diaz-Chamorro forces holding only the capital.

Mena was soon to regret his belated opposition to the railroad giveaway. Together with the lake and river steamers, which belonged to the same company, the railroad was the principal means of transport for troops and munitions. Naturally, Mena and his allies immediately took control of a large portion of both. But as soon as they did, Thomas O'Connell, who had recently arrived in Nicaragua to manage the railway for Brown and Seligman, called upon US Minister Weitzel to rescue this "American" property from the rebels. Although the government of Nicaragua was still the sole stockholder, the railroad and steamship company had been incorporated in Maine and put in the care of the New York bankers; that was enough. O'Connell was joined in his plea by Bundy Cole, manager of the National Bank of Nicaragua, Inc., another "American" corporation.

On July 29, when the fighting began, the US minister took personal charge of reorganizing the Managua police force. He held several consultations with Diaz at the US Legation, apparently coaching him on how to handle the situation. Nevertheless, in good diplomatic form, Weitzel penned a note to the Nicaraguan Foreign Ministry requesting protection for United States property. With equal gravity, Foreign Minister Diego Chamorro replied that, since it had its hands full, "my Government desires that the Government of the United States guarantee with its forces security for the property of American citizens in Nicaragua and that it extend its protection to all the inhabitants of the Republic."[29]

A contingent of ninety-five sailors from the *USS Annapolis,* anchored at Corinto, arrived in Managua the following day, August 4, 1912. Under the guise of protecting the US Legation, which was located close to the presidential palace, they immediately took part in repulsing a rebel assault on the city. Two days later another contingent landed at Bluefields, and President Taft quickly approved Weitzel's request for more troops. On August 14, Major Smedley Butler, a participant in the 1910 intervention at Bluefields, arrived from the Canal Zone at the head of 350 Marines. Soon there were nearly 3,000 sailors and Marines on Nicaraguan soil, supported by eight warships off the coasts.[30]

Hostile demonstrations met the arriving Marines in León and elsewhere, and several demonstrators were killed in clashes with the landing force. The divergence between the stated purpose of intervention—to protect lives and property—and the actions of US troops in Nicaragua soon prompted expressions of concern both in Central America and the United States. When President Manuel Araujo of El Salvador cabled his misgivings to President Taft, he was told that the United States was acting "under the moral mandate of the Washington conventions." The US alone could do this, Taft told Araujo, "because of its entire aloofness from those political interrelations which might be used to challenge and frustrate the efforts, however sincere, of any one of the Central American republics." Meanwhile, Salvadoran diplomats were warned that "the quality of the friendship of Salvador will be measured by its attitude in the premises." But Araujo rejected the assertion that the Washington Conference had given the United States any mandate to intervene:

> I see with pain that the agreements contracted in Washington by the Central American delegates, merely under the good offices and generous hospitality which ex-President Roosevelt tendered them, are apparently being invoked in favor of the attitude recently assumed. Salvador, being one of the contracting parties, deems it its undeniable duty . . . to declare to President Taft in the most frank and respectful form that the good offices which the United States and Mexico afforded to the Central American plenipotentiaries are always remembered with gratefulness, but that they should be limited to that which they in good faith signify.[31]

To deflect the mounting criticism, the State Department issued a major policy statement early in September. The purpose of the Nicaraguan intervention, it said, was "to take the necessary measures for an adequate legation guard at Managua, to keep open communications, and to protect American life and property." But the statement did not stop there. There were "important moral, political, and material interests to be protected," including the Emery claim, "the indemnity for the killing of Groce and Cannon in the Zelaya war," and "various American claims and concessionary interests." It reiterated the assertion that the United States had a moral mandate from the Washington Conference of 1907 "to exert its influence for the preservation of the general peace of Central America, which is seriously menaced by the present uprising." While elaborating these several aims, the State Department made no pretense of neutrality: the United States, it said, not only opposed Zelaya the individual, but "the system" as well; it "could not countenance any movement to restore the same destructive regime." It accused the current rebellion of having committed all manner of atrocities, labeling it "the most inexcusable in the annals of Central America." It asserted that the United States intended to bring about the "restoration of lawful and orderly government in order that Nicaragua may resume its program of reforms unhampered by the vicious elements who would restore the methods of Zelaya."[32]

US intervention forces first declared the capital a "neutral zone," removing any possibility that Diaz could be overthrown. Later, under the pretext of reopening the railroad and rescuing foreigners who were said to be in danger, US troops played the major role in recapturing for the government the other important cities of western Nicaragua.

General Mena, who occupied Granada, acceded to a US ultimatum late in September, and surrendered to the commander-in-chief of United States forces, Admiral Southerland. He was conducted to the Canal Zone aboard the *USS Cleveland* and held there in detention until Diaz judged it safe to release him. But former Zelayist General Benjamin Zeledón, the leader of the Liberals holding Masaya, refused to surrender. Instead, he sent Admiral Southerland his "most energetic protest" against the violation of Nicaragua's sovereignty. Such conduct he said,

> extraordinary in any nation of the civilized world, is yet more so in the United States, which complained bitterly about the government presided over by General Zelaya, characterizing it as despotic, and thus establishing a precedent unique in international law: that of suppressing the internal despotism of a country in order to establish a foreign despotism . . . It is not by acts such as those related that the doctrines of Pan-Americanism, whose commentaries have for so long filled the pages of the world press, are put into practice.[33]

US troops were heavily involved in the final actions in and around Masaya, the most important being led or conducted entirely by Marines and navy "bluejackets." According to the Annual Report of the Secretary of the Navy for 1913,

> the most notable event during the campaign was the assault and capture of Coyotepe, resulting in entirely crushing the revolution and restoring peace to Nicaragua; this assault lasted 37 minutes under heavy fire from the rebel forces before the position, which was considered impregnable by the federal forces, could be taken.[34]

After US forces had enabled them to capture Masaya, Diaz's troops took Zeledón prisoner. Major Butler wired Admiral Southerland:

> Government forces have captured Zeledon and have asked me if we want him . . . If you direct I can have Zeledon sent back here under guard or protected by my men in Masaya. Personally [I] would suggest that through some inaction on our part some one might hang him.

Southerland's reply to Butler, if any, is not known. But Zeledón, apparently wounded during capture, died mysteriously shortly afterward. Later, as a lesson to others, his body was paraded through the streets on the back of a horse.[35]

With the country under martial law, the principal cities occupied by US sailors and Marines, the National Assembly dissolved, and all those who supported the uprising disenfranchised, a presidential election was held. Marines guarded the polling places and there was but one candidate for president: Adolfo Diaz. George Weitzel, the US minister, reportedly intervened in the councils of the Conservative Party to ensure that Diaz, not Emiliano Chamorro, was the candidate. In return for supporting Diaz, Chamorro was given the job of minister to Washington with the promise that he would be president at the next election. Only three or four thousand people were allowed to vote—according to one report only eighty voted in León, the second largest city. In his report to Secretary Knox, Weitzel seemed pleased that the election had fulfilled the requirements of the Nicaraguan constitution and the Dawson Pact.[36]

US troops began to leave after the election. But Weitzel advised keeping a token force in the country, since "withdrawal of all marines would be construed as the tacit consent of the United States to renew hostilities."[37] Accordingly, a "legation guard" of about one hundred Marines remained in Nicaragua for the next thirteen years, a reminder of United States support for Diaz and his successors.

Diaz and his allies, most notably the Chamorro and Cuadra families, knew how to turn the failed uprising of 1912 to good account.* Once again all manner of claims were presented for losses purportedly suffered during the revolt. These new claims could no more withstand scrutiny by the Mixed Claims Commission than could the earlier ones, and since the National Bank had been given sole power to issue notes, the treasury could no longer simply print paper money to pay them. Therefore, Pedro Rafael Cuadra, the minister of hacienda (treasury), handed out letters of credit in amounts reportedly totaling $3 million. These were later exchanged for internal bonds or otherwise recognized as valid national debt; they were then paid off with new loans negotiated in the United States. Thus an internal bond issue of 1913, having a nominal value of $480,000 brought only $72,000 cash into the treasury; the letters of credit made up the balance. While proceeds from these bonds were intended to pay the back salaries of government employees, the money ended up going to Diaz himself for repayment of another of his "loans" to the government.[39]

Before 1910, the state monopoly on the sale of tobacco and alcohol produced annual revenues of $1.5 million, enough to service the foreign debt and pay some domestic expenses besides. This important source of revenue now began to dry up as the Diaz regime failed to pay the tobacco harvesters and *aguardiente* distillers with whom the government had contracts. The proceeds of a $240,000 loan, obtained from New Orleans bankers to pay arrears to tobacco producers, reportedly went directly into the hands of the minister of hacienda, in violation of the fiscal laws, and never reached the intended recipients. Furthermore, when the lender protested that he wasn't receiving payments regularly, it came to light that Diaz had been speculating with the revenues intended to pay off the loan.[40] Charges of misappropriation of funds were legion; corruption was the norm of public life.

Undemocratic as it was, not even the 1912 election could give Diaz a rubber stamp legislature. As soon as the new Congress was seated, it once again broke up into factional cliques. As a result, Diaz and his cronies were constantly challenged by those seeking to make political capital from the regime's peculations. In 1913 the Congress passed a budgetary law in an effort to bring corruption under control. Diaz ignored it, and for his entire term in office the nation never had so much as a proper budget. For the fiscal year ending June 30, 1914 nearly $800,000 was missing from the treasury. At the end of that year, a document read in the Congress alleged that $100,000 of a new loan had gone to pay Diaz's personal bills. Not-

---

* There were said to be at least a dozen Cuadras holding important positions during Diaz's term in office. Under the Emiliano Chamorro government that followed, seventeen Chamorros held important posts.[38]

withstanding all the measures supposedly directed toward financial and economic stability, the country went ever deeper into hock, and the economy deteriorated steadily.[41]

Teachers went without pay for periods of three to six months; postal employees were paid in stamps, which they then sold in the street at a discount. Public workers were evicted from their lodgings for inability to pay rent, and many were simply forced to abandon their posts and seek work in the coffee harvest. The result was a virtual collapse of public services. By late 1914 the situation had become so acute that the capital was threatened by an uprising of government workers.[42]

In order to meet this new emergency, a special emission by the National Bank of 1.5 million córdobas was authorized in December 1914. Of the 500,000 earmarked to pay public workers, 230,000 was diverted to Diaz to repay more of his undocumented loans. The printing of new money caused a 30 percent inflation of the córdoba—the just-instituted monetary unit that was supposed to remain at par with the dollar. Moreover, the New York bankers and Ethelburga bondholders consented to a moratorium on loan repayments so the customs receipts and other revenues pledged to them could be used to meet the crisis. These measures, in turn, undermined the economy and created a financial panic.[43]

WITH A SPLIT in the Republican Party and Theodore Roosevelt running on the "Bull Moose" ticket, President Taft failed to win a second term; the 1912 election went to Democrat Woodrow Wilson. Diaz was desperate for a new loan, but Brown Brothers and Seligman would not, in the words of the US minister, "advance another dollar . . . until they are certain that the incoming administration at Washington will continue the present policy." Despite Secretary Knox's assurance that "there is no foundation for the rumor that the incoming administration will change the present policy of the United States toward Central America," the bankers continued to be wary.[44]

Their fears were not allayed when Wilson declared in March 1913, just a few days after his inauguration, that he sought to extend a "hand of genuine disinterested friendship" to Latin America—a seeming break with the policies of his predecessors. Nor were they comforted by the new president's choice of William Jennings Bryan to head the State Department; Bryan, after all, had run for president in 1900 as an "anti-imperialist." Now secretary of state, he asserted that "the policy inaugurated by President Wilson seeks to bring international dealing into harmony with universal conscience."[45]

It turned out that Bryan's idea of how to combat the excesses of dollar diplomacy was for the United States government, not private enterprise, to assume the responsibility for making loans. Not only would the deal-ings be cleaner that way, they would, as he put it, give the US "increased influence." But Wilson rejected the plan; getting congressional approval for what was then a novel idea was too problematical. Seeing, therefore, no alternatives that it considered acceptable, the new administration was, in the words of Ray Stannard Baker, Wilson's authorized biographer, "ir-resistibly forced into arrangements that did not differ greatly, in aggravat-ed cases like that of Nicaragua, from those of Taft and Knox." The war against dollar diplomacy was a short one, and, as a Bryan biographer chose to phrase it, "not productive of any notable results."[46]

The Wilson Administration not only gave the go-ahead to Brown Brothers and Seligman, it embarked upon a policy in Nicaragua that, ac-cording to the *New York Times,* "outdoes the so-called dollar diplomacy of previous Administrations and opens an entirely new chapter in the his-tory of our foreign relations." In comparison with this new policy, the paper said, the old policies "more nearly resemble ten-cent diplomacy."[47]

Just one month before leaving office, Taft had submitted to the Senate for consideration the draft of a treaty negotiated by Minister Weitzel and Diego Chamorro, the Nicaraguan foreign minister. For a one-time pay-ment of $3 million, the United States would get exclusive rights to build a canal across Nicaragua and ninety-nine-year renewable leases on the Corn Islands in the Caribbean and on a site for a naval base in the Gulf of Fonse-ca. With the full approval of Wilson, Secretary Bryan and Emiliano Chamor-ro, Diaz's envoy to Washington, renegotiated the agreement. The Bryan-Chamorro Treaty, as it became known, added the provisions of the Platt Amendment to the draft treaty negotiated by the Taft Adminis-tration.[48]

Part of a 1901 Army appropriations bill, the Platt Amendment had speci-fied conditions for the withdrawal of US occupation forces from Cuba af-ter the war with Spain. In return for nominal independence, Cubans were required to adopt an amendment to their constitution giving the United States the right to supervise Cuban foreign policy and to intervene in Cu-ba's internal affairs whenever it saw fit. Cuba had not previously enjoyed an independent existence, so the excuse was advanced that the United States had a duty to "protect" the fledging nation it had "liberated" from Spain.

But Nicaragua had a long history of formal independence. The attempt to extend the Platt Amendment to Nicaragua, therefore, heralded what the *Times* buoyantly called "a new era in our Latin American rela-tions . . . due to a cheerful acceptance and amplification by President Wil-son's Administration of the much-condemned dollar diplomacy of his predecessors." It appeared that such "protectorates" were not to be the exception but the rule, "the entering wedge in a general programme of bringing all the weaker countries on this hemisphere, and certainly all those of Central America, under the guardianship of the United States."[49]

The idea of applying the Platt Amendment to Nicaragua originated with Adolfo Diaz and was repeated by him on several occasions. The Taft Administration had chosen to ignore the suggestion, apparently believing that the never-ratified Knox-Castrillo loan agreement and the canal deal would give the US all the leverage it needed in Nicaragua. But for Bryan, this was an opportunity not to be passed up. He wrote President Wilson:

> While the Platt amendment provision is asked for by the Nicaraguan government, and is intended for the benefit of that government, still I think that it is of advantage to us, in that it will give us the right to do that which we might be called upon to do anyhow. We cannot escape the responsibilities of our position, and this is an opportune time for us to secure the necessary treaty provision, as we can secure it at their request.[50]

Woodrow Wilson wired Diaz:

> I am gratified to learn that the policy of this Government toward Cuba has so favorably impressed you. Having the assurance that these provisions of the proposed treaty embodying the substance of what is known as the Platt amendment have been written at your request . . . it will give me great pleasure to give the treaty my cordial approval.[51]

Adolfo Diaz

Emiliano Chamorro

The attitude of Diaz and his successors, Emiliano and Diego Chamorro, toward a US protectorate was understandable. Without doubt there had been corruption in the Zelaya Administration that preceded them, but it was the kind of corruption that accompanied the rise of capitalism everywhere, including the United States. At the same time, the rule of the dynamic class of coffee grower-exporters that Zelaya represented brought many progressive reforms and structural improvements. The regime installed by the United States, on the other hand, was totally parasitic. For Diaz and company, corruption was not a sideline, it was a way of life; they were not capitalists, they were outright thieves. Lacking a social base beyond the circle of graft, they looked to the protection of the US to sustain them in power.

During Senate hearings on the Bryan-Chamorro Treaty, W. Bundy Cole, manager of the National Bank of Nicaragua, Inc., was asked whether he thought Diaz could remain in power without US support. Cole, who literally paid Diaz's salary, and who, as an employee of the New York bankers, was certainly not hostile to his regime, replied, "I think the present government would last until the last coach of marines left Managua station, and I think President Diaz would be on that last coach." Emiliano Chamorro reportedly boasted that his treaty with Bryan would insure Conservative domination for at least a hundred years.[52]

The proposed treaty produced a storm of protest throughout Latin America. The Central American states in particular felt their independence threatened. Moreover, the canal option and proposed naval base in the Gulf of Fonseca violated existing treaty rights of Costa Rica and El Salvador. Wilson, according to his biographer, "rarely gave the [Latin American] subjects under consideration his full attention," preferring to leave such matters to Bryan. It seems he only learned the Central American states were upset with the treaty from reading about it in the newspapers. But the Senate, or at least a part of it, was more attuned to the attitudes of the "backyard" neighbors, and the treaty had a difficult time before that body. It was not ratified until two years later, and then only after the "Platt Amendment" clause had been scrapped and a proviso added "that nothing in said convention is intended to affect any existing right" of Costa Rica, El Salvador, or Honduras.* As for the Nicaraguan Congress, it reportedly ratified the treaty after its text was read to them in English with US Marines stationed outside the doors.[54]

The treaty modifications did not placate Central Americans, however.

---

* Convenient for those seeking to overcome senatorial objection to the treaty, a story circulated in November 1915 that Canadian investors were trying to get a jump on the US by negotiating a contract to build a trans-Nicaragua railroad.

In a memorandum to the Senate Foreign Relations Committee accompanying the final

Both Costa Rica and El Salvador brought suit against Nicaragua before the Central American Court of Justice. While the court ruled that it lacked authority to nullify the Bryan-Chamorro Treaty, as it involved a power not formally signatory to the Washington Conventions, it did find that the rights of Costa Rica and El Salvador had been injured. Regarding the Gulf of Fonseca, it ordered Nicaragua to use whatever means were available under international law to restore the pre-treaty rights of El Salvador.[55] Supported by the United States, however, Nicaragua ignored the ruling. In doing so it delivered a blow from which the court never recovered.

The Central American Court of Justice had been an outstanding achievement for the 1907 Washington Peace Conference, notwithstanding that it resulted largely from Roosevelt's diplomatic intervention in Central America. During its ten-year existence the court remained aloof from the frequently petty factional squabbles of Central America; it set an example for the World Court of Justice at the Hague that came afterward. But the Washington Conventions were useful to Washington only so long as they served the strategic objectives of the US. The Taft Administration violated the spirit of the treaties by supporting the Estrada-Diaz uprising and ignoring the newly-created arbitration machinery, only to turn around three years later and cite them as a "moral mandate" to intervene militarily in support of Diaz. Now that the court—the only operative product of the Washington Conference—was upholding Central American rights against the United States itself, the Wilson Administration evidently felt that it had outlived its usefulness. But that was not all.

The ember of Central American unity had continued to glow ever since the federation broke up in 1838. The perennial projects of reunion always came to grief over the manuevering or paranoia of one political faction or another, but the eventual success of the endeavor was taken for granted by all; indeed, Central Americans generally considered themselves members of one nation. The last, and seemingly final, effort to revive the federation occurred during 1920-21. On that occasion Nicaragua—no doubt coached by the United States—insisted that the projected federal constitution include a clause formally recognizing the Bryan-Chamorro Treaty and, by implication, repudiating the rulings of the Central American Court of Justice. It was an obvious maneuver to sabotage the talks, and it worked. Believing a territorially fragmented federation without Nicaragua to be impractical, Costa Rica pulled out. El Salvador, Honduras, and Guatemala decided to unite on their own, and their merger had been formally con-

version of the treaty, Bryan wrote, "The question of including these [Platt Amendment] paragraphs in a separate treaty is reserved for future consideration."[53]

summated when a right-wing uprising began in Guatemala. Refusing to recognize the union, the United States invoked the non-intervention provisions of the 1907 Washington treaties to bar Honduras and El Salvador from aiding the Guatemalan government, whose overthrow put an end to the experiment.[56]

THE INTEREST of the United States in the Bryan-Chamorro Treaty did not stem from any plan to build a second canal; quite the contrary. In a memorandum to the Senate Foreign Relations Committee accompanying submission of the treaty for consideration, Secretary Bryan wrote:

> While at the present time the Panama Canal offers every prospect of being satisfactory, yet in all human affairs there are always contingencies which must be taken into consideration, and dealing with a great subject it is wise to consider all the possibilities that may enter into the problem. The price at which the canal route is to be bought is so reasonable that we can afford to purchase it even though there may be no immediate need for the construction of a canal along that route. In the second place, the Nicaragua route offers a prize to revolutionists, who, so long as it is open to negotiation can offer it as a contingent pledge for the securing of funds to carry on insurrection. Our interest in the peace and stability of the Government of Nicaragua is sufficient to justify such an expenditure as an aid to the maintenance of orderly government in Nicaragua. Third, as long as the canal route is upon the market for sale, we shall be continually disturbed by the reports, even if they be without foundation, that other governments are trying to secure the right to build a canal . . . The money which it is proposed to pay for the option on the Nicaraguan Canal route will be well spent if it does nothing more than remove from the arena of discussion the possibility of sale to other countries.*[58]

The $3 million payment was not released until July 1917. The treaty specified that the money could be spent only with the approval of the US

---

* Testifying on behalf of the Bryan-Chamorro Treaty, George Weitzel—the former US minister to Nicaragua and co-signer of the treaty in its original form—tried to prove the existence of a danger that an extra-hemispheric power might build a rival canal through Nicaragua. He introduced what he said was a translation of excerpts from an instruction of Zelaya's foreign minister to the Nicaraguan representative in Paris, written in 1908. The document mentioned efforts by Colombia to interest Japan in an alternate canal route and suggestions by an English consul that Britain and Japan together might want to build a canal through Nicaragua. It instructed the minister to suggest to the Japanese ambassador in Paris, confidentially and unofficially, that any "overtures" Japan might make would be well received by Nicaragua. The evidence, open to question on several counts, appears to be the sole basis for the claim, frequently repeated in print, that the Zelaya government sought to sell canal rights to Japan, Germany, or Britain.[57]

secretary of state; accordingly, $2.5 million was applied to Nicaragua's debt payments, suspended since 1914, and most of the funds never left the United States. The remainder was used to pay salary arrears of Nicaraguan government employees.[59]

All the while Nicaragua's debts continued to mount, though the country had nothing to show for them. The bankers made new loans and exercised their option to buy 51 percent of the railroad shares—for $1 million, a price well below their estimated value. They acquired 51 percent of the National Bank stock for a mere $153,000. The National Bank, in turn, took over collection of the internal revenues from tobacco and *aguardiente;* it became the sole depository for government funds and served as paymaster.* It didn't pay interest on government deposits, however; instead it collected a commission. On one sum of $158,000, deposited for payment of claims adjudicated by the Mixed Claims Commission, for example, the bank reportedly charged the Nicaraguan government $8,047.23 for expenses. To top it off, the National Bank of Nicaragua, Inc. was exempt from all Nicaraguan taxes. Meanwhile, the US-owned bank used its depositors' funds to create the Compañia Mercantil de Ultramar, through which it obtained control of the export of Nicaraguan coffee and other products.[61]

The monetary reform was the centerpiece of North American financial intervention. It was supposed to make the country attractive to US investors by creating a stable currency, on par with the dollar, that would simplify credit and exchange. Its chief architects were Charles A. Conant and Francis Harrison. Conant, one of the leading banking and monetary experts of the day, had served under President Taft during the latter's term as governor of the Philippines, designing the new US colony's currency system. Conant was a theorist, moreover, who devoted considerable attention to the role of the United States in the world economy. As an influential employee of the US government, his views shed light on the intervention in Nicaragua.

According to Conant, the empires of the future would be financial and economic—not necessarily territorial—in nature. In a book published in 1900, *The United States and the Orient,* he wrote:

> Whether the United States shall actually acquire territorial possessions . . . whether they shall adopt the middle ground of protecting sovereignties nominally independent, or whether they shall content themselves with naval stations and diplomatic representatives as the basis for asserting their rights to the free commerce of the East is a matter of detail.

---

* The bank reportedly withheld the salaries of Nicaraguan congressmen until they approved the railroad sale.[60]

Conant saw the importance of "free commerce" not so much in terms of exporting surplus products, but of exporting surplus investment capital. He was saying—from a pro-capitalist standpoint—the same things as anti-capitalist contemporaries like Lenin. And, like them, he felt that government had an important role to play:

> it is when the "trust" has swallowed up its rivals for the control of the local market, and reaches out for the control of foreign markets, that it seeks to bring political power to the aid of economic efficiency or inefficiency . . . It is the struggle between great political powers of the world for bolstering up national economic power which constitutes the cardinal fact of modern diplomacy.[62]

Whether through Conant's efforts or not, US investment in Nicaragua did increase dramatically during the period in question and, regardless of US government intentions, political (including military) power played the leading role in making that possible.

In practice the monetary reform proved to be another highly profitable operation for US bankers and an added disaster for Nicaragua. A large part of the funds loaned for the monetary conversion were used to buy up the old paper pesos in amounts necessary to reduce the rate of exchange from 20 to 1 down to 12.5 to 1. That conversion to the new córdoba would take place when the value of the peso had been stabilized at 12.5 to 1 was supposed to be a secret, to thwart speculators. But the friends of the government, who had received the biggest handouts of paper pesos in the first place, knew the conversion rate in advance. What is more, it was charged that Brown Brothers and Seligman, who had inside information, themselves made huge profits by buying up pesos at 20 to 1 or 15 to 1 and later converting them at 12.5 to 1. In reality it made little difference whether one had advance knowledge of the conversion rate or not; it required a dull wit indeed not to perceive that as the paper money was retired from circulation the value of the remaining bills could only increase. Whether or not the monetary conversion was in itself a good idea, the curious decision to first buy up large quantities of old pesos in order to reach an arbitrarily established rate of exchange proved to be extremely costly for Nicaragua. The conversion also had the unintended effect of raising prices, which, of course, most harmed the country's many poor. And the new currency was in circulation barely a year when the previously mentioned special emission of 1.5 million in unbacked paper córdobas began to destabilize it all over again.[63]

By 1917 Nicaragua's economy was a mess. The country had lost control of its customs receipts; a majority of the shares in its railroad and National Bank had been sold and the remainder mortgaged. Payments on most of the republic's debts, both external and domestic, had been suspended pending receipt of the $3 million from the Bryan-Chamorro Treaty, and many obligations had to be refinanced every six months. Added to all this, the Mixed Claims Commission, which completed its work in 1915, had recognized more than $5 million in claims that had to be paid.

To the State Department it was clear that something had to be done to straighten out the situation created by its Nicaraguan protégés and its banker friends. The "Lansing Plan" of 1917 was advanced as the solution. Named after Robert Lansing, who replaced William Jennings Bryan as secretary of state in 1915, it amounted to placing Nicaragua in formal receivership. Lansing demanded that the Nicaraguans adopt the new financial plan before he would approve disbursal of the proceeds from the Bryan-Chamorro Treaty.

Under the Lansing Plan, Nicaragua's monthly budget for government expenses was fixed at an austere 95,000 córdobas. The republic had to turn over a minimum of 180,000 córdobas quarterly from those internal revenues it still controlled; otherwise, collection of those, too, would be taken over by Clifford Ham, the US-appointed collector-general of customs. Ham was to receive the proceeds from all sources of income, which he would pay directly to foreign lenders or to the National Bank, where they would be apportioned out to other creditors. The plan established a High Commission, composed of one Nicaraguan and two North Americans appointed by the secretary of state, to supervise the entire financial life of the republic, and to rule on any complaints Nicaragua might have about the bankers or about Ham. The latter was to remain as collector-general until all Nicaragua's debts were paid.[64]

For his part, Clifford Ham was in no hurry to leave. He had found himself a comfortable sinecure as Nicaragua's head customs collector: he received a $10,000 annual salary—a small fortune at that time—plus a liberal expense allowance. Concerned that the US might pull out and leave him without a job, he argued for continuance of the protectorate in a magazine article titled "Americanizing Nicaragua." Wrote Ham:

> It would be a crime to withdraw the Marines and stop the baseball craze in Nicaragua. It is the best step towards order, peace, and stability that has ever been taken . . . People who will play baseball and turn out by the thousands every week to see the match games, are too busy to participate in revolutions.[65]

Colonel Ham would not retire from the collector-generalship of Nicaraguan customs until June 1928, after a seventeen-year career.

The "election" of Emiliano Chamorro to the presidency of Nicaragua in 1916 was a virtual carbon copy of the one that gave the office to Adolfo Diaz in 1912. Like Weitzel before him, US Minister Benjamin Jefferson intervened to compel Conservative Carlos Cuadra Pasos to relinquish his candidacy in favor of Chamorro, who, Jefferson had decided, "represents the most popular element of the Conservative Party." The Liberals had nominated Dr. Julian Irias, a former minister in the Zelaya government. But Jefferson informed Irias

> that any candidate would be unsatisfactory to the Department who would cause a disarrangement of the present arrangements between the present Government of Nicaragua and the United States, canal treaty, financial agreements and reforms, and the restoration of the republic's economic system . . . that the candidate must give satisfactory proof of not having taken an active and objectionable part in the administration of President Zelaya . . . that these objections being removed the Department will remain neutral between candidates.

Irias withdrew, leaving Chamorro the only candidate, and, in the words of Minister Jefferson, "President Diaz extended all liberty and freedom to any of those who cared to vote."[66]

But with the Lansing Plan the High Commission became the supreme power in Nicaragua; Emiliano Chamorro was reduced to the role of a subordinate administrator. As part of a new loan contract signed with Brown Brothers in 1920, not only were the provisions of the Lansing Plan reconfirmed, but the High Commission's control over Nicaraguan finances was extended in several particulars.[67]

Because the Nicaraguan government was unable to reach agreement with Brown Brothers on the price for a planned bond issue, most provisions of the 1920 loan contract never became effective. One section that was carried out, however, provided for repurchase by Nicaragua of the railroad stock that had been sold in 1913. For the shares they had acquired for $1 million, the bankers received $300,000 cash and $1,450,000 in treasury bills bearing 9 percent interest. It was a healthy profit, especially since the railroad had been severely decapitalized under their administration. In 1919, before signing the repurchase agreement, Nicaragua commissioned two US engineers to make a survey; they reported that only 43.7 percent of the track and roadbed were in good shape. In seven years of North American ownership the line had been shortened by twenty miles—the Chinandega-El Viejo branch had been allowed to deteriorate to the point that it was unserviceable. No new locomotives and few cars had been purchased, and exorbitant expenses had been incurred through the White Managing Corporation of Baltimore, which received a commission on purchases of equipment for the line plus $15,000 a year to manage it. All the steamers on the San Juan River and most of those on the Great Lake had sunk due to neglect; as a result, the sole route of communication with the Atlantic had been entirely cut off. Yet regular dividends were paid to stockholders, as much as half the gross income by one account.

Even more harmful in its long-term consequences was another result of North American management: the first fifteen miles of the Atlantic Railroad, completed before Zelaya was driven from office, had been torn up. Two thousand tons of rails had disappeared along with other equipment, including locomotives. No trace remained of the grand project for which the Ethelburga loan had been contracted, an obligation that Nicaragua nevertheless continued to pay. As a final humiliation, Nicaragua had to make a $90,000 settlement with the German engineering firm for cancellation of its contract. For all of this, too, the State Department shared responsibility—it maintained an appointee on the railroad's board of directors for the entire period as part of the 1913 agreement that gave the New York bankers control.[68]

THE ADVENT of the 1920s found United States policy in Nicaragua caught in a seemingly insoluble contradiction. The ostensible aim of intervention had been the achievement of stability. But despite the crushing of the 1912 uprising and the continued presence of Marines, no less than ten revolutionary attempts occurred during the years 1913-1924, and the country was under martial law for virtually the whole time.[69] When the State Department allowed the Nicaraguan Conservatives and the New York bankers a free rein, their looting produced economic chaos, popular indignation, and greater instability. When, on the other hand, it tried to bring their excesses under control by creating the High Commission, the increased interference only intensified nationalist opposition to North American control. And new factors were making the situation more volatile still.

The Marines had begun to manifest the degenerative symptoms characteristic of occupation armies. Brawls with Nicaraguans and other incidents became commonplace. On February 8, 1921, Marines wrecked the office of the Managua newspaper *La Tribuna* after it published an article they didn't like. In December of the same year, another group of Marines killed three Nicaraguan policemen who tried to break up a Managua cantina brawl in which they were involved. The following January, four more policemen were killed and five wounded while trying to apprehend four Marines who had gone AWOL.[70]

Then, too, Nicaragua was feeling ripples from the revolutionary wave that came in the wake of the First World War. The period saw the emergence of the country's first true labor unions, influenced by radical ideas, and based at the US-owned mining, lumbering, and banana operations. In 1921 and 1922 big strikes hit the Cuyamel Fruit Company and the Cukra

Development Company, a lumbering enterprise. Labor organization added a new dynamic to Nicaraguan politics.[71]

It was in this explosive context that President Diego Manuel Chamorro, Emiliano Chamorro's uncle, died in office in October 1923. He was succeeded by the vice president, Bartolomé Martinez. Though a member of the Conservative Party, Martinez didn't belong to the traditional Granada-based oligarchy; he was a coffee grower from the northern department of Jinotega, and represented a sort of left wing in the party. Viewed as an "outsider" by the Granada clique, his inclusion in the cabinet had been intended solely to broaden the government's base of support.[72]

Pressed on one side by nationalist popular sentiment and on the other by the propertied classes' fear of radical social upheaval, the Martinez government tried to distance itself to some extent from the policies of its Conservative predecessors. The Republican Conservatives, as Martinez's faction called themselves, sought to conciliate the Liberals by facilitating their participation in local administration. The Liberal majority, known as Nationalist Liberals, favored accommodation and formed a bloc with the Republican Conservatives that became known as the *Transacción*. By ending their traditional animosity and asserting a degree of independence from United States control, this "national unity" coalition sought to reestablish the traditional parties' hegemony over the increasingly restive populace.

The State Department, meanwhile, was seeking a way out of the dead end to which interventionism had led. The Marine occupation of Nicaragua was politically expensive. As Secretary of State Charles Evans Hughes phrased it, "a continuance of American forces in any of those countries is fraught with many possibilities of misunderstanding." The presence of the Marines in Nicaragua, he acknowledged, had

> at times given rise to the assertion, however unjustified it may be, that the United States Government is maintaining in office a government which would otherwise perhaps not be strong enough to maintain itself against the attacks of its political opponents.

In evident contradiction to the foregoing, Hughes added that the Marines could not be withdrawn immediately because "political disturbances might ensue."[73]

Thinking somewhat along the same lines as the Nicaraguan politicians of the Transacción, the State Department saw the need to establish a government in Nicaragua with enough popular support to survive withdrawal of the Marines and permit a more low-profile US involvement. The means to that end were, as Hughes saw it, "to aid the Nicaraguan Government in having an election which would be so fair and free that the people would be contented with the result."[74]

After the experience of 1916, most Liberal leaders had yielded to the philosophy that there was no political future in opposing the United States. Going out of their way to manifest "friendliness," they convinced the State Department that they were ready to accept US "influence" in Nicaragua; as a result they were allowed to participate in the 1920 presidential election. But massive fraud had prevented their victory. Major Jesse Miller, the US military attaché assigned by the State Department to observe the election, had concluded that "a free and honest election is practically impossible under the existing law."[75]

As a consequence the US had imposed on the elder Chamorro, as a condition for recognition, the requirement that he request a North American expert to write a new electoral law. Through the medium of the State Department, on December 15, 1921 Chamorro's government signed a contract with Dr. Harold W. Dodds. Later, after Dodds had written a new electoral law, the US pressured the Nicaraguan Congress to adopt it; that was accomplished in March 1923. The State Department hoped the Marines could be withdrawn after the presidential election of October 1924, the first that would be held under the new law.[76]

Though pursuing parallel aims (stability through a more broadly-based government), the State Department and the Transacción soon found themselves at loggerheads over how to achieve them. Washington policymakers didn't trust Nicaraguans to implement the law in such a way as to guarantee a result that would have popular support. They insisted that the elections be supervised by Dodds and a team of US advisers. The Martinez government vacillated, responding to the influences of disparate elements; some of these opposed US supervision on nationalist grounds, others feared the political consequences of association with the United States but dared not oppose the State Department directly. Martinez allowed Dodds and a few assistants to come to Nicaragua to oversee the registration process, but balked at having US advisers in the country for the voting itself. Failing to agree on a formula for US advisers, the Nicaraguan government accepted the idea of having members of the Marine "legation guard" act as unofficial observers. Even this compromise failed, however, when Secretary Hughes hotly rejected the Nicaraguans' insistence that the Marines appear in civilian clothing.[77] There was clearly little room for nationalism in US Central American policy.

In July 1924 the parties of the Transacción formalized their alliance, nominating Carlos Solórzano, a Republican Conservative, for president and Juan Bautista Sacasa, a Nationalist Liberal, for vice president. Both parties named the same number of candidates for other offices on the fusion ticket, and agreed that appointive posts would likewise be shared equally.[78]

In the election held on October 5, Solórzano defeated Emiliano Chamorro, *caudillo* of the traditional Conservative oligarchy, by a large margin. Not surprisingly, Chamorro supporters, including Adolfo Diaz, protested to the US legation that the results were fraudulent. But the US decided to recognize Solórzano after he signed a statement promising that he would immediately form a "constabulary"—with assistance from the US—to maintain order when the Marines were withdrawn, and that he would "undertake adequate and satisfactory measures with which the Government of the United States could cooperate for the solution of the economic problems of Nicaragua."[79]

It was planned that the Marines would be withdrawn at the end of January, after Solórzano's inauguration. But the new Nicaraguan president, citing fears of "political and economic disturbances," requested that their departure be postponed. The US agreed to keep them in Nicaragua long enough to train a national guard.

The guard had already become a sore point between Washington and the Transacción. Before the election Martinez had agreed to the creation of a "non-political" constabulary to keep order when the Marines left. Implementation was continually postponed, however, no doubt due to disagreements within the shaky coalition over control of the force, its functions, and the role of US advisers. Pressed by the United States to begin formation of the national guard, the Solórzano Administration's sensitivity to nationalist counterpressures became evident. The Nicaraguan Congress didn't approve a US blueprint for the force until May, and only then gave its assent after making substantial changes. Secretary of State Kellogg gave the go-ahead anyhow, only to have the plan run into further trouble over details of how US instructors would be employed. When Nicaragua appointed a nationalist general to prepare the guard regulations and act as liason with the US legation it further increased Washington's displeasure with Solórzano.[80]

The election and the national guard were not the only—nor, perhaps, the most important—points of contention between the United States and the Martinez and Solórzano governments. The independence of the Transacción in economic matters was also apparent. A Nicaraguan economist had drawn up a balance sheet for President Martinez showing that Washington's dollar diplomacy had cost Nicaraguans over $33 million, of which more than $8 million represented profits on various dealings or exorbitant salaries paid to North American officials. Martinez, Solórzano, and their allies took some tentative measures designed to rectify the situation. Martinez's administration completed the repurchase of the railroad and sought to liquidate the loans that formed the pretext for US receivership of the country's finances. When, in 1924, the Bank of Central and South America was negotiating the sale of its assets, Martinez seized the opportunity to buy back its 51 percent interest in the National Bank of Nicaragua.* It cost the country $300,000—nearly twice what the New York bankers paid for the shares. And as part of the deal it had to purchase the Compañia Mercantil de Ultramar for another $300,000. The latter was by that time on the verge of bankruptcy owing to a depression in coffee prices; when the government turned around and sold its assets, it netted only $100,000.[82]

Buying back the stock of the National Bank and gaining control over it were not the same thing, however. North American bank employees, reportedly aided by the high commissioner and customs collector, spread word that Nicaraguan control would result in currency depreciation. The ensuing panic forced Martinez to retreat from a plan to recharter the institution in Nicaragua (it was still a Connecticut corporation). Instead he asked the State Department to send a financial advisor. Meanwhile, three North Americans remained on the bank's board of directors; its president was still Robert F. Loree, a vice president of the Guaranty Trust Company.[83]

The financial advisor appointed by the State Department was Dr. Jeremiah Jenks. A professor of economics and political science at New York University, Jenks was a frequent appointee to government commissions over a period of thirty years. He had been a member of the High Commission for Nicaragua since its formation in 1917; he was also the State Department's appointee on the boards of directors of the bank and railroad. Arriving in Managua a few days after the inauguration of the new president, he advised Solórzano to resell to foreigners the National Bank shares that Nicaragua had just recovered. Jenks reportedly told Solórzano that if his advice were not followed, the bank's customers would withdraw their deposits. The Nicaraguan government agreed, for it was, in the words of Toribio Tijerino, a Nicaraguan member of the bank's board, composed of "very timorous individuals." But plans to sell the shares to Loree, the bank's North American president, were cut short when some not-so-timorous members of the government prevailed on Solórzano to change his mind.

The Nicaraguan majority of the bank's directors then voted to move the deposits to the Royal Bank of Canada, which offered higher interest, while the Nicaraguan Congress rejected a loan contract with Loree's Guaranty Trust Company. "The anti-American sentiments and utterances of most of [Solórzano's] probable collaborators are fully known to the Legation," wrote Chargé Thurston to the State Department at the start of the new Nicaraguan president's term. No doubt his estimation was based

---

* The Bank of Central and South America, of which the National Bank of Nicaragua had become a subsidiary, was a US-based company owned jointly by Brown Brothers, J. and W. Seligman, J.P. Morgan & Co., the Guaranty Trust Co., and W.R. Grace & Co., among others.[81]

on suspiciously independent measures like these.[84]

In September 1925, at the prompting of the Nicaraguan majority on the railroad's board of directors, the Solórzano Administration decided to cancel the contract of the White Managing Corporation. But when it gave notice of the cancellation, Dr. Jenks went to Washington and sent Solórzano a telegram in State Department code, by way of the US minister. The message asked that the White contract be extended for a period of months. Coming as it did, it appeared to Solórzano to be an official request, and he instructed his representatives in the US to comply. At the next meeting of the railroad directors (they were still being held in New York) a Nicaraguan member asked Jenks to explain the purpose of a few months' extension of the White contract. Another of the North American directors replied that many things could happen in Nicaragua during that time.[85]

Less than one month later, on October 25, 1925, Emiliano Chamorro seized La Loma fortress overlooking Managua and presented the governmet with a list of demands; chief among them was expulsion of the Liberals from the government. The Marines had withdrawn on August 1, and *Chamorrista* troops surrounded the fledging National Guard, which had just begun training. Solórzano capitulated. He purged twenty-one Liberal and Republican Conservative congressmen and numerous other officials. Vice President Sacasa was charged with conspiracy. Receiving death threats, Sacasa fled the country. When he refused to return to face the charges the vice presidency was declared vacant.

Chamorro prompted a friendly senator to resign and got himself elected to the seat. Then, as there was no vice president, he had the rump Senate name him first designate to the presidency. Pressuring Solórzano to quit, on January 17, 1926 Emiliano Chamorro again became president of Nicaragua.[86]

X
ALL BUT ONE

*The sovereignty of a people is not up
for discussion—it is to be defended
with arms in hand.*

—Augusto César Sandino, 1929.

THOUSANDS of US Marines and sailors went ashore in Nicaragua
in 1912 to save the Conservative government of Adolfo Diaz—a
government singularly "friendly" to the economic and geopolitical
interests of the United States. A "legation guard" remained for the next
thirteen years to keep Diaz in office, and after him Emiliano Chamorro,
and finally Emiliano's decrepit uncle Diego. These Nicaraguan presidents
acted only with the sufferance of the high commissioner, customs collector, and sundry other officials and advisors appointed by the New York
bankers and the State Department.

But the long-term military occupation of Nicaragua, even by a token
force of one hundred Marines, became a heavy political burden in the post-
war world that the United States had just made safe for democracy. It was
especially so in Latin America, where the Nicaragua intervention brought
esteem for Uncle Sam to a new low. Under Secretary Hughes, the State
Department drafted a plan to oblige its Nicaraguan protégés to hold an
election from which, it was hoped, would emerge a government with a
broad enough base to remain standing when the prop of the Marines was
removed. The plan looked good on paper, from the State Department's
point of view, but it failed miserably in practice. Having once upset the
equilibrium of Nicaragua's internal development, no amount of Yankee
tinkering could set it right again.

It was soon clear that the government resulting from the 1924 election
was shaky. Just a few days after Solórzano's inauguration, the US legation
in Managua advised the State Department that an uprising by the *cachurecos,* as the right-wing Conservatives were known, would immediately follow Marine withdrawal. By the same token, the election had brought to

power a regime whose political coloration was not entirely to Washington's liking, a development seemingly not anticipated by the withdrawal scenario. Some of its members were nationalists ("anti-Americans" in State Department parlance) who were suspiciously insistent that Nicaragua own and control its National Bank and railroad, and be financially independent of the United States. Washington was frustrated with the Nicaraguans' foot-dragging over establishment of the National Guard. Finally, the State Department was being urged to oppose Solórzano by US business interests, and by Chandler P. Anderson, a former Department counsellor serving as Chamorro's Washington lobbyist.[1] If these considerations did not in-spire the decision to now withdraw the Marines—the symbol of US support—and allow the fledgling government to fall, they certainly made that decision a lot easier.

Obviously, military occupation could be used as a tool for controlling governmental succession in Nicaragua. As it turned out, the end of that occupation, or at least its timing, could do the same thing just as effec-tively. Commented *New York Times* correspondent Harold Denny, "Sel-dom if ever has a nation, having full knowledge of the danger, taken deliberately a step whose disastrous results were more thoroughly a mathe-matical certainty than the United States took in ordering this with-drawal."[2]

In any event, once Chamorro had staged his coup, the United States devoted its efforts not toward restoring the purged Liberals and Nation-alist Conservatives to the government, but to giving the coup the appear-ance of constitutionality. In December 1922 Secretary Hughes had summoned Central American representatives to a second Washington con-ference, which resulted in a new set of treaties banning revolution and pledging the maintenance of constitutional government. Now, in 1925, the State Department headed by Frank B. Kellogg was faced with a dilem-ma: it could not recognize Chamorro in flagrant violation of the United States' own injunctions.

The plan that US Minister Charles Eberhardt considered "least danger-ous" consisted in having the Senate reappoint Adolfo Díaz, who was then a senator, to the presidency. Eberhardt warned Chamorro that "were he to become President in this way . . . especially within three months of his armed intimidation of President Solórzano, that step would be of such doubtful legality that the Government of the United States would almost certainly feel compelled to withhold recognition." But Chamorro rebuffed the US envoy, determined to have the presidency for himself.[3]

Chamorro, who as a representative of Uncle Diego had personally signed the Washington treaties, was surprised that the Coolidge Administration did not want him in the presidential palace. "I didn't think they meant it," he reportedly told a friend. "They had taken the marines away. What was I to think?" Meanwhile, Vice President Sacasa, the constitutional successor, tried to appeal to the Washington agreements, declaring from exile, "The Americans are responsible for everything that happens in Nicaragua, and they are obliged to take me there in one of their warships and give me possession of the presidency." Making a pilgrimage to Washington, Sacasa was told that the United States could not use force to put him in power. As it turned out, the US would not allow the Constitutionalists—as supporters of the deposed government called themselves—to use force to put him in power either. Instead the United States pursued a policy toward the Chamorro regime that Minister Eberhardt termed "benevolent non-recognition."[4]

There was a Liberal (Constitutionalist) uprising in Bluefields in May 1926. The Marines promptly landed and declared the town a "neutral zone." The poorly prepared revolt was soon crushed by Chamorro's troops and the Marines left. But in August, armed Liberal exiles landed at several points on the Atlantic Coast. It was clear that Chamorro now faced a serious threat, and Secretary Kellogg exerted renewed pressure for him to resign. Meanwhile, a well-rehearsed formula averted the imminent capture of Bluefields by Sacasa forces: Chamorro's local chief declared himself unable to protect the lives and property of foreigners, and the obliging Marines once again proclaimed a neutral zone. On September 15, President Coolidge embargoed arms shipments to Nicaragua after it became known that Constitutionalists were buying weapons in the United States.[5]

Under pressure from the United States and from business interests, the two sides agreed to a cease-fire in October. They sent representatives to a peace conference aboard the cruiser *USS Denver* at Corinto, supervised by Chargé Lawrence Dennis, who was managing US Nicaragua policy in the absence of Minister Eberhardt. The talks broke down after eight days of fruitless negotiation: the Chamorristas refused to relinquish the presidency they had usurped the previous year, while the opposition insisted on Sacasa's constitutional right to be president on the basis of the 1924 election. Sacasa supporters were willing, however, to submit the question to international arbitration involving the US and the other Central American states. Chargé Dennis declared the idea of foreign arbitration of an internal Nicaraguan political matter to be "preposterous."[6]

Still hoping to persuade Washington to support their cause, the Liberals threatened to continue the armed struggle and to appeal to Mexico for help if they failed to get US backing. Dennis urged the State Department to make "a clear, forceful statement . . . with respect to the continuation of the revolution with the aid of other governments, especially that of Mexico." Such a statement, he said, would "avert disaster" and "smash the doctrine of constitutional restoration by means of foreign aid to revolution, once and for all."[7]

However preposterous foreign arbitration may have seemed to Dennis, the United States now proceeded to its own arbitration of the matter. The *cachurecos* were told that US recognition—necessary to defeat the Constitutionalists—would not be forthcoming so long as Chamorro retained the presidency. The Nicaraguan Congress would have to replace him in such a manner that the proceedings would appear constitutional. Secretary Kellogg told Dennis:

> It is not the desire of the Department to suggest or favor any candidate for the Congress to designate, but should Adolfo Diaz be designated he would be a wise choice. According to the best information now before the Department he is honest and capable and has that firmness of character which is absolutely essential for any person called to fill the difficult position of President of Nicaragua.

Kellogg cautioned the chargé to "use the utmost care to avoid any criticism that the Government of the United States is endeavoring to direct Nicaraguan internal politics."[8]

Following the scenario outlined by Kellogg, Chamorro resigned and Diaz, designated to take his place, was inaugurated on November 14. Official US recognition came three days later. Chamorro received $20,000 from the national treasury to take a junket to Europe, and left the country in December.[9]

The State Department seemed to think that by stage-managing Chamorro's replacement and granting recognition to Diaz, it would defuse popular opposition and convince recalcitrant Liberals that resistance was futile. But on December 1 Sacasa returned from exile in Guatemala, declared himself constitutional president, and established a provisional government at Puerto Cabezas. Mexico granted him recognition. And to Kellogg's surprise, Minister Eberhardt cabled warning of a possible general uprising against Diaz.[10]

Diaz asked for US help, alleging that Nicaragua was the victim of a Mexican invasion. Reluctant to openly take sides in the war, Washington clung to a mask of neutrality, while its actions weighted the scale more and more heavily in Diaz's favor. The Marine occupation of Bluefields prevented the Constitutionalists from capturing that city, and the extension of the "neutral zone" to the customs house at El Bluff preserved an important source of revenue for the Conservatives. The State Department lifted the embargo on arms shipments to Diaz on December 18. Five days later, Marines landed at the Constitutionalist's stronghold of La Barra de Rio Grande and at Puerto Cabezas, their provisional capital. They seized arms stockpiles, declared the areas neutral zones, and gave Sacasa twenty-four hours to get his troops and munitions out of Puerto Cabezas. Then they banned all transmissions dealing with political or military matters from the Puerto Cabezas wireless station, largely cutting Sacasa's communication with the outside world. They prevented his government from collecting taxes or customs duties, even though the US had upheld such collections by anti-Zelaya rebels in 1909-1910. Later, the Marines extended the neutral zones to Las Perlas and other areas of the Atlantic Coast, while US ships tried to prevent arms shipments from reaching the rebels. Despite all this, when protests by journalists compelled the lifting of radio censorship, Sacasa expressed his continued confidence that "President Coolidge will do justice to Nicaragua."[11]

US help notwithstanding, Diaz's position continued to deteriorate. His troops abandoned the eastern half of the country entirely. When the Constitutionalists began a westward advance on the Rio Escondido, Diaz asked that Rama, the gateway to western Nicaragua, be declared a neutral zone. The US obliged, Minister Eberhardt expressing the hope that "with the neutralization of Rama . . . Sacasa might be more inclined to treat with [the] Diaz government." Moreover, the United States announced that the neutral zones, which now included all important areas of the Atlantic Coast, could not be used by the rebels as supply bases.[12]

The neutral zones on the Atlantic Coast denied the Constitutionalists staging and logistical support areas, and impeded their movements. Those on the Pacific side, however, aided the Diaz government: they eventually included most of the important cities, relieving the Conservatives of the need to maintain garrisons, and affording them safe bases for rest, recuperation, and supply.

I N THE UNITED STATES, the increasingly obvious disparity between the disclaimers of partisanship in Washington and the actions of the navy and Marines in Nicaragua evoked growing criticism from Congress and the newspapers. At a December 31, 1926 press conference, President Coolidge insisted that US involvement had the sole aim of protecting lives and property and that his administration continued to follow a policy of strict neutrality. He accused the press of injuring the US image in Latin America by questioning that policy, and of creating a false impression that domestic opinion was divided. Coolidge called on the newspapers to take an "American attitude" by presenting US foreign policy in a good light and helping to generate support for it.[13]

The attack on the press failed to silence criticism. Early in January 1927, Montana Democrat Burton Wheeler introduced a resolution in the Senate calling for withdrawal of US forces; Representative Huddleston of Alabama proposed a similar measure in the House. Wheeler told a rally sponsored by the Non-Intervention Citizens' Committee at New York's Lyric Theatre, "'Protection of life and property' is the classic mask worn by dollar diplomacy when it turns its face toward the American people." He gave his listeners a detailed account of US involvement, concluding, "The State Department has literally gutted the sovereignty of Nicaragua. At this moment it has the little republic hog-tied . . . Every strategic post, fiscal and military, is in the hands of the appointees of the State Department." He described the current policy as "utterly inconsistent with that good-will on which depends international comity and international trade," and said he could "no longer sit silent" to see "the country's legitimate material interests jeopardized by ruthless international bankers and their bureaucratic puppets in the State Department."[14]

Criticism such as Wheeler's forced the Coolidge Administration to search for arguments that could rally support behind its Nicaragua policy. Shortly after Diaz appealed for US aid, reports emanating from both Managua and Washington began to elaborate on the Mexican invasion theme. A November 17 Associated Press dispatch found "the spectre of a Mexican-fostered Bolshevistic hegemony intervening between the United States and the Panama Canal." On December 11, Diaz expanded his previous charges of a Mexican invasion. The Liberals, he said, "in the blindness of political passion," had "allied themselves with the forces of communism, radicalism and religious persecution now in control and running rampant in Mexico." This sinister alliance, the statement continued, was bent upon erecting a regime that "would confiscate property, deny religious freedom, close churches, banish ministers of religion and establish in general in Nicaragua the manifold evils of communism and political disorder now only too apparent in Mexico."

Two weeks later Emiliano Chamorro, en route to Europe, embellished the theme further in a special cable to the *New York Times:*

> There is a secret treaty between Mexico and Sacasa, who is in direct communication with Soviet Russia through Mexico. A union of Central American republics is planned, headed by Mexico, which aims to replace the United States influence in Nicaragua, then Guatemala, Honduras and Salvador.[15]

Anonymous Washington sources, meanwhile, stressed the importance of keeping Diaz in power to foil the plot to "establish a Bolshevist wedge between continental United States and the Panama Canal." Just a week after Coolidge angrily insisted that his policy was one of strict neutrality, the *New York Times* noted, "There is scarcely a pretense at Washington of impartiality, nor is it denied, except feebly and with a sort of sheepish smile, that we have in fact intervened in Nicaragua."[16]

In a statement to Congress on January 10, President Coolidge accused Mexico of providing large quantities of arms to Nicaraguan Liberals, and of trying to establish a government there hostile to the United States. The Mexican-backed Liberals, he claimed, "put in jeopardy the rights granted by Nicaragua to the United States for the construction of a canal" and threatened "large investments in lumbering, mining, coffee growing, banana culture, shipping and also in general mercantile and other colateral business," as well as the security of foreign-held bonds. "There is no question that if the revolution continues American investments and business interests in Nicaragua will be very seriously affected, if not destroyed," he concluded.[17]

Two days later Secretary Kellogg appeared before the Senate Foreign Relations Committee to present evidence to back up the administration's new policy justifications. He passed out a statement entitled "Bolshevist Aims and Policies in Latin America," which contained lengthy quotes from US Communist, Soviet, and other radical sources manifesting their desire to support anti-imperialist movements in Latin America. But the Kellogg paper contained no evidence of any "Bolshevist" links with the Mexican government; it did not even mention Nicaragua, much less provide proof that Mexico was arming the Nicaraguan Liberals. Still, it was reported widely as proving "that the Calles government of Mexico is seeking to establish in Nicaragua a Bolshevist regime hostile to the United States."[18]

"AHEM!"

—Sykes in the Philadelphia *Evening Public Ledger.*

Policing the "backyard": a pro-Coolidge cartoonist's view of US intervention

Regardless of whether the red scare propaganda originated in the bureaucratic cubicles of the State Department or the oligarchic salons of Granada, it largely failed to achieve its objective. Overseas it was ridiculed by friend and foe alike; at home many feared it was part of a plan to get into a war with Mexico, which was then threatening to nationalize the holdings of US oil companies.[19]

Soon the charges of Mexican-Bolshevik subversion were put on the back burner, and new arguments were advanced to support the Nicaragua intervention. At the end of February a British cruiser was reported to be on its way to Corinto to provide a haven for endangered British subjects. Pro-administration publicists exploited the report to focus attention on the State Department's claim that the lives and property of US and other foreign nationals were at stake, and to mobilize vocal Monroe Doctrine fanatics behind further "preventive" intervention by the United States. The British ship mysteriously turned around and left after staying in Corinto only a few days. Circumstantial evidence suggested that the British and US governments had jointly engineered the incident.[20]

On March 1, Acting Secretary of State Joseph Grew wrote Chairman Porter of the House Foreign Affairs Committee that new Marine units were being sent to Nicaragua to avert a danger that "armed bands of revolutionaries might interrupt communications on the railroad and possibly destroy a portion of the railroad." It was necessary, he said, to keep the line open to maintain a link "between the Legation and the marine guard at Managua and the sea." To accomplish this, neutral zones were declared the entire length of the track, including the cities of León and Chinandega. The trains themselves were not neutralized, however, which enabled Diaz to continue to use them for his troops and supplies—under Marine protection.[21]

The State Department or its supporters advanced at least four distinct justifications for renewing the US military intervention in Nicaragua during the Constitutionalist War.[22] These were the alleged need to protect life and property, including investments, the "Bolshevik menace" to the Panama canal area, the need to safeguard the Nicaragua canal option, and the Monroe Doctrine—intervening to forestall intervention by Europeans. The theory seemed to be that each new argument would increase the support for intervention, even if it was discovered after the fact. Then too, a multiplicity of justifications would diminish the impact of a compelling challenge to any one.

WITH HIS situation becoming weaker and weaker, Diaz again asked the US to make Nicaragua a formal dependency and, in the words of Foreign Minister Carlos Cuadra Pasos, "establish *de jure* what time and history have created *de facto* between our two countries." With its policy already under heavy fire at home and abroad, the Coolidge Administration lost no time denying that it had any intention of taking Adolfo up on his offer, even though it came with the endorsement of Minister Eberhardt.[23] As the *New York Times* put it:

> President Diaz was "our man," kept in office only by American bayonets, and for him to come gayly forward and succeed in placing his distracted country under the protecting wings of the American eagle would have been a sight to make international laughter hold both its sides. It is well for our Government to have stopped that farce before it went any further.[24]

Afraid of rekindling the attacks on dollar diplomacy, the State Department also scotched a plan by Diaz to resell the Nicaraguan railroad and National Bank to the New York bankers.[25]

Despite all the assistance it received from the United States, the Diaz army was faring badly. Though better armed than its adversaries, its morale was very low; mutinies and desertions were common. It was largely composed of hapless individuals shanghaied en mass by recruiting squads, handed a rifle, and sent to the front. Even Customs Collector Clifford Ham's Nicaraguan underlings at Managua and Corinto had to eat and sleep in their offices on several occasions to avoid the "recruiting" parties.[26]

The Constitutionalists won a decisive victory at Pearl Lagoon on the Atlantic Coast at the end of December, compelling government forces to retreat to the Pacific zone. It was thought that the neutralization of Rama would hold Sacasa's army in the East, but new Constitutionalist forces appeared in the Northwest, and in February, captured Chinandega. The Conservatives were only able to retake the city after it had been bombed by airplanes piloted by North American mercenaries. Meanwhile, the bulk of the Liberal army reached the Pacific zone by making a difficult trek across the northern jungles and mountains. After inflicting a series of defeats on Diaz troops in the hinterlands of Matagalpa, the Constitutionalists dug in near Boaco, dangerously close to the capital.[27]

J UAN BAUTISTA SACASA, a physician from León and president of the Constitutionalist government, was a well-meaning but weak man. Sacasa had a faculty for appointing the wrong people. The most notorious result of this tendency, and the one with the most far-reaching consequences, was his choice of José Maria Moncada to be minister of war and commander-in-chief of the Constitutionalist army. Described as "a newspaperman posing as a soldier," Moncada began his political career writing for a Conservative clericalist newspaper in Granada. Spending the Zelaya years exiled in Honduras, he served for a time in the Conservative Honduran government of General Manuel Bonilla. He returned home to join the US-backed Conservative uprising against Zelaya, and became interior minister in the Estrada-Diaz government installed by the Dawson Pact. Ousted along with Estrada, he went into exile in the United States. Moncada was no ideologue. Finding his ambitions blocked under the two Chamorro regimes, he made a political comeback in the Liberal-influenced coalition that won the 1924 election.[28]

The success of the Constitutionalist army was not due to any genius on the part of its commander-in-chief, but to the higher morale of its troops, which reflected the popular support enjoyed by the Constitutionalist cause. It was due also, perhaps, to a certain amount of luck. Moncada demonstrated his lack of military skill by failing to take advantage of the panic that the arrival of his army in western Nicaragua initially caused in the Diaz ranks. Instead, he soon found the tables turned and his own forces surrounded and facing annihilation. Such reversals of fortune were common when the title "general" was freely handed out to, or assumed by, those influential politicos or wealthy landowners who could dragoon the most peasants for the war effort.[29]

There was one general in the Constitutionalist army, however, who differed from the rest. With no military training or experience at the outbreak of hostilities in 1926, Augusto César Sandino had nevertheless earned the title of general, which, he said, his men had bestowed on him.

Sandino was the "natural" offspring of a moderately well-to-do coffee planter and a peasant woman who worked on his farm in the department of Masaya. As an illegitimate child he suffered the privations of his mother to the extreme of accompanying her, at the age of nine, into debtor's prison. Later, however, he was taken into his father's household where life was easier, and he received an education through secondary school. He developed a thriving business as a produce merchant while still a teenager, and apparently, acquired some land. But in his twenty-fifth year Sandino seriously wounded a local politico in a quarrel, and had to flee his native village.[30]

Making his way north to La Ceiba on the Atlantic coast of Honduras, he got a job as a watchman at a US-owned sugar refinery. But abstemious, serious, hard-working, and more than a little ambitious, Sandino desired to see "more civilized" countries where, as he wrote his father, "if I can't make any money, at least I can gaze upon the broad, clear light of civilization and gain something by it."[31] Moving on to Guatemala, he was employed for a time as a laborer on a United Fruit banana plantation, and then continued north to Mexico, where he found work at the US-owned oil companies in Tampico and Veracruz.

In those days the boisterous oil town of Tampico was a center of anarcho-syndicalist, socialist, and *Zapatista* agitation. The expatriate Nicaraguan kept company with a group of friends who liked to discuss politics, especially "the prostration of our peoples of Latin America" before Yankee power. He read widely on social problems, theology, and even spiritualism.[32]

Taunted by Mexican companions who considered all Nicaraguans to be sellouts and traitors, Sandino felt an acute sense of shame at the status of his own country as a vassal of the United States. At first he didn't think that he personally deserved the epithets, but after a period of reflection he "understood that they were right, since, as a Nicaraguan, I had the duty to protest."[33]

In May 1926, when Sandino learned of the revolutionary outbreak in Nicaragua, he was a supervisor of gasoline sales at the Huasteca Petroleum Company refinery in Veracruz. Taking some money saved from his earnings, he returned to his homeland. There, to his dismay, he found that the politicians—Liberal as well as Conservative—were a "bunch of scoundrels, cowards, and traitors, incapable of leading a valiant and patriotic people." They fought each other, he thought, "like cats and dogs in a sack" merely "to attain a presidency supervised by foreigners."[34]

Sandino worked for a few months as a payroll clerk at the US-owned San Albino gold mine in northern Nueva Segovia. He quit in October 1926, having convinced twenty-nine of his fellow workers to join him in taking up arms for the Constitutionalists. With part of his savings, he bought a few old rifles from the smugglers who operated along the Honduran border, and in early November the small band attacked the Conservative garrison at El Jicaro.

The action was a failure. It convinced Sandino to travel to Puerto Cabezas in the hope of obtaining more and better weapons from the Constitutionalist commanders. Accompanied by a few aides, he made the long and difficult canoe trip down the Rio Coco to the Atlantic Coast. But at Puerto Cabezas Moncada refused his request, treating with disdain the man he considered an upstart nobody. If he really wanted to fight, Moncada told him, he should join one of the existing units. But Sandino didn't give up; despite his inexperience in military matters, he was convinced it was necessary and possible to open a second front in the Segovian mountains.

When Admiral Latimer declared Puerto Cabezas a neutral zone on December 23, Sandino was still there trying to interest Liberal leaders in his plan. With the help of six of his men and a group of local prostitutes, he hauled thirty rifles and 6,000 rounds of ammunition—equipment abandoned by Moncada's troops—outside the zone before the Marine deadline.[35]

Returning with the arms to the northwestern mountains at the end of January, Sandino and his followers routed Conservative troops in a series of small encounters. They captured more arms as they went, and soon attracted large numbers of volunteers. Within two months the column had grown to 800 well-armed fighters and controlled large portions of the northern departments. Flying distinctive red and black banners with the inscription "Liberty or Death," Sandino's cavalry stormed the city of Jinotega on March 28. Marine Major M. S. Berry, who visited Sandino at that time, found his troops to be the best he had seen in Nicaragua.[36]

In April, Sandino received a desperate note from Moncada, whose army was then surrounded one hundred miles to the southeast. If he failed to furnish aid at once, said Moncada, he would be held responsible for the resulting disaster. Sandino's column did relieve the Liberal army, smashing through Conservative lines at the battle of El Bejuco, capturing the enemy headquarters and large quantities of arms. Their encirclement of Moncada broken, Diaz's battered forces retreated toward Managua, their last stronghold. The balance had tilted to the Constitutionalists once more. On May 2, occupying the forwardmost position of the rebel army, Sandino's column poised for an assault on the town of Boaco, the last remaining Conservative redoubt between the Liberals and the capital.[37]

THE COOLIDGE Administration closely identified the Diaz regime with US interests, and feared the deteriorating government military position could soon lead to a situation in which the Marines in Nicaragua (now approaching 6,000) would become involved in combat. Public opinion in the United States was sharply divided over the desirability of a war in the tropics, a situation exacerbated by the inability of the State Department to come up with a coherent rationale for intervention. Coolidge was determined, as the London *Spectator* put it, to get control of his slide down the "slippery" "slope of imperialism" where "the best intentions prove of no avail and where force of circumstances is always in charge."[38] To that end he dispatched Henry L. Stimson, a law partner of Elihu Root and former secretary of war, as his special representative to Nicaragua. The move was a public relations success even before Stimson's departure, as previously critical newspapers greeted the Stimson mission as a sign that Coolidge was backing away from military intervention in favor of a negotiated settlement.

Stimson was given a broad mandate to arrange matters any way he could short of a Liberal victory. Arriving in Managua on April 17, he found the military situation even more precarious than Washington had been led to believe. He reported that the predicament of the Diaz forces, which had briefly regained the initiative only to lose it again despite being "amply furnished with men and munitions," could only be explained by "complete incompetence or treachery or both."[39]

But after he conferred with Sacasa representatives, Stimson found that political prospects were considerably brighter. The Liberal politicians, he reported, "asserted that their party recognized that the United States had a legitimate zone of interest and influence extending as far south as Panama and that they considered this fact natural and beneficial in its results to Nicaragua." The Constitutionalists were willing to lay down their arms in return for US supervision of the 1928 presidential elections. The only sticking point was their refusal to accept Diaz in the presidency for the interim. But Stimson was adamant about retaining Diaz, who, he said would "cheerfully" accept the limitation of his authority necessary for a compromise and would

> loyally cooperate with execution of [the] plan. After careful considera-
> tion we know no other Nicaraguan whom we could trust to so cooper-
> ate . . . I told him I was insisting upon his retention, not for himself
> alone but because he was essential to successful settlement and my own
> country's honor.[40]

Stimson decided to seek out Moncada, a man he thought would be more flexible. It was known, wrote Stimson, that the Constitutionalist commander "in former times had put himself on record publicly in support of the right of the United States to intervene in Nicaragua to assist in the establishment of order and liberty." Moncada had been well known in the State Department for a long time. After the fall of Zelaya, he had urged the US to take over not only the National Bank, railroad, and steamships, but the telegraph and the national treasury as well. He once wrote Assistant Secretary of State Huntington Wilson, "We Nicaraguans are accustomed to designate the State Department as the arbiter of our fights and differences."[41]

Ignoring the counsel of his subordinates, Moncada agreed to talk with the special envoy of the Yankee president. The two met in the village of Tipitapa, fifteen miles east of Managua, on May 4. Sitting down under an *espino negro* (blackthorn tree) just outside town, Stimson apprised Moncada of the peace plan he had worked out with Diaz. There would be an immediate truce followed by disarmament of both sides and a general amnesty; Adolfo would remain in office until the next regularly scheduled election, which the United States would supervise; Liberals would be rewarded with cabinet posts in the interim; finally, a "nonpartisan" National Guard would be organized and commanded by US officers, while US Marines continued to occupy the country. Stimson then made the Constitutionalist commander the offer he couldn't refuse: if his troops did not lay down their weapons they would be forcibly disarmed by the United States.[42]

If Moncada was upset that the cause he had fought for was being robbed of certain victory, he failed to show it. "In less than thirty minutes we understood each other and had settled the matter," Stimson reported. Indeed, Moncada seemed anxious to cooperate: yes, he was against Diaz remaining in office, he said, but if Stimson insisted how could he possibly oppose the will of the United States? The only problem remaining was to convince his subordinates. Stimson had a "long talk" with Moncada "about methods of breaking news to his men." Diaz would appoint Liberals to head six departments in the Liberal Northwest—such patronage jobs were powerful inducements to "practical" commanders. Soldiers would receive ten dollars for every rifle they turned in, along with other material benefits. The threat of forcible disarmament by the United States would prove extremely useful in selling the plan: Moncada could tell his subordinates there was no alternative but to submit to the US, while he himself would appear to be acting only under compulsion from superior force. Although he had no authorization to make an arrangement with Stimson, and had not even consulted his generals, Moncada traveled to Managua the next day to work out the details of the pact.[43]

A few months later, for the readers of the *Saturday Evening Post,* Stimson gave the story of his "peacemaking" in Nicaragua a Hollywood touch:

> As we sailed away there remained with me as an earnest of the hopeful future of Nicaragua the memory of two patriotic men, one a Conservative and one a Liberal, each willing to sacrifice personal ambition and party interest to the higher welfare of his country and each willing to trust in the honor and good-will of the United States—Adolfo Diaz and José Maria Moncada.[44]

But Stimson's happy ending was premature.

WITH HIS TROOPS poised to attack Boaco, General Sandino received a note telling him that, contrary to advice, "General Moncada has departed [for Tipitapa] and must be playing up to the Yankees at this very moment." The next day a message came from Moncada ordering him to reconcentrate his troops because peace had been arranged. Seeking an explanation, Sandino went to see the commander-in-chief in person. The latter, reclining comfortably in a hammock, enumerated the terms of the arrangement. He told Sandino that he had been chosen to be *jefe politico,* or governor, of the department of Jinotega. What was more, the Diaz government would buy all the horses and mules used in the war; for purposes of payment, Sandino, personally, would be considered owner of those under his command, plus he'd be paid ten dollars for each day of his service. "I smiled maliciously," Sandino remembered afterward.[45]

Moncada tried to convince him of the insanity of trying to fight the United States. But making plain his disapproval of the peace plan, Sandino told Moncada that for him "liberty or death" was a duty, not merely a phrase, and that the war had kindled the hopes for liberty in the entire people. Wrote Sandino:

> [Moncada] smiled sarcastically and replied in a deprecating tone, "No, man, why do you want to sacrifice yourself for the people? The people don't appreciate it. I tell you this from my own experience. Life ends but the country remains. The duty of human beings is to enjoy and live well and not worry too much."

As Sandino and his aides left the meeting with Moncada, "we all understood that he already carried in his pocket the promise of the presidency of Nicaragua."[46]

Moncada invited the Constitutionalist commanders to come to Boaco on May 8; he would hear the opinions of all regarding the settlement. When Sandino and his staff arrived for the meeting they found their commander-in-chief in one of the principal houses, seated in a rocking chair. No longer in campaign attire, he was now wearing shined shoes and a "Palm Beach suit." Moncada told them the conference of military leaders was already over; all had agreed to disarm, and it was their duty to go along with the majority. Sandino and his aides had previously agreed it would be foolish to argue with Moncada where they might be arrested and their troops forcibly disarmed. Sandino told Moncada he would submit to the will of the others, but hedged on the details of disarming his men.[47]

> Moncada accepted, but told me it was necessary to sign the disarmament document the others had already signed.
>
> In that instant it appeared that my dreams of liberty were dashed, because if Moncada had insisted that I sign, I was disposed to let him have a bullet.
>
> I made a great effort to regain the composure required by the circumstances and replied, "You're in command. I give you full authority to sign for me."[48]

Ignoring a pledge to Moncada to await instructions from the Marines regarding the surrender of arms, Sandino led his men back to Jinotega. From there, on May 12, he sent a telegraphic circular to all departments announcing his rejection of the Espino Negro pact.* In another, dated the

---

* The pact between Stimson and Moncada was known in the United States as the Peace of Tipitapa.

19th, he explained his decision to continue the fight, concluding, "What does it matter if the whole world comes down on me? We shall fulfill a sacred duty . . . If there is no one to second me I will protest on my own account."[49]

From San Rafael del Norte in the department of Jinotega, Sandino withdrew farther north into the rugged mountains of Nueva Segovia near the Honduran frontier. He informed the jefe politico in Ocotal that he could continue in office there, but would exercise no authority in the rest of Nueva Segovia. That would be administered by Sandino's forces pending the establishment of an "honorable Liberal government." The flinty general then appointed one of his subordinates jefe politico of Nueva Segovia. The new capital would be at El Jicaro, where Sandino began his revolutionary career, "which henceforth shall be called Ciudad Sandino."[50]

Marines were sent to garrison Ocotal, Jinotega, and San Rafael. Their commander, Captain G.D. Hatfield, issued a proclamation declaring Sandino "an individual outside the law." But none of the US representatives seemed to think Sandino represented much of a threat. They wrote letters trying to persuade him to reconsider his resistance to the Espino Negro pact, but made no immediate plans for military action against him.[51]

At the end of June, however, Sandino and his followers occupied the US-owned San Albino mine, his former place of employment, removing gold and dynamite. Sandino had now become dangerous. Admiral Latimer passed orders down to Captain Hatfield to issue one last ultimatum: if the recalcitrant still refused to surrender, the Marines would proceed against him.[52]

Sandino received Hatfield's message. "Nicaragua has had its last revolution," declared the Marine. He called on the Nicaraguan to follow the example of Aguinaldo in the Philippines, who had given up his resistance to become "a splendid friend of the United States." Hatfield would overlook Sandino's earlier "insolent responses" and give him "one more opportunity to surrender with honor." But if he failed to accept the offer within two days the Marines would "finish with you and your forces once and for all."[53]

"I will not surrender and await you here," was Sandino's terse reply from a place called "Campamento del Chipote." But he did not wait for Hatfield at his camp. Instead, on July 16, the date the ultimatum was set to expire, Sandino attacked the Marine garrison at Ocotal. He brought with him 800 local peasants, whom he invited to sack the Conservative town "in order to demonstrate that the invader was incapable of giving guarantees [of security]."[54]

A CCORDING to Sandino's version, he had only sixty actual combatants at Ocotal, against six hundred Marines and members of the
newly-reorganized *Guardia Nacional.* The Marines claimed the opposite:
they numbered thirty-nine with forty-seven *Guardias,* against hundreds
of attackers. Both agreed that the Sandinistas sustained the battle for fifteen
hours and the defenders were reduced to their compound—two fortified
stone buildings. Sandino withdrew when a squadron of airplanes arrived
the following afternoon and conducted what was said to be the first dive-
bombing attack in history.[55]

The Marines reported losing only one of their number killed, with
another Marine and several Guardia injured. Captain Hatfield told reporters
that Sandinista losses were 300 killed and another 100 wounded. It was
later admitted, however, that there was no actual "body count," and the
estimate of Sandinista dead was scaled down to about sixty. The Marine
version pictured a town heroically defended against overwhelming odds:
the Sandinistas were sent fleeing in disorder; the heavy casualties they sustained would end effective resistance. Both the squadron commander who
led his planes through a tropical storm to save the Ocotal garrison and
Captain Hatfield were awarded the Navy Cross. For his part, Sandino conceded that his own losses had been heavy, while claiming to have killed
eighty Marines.* But he considered the attack a victory. He had proven
his point, capturing most of Ocotal. And, according to his version, the
Sandinistas made an orderly withdrawal after the peasants plundered the
town, taking with them captured supplies and munitions.[57]

Regardless of who won the battle of Ocotal, the news that Marines were
engaged in open combat with Nicaraguans did not make good public relations for the Coolidge Administration. The Pan American Federation of
Labor was meeting in Washington at the time. On behalf of the gathering, William Green, president of the American Federation of Labor, addressed a protest to the State Department against the continued Marine
presence in Nicaragua. In reply, Secretary Kellogg defended the role of
the Marines as peacekeepers who, he said, were fulfilling the commitment
made by the United States in the Stimson agreement; Sandino and his
followers were nothing more than "common outlaws" whose "activities

---

* The evidence indicates that in this and later engagements both sides reported their own
casualties more or less accurately, but grossly exaggerated the number inflicted on their opponents. In a report to the Senate, Secretary of the Navy Wilbur gave the number of casualties through April 16, 1928—the entire first phase of the war—as 21 Marines killed and 45
wounded, 8 Guardia killed, 4 wounded. He put the Sandinistas' dead at 202, based on actual count—a figure that may have included some civilians killed in bombing raids. This estimate of Sandinista deaths was much lower than the extravagant numbers reported in the
press.[56]

cannot be considered to have had any political significance whatsoever." Kellogg apparently thought Ocotal had ended Sandino's "activities."[58]

Nine days after Ocotal, Sandino suffered what he regarded as his first defeat when the Marines caught up with him at San Fernando. He himself was nearly killed and his men were dispersed in disorder. Then came another beating at Las Flores, where the Sandinistas tried to defend fixed positions against the pursuing "leathernecks." Under such conventional warfare conditions they proved no match for the Yankees' aircraft and superior tactics. By Sandino's account, the "more than sixty" casualties he sustained at Las Flores were the most losses in a single engagement during the entire first two years of his war with the Marines.[59]

On August 1, Minister Eberhardt reported from Managua that Sandino, having disbanded his troops, was fleeing down the Coco River toward the Caribbean. If it was impossible to know for certain the whereabouts of the rebel leader, said a Marine intelligence report, it was only because of Sandino's "demented condition." Brigadier General Logan Feland, Marine commander in Nicaragua, assured reporters, "The time is past when it is necessary to use force to maintain peace in Nicaragua"; Sandino "is through." In light of such terminal pronouncements, the Marine withdrawal from Nicaragua proceeded apace.[60]

Defeats notwithstanding, Sandinista ranks continued to grow. After Ocotal, Marine and Guardia harassment of the local peasantry caused many to abandon their homes and join the rebels. "All people encountered are unquestionably strong for Sandino," said a report by the pursuing Marines' commander.[61]

It quickly became clear to the rebel leader that his "Army for the Defense of the National Sovereignty," as he called it, would not last long in conventional warfare with the United States. The only hope against overwhelming odds was to fight exclusively at the times and places of his own choosing. Ten days after the defeat at Las Flores, his forces slipped behind the Marine lines to make a nighttime attack on the town of Telpaneca. The Sandinistas captured the high ground, and while their machinegun fire pinned down the Marine garrison in its barbed wire-enclosed compound, they called on the local populace to loot the town. When the bombers arrived at dawn, the Sandinistas withdrew.[62]

Two weeks later the guerrillas downed their first plane. They captured the pilots, put them on trial, and executed them. Then they ambushed the Marine rescue patrol.[63]

An Associated Press dispatch dated October 22 reported that "conditions in the northern part of Nicaragua are growing from banditry into a state of insurrection." Sandino's forces held virtually the entire department of Nueva Segovia, and most of Esteli and Jinotega outside the depart-

mental capitals. North American mining engineers told reporters that
whereas the people in the region were formerly "friendly to Americans
and worked contentedly in the mines," they were now "anti-American,"
having been converted to "radicalism and Bolshevism" by Sandino. In December, a Marine commander said that "practically every coffee and cattle
plantation" in the country had asked for Marine protection, and Standard
Fruit, operating on the Atlantic Coast, complained that it had to hire guards
at yearly salaries of $10,000.[64] Washington's optimism had suddenly given
way to alarm.

Dana Munro, chargé of the US legation in Nicaragua, wired the State
Department asking that Diaz be given the go-ahead to declare a state of
war in northern Nicaragua. "The authorities," he said, "are placed in a
most embarrassing position when suspects or prisoners of war bring habeas
corpus proceedings and the marines and *guardia* are being hampered in
the actual conduct of operations against the bandits." A state of war declaration would mean suspension of bothersome legal guarantees. But the
secretary of state refused: "A formal declaration of a state of war by the
Nicaraguan Congress would probably have the effect of converting Sandino's status from that of a mere bandit to that of leader of an organized
rebellion," reasoned Kellogg, "with possibilities of a recognition of his belligerency by any nation which might deem it desirable to act in that
sense."[65]

At the end of November, Marine Headquarters warned all travelers and
pack trains in the northern region to give prior notice of their movements
to avoid being bombed by patrolling aircraft. The region was so deficient
in roads and other communication facilities, however, that the Marines
themselves had to devise a method for planes to pick up messages suspended from a wire strung between two poles. Under such conditions isolated peasants were not even aware of the Marine warning, much less able
to communicate their travel plans in advance. The inclination of pilots to
attack anything undoubtedly caused a significant number of civilian casualties. Sandino told a story of three planes that repeatedly bombed and
machinegunned a hill some two kilometers from his encampment. Sending an aide to learn what the Yankees were up to, the man returned to
report finding nothing on the site but an old lame ox, put out to graze.
The area all around had been blackened by the bombing, but the ox itself
was miraculously unscathed.[66]

T HROUGHOUT 1927 the Marines hunted for Sandino's mysterious
mountain fortress called El Chipote. Marine columns passing through
the rugged Segovian mountains were ambushed continually. Harold N.
Denny, sent to Nicaragua to cover the war for the *New York Times,* report-

ed that members of the "American colony," celebrating New Year's Eve at Managua's International Club, had their spirits dampened by news that a Marine unit had been ambushed on its way to Quilali, near El Chipote, and that its commander was among the first casualties. According to Denny, "the bandits" who laid the ambush had worn khaki uniforms "instead of their former nondescript rags," and "evinced a military training lacking heretofore."[67]

Charles Lindbergh was then about to depart on a good-will tour through Central and South America after his historic trans-Atlantic flight. Expected to overfly northern Nicaragua, he was seriously advised to keep his plane at high altitude to avoid being shot down by Sandinistas. When Lindbergh landed in San Salvador he was handed a note calling for the US to get out of Nicaragua.[68]

The Marine force reduction was halted. A thousand additional Marines were dispatched. Dock workers at Corinto went on strike—reportedly influenced by Sandino, and a group of Guardia deserted their Yankee commander and joined a Sandinista force attacking Somotillo. US delegates at the Sixth Pan American Conference underway in Havana maneuvered to block passage of a censure resolution, and humorist Will Rogers poked fun at official explanations for United States involvement.[69]

Marine flyers finally pinpointed El Chipote at the end of November. Men and supplies were brought up, methodically closing a ring around the Sandinista stronghold. In January the assault began. Leathernecks on the ground worked their way up the sides of the mountain, while day after day, waves of planes bombed the summit. But when the Marines finally reached the top on January 26, they were confounded to find the earthworks occupied by straw-filled dummies. Sandino had slipped away under cover of darkness, relating afterward that the planes bombed the dummies for two days before the position was taken. Nevertheless, *Times* correspondent Denny reported that Sandino had been killed or seriously wounded in the bombing. "So thorough was Sandino's defeat," announced an Associated Press dispatch, "that a majority of his men deserted him."[70]

On February 4, Marine Headquarters announced that Sandino was still alive but fleeing southward, his forces completely routed. The very next day he was reported active in the department of Matagalpa, and Marine reinforcements were rushed to the area. The day after that the elusive "bandit" was spotted far to the north; on February 9 he was again reported in Matagalpa and about to sweep through North American-owned coffee plantations; two weeks later the Associated Press had him in position to strike Atlantic Coast points. Sandino did stop long enough to have dinner at a British coffee plantation in Matagalpa, where he left a defiant note for delivery to the Yankees.[71]

"The wily Sandino is a maddening problem for the Marines because of his swift shifting," wrote Denny in the February 12, 1928 *Times,* "and many officers declare earnestly they would give a year's pay only once to come to grips with him." Yet, just the day before, Secretary of the Navy Curtis Wilbur had appeared before the Senate Foreign Relations Committee to again offer assurance that Sandino was "finished."[72]

Back in Managua, General Feland explained that "in the army, we use the word 'bandit' in a technical sense, meaning the member of a band." In early March, however, the Marine Corps announced that Sandino had met the official criteria necessary to be designated a "guerrilla." On March 14, Feland ordered his men to wipe out the "guerrilla" within two months. The same day the US Senate received a message from Sandino demanding immediate withdrawal of the Marines, or the safety of all North Americans in Nicaragua would be in jeopardy. Two days after that another 1,000 Marines were dispatched for Nicaragua duty—a group of young men who had just joined the Marine Corps to become musicians found themselves slogging through Nicaragua's Atlantic swamps and jungles.[73]

At the end of April Sandino suddenly turned up far to the east in the Atlantic Coast region, destroying the La Luz and Bonanza gold mines. He left the following note for the La Luz mine manager:

> Your mine has been reduced to ashes by order of this command to make more tangible our protest against the warlike invasion your Government has made of our territory with no other right than that of brute force . . . You, the capitalists, will be appreciated and respected by us as long as you treat us as equals and not in the erroneous manner of today, believing yourselves lords and masters of our lives and property.

In the meantime, Sandino advised the mine owners to bill President Coolidge for the damages.[74]

Amidst the barrage of conflicting reports on the whereabouts of the bandit guerrilla or guerrilla bandit, North American writer Carleton Beals was telegraphing the first of six dispatches to *The Nation.* Making a difficult journey across the Honduras border, Beals had evaded both Honduran troops and US Marines. He caught up with Sandino just after his abandonment of El Chipote. The first journalist to reach Sandino since he began his war against the Marines, Beals furnished the North American public with a glimpse of a nationalistic leader who was neither defeated nor the rapacious bandit they had been led to believe. The writer concluded his final dispatch with the following:

> "Let me repeat," declared the General, "we are no more bandits than was Washington. If the American public had not become calloused to justice and to the elemental rights of mankind, it would not so easily

forget its own past when a handful of ragged soldiers marched through the snow leaving blood-tracks behind them to win liberty and independence. If their consciences had not become dulled by their scramble for wealth, Americans would not so easily forget the lesson that, sooner or later, every nation, however weak, achieves freedom, and that every abuse of power hastens the destruction of the one who wields it."[75]

Beals' portrait of Sandino no doubt helped spread opposition to Coolidge's Nicaragua policies within the United States. There were speeches and resolutions in Congress: "Never in the history of the country has a President sent armed forces to a country and kept them there a year without the authority of Congress," declared Senator Dill of Washington. There were petitions and peace delegations and protesters arrested in front of the White House. Sandino's half-brother Sócrates made a speaking tour of the US, and the All America Anti-Imperialist League sold "postage stamps" with the caption, "Protest Against Marine Rule in Nicaragua," which were pasted on the backs of envelopes. Citing a section of an obscenity law, the US Post Office refused to deliver letters that bore the stickers.[76] Later, the same committee organized a drive to collect medical supplies for the Sandinistas.

A MARINE captain described an expedition down the Coco River that failed to make contact with the rebels:

The health of the personnel suffered severely. The waterproof seabags sprang leaks. The rains wet the blankets. The high, steep banks of the river, the fogs, the low-flying clouds, and the afternoon rains, allowed so little sun-light to strike the Coco bottoms that from Telpaneca on the men's clothing and blankets were never dry . . . When it is considered that the men spent an average of eight to twelve hours per day in the water, handling the boats and the lines, slept in wet bedding and were at the mercy of mosquitoes, fleas and gnats (the latter very bad) during the day, it is easy to understand why 37 men of the expedition were sick at one time or another . . . At the time of its recall, the expedition had 18 men on the sick list, three of the above were stretcher cases. The lack of sunshine, the exhausting labor and the constant state of wetness had sapped the vitality to a low ebb and left disease an easy entrance. Add to this that cuts, bruises and lacerations were constantly being acquired from boats, rocks, and thorns, these became infected by lengthy exposure in dirty river water, and that few of the personnel escaped them. One member of the expedition was drowned. Another suffered a cerebral concussion and facial wounds . . . Under conditions ceaselessly perilous as those encountered, narrow escapes became commonplace and saving and being saved routine stuff.[77]

By the end of the first nine months of the war against Sandino all the elements had appeared—in miniature—that would become so familiar forty years later during Vietnam: a terrain alien and difficult for the foreigner, an elusive enemy, a hostile and seemingly inscrutable population. There were peasants who took rifles from hiding places at night and resumed innocuous rustic tasks at dawn. There were the inevitable barbarities and the difficulties of trying to explain this "police action" being conducted against those who were, it was asserted, merely a group of outlaws. There were even three Marines who deserted to join Sandino.[78]

There were other "pioneering" aspects to the war as well. Harold Denny told *Times* readers in a dispatch from Ocotal that "the present activities furnish the first practical laboratory for the development of post-war aviation in coordination with ground troops. Never before have planes participated in [guerrilla] warfare, but they have proved themselves a most deadly weapon against hidden enemies." The aircraft were doing the work of artillery, Denny reported, breaking up enemy concentrations with their bombing attacks and following these up with "diving charges ending with bursts of machinegun fire"—the word "strafing" had not yet come into usage.[79]

A few years later the Japanese would find such a "practical laboratory" in China. In fact, when Henry Stimson became Hoover's secretary of state, recommended for the job in part by his "peacemaking" efforts at Tipitapa, he protested against the Japanese invasion of Manchuria, only to find his own country's activities in Nicaragua to be a considerable embarrassment: Japan claimed that it, too, was simply protecting the lives and property of its citizens.[80]

THE POSSIBILITY that Sandinista activity would disrupt the 1928 voting became a major worry for the United States. The US-supervised presidential election was the cornerstone of the Stimson/State Department plan for Nicaraguan "stability" imposed at Tipitapa the previous year. "Getting Sandino was a matter of vital importance to the United States," said Dana Munro, US chargé in Managua. The defiant Nicaraguan who had stepped from nowhere to the center of the world stage had already caused the United States a great deal of discomfiture, and now jeopardized its entire Caribbean policy. To cope with the threat, Marines and naval personnel in Nicaragua, reduced to less than 2,000 after Espino Negro, were increased to nearly 6,000 again in 1928. By April the Marines had established forty-eight garrisons throughout Nicaragua, supported by numerous airstrips.[81]

Though the continued inability to "get" Sandino never ceased to be a source of frustration, the military escalation was not without results. By

Sandino's own account he came close to being captured or killed on several occasions.[82] His troops learned to shun combat with large Marine and Guardia units and to avoid being sighted by the airplanes. But the Marine-Guardia columns likewise learned to be wary of Sandinista ambushes. As 1928 advanced, the number of clashes became fewer and fewer. The harsh reality of a seemingly unwinnable war, the electoral propaganda, and offers of amnesty all took their toll on Sandino's followers. The guerrilla leader confronted defections and treachery, seeing his force reduced to a few hundred at most. Though unable to defeat Sandino, the Marines managed to keep his locus of operations confined to remote and sparsely populated areas where he could not mount a serious challenge to the election.

Augusto César Sandino

"So far as Nicaraguan internal politics are concerned, in fact," wrote Minister Eberhardt to Secretary Kellogg, "the Sandinista movement has lost practically all of its significance." In regard to the 1928 election Eberhardt was not far wrong. On August 1 Sandino issued a manifesto denouncing the election, saying that both candidates were merely tools of US policy, and declaring his intention to prevent it from going off as planned.[83] But the manifesto was about the only real opposition he could mount.

The State Department had other difficulties with the election, however. Emiliano Chamorro wanted to be president again, but he was out of favor in Washington. Chamorro was as cooperative as could be with US investors and with Washington's strategic/canal objectives, but he expected in return the perpetuation in power of the Conservative Party's right wing, which he headed. Chamorro did not share the State Department's squeamishness about constitutional forms. If it took US troops to keep him in power, it was fine with him. But that was definitely not what Washington had in mind.

Chamorro made a trip to Washington in October 1927 seeking support for his candidacy. Chargé Munro urged the State Department to use the occasion to tell him, in no uncertain terms, that he could not run. Argued Munro:

> Even if he were eligible for the Presidency, his election in 1928 would be disastrous to Nicaragua because it would intensify the hostility of the two parties to such a degree that the establishment of a satisfactory government would be impossible . . . I believe the above points outweigh the obvious disadvantage of appearing to do anything to influence the selection of candidates by either party.

The advice was taken. Assistant Secretary of State Frances White handed Chamorro a written statement informing him that he would not be considered constitutionally eligible for the presidency.[84]

But the *caudillo* was not to be jilted so easily. Coolidge had dispatched Brigadier General Frank R. McCoy to supervise the election, and Harold Dodds returned to revise his 1923 law to allow for North American electoral officials and Marine poll watchers. Chamorro, wanting to prevent Yankee interference with the electoral shenanigans traditionally employed by the Conservatives to keep themselves in power, put on a show of nationalist indignation at this foreign interference; his faction in the Congress refused to approve Dodds' revised law. US strong-arming to get the law passed was of no avail. Finally it was necessary to have Diaz promulgate the law by decree after Congress adjourned, notwithstanding the apparent unconstitutionality of such a procedure.[85]

Nor did the troubles end there. Habitual factionalism split the Conservative Party, which held two separate conventions. But McCoy ruled that only one Conservative candidate could run, and ultimately forced the two factions to agree on Adolfo Bénard, the "Sugar King." To insure that there would be no "anti-Americans" on the ballot, or any possibility that the election could be thrown into the troublesome Congress, McCoy refused to allow the participation of third parties. Carleton Beals found McCoy to be a man who "had hit upon an ideal scheme for the salvation of Nicaragua—a utopian democratic perfection, which he was putting over with the faith of a Loyola and the same inquisitorial methods."[86]

The Liberal candidate was José Maria Moncada. Even beyond Sandinista ranks there was much speculation that Moncada had been promised the presidency as part of his deal with Stimson. Whether or not he had any promise or hint of US support is of little importance; Moncada didn't need it. He was a shrewd enough politician to parlay his friendship with Stimson and Yankee military personnel, and a trip to the US capital, into the appearance that he was Washington's man. That was enough.[87] After seventeen years of North American control, most Nicaraguans were resigned to the idea that the US choice would be president; if they had to humor the Yankees by putting a piece of paper in a box, so be it.

The Coolidge Administration strenuously denied being partial to Moncada, but it couldn't convince the US press of that, much less the Nicaraguans. Not that it wasn't pleased at Moncada's election. "Have we the right to deny the United States the right of intervention in our affairs?" Moncada had asked rhetorically in 1911. "By no means," was his categorical reply. These views were well known at the State Department. Stimson regarded Moncada as "our strongest real friend in Nicaragua," someone "brave enough to stand for friendship with the United States."[88]

The Department also knew that its open endorsement of Moncada was not necessary. The Liberals had long been known to be the majority party. All that was needed for Moncada's election, if that was what the United States wanted, was to insure that the Conservatives didn't control the voting and that nationalistic Liberals had no alternative candidate they could vote for. McCoy and the Marines saw to it that both those conditions were met.

So far as the Liberal Party was concerned, it was no longer the party of Zelaya, the party the United States had deposed in 1909-10. Among its leaders, nationalists were now in a minority, some having gone over to Sandino. The majority saw no future in opposing the United States. If Moncada's ostentatious toadying was the road back to power after their long exclusion, Liberal Party leaders were ready to take it. Their attitude no doubt infected much of the rank and file who looked for some good to come from Moncada's election, no matter how distasteful they found him personally.[89]

The inauguration of Moncada in January 1929 was accompanied, no doubt, by sighs of relief and self-congratulation in the State Department and the Managua legation. They had taken a major step forward in realizing the pacification plan embodied in the Espino Negro pact. The election had come off, after all, without a major hitch. Never mind that armed Marines had been posted at every polling place. The election looked honest and they could hold it up as an example of democracy in action. The world, especially Latin America, would see that the United States truly was fulfilling its vaunted mission of teaching its wards to "elect good men." Moreover, Nicaragua's president, put in office by the popular will, was a man in complete sympathy with United States interests. If the damned Sandino wasn't completely out of the picture, at least he'd been pushed into the background. More supervised elections would be needed to make this kind of stability habitual, but in the meantime Moncada could be trusted to cooperate in strengthening the Guardia Nacional. In the forseeable future this native force would replace the Marines hunting Sandino and the United States would be relieved of its chief international embarrassment. In short, there was light at the end of the tunnel, and guarded assurances could be given to incoming President Hoover, who was understandably reluctant to take up where Coolidge left off with the foreign policy nightmare called Nicaragua.

F OR SANDINO it was a time of reflection and reorientation. When he reached his difficult decision to oppose what he considered the shameful and humiliating betrayal of Espino Negro, he did so more with the idea of offering himself as a sacrifice, an example for future generations, than with the expectation of successfully resisting the power of the United States. It was a modest objective. He had declared in one of his first manifestoes, "I want to convince the unconcerned Nicaraguans, the apathetic Central Americans, and the entire Indohispanic race that in a spur of the Andean cordillera there is a group of patriots who know how to fight and die like men." He had asked his followers to embark upon a consciously suicidal mission. "We are alone," he told his assembled troops at Jinotega after Moncada's capitulation, "the cause of Nicaragua has been abandoned. Henceforth our enemies will be, not the forces of the tyrant Diaz, but the Marines of the most powerful empire that history has known . . . We will be vilely murdered by the bombs that terrible airplanes rain down upon us; slashed with foreign bayonets; riddled by modern machineguns." He dismissed from the enterprise all who had family obligations.[90]

But when the confrontation did not end in the dramatic finale of blood and fire, thoughts of self-immolation gave way to more ambitious projects. As the months went by and the movement survived, gaining strength and self-confidence, the idea emerged that if it was not possible to defeat the United States militarily, perhaps sustained resistance could so impede North American plans as to compel their eventual abandonment. Actions were aimed at embarrassing the United States by demonstrating the vulnerability of its power. A special target was the Yankees' claimed right to protect lives and property: those who appealed for US protection, whether foreigners or Nicaraguans, were singled out for summary and sometimes brutal treatment, but those who forswore such protection were left alone. The war became a kind of armed propaganda. When the United States became convinced that it could not forcibly pacify the country, it would have no choice but to give up trying to impose a Diaz or a Moncada; it would resign itself to allowing Nicaragua to choose its own government in its own fashion. The Sandinistas would then put down their arms. This was the often-repeated pledge—peace when the Marines were withdrawn, not before.

Early manifestations of support in both Latin America and the United States had been encouraging. But the adulation of poets and declarations of solidarity by isolated groups were not enough, and as the struggle dragged on Sandino's hopes of more substantial international aid were disappointed. Both Nicaragua and the outside world seemed to be losing interest, succumbing to venality.

As the 1928 elections drew near Sandino gave vent to his disillusionment. In a "Letter to the Rulers of America," dated August 4, 1928, he chided Latin American leaders for their lack of support. For fifteen months, he said, his army had singlehandedly stood up to the Yankees. "During this time, Gentlemen Presidents, you have not attended to the fulfillment of your duty, because as representatives of free and sovereign peoples you are obliged to protest diplomatically or, if necessary, with the arms the people have entrusted to you," against the US actions in Nicaragua. "Perhaps the governments of Latin America think the Yankees only desire the conquest of Nicaragua and will content themselves with that," he continued. Had they forgotten that "of the twenty-one American republics six have already lost their sovereignty"—Panama, Puerto Rico, Cuba, Haiti, Santo Domingo, and Nicaragua? To concede to the United States any right of intervention in Latin American affairs, as some had done at the Pan American Conference, would bring disastrous consequences. If Latin governments were conscious of their historic responsibilities they would come to Nicaragua's aid rather than waiting until "conquest inflicts its ravages on their own soil."[91]

Nor had attitudes in the United States lived up to Sandino's expectations. "For some time I believed that the North American people were not in agreement with the abuses committed by the government of Calvin Coolidge in Nicaragua," he wrote in October 1928, "but I have become convinced that in general the North Americans applaud the interference of Coolidge in my country." For that reason, he declared, "all North Americans who fall into our hands have reached their end."[92]

From the conclusion that Latin American leaders had defaulted on their duties in the face of the Yankee threat, Sandino developed ideas even more ambitious than the mere thwarting of US plans in Nicaragua. Perhaps he had been called to complete the project of Morazán, reunifying Central America, or even to take up where Bolívar had left off, forging from Latin America one great nation. "In the destiny of our peoples it is said that humble and outraged Nicaragua will be the one designated to call us to unification," he wrote the president of Argentina. He had in mind a Nicaraguan canal, constructed jointly by the Latin America states in their mutual self-interest. If Latin Americans lacked the necessary capital for the work, at least by banding together they could extract a pledge of non-intervention from the United States in return for the concession. He proposed that Argentina host a conference to discuss these ideas.[93]

Receiving no response, Sandino conceived an even more ambitious "Plan for the Realization of the Great Dream of Bolívar." His army, he wrote in his introduction to the plan, could continue to resist the United States for years. But without the support of other Latin countries, it would ultimately be vanquished by the superpower. He urged the Latin American states to join in a formal alliance to maintain their independence "in the face of the pretensions of the imperialism of the United States of North America, or in the face of any other power that tries to subordinate us to its interests." The forty-four points of his plan included formal recognition of a single Latin American nationality, a declaration of the abolition of the Monroe Doctrine, establishment of a Latin American Court of Justice to resolve differences between states, provisions for mutual self-defense, and regulation of foreign investments. He would create a pan-Latin American armed force to step in and provide guarantees during outbreaks of civil war, thus avoiding foreign intervention on the pretext of protecting lives and property. He even included provisions for regulating tariffs and promoting tourism between Latin countries. All this pointed toward eventual unification.[94]

To promote the plan and to renew contacts with the outside world that were broken off by the resignation of Froylán Turcios, his representative in the exterior, Sandino traveled to Mexico in July 1929. He placed great faith in Mexico and hoped to get help there. But the Mexican government was cool to him. He waited at Mérida, Yucatán for six months before President Portes Gil would receive him, and no offer of support resulted from the meeting. In fact, unknown to Sandino, the United States had made a deal with Mexico to expedite the trip, hoping to keep him a virtual prisoner there. Finally, in May 1930, he managed to outwit his surveillants, and returned to Nicaragua to resume the struggle. He had been absent for nearly a year. Though Central American exiles, labor organizations, and the Mexican people in general had greeted him with enthusiasm, his trip was a disappointment; the project of a Latin American alliance in support of Nicaragua had come to nothing.[95]

But appeals to Latin American governments were not Sandino's only strategy for breaking the impasse his movement seemed to have reached. Though he never abandoned the dream of a unified Latin America, he also began to develop a political strategy based on the day-to-day concerns of the Nicaraguan people themselves.

In January 1929, after Moncada's inauguration, Sandino had publicized a series of proposed bases for peace. The Sandinistas promised to recognize Moncada's presidency and lay down their arms, provided that he fulfill certain conditions. He must demand the immediate withdrawal of all US forces from the country and an end to US intervention. He must also agree to a series of reforms, including the abolition of the state tobacco monopoly (a measure favored by small peasants in the North), an eight-hour day for all workers, abolition of wage payments in scrip, equal pay for equal work for women, the regulation of child labor, and the recognition of workers' right to organize. Sandino never expected Moncada to agree to these conditions, but the proposal served to draw a clear line between the two camps regarding Nicaragua's social problems. A manifesto issued shortly before the guerrilla leader returned from Mexico was equally significant. It called on Nicaraguan labor to unionize: only the organized force of the peasants and workers could achieve victory, it declared.[96]

Sandino's return to Nicaragua and the new orientation coincided with the start of the Great Depression. Prices for coffee, the country's chief export, plummeted; mines and lumber companies on the Atlantic Coast closed down. Many more people were thrown out of work by a fungus that infected large sections of the banana growing region and halted operations. Moncada closed schools and paid public employees with bonds. When workers on the Managua-Rama road project were fired without pay in mid-1931, they revolted and joined a Sandinista attack on the Guardia post at Rama.[97]

The Moncada government responded to unrest by stepping up repression, not only against suspected Sandinista supporters but against traditional political opponents as well. Because US Marines officered the National Guard, the nation's sole military and police force, it was the United States that carried out Moncada's repressive measures. With the approval of the Marine commander, General Feland, Moncada formed "volunteer" paramilitary units in the northern regions. Composed of his personal loyalists and commanded by a Mexican mercenary, General Juan Escamilla, these bands terrorized peasants suspected of Sandinista sympathies and summarily executed a number of persons. Some of the killings were carried out with the complicity of accompanying Marine officers. Moreover, some 200 women and children relocated by the "volunteers" died from starvation or exposure.[98]

General Feland defended the *voluntarios* as more efficient and aggressive than the Guardia. But the State Department worried that their activities would reflect on the US. Secretary of State Stimson cautioned the new US minister, Matthew Hanna, to insure that the voluntarios not be identified with the Guardia, and that they be disbanded "as soon as practicable."[99]

In 1930, the Marine officer commanding the Guardia in the northern region developed a plan to forcibly relocate peasants. Like the "strategic hamlet" program tried in Vietnam, its purpose was to deprive the guerrillas of their support base. The plan was soon abandoned, however, presumably for fear of adverse publicity.[100]

The Sandinista movement grew rapidly. It developed a network of collaborators and spies reaching into the Guardia and onto the Marine bases. It published a clandestine newspaper and minted gold coins to circulate in areas under its control. 1931 was a year of "general offensive," and Sandinista military actions extended to several new regions. Moncada had to declare martial law in the departments of León and Chinandega, where Sandinista activity had previously been minimal. Sandinista attacks forced US businesses on the Atlantic Coast to shut down. By November 1931 the situation was, in the words of US Chargé Beaulac, "as grave as, or graver than, at any time since I have been in Nicaragua." He reported to Washington that many of his Nicaraguan contacts "fear that the movement has attained a revolutionary character."[101]

The Hoover Administration faced difficult decisions. When the Stimson pacification plan was imposed in 1927, it was thought the Marines could be reduced to a token force that could then be withdrawn after the 1928 Nicaraguan presidential election. Sandino's revolt had radically altered those calculations. Nonetheless, in the flush of optimism caused by the lull in Sandinista activity during and after the election period, the number of Marines had been reduced again to 3,100 by May 1929, or just over half. But Moncada and the US legation opposed further withdrawals; Hanna advised that despite the lack of activity, Sandino's influence had grown since his departure for Mexico.[102]

Other pressures, however, compelled Hoover to continue the troop reductions despite Sandino's resurgence. The 1929 stock market crash laid economic problems on the White House doorstep that were more than enough to occupy the president. The public, including much of the business sector, was tired of the long and costly Nicaragua intervention, and that reality was reflected more and more in Congress. Then, too, the Marines were just not proving effective in combating Sandinistas. In November 1930, the Foreign Policy Association reported the findings of an investigation it had conducted on the progress of Nicaraguan "reconstruction" since the

Espino Negro pact. It did not express optimism that Sandino could be defeated by military means. Concluded the report:

> If the common population of Nicaragua and Honduras did not believe that the fighting in Nicaragua was between so-called "patriots" and the United States, but was merely what the American government represents it to be—a campaign against "common outlaws"—the problem of the suppression of banditry would be much easier.

Economic problems, it found, were also a significant factor in generating "banditry." Then, too, there were signs of demoralization in the State Department: Secretary Stimson lamented that, in contrast to the Philippines, the Marine record in Nicaragua "simply hasn't been a good job well done."[103]

By June 1930 US personnel in Nicaragua had been reduced to 1,248. That figure nearly doubled again for the 1930 congressional elections, but declined again afterward. By this time the Guardia Nacional had been built up to 2,176, including 203 US officers and trainers. As far as the development of the Guardia permitted, the policy was to keep Marines out of actual combat so as to minimize casualties. But on December 31, 1930, Sandinistas ambushed a patrol of ten Marines in Nueva Segovia, killing all but two. The dramatic attack brought to a head the domestic opposition to intervention, resulting in a new series of protests and congressional withdrawal resolutions. The administration had little choice but to respond to the pressure. On February 13, just hours before a crucial House vote, Stimson announced that the remaining Marines would be withdrawn after the 1932 Nicaraguan presidential election. In the interim, all "police powers" would be turned over to the Guardia, with the Marines confined to garrison duties. Stimson's plan would handle the Sandinistas by building roads into rebel strongholds and increasing the size of the Guardia. The bill before the House, which would have compelled Marine withdrawal six months ahead of Stimson's timetable, was defeated by a margin of 191-133.[104] But without the secretary's prior withdrawal announcement the vote might easily have been reversed.

Development of the Guardia had been slow and difficult. There were nine mutinies in the native force, in which two US officers were killed. Nicaraguan politicians argued over who would control it. No faction, not even Moncada's, wanted to facilitate the growth of a military organization independent of itself. Likewise, there were jealousies and rivalries between the Marine and Guardia command structures. The Marine officers in charge of the Guardia were nominally subject to the regular Marine chain of command, but at the same time were supposedly independent of it. Thus Marine Lieutenant Colonel Beadle, a subordinate of General Feland, was, as *jefe* of the Guardia, a general himself. Naturally Beadle favored independence from the Marines, while Feland maneuvered to bring the Guardia under his own sway. The State Department, meanwhile, wanted to keep the Nicaraguan Sepoys beyond the reach of local political controversies. It was thought this would lead to greater political "stability" and, incidentally, to greater US control. The military men didn't concern themselves with such questions; they argued that letting Moncada have his way with the Guardia would mean greater "efficiency." The process was not totally without comic relief, however: at one point the Yankee Guardia command had the penitentiary painted green, unaware that green symbolized the Conservative Party, Moncada's opponents.[105]

As the 1932 presidential election—and the scheduled US withdrawal—drew near, presidential candidates Adolfo Diaz and Juan Sacasa signed an agreement to make peace with Sandino "the prime objective" of the victor. The pact, made at the behest of the independent *Grupo Patriótico,* was kept secret from the Moncada faction.[106] Anastasio Somoza, Moncada's acting minister of foreign affairs, attempted in the interim to convince the US to abandon its plan to withdraw after the new president's inauguration. US Minister Hanna tried to reassure Somoza:

> I have pointed out that the possibility of conciliating Sandino will be greater if no marines remain in Nicaragua and that even if conciliation proved to be impossible, a united Nicaragua, having deprived Sandino of his principal excuse for continued belligerency, that is, the presence of American Marines on foreign soil, might be in a better position to eliminate banditry than the present Government assisted by the Marines.[107]

Hanna compelled the two candidates, Sacasa (Liberal) and Diaz (Conservative), to sign a pledge to maintain the National Guard as a "nonpolitical" force, and plans were made to turn its command over to Nicaraguan personnel. As the Guardia had only a few recently-trained Nicaraguan officers, who held junior ranks, civilians would have to be appointed to the higher posts.

Hanna's choice to head the Guardia was Anastasio Somoza. Both the aging minister and his younger wife, it was said, were "bewitched" by Somoza's "effervescent personality." Mrs. Hanna reportedly found him to be a charming dancing partner.*[109] To the State Department Minister Hanna wrote:

---

* William Krehm, a *Time* magazine reporter, wrote that Moncada told him some years later that Hanna originally insisted on Somoza being the Liberal presidential candidate, but as Sacasa had already been nominated, Moncada suggested the Guardia appointment instead, both to please Hanna and to spite Sacasa, whom Moncada didn't like.[108]

I look upon him as the best man in the country for the position. I know no one who will labor as intelligently and consciously to maintain the non-partisan character of the Guardia, or will be as efficient in all matters connected with the administration of the Force.[110]

Juan Sacasa, the winning presidential candidate, was sworn in on January 1, 1933. During the preceding four years he had reestablished his credentials with the United States, serving as Moncada's ambassador to Washington. The next day, the last of the US occupation forces departed from Corinto.

Negotiations between representatives of Sacasa and Sandino progressed rapidly, impelled in part, perhaps, by mutual apprehension about the intentions of the new National Guard commander. For his part, Somoza publicly opposed the negotiations, fearing they would result in a reorganization of the Guardia. Nevertheless, Sandino flew into Managua, where he was greeted by an enthusiastic mass outpouring. His main precondition for laying down arms—a US withdrawal—had already been met. In addition, the agreement he signed with Sacasa on February 2 provided his followers with a large tract of land in the Coco River Valley on which to develop an agricultural cooperative.[111]

Typically, both Sandino and the United States claimed victory. The Sandinistas believed their five-and-one-half-year resistance had forced the US to withdraw the Marines.

Dana Munro tried to draw up Washington's balance sheet in the July 1933 issue of *Foreign Affairs* magazine. Munro had played an important part in shaping US Nicaragua policy: he was in charge of Central American affairs at the State Department under Coolidge, served as US chargé in Managua during the war against Sandino, and authored several influential books on Central America. Munro downplayed Sandino's significance. US intervention in Nicaragua had ended, he wrote, "with the withdrawal of the marines and the capitulation of Sandino." He did not, he said, propose to take up the question of whether the intervention had been right or wrong, "a question which could not be discussed adequately without a comprehensive examination of the fundamental bases of the foreign policy of the United States." But as he saw it, the intervention had certainly

increased the prevalent suspicion and dislike of the United States, with noticeable results not only in the sphere of diplomacy but also in commerce. Commercial rivals and other elements interested in creating anti-American sentiment were prompt to seize upon the opportunity for hostile propaganda, and distorted and misrepresented the details of a policy which in any case was highly offensive to Latin American public opinion.

On the other hand, he concluded, "There can be no doubt . . . that the intervention was beneficial to Nicaragua." The US had halted a civil war; its policy, "ably and tactfully carried out by the American representatives in Nicaragua" had helped foster a "spirit of conciliation" between the traditional political parties, and this had been augmented by "a series of free elections." He was hopeful that, thanks to the benevolent influence of the United States, the Nicaraguan Liberals and Conservatives would now be able to "cooperate loyally in a program to establish permanent peace."[112]

Nearly thirty years later, in 1961, Munro had changed his evaluation: "The continent-wide reaction" to the war with Sandino, he wrote, "made the Nicaraguan intervention one of the most disastrous things that ever happened to our Latin American relations."[113]

In a sense, both sides had won a victory. It was partly true that Sandino's guerrillas had compelled withdrawal of the Marines. More precisely, the Marines had been withdrawn in the face of the opposition to intervention, both domestic and international, generated by the Sandinistas' stubborn resistance. Perhaps more important, a Latin American army, and a small one at that, had successfully demonstrated that the United States was not invincible. Operating on the contrary thesis a quarter of a century earlier, Zelaya had resigned his office at the mere threat of intervention.

But the US government had also won. It had disposed of the embarrassing "Sandino affair" and put itself in position to step forward as the "good neighbor" of Latin America. And it still had cards to play in Nicaragua.

At first all went well with the peace between Sandino and Sacasa. Sandino's followers, except for a personal bodyguard of one hundred, disarmed according to plan. But Sandino's political activity on the one hand and ominous moves by Somoza's Guardia on the other heightened tensions as the year progressed. Sandinistas and Guardia clashed. It became increasingly clear that the weak Sacasa could not control Somoza, despite his assurances to Sandino. Under the circumstances Sandino was reluctant to carry out the provision of the peace plan that called for the disarming of his bodyguard. Instead he denounced the Guardia as unconstitutional and demanded its reform. He returned to Managua one year after signing the peace treaty to try to resolve the matter. Leaving the presidential palace after a dinner with Sacasa on the evening of February 21, 1934, Sandino, his brother Sócrates, and two aides were arrested by members of the Guardia, taken to the Managua airfield, and machinegunned.[114]

GOOD NEIGHBORS

> *The third alternative is a policy whereby the United States would merely guarantee stability in Nicaragua, regardless of whether this involved the maintenance of unrepresentative or dictatorial government . . . This policy would have the merit of simplicity—it would be the easiest policy for the United States to apply.*
>
> —From a 1930 report summarizing policy options under consideration by the US State Department.

ANASTASIO SOMOZA GARCIA was born in 1896 in the village of San Marcos, just a few kilometers from Niquinohomo, birthplace of Augusto Sandino the year before. His father, Anastasio Somoza Reyes, was, like Don Gregorio Sandino, a coffee planter. Somoza Reyes worked the farm his wife had inherited; though less successful than Sandino's father, he was nevertheless well-connected. As a senator during the Conservative regime inaugurated by the Dawson Pact, he was able to send his son "Tacho" to school in Granada under the guardianship of the country's foreign minister (and later president), Diego Manuel Chamorro.[1]

But apart from the coincidence of the time and place of their birth and the similarity of family and educational backgrounds, Tacho Somoza and his future victim Sandino could not have been less alike. Though Somoza's father was a Conservative politician, young Tacho at first showed no interest in politics. After getting the maid pregnant, he was sent to live in Philadelphia with his uncle, a wealthy physician. There he attended business school, studied bookkeeping and advertising, and worked at several jobs, including it seems, that of used car salesman. The selling of used cars would have been an apt choice for Somoza, because all the traits popularly associated with that profession—backslapping unctuousness, gaudy bad taste, braggadocio, sleezy lowbrow humor, and dishonesty—fit him to a tee.

Business acumen was the one thing Tacho lacked, however. When he returned to Nicaragua several years later his business ventures—opening a store and later an automobile dealership—were failures. Though he married into a wealthy León Liberal family, the bride's father was not disposed to support his uncouth son-in-law. Tacho had to try his hand at various jobs, even that of outhouse inspector for the Rockefeller Foundation Sanitation Mission. But he soon tired of such efforts to support himself and his family. Arrested for participation in a counterfeiting scheme, he was saved from prison by the former guardian who was now president of the republic, Diego Chamorro.

The events of 1925 and 1926—the coup by Emiliano Chamorro and the Constitutionalist uprising—at last awakened Somoza to the possibilities of a career in politics. Sensing the direction of political fortunes, he took up the Constitutionalist cause, and persuading some of the locals to join him, tried to seize control of his home town, San Marcos. Chamorrista troops quickly squashed the clumsy effort and captured its ringleader. But once again the old family ties with the Chamorros came to Tacho's rescue, and he was pardoned on a promise of good conduct. Bestowing on himself the title of "general" for his role in the San Marcos putsch, Somoza sat out the rest of the war in exile in neighboring Costa Rica.

With US intervention and the arrival of the Stimson mission, however, Tacho saw his chance, as did fellow opportunist and distant relative Moncada. The return of North American tutelage would mean political rearranging, and he was not about to be left out. Back in Nicaragua, he parlayed his ingratiating manner, his fluency in English (generously laced with North American slang), and credentials as the son-in-law of an influential Liberal into a job as a translator and constant companion of the Yankees. Stimson himself was so favorably impressed that he wrote in his diary, "Somoza is a very frank, friendly, likeable young Liberal and his attitude impresses me more favorably than almost any other." Tacho stuck close to the US military personnel charged with setting up the National Guard, and when Moncada became president he was given a job in the Ministry of Foreign Affairs with special responsibility for acting as a go-between with the North Americans.[2]

Nicaraguan "yanquistas," as Sandino called those who identified their interests with the United States, were quick to play on the vanity of some US military personnel. Much to the consternation of the Managua diplomatic corps—including the US legation—Marine commander Brigadier General Feland and Special Service Squadron chief Rear Admiral Sellers had insisted on being accorded special diplomatic status by the Moncada government. This enabled them to take precedence over the chargés of other countries in matters of diplomatic protocol. Feland, in particular, jealously clung to this privilege. Taking his cue from Moncada, who made a major production of presenting Admiral Latimer with an improvised medal after the Espino Negro settlement, Tacho began arranging for medals to be awarded regularly to US officers. These trinkets of gold, silver, and bronze (according to the rank of the recipient) soon became much sought after, and the wives of officers who received lesser awards clamored after Tacho for the more prestigious ones.[3]

Somoza's Philadelphia bookkeeping course may not have taken him far, but he put to good use the things learned in the States about North Americans. Whether dangling medals, charming Minister Hanna's wife with his ballroom dancing, entertaining journalists with locker room jokes, or manipulating Yankee anticommunist paranoia, throughout his career he was a master at getting the gringos to do what he wanted. Under the circumstances it was not surprising that Tacho became the first Nicaraguan commander of the Guardia Nacional.

Of course, the manipulation was not all one-sided. Somoza was made Guardia chief because he was known to be friendly to US interests. The Guardia was to be a "non-political" force that would maintain a stable, pro-US government by mediating between the fractious Liberals and Conservatives. The Yankee arbiters of Nicaragua's destiny could not have been blind to the consequences of an organization like the National Guard headed by someone as unscrupulous as Somoza. Six years earlier, as head of a similar US-organized and -trained "non-political" army, Rafael Trujillo had seized control in the Dominican Republic after formal US control had ended there; that fact certainly had not escaped the notice of analytical State Department minds. The danger was clear to both Sandino and Sacasa as soon as Somoza became Guardia *jefe.* Likewise, Arthur Bliss Lane, who replaced Hanna as head of the US legation at the end of 1933, was soon sending the Department an accurate picture of goings-on in the country. In any case, soon after Sandino's murder it was widely accepted that Somoza was the real power in Nicaragua.[4]

Fearing that Sandino could foil his plans even from the grave, Tacho soon began orchestrating a drive to discredit the memory of his dead enemy. He published a ghostwritten book titled *The True Sandino,* which portrayed the late rebel leader as a menace to society. Somoza, his ally Moncada, their supporters, and the newspapers under their influence depicted Sandino's assassination as a patriotic act. Before long Somoza felt confident enough to publicly acknowledge his responsibility for the deed, claiming it was done with the acquiescence of US Minister Lane, a charge made also by Sandino's lieutenants. Lane and the State Department hotly denied complicity, and indeed, there was no evidence of direct United States involvement. But neither were US representatives upset over Sandino's death. Lane rebuked Somoza for having violated his "word of honor" to "take no action against Sandino without my consent," but that was all.[5] For his part, Tacho must have felt certain that if the United States did not look with favor on Sandino's murder, at least it would not react strongly; otherwise he would never have undertaken it, much less admitted his authorship. For Tacho well knew that those who incurred the displeasure of the US could find their ambitions vetoed just as those of Emiliano Chamorro had been in 1926. He understood that the death of Sandino was to the advantage of the United States: so long as the radical *guerrillero* remained alive he represented a threat not only to Somoza but to the whole "American program" in Nicaragua.

Most Nicaraguans simply assumed the United States was behind Somoza. Minister Lane made an effort to restrain him and to strengthen the Sacasa government, but did not receive State Department backing. Lane repeatedly asked his chiefs in Washington to publicly disavow partisanship for the National Guard jefe and to reiterate the policy of the 1923 Washington accords denying recognition to regimes that came to power by violent or unconstitutional means. His requests were always turned down, with the explanation that the Department wanted to avoid the impression of trying to control affairs in Central America. The Roosevelt Administration had embarked on its vaunted Good Neighbor Policy and such public statements, they said, would give the appearance of intervention.[6]

Roosevelt and his secretary of state, Cordell Hull, were certainly sincere in their desire to disentangle the US from its long and costly Nicaragua involvement. They had much bigger things to worry about, as did Herbert Hoover before them who first used the "good neighbor" phrase.[7] But the United States had unleashed Somoza and the National Guard on Nicaragua, and Latin Americans familiar with long-established US policy goals in the region found the disavowal of further responsibility—in the name of good-neighborliness—a bit hard to swallow.

Putting his own followers in key Guardia posts and cultivating the allegiance of junior officers unhappy at seeing politicians appointed to fill the higher ranks, Tacho swiftly consolidated his power. Lane immediately saw that Somoza had "sacrificed respect of his men for popularity," and that Sacasa, in turn, had little or no control over the National Guard commander. In fact, an atmosphere of siege gripped the presidential palace. As the head of the only legal armed force in the country, which acted as both army and police, Tacho could attract the support of opportunistic anti-Sacasa political factions like those headed by Moncada or Emiliano Chamorro, and could intimidate others. His influence over the Congress was such that by August 1934 he had pushed through a bill exonerating the National Guardsmen accused of killing Sandino. He used the same leverage to have relatives appointed to government jobs.[8]

Lane advised the State Department in March 1935 that Nicaraguans still believed the US would choose the next president of their country, and the choice would be Somoza. Tacho himself was doing everything he could to foster the impression that he was Washington's man—something he and his offspring would do for the next forty-three years. At last the Department did give Lane a go-ahead to issue a vaguely-worded public statement to the effect that, in line with the Good Neighbor Policy, the US would not favor any candidate for the 1936 election. But not even Lane wanted to take a position opposing Somoza's presidential bid, despite the unfavorable impression Tacho's ascension would make. Ultimately, however, Lane concluded that the National Guard was "one of the sorriest examples on our part of our inability to understand that we should not meddle in other peoples' affairs."[9]

Nicaragua's incipient fascist movement, the *Camisas Azules,* or Blueshirts, staged rallies and demonstrations in which they hailed the killing of Sandino and compared Somoza to Mussolini and Hitler. Proving he had learned a few things from *Il Duce* and *Der Fuehrer,* El Jefe Somoza used fascist gangs to create disturbances so the National Guard could declare martial law; he, not the civil authorities, would then be in charge. Later Tacho rewarded the fascists by appointing their leader to head the Ministry of Education. Orders from President Sacasa were ignored or openly defied, while Somoza's own newspaper denounced the weakness and vacillation of the government. Nicaraguans told Lane the Guardia was making extravagant and unauthorized expenditures, imprisoning government officials without trial, and assassinating innocent people. Many of Sandino's remaining followers were massacred, including their wives and children, and critical newspaper editors were harassed, arrested, or kidnapped. On at least one occasion, Camisas Azules, acting with the aid of the Guardia, burned a newspaper office.[10]

Sacasa and the members of his government worried over what to do about Somoza. They asked Washington for permission to reorganize the Guardia. Assistant Secretary of State Sumner Welles replied:

> the Department does not feel that it could comment officially on the proposed reorganization of the Nicaraguan Guardia any more than it could on the reorganization of the military forces of any other independent, sovereign nation. It is the Department's opinion, nevertheless, that

the continued maintenance of a Guardia Nacional organization substantially as at present is important to the future peace and welfare of Nicaragua.[11]

Whatever their intent, such equivocal declarations did not serve to strengthen the self-confidence of Nicaraguan politicians. They encouraged Somoza and discouraged the resistance to his rise. The "opinion" of the State Department had been law for so many years that neither Somoza nor his opponents seriously believed the Rooseveltian "hands off" declarations, no matter how often they were repeated.

A "person very close to the President"—apparently Sacasa's wife—came to Lane to advise him that the government intended to force Somoza to resign, relying on military assistance from El Salvador and Honduras in the event of Guardia resistance. Secretary Hull instructed his minister to indicate that it "would be a matter of profound regret" if any action were taken to bring about intervention by other Central American countries. When it became clear that Somoza would be a candidate to succeed Sacasa despite his constitutional ineligibility (relatives of the incumbent—Somoza's wife was Sacasa's niece—and those holding high military rank were barred from running) the US legation was again requested to make a statement. The curt reply was that only the Nicaraguan courts could rule on constitutional questions.[12] To a powerless government, such high-sounding advice was little more than a death sentence.

As the 1936 election approached, Liberals and Conservatives agreed to run a joint candidate in a last ditch effort to stop Somoza. In response, Tacho administered the *coup de grâce* to the government. In early June he surrounded the presidential palace with National Guardsmen and forced Sacasa to resign.[13]

Just a few months earlier the US had granted recognition to Salvadoran General Hernández Martínez who had come to power through a coup, and had formally announced its abandonment of the non-recognition provisions of the 1923 Washington accord. Though this change in policy was intended to bring the US into line with generally-accepted international practice, the timing had the effect of giving a green light to Somoza. Significantly, as Somoza's coup got underway, Secretary Hull refused the Managua legation permission to join representatives of Latin and European nations in appealing to Somoza to renounce the use of force.[14]

Like Emiliano Chamorro eleven years before, Tacho demonstrated an incongruous punctilio for the formalities of constitutional procedure, despite the scrapping of the 1923 Washington pact. Through a submissive Congress, he had a proxy, Carlos Brenes Jarquin, designated to finish out the remaining months of Sacasa's term. Jarquin dutifully pushed the election back to December so as to insure the constitutionally required six-month interval between his boss' election and the incumbency of Sacasa. Somoza also gave up his Guardia post for a short time to circumvent the prohibition on the election of military officers. Washington avoided the question of recognition by merely sending the new foreign minister a note acknowledging the changes in government personnel.[15]

Since the traditional Liberal and Conservative parties had jointly nominated Leonardo Argüello for the presidency, Tacho formed his own "Nationalist Liberal" and "Nationalist Conservative" parties. Given the climate of repression and the unlikelihood of winning an election supervised by Somoza's Guardia, Argüello and his supporters boycotted. Needless to say, when the ballots were counted Somozaism had won the first of many landslide electoral victories—107,000 votes for, 169 against.[16]

Exiled former presidents Juan Sacasa, Emiliano Chamorro, and Adolfo Diaz arrived in the United States shortly before the election. As three of the four Nicaraguan signers of the 1932 agreement that turned the Guardia Nacional over to Nicaraguan control, they addressed the following appeal to Secretary Hull:

> Previous to the signing of the agreement, we called the attention of the American Minister, Hon. Matthew E. Hanna, to the danger that the maintenance of the National Guard, under the new command called for in the plan, would eventually constitute a threat to peace and order, for, under such command, it would hardly retain the non-political character it had previously enjoyed. To this, Minister Hanna replied that we could rest assured that the American Government would morally guarantee the agreement . . . Trusting in this promise . . . we agreed to sign the proposed agreement. The independence from Government control which it had been considered convenient to give the National Guard at the time of its establishment in 1927 under American officers, took away from the Executive all effective interference in the management of that institution. Therefore, when the United States Marines withdrew, the new Nicaraguan Government . . . was left, except for promised United States moral support, entirely at the mercy of the Guard.

They went on to recount the illegal steps taken by the Guardia chief up to the coup that forced Sacasa from office. Since that time, they said, Somoza "holds sway over the country by armed force and violence, treading on liberty and suffrage." They pointed out the "lack of guarantees which make impossible all electoral activity" and called upon the United States to "lend Nicaragua in these times of need the valuable moral support of its friendly influence to the end that all the evils emanating from the National Guard" might be remedied. They did not ask, they said, for renewed occupation or for the support of any political faction. But

the principle of non-intervention, dear to all the Latin American peoples and on which is based the policy of "good-neighbor" so full of prestige and so emphatically proclaimed by President Roosevelt, must not
exclude the friendly cooperation between the American countries, in
as much as indifference to the struggles and misfortunes of a friendly
or sister nation can in no way denote goodwill towards her.

In particular, they added pointedly, "in the present case of Nicaragua, such
cooperation from the United States follows as a natural sequence of the
international origin of the National Guard."[17]

But Diaz, Chamorro, and Sacasa, who in the past had demonstrated
canine faithfulness to the United States, no longer had the ear of the State
Department. The US minister attended Tacho's inauguration to Nicaragua's
highest office on January 1, 1937, and if the Roosevelt Administration dis-
approved of anything he had done to get there, it was a well-kept secret.

Even while still an obscure figure on the Nicaraguan political scene, Tacho
had acquired the nickname "El Yanqui" for his command of North American slang, his mannerisms, and his apparent preference for the company
of US military and diplomatic personnel. Once installed in the presidency
he lost no time in making his "friendship" for the United States known
to everyone—he had not studied advertising for nothing. Within months,
articles began to appear in US newspapers and magazines portraying Somoza as "intensely pro-American." References to the murder of Sandino or
to the methods Tacho used in his ascent to power miraculously disappeared.
He was now depicted as progressive, a "builder" who brought stability.
After all, as an article in *Harpers* put it, the US "cannot get cooperation
from a nation torn by civil war."[18]

T HE CAMISAS AZULES had helped Somoza in his rise to power. The
fascists greatly admired Tacho, or at least saw him as the only promising
candidate to be Nicaragua's Mussolini. The real Mussolini demonstrated
his regard for Somoza by presenting him with a Fiat mini-tank, and Tacho,
in turn, looked up to the fascist leaders, especially Spain's Franco. But the
Nicaraguan dictator had a keen sense of international as well as domestic
political expediency; it didn't take him long to perceive how world align-
ments were shaping up for the coming war. Somoza understood that he
must fall in behind the powerful neighbor whose "backyard" he occupied.
He knew well the value of having his anticommunist credentials in order,
having lived in the United States during the era of the Palmer Raids and
having watched as his predecessors Diaz and Moncada played the anticommunist card. In fact, Tacho began discovering communist plots even
before becoming president. But now he turned on the fascists as well, and
quickly became one of the foremost defenders of democracy in the

hemisphere. He was, he said, "checking every anti-democratic attempt in my country, wherever it originated," and announced that he was not only "granting complete freedom to all free and democratic institutions" in Nicaragua, but defending the "democratic traditions of the Americas" against all "foreign systems," whether fascist or communist, as well.[19]

Of course, US diplomats and journalists alike knew Somoza's democratic talk was so much hot air for consumption up north. US Minister Merideth Nicholson told Secretary Hull that Somoza "sees in democracy only a device for the easy domination of his country, with abundant opportunities for plunder to the strains of the national anthem." Thanks to Nicholson, the State Department was kept well-informed of Somoza's real activities, though it chose to say nothing about them. Nicholson told of a web of repression and brutality that included wholesale political killings. But Somoza was smart enough not to kill well-known opponents: "While prominent Conservatives are not killed, they are apprized of the Executive's displeasure by the murder of their ranch employees," wrote the US minister. To reporters, Tacho confided that his version of democracy was stronger medicine than the usual stuff. Nicaragua, he told them, was a sick child, and "when a boy's sick, you've got to force castor oil down him whether he likes it or not. After he's been to the toilet a few times he'll be all right."[20]

Somoza's appeal had a dollars and cents side, too. He wanted it to be known that he welcomed US capital in Nicaragua, and was soon reported to be signing contracts that granted "liberal aid and concessions" to Yankee investors.[21]

Tacho may have acted the buffoon at times, but he was no fool; he wanted something in return for his friendship. An early ambition was to cajole the North Americans into coming across on the Bryan-Chamorro Treaty and finally digging the Nicaragua canal.

Having completed the canal at Panama, the United States extracted the Bryan-Chamorro Treaty as an insurance policy and as an added measure of control over Nicaragua, not with any intention of building another waterway. Nevertheless, the increase in traffic through Panama during the post-World War I economic boom was so great that for a time many thought a second canal would be necessary. US engineers made new surveys of the Nicaragua route in the late 1920s. Then came the Depression; the great merchant fleets lay rusting at anchor and no funds were available for such projects. But Tacho's consolidation of power coincided with a partial revival of trade; that and the looming prospect of another world war stirred anew the talk of a Nicaragua canal. However insignificant the flap may have been, it was enough to excite Somoza, who quickly acquired strategically-located properties for his own account. Hoping to finally pin the US down to a commitment, he suggested that, as a first step, the United States finance the dredging of the San Juan River to Lake Nicaragua. That part of the project would cost relatively little—perhaps only $3 million—and the rest would come later. In return he offered to let US troops use the waterway and complete the crossing from Lake Nicaragua to the Pacific by rail.[22]

He began angling for an invitation to Washington to discuss the plan with Roosevelt. "Ever since I began my political life I have appreciated the importance to Nicaragua of cultivating cordial relations with the United States," said Tacho in a bit of understatement. Playing his hand close, he told reporters there were many reasons why Roosevelt would want to talk to him: "I am sure Nicaragua can, as a small nation, contribute her views to the great ideals of democracy which are being tested by the grave problems of Europe." The invitation to visit the United States was soon forthcoming, despite the State Department's belief that the trip "would be a political move to strengthen the position of the Nicaraguan President in his own country."[23]

Meanwhile Somoza demonstrated his concern for the practical application of democratic procedures. He called a Constituent Assembly to revise the constitutional prohibition on presidential second terms. While the delegates were at it early in 1939, they obligingly voted to extend Tacho's stay in office until May 1, 1947, saving the voters the trouble of going to the polls.[*25] The timing of Somoza's visit to the United States—just six weeks later—had the effect of putting Washington's stamp of approval on these antics.

Good neighbor Roosevelt pulled all the stops for Tacho's visit. He went to Union Station to meet his guest at the train, the first time FDR, disabled by polio, had left the White House to greet a head of state since entering it in 1933. The two leaders of the free world left Union Station together in an open car. Five thousand soldiers, sailors, and Marines in full dress uniform lined the route to the White House, presenting arms as Somoza passed; joining them were thousands of federal employees who had been let off work to attend. Field guns boomed a twenty-one gun salute and forty-two airplanes flew overhead. Tacho was treated like European royalty. The *New York Times* thought perhaps the display was meant "to make it clear to the people of Latin America that the good neighbor to the north is also a strong neighbor and a useful friend in time of trouble." Roosevelt himself, in preparing for Somoza's visit, reportedly stated the matter more bluntly: "He's a sonofabitch," said FDR, "but he's ours."[26]

---

* Despite Somoza's growing coolness toward them, the Camisas Azules delegates played an active role in the Constituent Assembly, proposing that El Jefe be proclaimed president for life.[24]

On May 8, Tacho addressed the US Senate, appealing for construction of a Nicaragua canal. The day before he had presented Roosevelt with a table whose top was elaborately inlaid in gold, ebony, and other tropical hardwoods. On one side appeared the likeness of Theodore Roosevelt above the Panama Canal, on the other, Franklin Roosevelt over the Nicaragua Canal.[27]

Speaking to the Pan American Society at the swank Waldorf-Astoria Hotel in New York City, Somoza offered his country for the "defense of the United States which is the defense of the continent," and added, "the democracy that is in the American continent we have learned from you of the United States." When he visited Philadelphia, his one-time home, Valley Forge Military Academy presented him with the "Order of Anthony Wayne."[28]

Tacho and FDR in 1939

In contrast to the public VIP reception, however, Roosevelt's offer of aid to Tacho was stingy; it was motivated, moreover, by considerations of national gain. An agreement signed on May 22 provided what was described as assistance to combat "economic penetration of Latin America by the totalitarian powers of Europe." Roosevelt did not offer to dredge the San Juan River, much less dig a billion dollar canal. Two million of the $2.5 million loan consisted of Import-Export Bank credits for the purchase of US-manufactured machinery, mainly for road-building; it was to be repaid at 5 percent interest. Another $500,000 in short term credit would go to stabilize the exchange rate for Nicaraguan currency, a measure explicitly intended to benefit US holders of Nicaraguan bonds. The United States would assign personnel to head a military academy for the Guardia Nacional and help Tacho set up an air force. The US would also send experts to study the possibilities for "non-competitive" agricultural products in Nicaragua. Finally, as a sop to Tacho, engineers would make another feasibility study for a Nicaraguan waterway—to add to the piles of studies collecting dust since 1852.[29]

Apart from repaying the loan, Nicaragua was pledged to encourage the investment of US capital and to make prompt payments on its outstanding bonds. Somoza's hosts had wanted to impose a new US financial advisor as part of the deal, but Tacho balked, explaining that public opinion in Nicaragua would not tolerate any more US-appointed overseers. Such supervision, he said, would have to be unofficial.

Commenting on the agreement, the *New York Times* wrote:

So far as our strictly commercial and financial relations are concerned, Nicaragua is a small factor. Our trade with her accounts for only about one-tenth of 1 percent of our total foreign trade. The importance of the treaty is elsewhere—in the strengthening of our bonds with a country that occupies an important strategic position in the Caribbean Sea, relative to the Panama Canal.[30]

Somoza left for home feeling his mission had been accomplished. Roosevelt had personally promised him that the US would finance construction of a shallow-draft barge canal in the San Juan River if the report showed it to be feasible. Tacho and his party "naturally were overjoyed with the President's intentions and act as though a barge canal was as good as already agreed upon," wrote Laurence Duggan, chief of the State Department's Division of American Republics, to Minister Nicholson in Managua. But, added Duggan, in his opinion no canal of any kind would be built regardless of what the survey showed.[31]

Canal or no canal, the lavish reception in the US was of tremendous value to Somoza. Any Nicaraguans who may have harbored doubts were now fully convinced that Tacho was Washington's man; and in Nicaragua that counted for just as much, if not more, than controlling the National Guard.

Six months later, a visiting US congressional delegation gave the dictator an opportunity to return Yankee hospitality. Tacho treated the North American legislators to one of the biggest banquets ever held in Managua, and the panegyrics were as abundant as the food and drink. After toasting Roosevelt, Tacho proclaimed, "If the United States should ever get into

a war, which is against our hopes, Nicaragua will put 10,000 well-trained
men at the service of the United States within twenty-four hours. There
will be 40,000 within sixty days, besides our landing fields and other facilities." Senator Elmer Thomas of Oklahoma replied with a toast to Somoza. "I have never visited a more friendly and hospitable country," said
Thomas, "It is my personal belief that the United States would more quickly
go to war on behalf of Nicaragua than for any other country."[32]

Somoza's gratitude to FDR was unbounded. He renamed Managua's
main street *Avenida Roosevelt;* he built a statue to the US president and
made his birthday a national holiday. Proclaimed Tacho, "President
Roosevelt seems like a brother to me or a member of my family. I shall
never forget our meeting in 1939, for in five minutes it seemed as if we
had been friends for years."[33]

When Secretary of War Stimson, early in 1941, advised Roosevelt on
the progress of the San Juan River survey report, the president replied that
"he no longer desired the completion of the report." The project was being dropped "because of the excessive cost and lack of sufficient economic
or political advantages" to the United States. But Tacho was led to believe
that the war was the reason the US couldn't help with dredging the San
Juan River. He was not about to release Roosevelt from his commitment
so easily, however. In 1942, when it became clear there would be no San
Juan canal, Somoza proposed that the US help instead with construction
of a road to the Atlantic Coast and the capacitation of the port at El Bluff
for deep-draft vessels. He stressed the project's "great strategic importance
for Continental defense."[34]

The State Department considered helping Somoza complete a road, already begun, as far as Rama, some sixty miles from El Bluff on the Escondido River. Asking for the opinion of the War Department on the military
value of the project, Acting Secretary of State Sumner Welles received the
following reply:

Washington, April 2, 1942

Dear Mr. Secretary:

   During a recent conversation which I had with Ambassador Boal and
Mr. Bonsal, of your Department, I was requested by the latter to forward to you the War Department's opinion as to the desirability, from
a military point of view, of building the Rama Road in Nicaragua.

   The subject of munitions of war under lend-lease for Nicaragua and
certain other military questions were also discussed.

   With respect to the building of the Rama Road, it is the opinion of
the Operations Section that the execution of this project will tend to
increase the stability of the country, and so minimize the possibility of
trouble with disaffected elements. The road would have a decided tac-

tical value, should it become necessary for United States troops to intervene, either because of attempted uprising by the enemy nationals along
the western coast, or because of an attempted hostile raid.

Sincerely yours,

Dwight D. Eisenhower*

It was agreed to provide $4 million from Roosevelt's discretionary Emer-
gency National Defense Fund for completion of the Pan American Highway through Nicaragua and for the road to connect it with Rama. The
US would also survey the remaining distance from Rama to El Bluff, but
would not finance the construction of that section, nor would it help with
deepening the port. In return, Somoza had to agree to make no further
mention of canalizing the San Juan and to release the United States from
any further obligation, explicit or implied, arising from the Bryan-Chamorro
Treaty or from the 1939 Roosevelt-Somoza meeting.[35]

The road to Rama turned into a boondoggle that dragged on for twenty
years; it was not completed until the 1960s.[36] The section from Rama to
the Caribbean was never built, and the port of El Bluff was not conditioned for large ships. Communication with Bluefields became somewhat
easier, but aside from that the Rama road served mainly to access Somoza
properties. It did little for the development of Nicaragua.

During the Second World War Nicaragua was assigned to produce raw
materials for the war effort. US PT boats and other naval vessels were built
with Nicaraguan mahogany; primary products from Nicaragua like rubber and citronella oil replaced those from areas of Asia under Japanese
control. The US Department of Agriculture set up a research station at
El Recreo for "stimulating production of crops complementary to the
agriculture of the United States." By mid-1943, 95 percent of Nicaraguan
exports were going to the big northern neighbor.[37]

Through Roosevelt's Export-Import Bank, the Inter-American Development Commission and other agencies, Nicaragua, along with the rest of
Latin America, was obliged to pledge itself to shun "economic nationalism" by reducing or eliminating tariffs, encouraging foreign (which meant
US) investment, and refraining from the use of customs protection to foster
new industries. Government was to promote private enterprise through such
measures as tax incentives and a minimum of regulation; it was not to enter
into competition with private capital. These parameters for "development"
would be continued and enforced after the war by the lending policies of
the Inter-American Development Bank, the International Bank for Recon-

---

* Eisenhower was then a major general and assistant chief of staff on the general staff of
the War Department; Pierre de L. Boal was US ambassador to Nicaragua; Philip W. Bonsal
was chief of the State Department's Division of the American Republics.

struction and Development (later known as the World Bank), and the International Monetary Fund.[38]

Good neighbors were tributary neighbors. Nicaragua became an economic satellite of the United States, its role to supply raw materials, buy US industrial products, and absorb a portion of excess US investment capital when required. Development of both industry and agriculture was limited to non-competitive products—those not produced by the United States. It was better than a colony: Nicaragua provided the economic and strategic benefits without the administrative and political overhead.

Tacho declared war on Japan on December 9, 1941, two days after Pearl Harbor. Though he never got the chance to send the Guardia Nacional to fight for the United States, World War II did provide him with other opportunities. He had already received $1.3 million worth of US arms under lend-lease—ostensibly for the purpose of hemispheric defense, making Nicaragua one of the first nations to benefit from the program. The United States built air bases in Managua and Puerto Cabezas as well as a naval base at Corinto; these were turned over to Tacho at the end of the war. The stationing of dollar-spending US personnel at these wartime bases was a boon to the entrepreneurial classes, especially the *somocistas,* but the resulting inflation imposed one more hardship on the people, already suffering from war-induced scarcities. Nicaraguan pilots received scholarships to train in the United States, and Somoza emerged from the war with a considerable air force. Keeping up his long-standing practice, he frequently awarded medals to members of United States military missions who visited Nicaragua, making many friends in the process. In 1943, Guardia cadets were sent for the first time to Fort Gulick in the Panama Canal Zone for training. By the end of Somoza rule, Nicaragua, with one of the smallest populations in the hemisphere, would have more than 4,000 National Guard members trained at the base, later called the "School of the Americas," more than any other Latin American country.[39]

During the war the properties of German and Italian nationals were confiscated and sold at auction. The Guardia made sure Tacho had no competition in the bidding for choice pieces of real estate, which he acquired for a fraction of their worth. He bought the properties of one German, valued at $1 million, for only $150,000—money he took from the National Bank of Nicaragua and never repaid.[40]

Somoza compensated for his lack of business ability with the advantages of being El Jefe—The Boss—as the Guardia members called him. National Guardsmen worked his farms, or laborers were simply listed on the government payroll as Guardia members. The Guardia also supplied the trucks and gasoline he needed. Government road and railroad building projects led to Tacho's properties or to those of his relatives. He manipulated the laws to favor his cattle exporting operations—he owned fifty-one cattle ranches by 1944—and used licensing procedures to restrict his competitors. In fact, everyone doing business in Nicaragua, at least those who weren't Somoza cronies or relatives, had to pay tribute to Tacho through one or another form of tax, licensing fee, or levy. The Guardia, meanwhile, for whom salaries merely supplemented graft and corruption, acted not only as the nation's sole military and police force, but administered a host of other activities including mail, telephone and telegraph, radio broadcasting, and customs inspection—not to mention prostitution and gambling. Just two years after Tacho came to power, US Minister Nicholson wrote, "What limit may be imposed to the man's rapaciousness . . . does not at this time appear." After ten years Somoza had become one of the wealthiest men in Latin America, with personal assets estimated at $120 million.[41]

José Maria Moncada—the former best friend of the United States in Nicaragua, one-time protégé of Henry Stimson, and mentor of Somoza—was accused of being unusually corrupt during his term as president. But, quipped Moncada, "now that Tacho is president, they say I was an honest man." Explained Somoza, "Godammit, I want to make sure that my family has enough to live on after I die."[42]

July 1944 witnessed mass demonstrations against the dictatorship, the first serious challenge Tacho faced since coming to power. His relationship with the United States immediately became an issue. The Roosevelt Administration's Good Neighbor image had already been tarnished by widespread criticism in Latin America of the practice of providing lend-lease arms to Caribbean dictators. Now, eighteen lend-lease aircraft arrived in Nicaragua the very week Tacho was shooting or imprisoning student demonstrators.[43]

US Ambassador James B. Stewart was a big booster of Somoza "stability." His practice of accompanying the dictator on political trips caused Emiliano Chamorro and Juan Sacasa to travel to Washington in 1944 to lodge a protest.[44]

Tacho, fond of puns, would refer to Stewart as "my steward." Invited to spend one Easter at Somoza's Montelimar estate, the US ambassador rolled up his sleeves and joined several of Tacho's cabinet ministers helping to load a boat with cement from the Somoza factory. An anti-Somoza journalist commented on the incident to *Time* correspondent William Krehm, "Frankly, there are moments when I'm pleased with Somoza—when he humiliates the representatives of the country to which Nicaragua owes so much humiliation."[45]

Colonel Irving A. Lindberg, who succeeded Clifford Ham as collector-general of customs in 1928, also headed Somoza's wartime price and commerce control board. In that capacity he signed an order for confiscation of any business that shut down in a planned anti-Somoza strike. Due in part to Lindberg's order, the strike failed to materialize. Lindberg was a US citizen; moreover, his appointment as customs collector had been approved by the State Department during the protectorate. Theoretically, at least, he was still answerable to the State Department. (To many natives, Lindberg proved that Nicaragua was still a protectorate.) Having signed the confiscation order without State Department consent, he was advised to refrain from political involvement in the future. But after considerable discussion the Department decided not to discontinue its ties with Lindberg, notwithstanding the repeated protestations that the "special relationship" with Nicaragua had ended with the Good Neighbor Policy. It was thought to be useful to have an "American" in the position of responsibility for payment of Nicaragua's foreign debts and for regulating the nation's imports, 95 percent of which were now coming from the United States.[46]

To add to US embarrassment, Tacho sent hundreds of arrested demonstrators to a prison camp on one of the Corn Islands. According to the Bryan-Chamorro Treaty, the two islands were under lease to the United States and were to be treated as part of the United States. Actually, the US had never taken possession, and the islands remained under de facto Nicaraguan control. But Secretary Hull asked Somoza to move the prisoners elsewhere, and Tacho complied.[47]

The US relationship with Somoza came under further strain the following year when Tacho announced he would be a candidate for "reelection" when his term expired in 1947. Nelson Rockefeller, then undersecretary of state, called in Somoza's ambassador and told him "unofficially" that the reelection of his boss would not be in the best interest of either Nicaragua or the United States. The US ambassador in Managua repeated the message directly to Tacho. To make the point more emphatic, when Somoza asked to buy 10,000 new rifles for the National Guard, he was told there were none available.[48]

The refusal considerably upset Fletcher Warren, the new US ambassador, who had taken to tagging along after Tacho, just as Stewart had done before him. "We have asked President Somoza for nothing that we haven't received," Warren wrote the Department; "I have confidence in the President and think that as long he is President we would be foolish to make an enemy out of a chief of state who has consistently been our friend." But the rifles weren't forthcoming, not just then anyway. And to add insult to injury, when Tacho announced plans to attend the graduation of his son Anastasio Junior (Tachito) from West Point, he was told the visit must be strictly unofficial, and asked to keep it as short as possible.[49] But

Ambassador Warren was instructed to discourage a rumored Guardia plot against Somoza; US discomfiture had its limits.

Tacho finally did renounce the intention to have himself reelected. Instead he nominated Leonardo Argüello, the aging one-time opponent who had withdrawn in protest from the 1936 election. Argüello had since fallen in to step with Somozaism and seemed a dependable puppet. His rival was Enoc Aguado, who had the backing of both the Conservatives and the recently-formed Independent Liberals. Political prisoners were released and press censorship relaxed; it looked like a real contest. Somoza opponents' hopes for a fair election were buoyed by public pronouncements against dictatorship by US Assistant Secretary of State Spruille Braden and by US denunciations of electoral fraud in Poland. But when the balloting took place on February 2, 1947, those planning to vote for Aguado were told to line up on one side and Argüello supporters on the other, each with their own ballot box. It seemed much easier for Argüello supporters to get through necessary procedures, because when the polls closed many opposition voters were left waiting in line. The Guardia counted the ballots and announced that Argüello had won by a large margin.[50] The United States was satisfied with the election; Poland was one thing, Nicaragua another.

Tacho's plan to rule by proxy ran into a snag, however. Old lawyer Argüello, apparently carried away by the size of his popular mandate, did not prove as trustworthy as Tacho had thought. The day after his inauguration he began removing or reassigning Somoza appointees, replacing many of them with opposition figures. Tacho still had control of the Guardia, though, and on the night of May 25-26, less than a month after Argüello took office, Tacho placed him under arrest. By 3:00 A.M. Tacho had the Congress in session, declaring the erstwhile president mentally incompetent, and choosing Benjamin Lacayo Sacasa to replace him. Guillermo Sevilla Sacasa, Tacho's son-in-law and ambassador in Washington, told the State Department that Argüello had been flirting with the communists.[51]

Most Latin nations refused to recognize the new regime, however, and the Truman Administration went along with the boycott. Wrote *Time* magazine, "What optimists now hoped was that international disapproval might goad Somoza into new elections, and that the elections would be honest."[52]

But Tacho had other plans. Acting on his orders, Lacayo Sacasa dissolved the Congress and called a new Constituent Assembly to write yet another constitution. The Assembly appointed Somoza's uncle, Victor Román y Reyes, to be the new president. Tacho was an early enlistee in the cold war, and his new constitution contained one of the hemisphere's first anticom-

El Jefe Somoza, 1947

munist clauses. He soon used "communist conspiracy" charges to justify
a new roundup of political opponents.[53]

Within a few months the United States had restored formal relations.
"The unappetizing fact was that a dictator had been given fresh prestige
at a time when fresh pressures from his democratic Central American neighbors had begun to threaten his 16-year reign," commented *Time*.[54]

Somoza derived his power from the Guardia Nacional, a private army
whose loyalty he assured by an elaborate system of patronage and by the
bonds of corruption that united members of an elite organization existing
above the law, or better said, that was the law. In the background of course,
and just as essential for maintenance of the dictatorship in the long run,
was the carefully cultivated support of the United States. But those were
not the only factors that gave the regime its "stability." On the "civil"
front there was the Somoza political machine, the Nationalist Liberal Party
(PLN), headed by Tacho himself or by one of his trusted relatives. Mem-
bership in the party was obligatory for government workers (it was financed
by a payroll dues check-off) and even for those employed in Somoza-owned
private enterprises. There was no such thing as a secret ballot in Somoza
elections; those who voted for El Jefe, or his stand-in, were given a pink
card that Nicaraguans irreverently called *la magnifica,* the name given to
a prayer card carried by Catholics as a talisman against unknown dangers.[55]
In Nicaragua, Tacho's *magnifica* was more likely to assure safe conduct than
any prayer card.

But the fact remained that Somoza's principal opposition for many

years—the Conservative Party—had so discredited itself during the long
US occupation that few Nicaraguans could relish it as an alternative to
Somoza. Its leader, Emiliano Chamorro, was literally and figuratively a relic.
Its supporters were the remnants of the Granada aristocracy, businessmen
excluded from the Somoza system, and the populations of certain traditionally Conservative rural areas. *New York Times* correspondent Sidney
Gruson found that "General Somoza's political opposition is led mainly
be members of the extremely wealthy class. Observers here say the opposition is more concerned with the increased commercial possibilities that
go with political power rather than with the principles of dictatorship versus democracy."[56]

There was also the Independent Liberal Party (PLI), formed by remnants of the historic Liberal Party who split away in 1944 as Somoza consolidated his control over the PLN. But support for the PLI was largely
confined to intellectuals, professionals, and artisans in the traditional Liberal
base of León. Also appearing in 1944 was the Nicaraguan Socialist Party
(PSN). Ideologically, the PSN was aligned with the Communist parties of
other countries, which at that time were subordinating all issues to the
war against fascist Germany and Italy. In practice, that meant uncondi-
tional support for those governments participating in the allied war effort;
in Nicaragua that was Somoza. Taking advantage of this policy, Tacho initially aided the PSN. By means of its support and the concession of certain social benefits, he was able to assure the passivity of the urban labor
movement for a time; thus the workers remained on the sidelines during
the 1944-45 protest wave.[57]

But the alliance with the PSN didn't stop Tacho from arresting its members during the post-war witch hunt a few years later. The beginning of
the Cold War coincided with renewed unrest in Central America, fueled
in part by the emergence of reformist governments in Costa Rica and
Guatemala. Tacho took no chances. On the pretext of fighting communism
he ordered PSN members arrested, and scooped up many Conservative
businessmen as "suspected communists" in the same net.[58]

With the opposition divided, discredited, and marginalized, and with
a favorable economic conjuncture brought on by the expansion of cotton
exports in the late '40s and early '50s, the Somoza regime could pass itself
off to the outside world as a stable, relatively "benevolent" dictatorship.
Killings of opponents were infrequent; brief jailings, beatings, or electric
shock treatments would usually suffice to keep things under control. Tacho
enhanced the "democratic" facade by allowing Pedro Joaquin Chamorro
to take pot shots at him from the columns of the Conservative organ *La
Prensa*. After all, 80 percent of the people couldn't read anyway—it was
radio programs he rigidly censored.[59]

Then, too, the Emiliano Chamorro faction of the Conservative Party gave the regime's image a big boost. After the failure of a feeble attempt at armed revolt in 1948, the seventy-seven-year-old Chamorro went into exile; but the following year he was allowed to return to be a candidate in the 1950 presidential election. His followers, meanwhile, made a pact with Somoza in which they became institutionalized as the loyal opposition. Another new constitution was written: it provided that the minority party would receive one-third the seats in Congress regardless of electoral results. Since the only legal parties were the Conservatives and the Nationalist Liberals, everyone understood the meaning of the terms "majority" and "minority." The Conservative Party, at least its dominant sector, thus became a mere appendage of the regime in return for patronage. In May 1950, just two weeks before the election, Victor Román y Reyes died in a Philadelphia hospital after an unsuccessful operation; Congress duly swore in Tacho, already the PLN candidate for president, to finish out his uncle's term. When Nicaraguans went to vote on May 23, they marked their ballots in the presence of two Nationalist Liberal Party members who stood on either side of the ballot box. As usual, those voting for Somoza were given a *magnifica*. Somoza won the expected landslide victory, but this time Chamorro and the Conservatives didn't complain, they quietly took their seats in Congress. On May 1, 1951 Tacho was sworn in for a new six-year term.[60]

These trappings of democracy made possible the jocular comments of visiting North American VIPs like President Truman's military aide, Major General Harry Vaughan. After being entertained by Tacho while visiting Managua in 1951, Vaughan declared:

He could just as easily be President of the U.S. After all, he and Harry [Truman] are just alike. They both like the same things—a friendly poker game, a good story and a stiff drink.[61]

According to Thomas Whelan, US ambassador to Nicaragua, "Somoza is not a dictator in the true sense of the word." In any event, having a dependable ally in charge of the strategically most important country in Central America was the overriding consideration for US policymakers during the Cold War, just as it had been during the recently-ended world war. As the *New York Times* noted:

In the United Nations, the Organization of American States and other international bodies, Nicaraguan delegates support United States policies so quickly and enthusiastically that they have given a new meaning to the phrase "me too."[62]

Tacho was better than a puppet. He did the right thing without prompting.

Somoza made another visit to the United States in 1952. Arriving in Washington on May 1, he told reporters, "I am very happy to be back in the United States. I feel at home here." No doubt he was sincere on both counts. Though the visit was "unofficial"—Tacho had come to have gallstones removed—he was welcomed at the White House and lunched with President Truman. In a pre-meeting briefing paper, Secretary of State Dean Acheson told Truman:

> His methods have often been criticized in the United States and Latin America. He has, however, restored order to Nicaragua and in recent years has been less repressive. Nicaragua now has a two party system and a free press. Recent delegations to international meetings have been bipartisan.

Later Somoza got the red-carpet treatment in New York City where the mayor presented him with a scroll and "medal of honor." Somoza told the VIPs assembled for the ceremony he considered the United States to be a "big brother." "We appreciate the kindness, protection and help you have given us," he said.[63]

BETWEEN 1952 and 1954 the US inaugurated several new military assistance programs for the Guardia Nacional. In a memorandum urging the State Department to approve more military aid, the embassy in Managua wrote:

> It seems to have been customary in some quarters to have attacked Somoza's character. The Embassy agrees that he appears to have an insatiable thirst for money and a considerable love of power. Nevertheless, the Embassy believes in his expressions of friendship for the United States. During the last war he virtually offered to turn this country over to us. He says (and we believe him), he would do so again. He has consistently instructed his delegates to United Nations Assemblies to cast their votes in support of the policy of the United States. He once offered his services in combating the spread of communism from Guatemala but cancelled his plans when he learned they were unacceptable to us. He has repeatedly said that he would do exactly as we say, and we know of nothing in his record that shows any inclination to fail us in international matters.

Written shortly before the end of the Korean War, the memorandum alluded to a plan in which Somoza was to play the leading role in an invasion of Guatemala to oust the reform-minded government of Jacobo Arbenz. The project was scrubbed partly because of its potential for negative propaganda impact. The United States was trying to mobilize world opinion against "communist aggression" in Korea and didn't want attention diverted to aggression in Central America. A few months after the memorandum was written, however, the Korean War ended, and a new Guatemala plan was drafted; it gave Tacho, at last, his opportunity to be of service.* A CIA-sponsored "liberation army" for Guatemala included Nicaraguan National Guardsmen; it trained in Nicaragua on one of Somoza's own estates, while CIA-piloted aircraft took off from Managua's Las Mercedes airport to bomb Guatemalan targets. In return for his help, Tacho got to keep much of the equipment left over from the operation, including the planes.[64]

In 1953 Nicaragua finally repaid the Ethelburga loan that President Zelaya contracted in 1908 to finance construction of the Atlantic railroad. The still uncompleted Rama road was no substitute for the rail project begun by Zelaya and scrapped under the US protectorate. As a result of the US-backed ouster of Zelaya in 1909, the country received not a single benefit from the loan for which its treasury was drained for forty-four years. The money had been doled out to a multiplicity of creditors, repaying a complex web of new, non-productive financial obligations imposed by the occupation: the short-lived monetary reform (a gold mine for corrupt Diaz-Chamorro regime politicians and Yankee bankers), the exorbitant salaries of a host of North American advisors, administrators, customs collectors, and high commissioners, and the real or claimed private losses resulting from the violence necessary to sustain the various Diaz-Chamorrista regimes in power. Moreover, with the failure of the 1911 Knox-Castrillo convention to gain ratification, the Ethelburga loan itself had become the pretext for the formal protectorate that ended in 1933 and for the financial supervision that continued, in the person of Customs Collector Irving Lindberg, for two decades longer.[65]

S OMOZA could well afford to brush off any suggestion of a domestic threat to his empire. He had the loyalty of a private army and the support of the United States; the politicans of the pseudo-opposition were housebroken, and the ubiquitous "ears" of the regime—the web of Guardia informers—kept the dictator one step ahead of any plot against him. As Tacho trotted around the dance floor of the Workers' Club in León on the evening of September 21, 1956, he had every reason to feel himself securely in control of the nation he had turned into a private hacienda. He was surrounded by well-wishing sycophants celebrating the announcement of his "candidacy" for a new term as president—it was a gay time and Tacho was in his element. But the system did have a flaw: it did not anticipate

---

* Tacho had volunteered to send the National Guard to Korea to help turn the "red tide," but his offer had not been accepted.

the possibility that Rigoberto López Pérez, a young poet, acting alone, would step out of the partying crowd and pump four .38 caliber slugs into the pudgy figure of the dictator.

For López Pérez it was over in a second. As he knew he would, he paid for his action with his life, instantly riddled with dozens of bullets from the guns of Somoza's bodyguards. But for Tacho it was no consolation. "I'm a goner. They got me this time, Tommy," he would tell his poker-playing friend US Ambassador Thomas Whelan in a line right out of a second-rate gangster movie. Learning of the attempt on Somoza's life at one o'clock in the morning, Whelan had immediately contacted Washington. The Eisenhower Administration spared no effort to save the dictator's life: it rushed a taskforce of US doctors to the scene, headed by Ike's own surgeon, Major General Leonard Heaton, commander of the Walter Reed Army Hospital in Washington. They took Somoza to Gorgas Hospital in the Canal Zone and operated for over four hours, but to no avail. Tacho expired a week later. Appropriately enough, the cause of death was diagnosed as "organic failure."[66]

As the Air Force plane with Somoza's body left Panama, US troops fired a twenty-one gun salute. In a message of condolence to the dictator's widow, Secretary of State John Foster Dulles wrote, "His constantly demonstrated friendship for the United States will never be forgotten."[67]

The New York Times thought "the fact that General Somoza has had a complete dictatorship, although a benevolent one as such regimes go, was no extenuation for trying to murder him." But for any Nicaraguans who might be reading its editorial page, the Times failed to suggest an alternative means for changing things. Instead, it assured readers that " 'Tacho' Somoza's personal popularity among a majority of his people was beyond a doubt."[68]

While the doctors in the Canal Zone were laboring to save Somoza's life, Ambassador Whelan in Managua was helping to arrange the dynastic succession. The country was led to believe that Tacho would recover and all would soon be back to business as usual. Meanwhile, Anastasio Junior, the thirty-two-year-old younger son of the dictator and head of the National Guard, rounded up some 3,000 suspected political opponents to prevent them from using the confused situation to their advantage. His thirty-four-year-old brother Luis, already president of the rubber-stamp Congress, was placed in Tacho's chair as head of state.[69]

FOR MANY years the US Embassy was situated atop *La Loma*, the hill formed by the extinct Tiscapa volcano that overlooks downtown Managua. It was part of a heavily-guarded compound that included the presidential palace and the various Somoza residences. No other nation's embassy was located there. Thomas Whelan, its occupant for more than a decade, could speak no Spanish, and since Tacho and his sons all spoke English he saw no reason to learn. Appointed by Truman to pay off a political debt, Whelan was himself a Republican, and he remained as ambassador throughout the Eisenhower years. Described as a farmer and football promoter, he viewed all opponents of the Somozas as communists. When anti-Somoza students at a US-funded journalism school tried to participate in student elections, he interceded with President Luis to have the entire school expelled from the National University. When, on July 23, 1959, the Guardia shot and killed four demonstrating students in León, Ambassador Whelan issued a statement denouncing the victims as reds.[70] The US Embassy in Managua was the symbol of an era. And Thomas Whelan personified for Nicaraguans the friendship of the United States for the dictatorship that ruled over them.

XII

THE LAST MARINE

Those who killed Sandino believed they had killed the revolution. They believed they had killed even the possibility of a revolution.

—*Tomás Borge*

I N FEBRUARY 1957, five months after Tacho's death, Somozaism held another "election." Luis soundly trounced the pseudo-opposition and "won" a six-year term in the presidential palace. In doing so, the heir to Nicaragua demonstrated his ability to carry on the tradition of political chicanery established by his father. It almost seemed as if nothing had changed, as if the act of Rigoberto López Pérez had been in vain. Indeed, Somoza rule had yet to reach its half-way mark. But while the four bullets from López Pérez's revolver did not topple the regime, the "organic failure" that claimed Tacho was beginning to affect the system as a whole, and *somocismo* would never fully regain its equilibrium.

Luis thought he could perpetuate Somoza rule by moving the family out of the limelight and ruling indirectly through the party. To that end he announced a "liberalization": some of those jailed after his father's death were released, and *La Prensa* was put on a longer leash. Dressing himself in a business suit, Luis left command of the Guardia to younger brother Anastasio Junior (Tachito). He had a one-term-only provision reintroduced into the constitution, and took various measures to rationalize the workings of the dictatorship. These efforts impressed Milton Eisenhower—Ike's brother—who visited Nicaragua in 1958, but they accomplished little else; every crumb of reform merely whetted the appetite of opponents and made hard-core Somocistas nervous.[1]

Luis Somoza inherited an economic crisis along with the dynastic mantle. The rapid extension of cotton acreage in a period of high world market prices had brought the country a measure of prosperity during the postwar years. But the price of the fiber fell sharply in the late 1950s, causing serious balance of payments deficits.[2]

The triumph of the 26th of July Movement in Cuba in 1959 coincided with and helped to stimulate an upsurge of armed challenges to the Somozas. These emanated from several sources, including old and new Sandinistas and a section of the Conservative Party resuscitated with the breath of Christian Democratic reformism. None of the abortive risings posed a serious challenge, but they did help increase the sense of autocratic insecurity that followed the fall of Cuban dictator Batista.

The Cuban Revolution had other important ramifications for Nicaragua. The United States was determined not to "lose" another country in the hemisphere. In March 1961 President Kennedy announced "a vast cooperative effort, unparalleled in magnitude and nobility of purpose" called the Alliance for Progress. He told Latin Americans that by the end of the decade "the living standards of every American family will be on the rise, basic education will be available to all, hunger will be a forgotten experience, the need for massive outside help will have passed, [and] most nations will have entered a period of self-sustaining growth." By demonstrating that "economic progress and social justice can best be achieved by free men working within a framework of democratic institutions," Kennedy's "revolution" would undercut the potential for revolutionary movements that challenged US interests. "Political freedom must accompany material progress," he said, and pointed to Cuba and to Trujillo's Dominican Republic as the countries he hoped would "soon rejoin the society of free men."[3] The Somozas were conspicuously absent from Kennedy's short list of hemispheric enemies of freedom, even though he had criticized them during his presidential campaign. As it happened, at the very moment Kennedy spoke, the CIA was busy preparing the Bay of Pigs invasion force that would set sail the following month from Puerto Cabezas, Nicaragua— the base obligingly provided by Luis and Tachito Somoza.

Two months earlier, Adolf Berle, the head of Kennedy's "Taskforce Latin America," had advised the president-elect that a "full-scale Latin American 'cold' war" was underway. Berle, a prominent New York corporation lawyer and veteran of Franklin Roosevelt's Brain Trust, had helped engineer the Good Neighbor Policy. "Social revolution is inevitable," Berle told Kennedy; "it must be dissociated from Communism and its power politics." Among the "political steps" Berle's group recommended was "stabilization of social revolution at left-of-center." To Berle that meant "substantially the Betancourt plan": in Venezuela, liberal President Rómulo Betancourt had embarked on a program of limited land reform and industrial development financed by that nation's large oil revenues. "Dying dictatorships" in the Dominican Republic, Haiti, Nicaragua, and Paraguay were not to be supported.[4]

Taskforce Latin America thought Kennedy should "fire [Ambassador Thomas] Whelan and negotiate a transition government in Nicaragua which wants just this." A central figure in Berle's scheme for a "left-of-center" government for Nicaragua, however, was his "old friend" Luis Manuel Debayle, Luis and Tachito Somoza's uncle. Debayle would later become known as "Tio Luz" (Uncle Light) for his ten-year stint as head of Nicaragua's National Light and Power Company, during which he reportedly embezzled $30 million. Berle met with Debayle periodically in an effort to arrange things in Nicaragua. During a visit by Berle to Managua in March 1962, Luis Somoza joined him at Debayle's place for dinner. Berle told Luis he needed to "legitimize his government by getting a clear popular mandate . . . in such fashion that everybody recognized it." The Kennedy aide congratulated "Luisito" for Nicaragua's material progress, including "a net of paved roads comparable to an American state."[5] Berle's exaggerated notion of Nicaragua's highway system may have resulted from his being chauffered directly from the airport to Debayle's estate, a route certain to be well tended with US aid dollars.

The $500 million that Kennedy held out to Latin America as seed money for the Alliance for Progress was ample incentive for the Somozas to continue their pretense of liberalization. Pressured by Berle and Aaron Brown, the new US ambassador, they allowed a puppet, René Schick, to assume the presidency in 1963. Luis and Tachito held on to real power as respective jefes of the Nationalist Liberal Party and National Guard. Schick's election—a ten to one victory over the *zancudos* (mosquitos), as Conservatives who helped legitimize the dictatorship were known—was as phony as any the regime ever staged; true Somoza opponents weren't even on the ballot.[6] But with Schick in office the Kennedy and Johnson Administrations were spared the embarrassment of dealing directly with a member of the family.

Berle's elitist reform plans for Latin America were never realized. "The difficulty of this State Department is that it will always come down on the side of the *status quo*," he wrote in his diary. But this self-styled enemy of "dying dictatorships" seems to have reconciled himself to Somozaism: in 1966 he concluded that in Nicaragua "the social standards were now higher than any other country in Central America."[7]

Alliance for Progress programs did give the Nicaraguan economy a big boost, but the main beneficiaries were the Somozas and their cronies. The $30 million in Alliance funds spent on road construction enabled the family to greatly expand its beef and dairy operations. The dollar influx also bloated the government payroll with bureaucrats and technocrats. To the extent that this increased the number of middle class dependents of Somozaism, it broadened the regime's base and helped give it stability.

A so-called land reform took some of the peasants dispossessed from the fertile and accessible lands along the Pacific and deported them to the Atlantic jungles. There they were left without transportation or marketing facilities, technical assistance, or access to credit, but where, it was thought, they would be less of a nuisance.[8]

A key component of the Alliance strategy in the region was the Central American Common Market or *Mercomún*. Initially a project of CEPAL, the United Nations Economic Commission for Latin America, the goal of the Mercomún was to resolve or alleviate the severe balance of payments problems of the Central American countries through "import substitution"—the encouragement of industry in order to reduce dependence on imported products. Because the vast majority of the people were extremely poor, however, the demand for manufactured goods was largely confined to small elites and middle class sectors; these restricted markets could not support industrialization on a national basis. Since the program took the social status quo for granted, it did not contemplate the thoroughgoing land reform that would be needed to broaden the market. Instead, it adopted the strategy of joining together the small existing markets of privileged consumers in a larger common market.[9]

In general concept, the program dovetailed with Washington's objectives of stabilizing the region against the "communist threat" and of providing new opportunities for North American investors. But certain features of the common market, as envisioned by CEPAL, worried the US: it would establish regional economic planning mechanisms and controls on investment and trade designed to insure that industrialization benefited all the countries equally. Economic planning, which had the ring of "socialism," was anathema to the United States, and the idea of controls conflicted with "free market" dogmatism. So the US decided to strong-arm its way into the Mercomún. By offering up to $100 million in assistance funds, Washington induced the Central American countries to scrap the planning features and subordinate balanced growth to unrestricted free trade. CEPAL was pushed out and replaced by the US Agency for International Development (AID).

Under North American tutelage, the Mercomún became little more than a mechanism for encouraging foreign investment. This rose from $388 million in all Central America in 1959 to $888 million ten years later—a 129 percent increase, compared to 37 percent during the previous decade. In Nicaragua, where US capital made up 70 to 80 percent of all foreign investment, United States companies undertook new ventures in food processing, fisheries, tobacco, textiles, chemicals and pesticides, forest products, packaging, steel rolling and fabrication, oil refining, household goods, and ceramics, as well as in such non-industrial sectors as tourism and banking.[10]

While some of the new production was directed toward local markets and did replace imported products, several negative factors more than offset these benefits. Unlimited investment incentives deprived the Central American countries of needed revenues from taxes and duties. Much, if not all, of the production was dependent on expensive imported machinery, semifinished goods, and even raw materials, most of which came from the United States. In Nicaragua, these new imports understandably accounted for 100 percent of the non-labor inputs in such industries as oil refining and chemicals, but even reached 35 percent or more in industries like leather goods and clothing, which could have been produced entirely from domestic raw materials. Then too, many were merely "phantom" industries that simply mixed, repackaged, or added simple finishing steps so as to take advantage of the tax incentives, free trade, and low-paid labor. In other cases the new investments consisted simply of buying out existing Central American companies; other local firms were forced out of business through competition. Moreover, with elimination of planning mechanisms, a disproportionate amount of new production took place in El Salvador and Guatemala, which were already the most industrialized of the five Central American countries. Even though Nicaragua had the highest economic growth rate in the region during the first half of the '60s, by the end of the decade both Nicaragua and Honduras were showing serious deficits in trade with their common market partners.[11] These problems caused the virtual collapse of the Mercomún in 1970.

Industrialization did not bring about an improvement in Nicaragua's balance of payments; quite the contrary. The country's foreign debt, which stood at $222 million in 1971, had grown to $1.2 billion by 1979, making Nicaragua one of the world's most indebted nations per capita. Furthermore, the world economic slowdown that began toward the end of the 1960s undid much of the industrialization that had taken place; 292 factories are said to have closed down between 1969 and 1974 in Managua alone.[12]

By the mid-'50s cotton had already taken over 80 percent of Nicaragua's staple food growing region on the Pacific littoral. During the Alliance for Progress decade the stimulation of large-scale agro-export projects produced one of the most extreme concentrations of land ownership in the world, despite the country's low population density. This land reform in reverse is reflected in the fact that between 1960 and 1977 the number of persons engaged in agriculture declined from 60 percent to 44 percent of the population. Such a decline in the agricultural labor force often indicates development, industrialization. But in Nicaragua it merely reflected the growing numbers of "marginalized" persons who congregated in shantytowns on the outskirts of Managua and other major cities with little or no possibility for employment. By the late 1970s half the Nicaraguan population was living on an average annual per capita income of $286. The *Alianza para el Progreso* did not rectify the severe socio-economic imbalances, nor, in the long run, did it succeed in stabilizing the system. Given a choice between the interests of the Central American countries and those of US corporate investors, the *Alianza* opted for the latter, just as it chose to identify with local elites rather than the needs of the destitute majority. By the end of the 1970s the problems the United States was supposedly going to help solve were worse than ever, exacerbated in part by the Alliance itself.[13]

At the end of the ten-year Alliance for Progress, former AID official Jerome Levinson and *New York Times* Mexico City bureau chief Juan de Onis published a critical appraisal called *The Alliance That Lost Its Way*. They found that as "the threat of Castro lost its urgency," social goals had been sacrificed for "technocratic considerations" such as monetary stabilization and growth of the gross national product. The objectives of literacy and universal primary schooling had been replaced by an emphasis on technical and higher education. Land reform had given way to efforts to improve the productivity of commercial farmers. Housing programs for the poor became transformed into housing programs for the middle classes and then were dropped altogether. "Abandoning the task of social integration, the Alliance sought to improve conditions within the core [elite] society and perhaps to expand the core over an extended period of time."[14]

"Conventional development assistance usually serves to accelerate the economic growth of the recipient country," Levinson and de Onis wrote, but "the economic benefits will tend to follow the recipient country's existing pattern of income distribution; unless they are accompanied by social or political restructuring, they will go primarily to those who already hold wealth and power." In Nicaragua that meant the Somozas.[15]

But the Somozas of Latin America were not the only beneficiaries of the Alliance for Progress. Between 1961 and 1968 US corporations operating in Latin America repatriated $2.16 in profits for every dollar of new investment. In fact, if the total of the various forms of capital repatriation to the US is subtracted from the $18 billion in US loans and grants during the Alianza, the net capital flow from the United States to Latin America was virtually nil. Meanwhile, by the late '60s the United States' favorable balance of trade with Latin America was offsetting nearly two-thirds of its trade deficit with Western Europe and Japan.[16]

As the Alliance for Progress visibly failed to exorcise the specter of radical social revolution, the emphasis shifted to counterinsurgency, the other, less publicized strategy to emerge from the Kennedy era. Regional cooperation in Central America underwent a parallel transformation: economic integration through the Central American Common Market gave way to military integration through CONDECA, the Central American Defense Council.

Originating in a proposal by the US Army Southern Command to combat "internal subversion" in the region, CONDECA was established in 1964. It involved the standardization of arms and military training, joint maneuvers, and a pact for mutual defense. CONDECA members also exchanged information on "subversives." Officers were sent to the US Army School of the Americas in the Canal Zone, where counterinsurgency training replaced classic military tactics, and anticommunist propaganda courses took as much as 20 percent of curriculum time. As the *Miami Herald* described it, "Little countries in Central America are setting a brisk pace for larger nations of the New World in combatting Red Cuban subversion as well as in lowering trade barriers."[17]

CONDECA-sponsored cooperation proved invaluable to the Somozas. In 1966 Guardia Nacional units participated in two major CONDECA counterinsurgency exercises; the Guardia put the training to use the following year when it crushed an attempt by the Sandinist Front to establish a guerrilla base at Pancasán in the Matagalpa mountains.

The counterinsurgency aid the "guardians of the dynasty" received through CONDECA was supplemented by direct military assistance from the United States. In 1961, the year Kennedy launched the Alliance for Progress, Nicaragua had seventy-four officers training at the School of the Americas, two to three times as many as any other Latin American country—Somoza's National Guardsmen consistently accounted for the largest number of the school's students. In 1963, direct US military assistance to Nicaragua was valued at $1.6 million, also disproportionately high. That same year the Sandinistas had unsuccessfully attempted to open a guerrilla front along the Coco River.

Testifying before the House Foreign Affairs Committee on behalf of the Military Assistance Program for fiscal 1968, General Robert W. Porter Jr., commander-in-chief of the US Southern Command, explained that Central America was

of particular strategic significance. It dominates the sea, land, aerial and other lines of communication between North and South America, and permits access by relatively defensible routes to the raw materials of South America.[18]

Military assistance to the Somoza regime paid off in other ways as well: in 1965 Nicaragua sent a Guardia contingent to join the US military intervention in the Dominican Republic. (The US declined Tachito's offer two years later to send the National Guard to help out in Vietnam.)

Though US military equipment and counterinsurgency training enabled the Guardia to contain the guerrilla threat for the time being, the regime showed other signs of decomposition. The year 1966 marked the end of the dictatorship's "reformist" experiment. The Nationalist Liberal (Somozaist) Party nominated Tachito, the head of the National Guard, to be its "candidate" for the 1967 presidential election. Two days later incumbent President René Schick died, apparently of natural causes, though his failing health was attributed to pressures from Tachito and his "hard line" faction.[19] Luis Somoza, the other exponent of Somoza-style liberalization, died of a heart attack the following year.

During Schick's term, as part of the Alliance for Progress-related facelift, a Guardia colonel was courtmartialed and sent to prison for the murder of three alleged "agitators." Tachito's appointee to finish out the remaining months of Schick's term, Lorenzo Guerrero, freed the officer, absolving him of all guilt.[20] The action cleared up any doubts Schick may have created: the Guardia was once again to be regarded as a law unto itself.

For the election campaign a National Opposition Union, composed of Conservatives, Independent Liberals, and the new Christian Democratic Party, nominated Conservative leader Fernando Agüero. Supporters of Agüero were subjected to systematic violence and harassment by a new Somocista paramilitary organization, AMOROCS—the Somozaist Military Association of Retired Officers, Workers, and Peasants—a precursor of the death squads that appeared later in other Central American countries.[21]

The prospect of once again having a Somoza in the presidency galvanized popular sentiment behind Agüero's campaign. On January 22, 1967, the candidate addressed a rally of 60,000 people in Managua, probably the largest demonstration held in Nicaragua up to that time. When the crowd began to march on the National Palace to protest Somocista violence, the Guardia opened fire, killing at least forty marchers and wounding more than one hundred others. More demonstrations took place during the following days, demanding the release of those arrested. On January 25, in the midst of the evening rush hour, Guardia members ran amok, shouting obscenities and shooting at demonstrators and innocent bystanders alike; their victims included many women on their way home from work or shopping. "This was the first of a long series of almost random acts of violence by the guard that I was to witness over a period of more than a dozen years," remarked *Time* magazine correspondent Bernard Diederich.[22]

The generalized violence that accompanied Anastasio Junior's election even spilled over into internal Guardia disputes. That same year Guardia Major Oscar Morales beat to death a former officer accused of subversive activities; he tried to cover up the murder by throwing the body down the

Anastasio Junior conferring with US military personnel

crater of Santiago volcano. But word leaked out, and the public outcry created dissension within the Guardia itself. Morales was tried and convicted
on minor charges and sentenced to prison in 1969. He remained free,
however, and the following year he shot and killed one of his accusers, a
fellow Guardia officer, on a downtown street in broad daylight. Finally
sent to prison, Morales was allowed to escape during the 1972
earthquake.[23]

With Tachito's constitutionally prescribed term as president set to expire in 1972, the *zancudo* Conservatives stepped forward once more to
legitimatize the continuation of Somocismo. Fernando Agüero, the bitter
opponent of four years earlier, signed an electoral pact with Somoza in
1971, under which his followers would share the spoils of office right up
to the executive. Following the well-rehearsed formula, Congress dissolved
itself to make way for a Constituent Assembly, which mandated the replacement of the presidency with a triumvirate. In May 1972, Tachito handed
nominal power to a three-man junta, with Agüero as its token Conservative member. But he retained command of the Guardia.

THE TREMOR that leveled central Managua in the early hours of December 23, 1972 measured 6.3 on the Richter scale; its epicenter was
directly under the downtown shopping and commercial area. While the
number of persons killed has never been definitely established, estimates
of the deaths have been as high as 20,000 or more. Three-quarters of the
city's population of 400,000 were left homeless. If the earthquake was a
terrible reminder of the geological faults underlying the city of Managua,
it revealed no less strikingly the decayed foundation of the Somoza dic-

tatorship. In the hours following the disaster, the Guardia Nacional virtually disintegrated. Many of its members joined in widespread looting; others abandoned their posts to look after their own families and possessions. It was days before any semblance of order could be restored to the Guard. Acting swiftly to protect the dictator, Ambassador Turner Shelton had 500 troops from the US Southern Command in the Canal Zone airlifted to Managua; they camped next to Somoza's El Retiro palace in the suburbs south of the city. Martial law was declared and, as head of the Guardia, Somoza assumed full personal control once again. Swept aside was the triumvirate, known to Nicaraguans as the "three little pigs," that had fronted for his regime for the past seven months. Tachito now ruled directly through a newly-formed National Emergency Committee that was supposedly directing relief efforts.[24]

Somoza's committee administered tens of millions of dollars in international relief funds and supplies. As there was no system of accounting, millions of dollars simply disappeared. The material aid pouring into the country provided lucrative business opportunities for Guardia officers, while the regime's higher echelon parasites made fantastic killings in real estate speculation. Food and other goods were distributed through Somoza's Nationalist Liberal Party; Guardia members and functionaries helped themselves. On his way to Managua to see that donations actually reached earthquake victims, Puerto Rican baseball star Roberto Clemente died in a plane crash. Exposés of corruption in *La Prensa,* the opposition newspaper, prompted the regime to pass a law levying fines against newsmen who "defamed" government officials.

Meanwhile the dictatorship did virtually nothing to help the sufferers. Many victims migrated to nearby cities where they had relatives or to seek whatever shelter churches and ad hoc civic committees could provide. In many respects this spontaneous assumption of governmental functions by the citizenry was a dress rehearsal for the insurrection that was only five years away.

The Nixon and Ford Administrations ultimately furnished $80 million in earthquake-related loans, more than any other single source. But because of the way the aid was administered and became identified with the regime, the US government received little credit from the Nicaraguan people. A 185-man US Army medical team operated from behind a barbed-wire barricade next to Somoza's residence. Aside from being one more symbol of US identification with a dictatorship that was now more than ever the object of its people's contempt, the location of the hospital put it far from the suffering population it was supposed to help. *Time* reported that a 50-person Cuban medical team located in a populous slum was treating 1,000 patients a day, four times as many as the much larger US Army unit.

Ambassador Shelton, who like "ugly American" Ambassador Whelan before him, spoke no Spanish, was at Somoza's side so frequently during the crisis that he seemed more like the dictator's aide-de-camp than a foreign diplomat. Meanwhile, due to the destruction of the US embassy compound, operations were moved to tents on the grounds of Shelton's mansion-residence. The ambassador refused to let embassy staff set up temporary offices inside, and his wife wouldn't permit Nicaraguan nationals employed by the embassy to use the toilets. Nevertheless, Secretary of State Rogers decorated Shelton for his earthquake relief activities.[25]

In 1975, columnist Jack Anderson called Shelton "the worst ambassador in the US diplomatic service." Shelton had begun his government career by witch-hunting "communists" out of the US Information Agency. Appointed to the Nicaragua post by Richard Nixon, he became so close to Tachito that local wags said a cabinet meeting was when Somoza and Shelton got together. When, in 1971, the US Senate agreed to abrogate the Byran-Chamorro Treaty, Somoza issued a twenty córdoba note depicting the exchange of documents. The engraving showed Shelton in a typical pose, head bowed to Tachito. "I think President Somoza is a very nice man," said Shelton, "He is very friendly to the United States, he does a good job and he's a hard-working leader who has done a lot to improve things in this country."[26]

Shelton had reportedly helped engineer the Somoza-Agüero pact of 1971. After the earthquake, it is said, the US ambassador tried to persuade Agüero to accept Somoza's open assumption of absolute power, and when the Conservative leader balked, he urged Somoza to replace Agüero and take over anyway. Nor did Shelton confine his matchmaking activities to political affairs. In 1972 he arranged for Howard Hughes to take up residence on the top floor or Managua's Intercontinental Hotel; there the billionaire industrialist apparently considered a number of joint business ventures with Somoza. But Hughes hurriedly departed after the earthquake, having done no more than buy a share of the dictator's Lanica airline.[27]

Presumably as part of the earthquake relief effort, a team of mental health experts from the Andromeda Mental Health Clinic for Spanish-speaking peoples in Washington, DC, traveled to Managua. They found a "rise of aggressiveness, depression and sense of revolt among the people," symptoms they attributed to earthquake-related trauma. Reporting on the team's findings, *New York Times* correspondent Marvine Howe concluded, "Many Nicaraguans admit that they are more irritable, and less willing to accept injustices attributed to the authoritarian Government."[28]

After the earthquake Somoza moved his headquarters into a new compound constructed of reinforced concrete and precast aluminum.[29] Tachito, like everyone else, referred to it as "the bunker." Unlike everyone else, however, the dictator seemed unaware that it was the perfect symbol for a regime that, in the aftermath of the earthquake, was besieged first by the hatred, and soon by the guns of its own people.

T HE SANDINIST FRONT for National Liberation (FSLN) burst onto the world stage in December 1974 with a daring raid on a Christmas party given in honor of Turner Shelton at the Managua residence of a pro-Somoza businessman. The Yankee emissary had already left the party, but thirteen guerrillas took a number of prominent guests hostage, including Somoza's brother-in-law. Holding out for three-and-one-half days, they won the release of fourteen political prisoners, $1 million in ransom, and the reading of a lengthy denunciation of the regime over radio and television. The guerrillas and the freed prisoners, who included Daniel Ortega,

US Ambassador Turner Shelton (right) at Christmas party given by Somoza crony José Maria Castillo Quant (left), just before FSLN raid, 1974

were flown to Cuba. "Almost overnight, the extreme left emerged as a political force capable of inflicting a stinging defeat on the Government and proving the vulnerability of the long-ruling Somoza regime," wrote *New York Times* correspondent Alan Riding, sent to Managua to cover the story. It was clear that Somozaism, so long supported as a retardant to social revolution, had now become the catalyst for radicalism. "The perpetuation of the Somoza regime has already increased class consciousness here and I'm worried that there will be even more polarization now," a member of the upper classes told Riding. The same concern would force a rethinking of the long-standing US policy of uncritical support for the Somozas.[30]

In fact, conditions propitious for the emergence of a revolutionary movement had begun to appear after the assassination of Anastasio I in 1956. The action of Rigoberto López Pérez gave a political impulse to growing unrest among important sectors of the population. The wholesale evictions that accompanied the expansion of cotton production alienated the peasants, while the extension of Somoza tentacles outside the traditional realm of agriculture antagonized many businesspeople; the grasp of the Somoza family and its hangers-on was strangling whole branches of commerce and industry.[31]

The new movement sprang from long-dormant roots. The crusade of Sandino had never ended entirely: a year after the *guerrillero's* death and the massacre of his followers at Wiwili, a number of survivors led by Pedro Altamirano tried to reinitiate armed struggle. But Altamirano was tricked and murdered by Somoza agents in 1937, and the brief flurry of guerrilla activity came to an end. The remaining Sandinistas dispersed in hiding or in exile, where they awaited favorable conditions to take up arms once more. Many remained loyal to the goal of a sovereign and independent Nicaragua under a socially equitable regime, but they possessed neither Sandino's leadership qualities nor the ability to hold the movement together under changed conditions. Episodic attempts by Sandino lieutenants to resume guerrilla activity haunted the Somozas over the years but invariably failed. Juan Gregorio Colindres was killed trying to open such a guerrilla front in the mountains of Jalapa in 1948; other efforts led to the death of Optaciano Morazán in 1954 and Ramón Raudales in 1958.[32]

But after the killing of the first Somoza in 1956, the hegemony that the ineffectual Conservative Party exercised over the opposition by default began to erode. This was particularly true after 1958-59 when the 26th of July Movement's defeat of the Batista dictatorship in Cuba gave a great impetus to activity outside traditional opposition channels. Although the universities had been centers of anti-Somoza agitation since the mid-1940s, the student movement now began to reevaluate the experiences of Sandino and, as is inevitable in 20th century revolutionary movements, to examine the ideas of Marx and the theoreticians of the Russian and other modern revolutions.

Carlos Fonseca stood out among the leaders of the Nicaraguan student movement in the 1950s. While he, too, studied the writings of Marx, and joined the Nicaraguan Socialist Party (pro-Moscow Communists), Fonseca was instrumental in reviving interest in Sandino. Arrested in 1956 after Tacho's assassination, he spent a brief period in prison and then traveled to the Soviet Union and East Germany. Returning to Nicaragua, he was wounded in one of the twenty or so armed attempts against the dictatorship that took place in the late '50s, most of them influenced by the success of the Cuban revolution. Fonseca escaped to Cuba where he recuperated from his wounds. When he left there he quit the Socialist Party, and in 1961, became one of the principal founders of the FSLN.

Also joining in the formation of the new Sandinista movement was Colonel Santos López, a surviving comrade-in-arms of Sandino. López led the FSLN's first unsuccessful guerrilla front at Bocay in 1963. Joining later were the three Ortega brothers, Daniel, Humberto, and Camilo, whose father had fought with Sandino.[33]

The defenders of the status quo, naturally, accused the new Sandinistas of being part of a Cuban effort to "export" revolution. But Nicaraguan student leaders had been denounced as "communists" or "Marxists" long before the triumph of the *Fidelistas*, as had virtually everyone, regardless of political beliefs, who opposed the Somoza regime. Like radicals in many other Latin countries, Nicaraguans tried unsuccessfully to repeat the Cuban guerrilla experience. In this they received moral and a small amount of material support from Cuba. On the other hand, there is strong evidence that the Fidelistas who fought in the Sierra Maestra had been influenced by Sandino's struggle, even trained by surviving members of the original Sandinista movement. It might easily be said, therefore, that to the extent the Cubans were involved, they were merely repaying a favor—"re-exporting," so to speak, a revolution they themselves had "imported" from Nicaragua.[34]

As serious revolutionaries, the Nicaraguans looked at the experiences of other countries, including Cuba and the Soviet Union, and examined the theories of Marx and of other thinkers to see what they could adapt to their own circumstances. In the same way, Sandino had endeavored to synthesize the variety of theories and experiences extant in his own time. But the Nicaraguan revolutionaries were home grown: they were radicalized by the gross injustice and inequality fostered by a dictatorship that maintained itself in power with the help of the United States.

Though the FSLN repeatedly met with failure in its military operations, the very fact that the new Sandinista movement persisted and defied the efforts of the dictatorship to eradicate it proved that it represented something more than the occasional armed attempts of the Conservative opposition; those, more than anything else, had been aimed at getting Somoza and the US embassy to take them seriously. In particular, the guerrilla front opened at Pancasán in 1967, though crushed the same year, succeeded in projecting the Sandinist Front as an opposition force on a national scale.[35] After the 1972 earthquake, the FSLN began to make significant headway in clandestine organizing in the cities.

SOMOZA responded to the 1974 Christmas party raid by launching a fierce repression. He imposed a state of siege that lasted for three years,

while an intensive counterinsurgency campaign tried to wipe out the FSLN
once and for all. Gradually, the outside world learned of a reign of terror
instituted by the National Guard in the departments of Matagalpa and
Zelaya. In June 1976, a US congressional subcommittee hearing testimony on human rights violations in Nicaragua received a letter from a group
of thirty-one North American Capuchin missionaries working in Zelaya
Department; it documented numerous tortures, rapes, and disappearances
among the peasants of the Atlantic Coast region. This was followed by a
pastoral letter issued in January 1977 by the Nicaraguan Bishops' Conference and signed by Managua Archbishop Obando y Bravo. Though suppressed in Nicaragua, it reached international news media, confirming the
existence of "widespread torture, rape and summary execution of civilians."
According to the bishops' letter, two mass executions totaling eighty-six
civilians—including twenty-nine children—had occurred in the mountains
of Zelaya in the previous weeks alone. The following August, Amnesty International published a report on Nicaragua that expanded on the earlier
revelations.[36]

In the wake of the Vietnam defeat, Watergate, and the disclosures of
CIA dirty tricks, many members of the US Congress reflected widespread
concern over the United States' association with repressive dictatorships.
Just before Jimmy Carter's election to the presidency, the Ninety-Fourth
Congress mandated the secretary of state to appoint a human rights coordinator who would issue an annual report on the status of human rights
in countries receiving US aid.[37] These human rights concerns were echoed
to a certain extent in Carter's presidential campaign; they paralleled a debate taking place in the highest circles of power over how best to contain
the advance of social revolutions in the Third World. On one side were
partisans of continued uncritical support for US allies with proven anticommunist track records—including many of the world's most notorious human rights violators like Somoza and the shah of Iran. On the other side
were those who believed that repressive dictatorships that provided no "safety valve" for opposition would surely hasten the very social revolutions the
US was determined to prevent. Ultimately this would require the sort of
large-scale US military intervention that had proven so costly and
problematic in Vietnam. Their solution was to elicit a certain amount of
liberalization from the heavies in the US camp by means of a carrot-and-
stick approach. Such reformist-managerial schemes were not entirely new;
indeed, the broadening of the political base of conservative Third World
regimes they sought to achieve closely resembled what the Alliance for
Progress had unsuccessfully tried on the economic level. But in the early
1970s such measures were seen to be even more imperative: "Vietnam syn-
drome" had made counterrevolutionary military interventions by the US

virtually unthinkable, at least for the time being. Even before Carter's election the liberalizers viewed Nicaragua as a "test case."

Nicaragua was selected as a proving ground for the new strategy because US "national security" concerns there were felt to be less immediate than in Iran or South Korea, which were also coming under attack for human rights abuses. Moreover, it was erroneously thought that the counterinsurgency campaign launched after the FSLN's 1974 Christmas party raid had eliminated "leftists" as serious contenders for power in Nicaragua. Such appeared to be the case after November 1976, when two principal FSLN leaders—Eduardo Contreras, who led the Christmas party raid, and Carlos Fonseca—were killed by the National Guard. (A few months later, fourteen members of the US Army's Southern Command had a first-hand look at the situation when CONDECA conducted its "Aguila Six" counterinsurgency exercises in the very region where Fonseca was killed.)[38]

Jack Anderson's columns, combined with criticism from within the State Department, had compelled President Ford to replace Ambassador Shelton with James Theberge in 1975. Theberge, like Shelton, was a professional anticommunist, though one of a different caliber. With an academic "think tank" background, he had authored such books as *The Soviet Presence in Latin America* and its sequel, *Russia in the Caribbean*. Ford assured Somoza that the replacement of Shelton "was not to be taken as representing any change in United States policy," but there is reason to believe the switch was more than cosmetic. Shelton's actions, openly identifying the US with Somoza, and his reports on the stability of the Nicaraguan regime had come under fire from more perceptive members of the embassy staff. Such clumsiness on the ambassador's part made him a serious obstacle to the employment of a more sophisticated policy toward Somoza. It is not unreasonable to suppose that liberalizers in the State Department leaked information to Jack Anderson precisely in order to force Shelton's removal.[39]

Theberge, who arrived at his post in August 1975, began meeting with members of Somoza's legal opposition. Headed by Conservative newspaper publisher Pedro Joaquin Chamorro, Somoza opponents had formed a united front called UDEL (Democratic Union for Liberation) with the aim of pressuring the US to withdraw support from Somoza. "American ambassadors have always been seen here as sort of viceroys or proconsuls and both the Government and the opposition have always tried to win their support," an unnamed "foreign official" in Managua told *Times* correspondent Alan Riding.[40] While Theberge's meetings with UDEL did not mean Washington was going to dump Somoza, this feeling-out of the opposition was a necessary precursor to more active management of Nicaraguan politics; it indicated that a policy shift on Nicaragua was in the works at least two years before the beginning of Carter's touted human rights campaign.

In an interview given in December 1979, FSLN leader Humberto Ortega charged that US pressure on Somoza for limited democratic reforms was deliberately withheld until it appeared that the FSLN had been crushed and no longer constituted a significant political force.[41] The pattern of Washington's subsequent actions lends credence to this charge: the "human rights" pressure on Somoza corresponded not to the actual level of abuses as documented by various human rights agencies, but to periods in which Somoza's grip appeared to be relatively secure and the Sandinistas either defeated or too weak to present a serious challenge. Conversely, at the times of Somoza's greatest weakness, renewed support in one form or another would be forthcoming, even though it was then that the most serious human rights violations took place. This pattern did not change until the very end, when Somoza's intransigence and world public opinion made further overt support unthinkable. In short, the object was not to replace Somoza but to "reform" his regime. This goal—as well as the widening gulf that separated it from reality—would become increasingly clear as Somocismo crumbled.

There were several operative factors that combined to give the Carter policy the appearance of confusion. In the first place, there was no unanimity in governing circles. Somoza's congressional supporters, led by Democratic Representatives Charles Wilson of Texas and John Murphy of New York (the so-called "Nicaragua Lobby"), who vigorously opposed any attempt to cut aid to the dictator, represented a more significant and entrenched opposition to the new policy within congressional and "national security" circles than appeared to be the case. The would-be reformers of Somoza were often compelled to compromise with this tendency. On the other hand, the Carter Administration opposed the efforts of more liberal congresspeople to cut assistance funds for Nicaragua. The carrot-and-stick approach was practicable only if Congress approved aid and the executive branch then withheld or dispensed it as the case seemed to require; congressional efforts to rein in Somoza through control of the purse strings restricted the administration's maneuverability. Perhaps the most glaring weakness of the managerial strategy, however, was that while it made perfect sense to those who understood and sympathized with it (State Department insiders and think tank associates), the gyrations it produced appeared ludicrous to the rest of the world.

The policy conflict over Nicaragua surfaced initially in June 1976, seven months before Carter took office, when congressional human rights hearings were pending. At that time Ambassador Theberge flew to Washington for a meeting with Representative Edward Koch of New York, a key critic of Somoza aid. Theberge tried to assure the congressman that Somoza's human rights violations were not "systematic," and therefore did not warrant a cutoff of assistance.[42]

Even after Carter took office and massive human rights violations were confirmed by the Capuchins and the Nicaraguan Bishops' Conference, the US embassy in Managua continued to take a low-profile approach. Said Theberge, "We have reason to believe that some of the allegations of human rights violations are accurate, and our concern has been made clear to the Nicaraguan government on various occasions in the past year." But, in the ambassador's opinion, the situation still did not warrant an aid cutoff. A few months later, Tachito suffered a mild stroke; the Carter Administration sent a US Air Force ambulance plane to take him to the Miami Heart Institute—evidence of its continued solicitude for the well-being of Somozaism.[43]

In August 1977 Congress approved $3.1 million in military sales credits for Somoza for fiscal 1978, after the State Department gave assurances that the money would not be made available until signs of human rights progress were forthcoming. But behind the scenes, the administration was striking a deal that would allow arms shipments to continue. Fiscal 1977 military sales credits worth $2.5 million had not yet been released, and authorization to spend military aid funds expired on September 30. After several conferences between US and Nicaraguan officials, on September 19 the Somoza regime rescinded the state of siege that had been in effect since 1974. The Carter Administration used the lifting of martial law to justify signing the $2.5 million military assistance agreement—just days before the authorization expired.[44] The theoretical reinstatement of constitutional guarantees did not help peasants who were being tortured, raped, or massacred, however, a fact that wasn't lost on critics of continued US aid for Somoza.

At the very moment it was giving the go-ahead for further military aid, the administration announced the suspension of $12 million in economic aid. Karen DeYoung of the *Washington Post* reported from Managua, "U.S. embassy officials here are confused by the apparent contradiction over whether Washington considers the human rights situation here to be better, as the military assistance approval implies, or not, as indicated by the economic aid deferral." If everyone else was perplexed, at least matters were clear back at the State Department—it was merely a question of juggling the carrot and the stick. Since military aid could not be deferred, it would be released as the reward for lifting the state of siege; economic aid, on the other hand, could be carried over into 1978, and it would be withheld as an inducement for Somoza's continued cooperation. Or, as Deputy Secretary of State Warren Christopher put it, "On the basis of our reasoning, we thought it was the right thing to do." Christopher felt Somoza had been given "a big enough signal for the time being."[45]

To the FSLN, the maneuvers around the lifting of the state of siege presaged a US-engineered arrangement: in return for certain superficial reforms, the conservative opposition would assent to Somoza's continuance in power till the end of his term in 1981. Even though they felt themselves to be ill-prepared, the Sandinistas resolved to launch a new offensive with the express purpose of sabotaging the plan. Their suspicions about US intentions appeared to be confirmed in December when Mauricio Solaun, President Carter's new ambassador, set up talks between Somoza and the opposition that were to begin on February 5, 1978.[46]

Before the date for the talks arrived, however, the FSLN offensive had set in motion a process that made accommodation impossible. It began on October 13 with a series of coordinated attacks in various parts of the country, including the city of Masaya just a short distance from the capital. The offensive was only partly successful from a military standpoint, and the guerrillas suffered significant casualties, though they emerged largely intact. But the political results were more important. The Sandinistas had reappeared in force precisely when almost everyone else considered them to be defunct.[47] Somoza, whose confidence was shaken, was only disposed to make concessions when he felt he had things under control; likewise, as events would prove, the United States would only exert pressure on him when the Sandinistas did not appear to be a threat. But the "moderate" opposition, sensing both Somoza's weakness and the political risk they took by compromising with him, were emboldened to demand changes that undermined the very foundations of the dictatorship.

In coordination with the FSLN military offensive, opposition political, business, and church leaders representing a broad spectrum of opinion, issued the "Document of the Twelve" from Costa Rica. Calling for the complete overthrow of the dictatorship and the inclusion of the FSLN in any political solution, it cut the ground from under any opposition politicians who might still be considering a deal with Somozaism.[48]

I T HAS BEEN said that the January 10, 1978 assassination of internationally-renowned journalist and perennial regime critic Pedro Joaquin Chamorro was Somoza's undoing. Certainly the act brought the anti-Somoza movement to a head. But Chamorro's murder was a symptom, not the cause, of Somocismo's terminal illness. It made little difference whether the killing was ordered by Tachito himself, as many assumed, or by his son Anastasio III, as others thought, or even by Cuban exiles who were running a blood plasma exporting racket in partnership with Somoza—literally bleeding the Nicaraguan people for profit—that

Chamorro had exposed just a short time before.[49] Engulfed by the hatred of its own people, the system headed by the Somozas was lashing out blindly and senselessly against a symbol of a world it could no longer control.

Just over a year later the fury of the dying order claimed the life of hapless ABC-TV reporter Bill Stewart—to Guardia goons he seemed to represent the treachery of the Yankees, who had turned against their ever-faithful friends in their time of agony. Unknown to the Guardsman who pulled the trigger, the much-maligned government headed by Carter went further to maintain the Somoza regime intact than anyone could reasonably have expected.

Less than a month after Chamorro's assassination—with Nicaraguan business and labor on strike demanding an end to the dictatorship, with the Guardia daily using teargas, clubs, and bullets to disperse anti-government demonstrators—the State Department issued the annual report on human rights that Congress had mandated as a precondition for foreign aid. The section on Nicaragua reported that while "serious abuses of the rights of persons were committed by the National Guard," allegations of new abuses "markedly diminished" after "President Somoza ordered the National Guard commanders to avoid any abuses whatever." Since the lifting of the state of siege, the report continued, "the political scene has been characterized by vehement and lively press and public debate . . . and steps toward a 'national dialogue' between the Government and opposition groups." The divergence from reality might have been attributed to its having been prepared several months in advance. But on February 16, two weeks after the report's release, Deputy Assistant Secretary of State Sally Shelton, testifying before a House subcommittee, reiterated the conclusions: "Although problems remain, it is our opinion that marked progress [in human rights] has been manifested since early 1977," she said. Furthermore, Shelton asserted that the National Guard had "thus far reacted in a generally restrained manner" since Chamorro's murder. She characterized the Guardia's actions in suppressing unrest as the fulfillment of "a duty to protect the population from terrorism and acts of violence."[50]

The military aid the administration requested for Somoza for fiscal 1979 amounted to a mere $150,000 training grant. Closer examination by a House subcommittee revealed, however, that the figure was really $600,000—the same level of training funds as the previous year. Intentionally or not, it had been made to appear, by a change in accounting methods, that funds for the Guardia were being reduced. Deputy Assistant Secretary Shelton asserted that continued aid to the Nicaraguan National Guard was necessary because it helped provide a "sense of security which is important for social, economic and political developments" and because it "helps to maintain our cooperative political relationship with that country."[51]

While releasing its own generally favorable report on Nicaragua, the State Department was trying to stifle a Venezuelan-sponsored initiative for a human rights investigation to be conducted by the Organization of American States (OAS). The US reportedly favored a "quiet, unpublicized approach." In fact, the State Department was afraid of upsetting the dialogue between Somoza and the opposition that it still believed to be possible. But "moderate and conservative foes of the regime" were worried by "the rapid surge to radicalism by workers, students and the poor," reported the *Times'* Alan Riding. To be seen selling out to Somoza could only increase that radicalism and destroy whatever influence the "moderates" still retained. In reality the opposition had ceased to be "moderate" or "conservative" after the killing of Chamorro, in the sense that it was unwilling to commit political suicide by endorsing any formula that would retain Somoza. Yet Washington, apparently trying to recycle its Espino Negro solution of 1927, was thinking in terms of an arrangement that would provide guarantees for an election to be held in 1981—three years away. Because of their fear of radicalism, the Nicaraguan conservatives could not embrace Somoza; the United States, for the same reason, could not let go of him.[52]

The amount of US aid for Tachito that was under discussion was of little importance in and of itself. Until the end the Guardia was relatively well-supplied. The repression eventually caused ammunition stockpiles to run low, but Somoza had taken the precaution to establish alternative supply sources in Israel and Argentina.[53] The important thing was the psychological effect of continued support from the United States. An encouraging word from the Carter Administration or a favorable vote in Congress for a few dollars' worth of aid was far more important than whether or not the aid ever arrived. The fight over the $150,000, therefore, was just as crucial as if it had been billions.

The State Department was trying to release enough aid to maintain its support for, and its leverage over Somoza. At the same time, it sought to appease the "human rights lobby" by downplaying the importance of the aid. Thus, when the Senate Foreign Relations Committee voted on May 11 to eliminate the fiscal 1979 military appropriation for Nicaragua, the Carter Administration responded by releasing the $12 million in economic aid that it had withheld the previous September. In a complete about-face from its previous position, it now claimed that the economic aid was being released because it benefited the poor, not Somoza, while military aid (the $3.1 million for 1978) was being delayed pending further human rights improvement. At the same time, however, it became known that several weeks earlier the State Department had quietly released $160,000 in equipment credits for a military hospital. "The Administration appears to be rewarding backward steps," a *New York Times* editorial observed.[54]

Tachito, himself, seemed to be confused about the "signals" from Washington. He told *Washington Post* reporter Karen DeYoung he thought his relations with the Carter Administration were "all right," while Alan Riding quoted him as saying that "those who historically have beaten up blacks and kept Indians as second-class citizens have nothing to teach us."[55]

The crisis continued at a rolling boil during 1978, with more daring actions by the FSLN and the first mass insurrection in the Masaya Indian community of Monimbó. On August 1 the press learned through a "leak" that Carter had sent a secret letter to Somoza, congratulating him on his promises to improve the human rights situation, just when the State Department was receiving reports of increased violations. This was no casual slip-up; the idea for the letter reportedly originated in the National Security Council, an indication of the seriousness with which the administration viewed the Nicaragua situation. Disagreement in the State Department over the move was apparently responsible for the text of the letter being made public.[56] The editors of the *Washington Post* were furious over the leak, even though their own paper broke the story ("A newspaper can hardly bite the hand that feeds it," they explained):

> It is very well to argue, as some State Department human-rights advocates evidently did, that President Carter risked undercutting the cause by writing a personal letter to Nicaraguan President Anastasio Somoza last month patting him on the back for certain human-rights improvements. Steering another country's social and political change is tricky, and there's room to debate tactical details.

But leaking the letter wasn't playing by the rules, they thought: "A president should be able to send a personal letter without worrying that those he consults in preparing it will blab."

They were even more concerned, however, that "the letter and the leak are premised on a view of Nicaragua that may be fundamentally wrong: that what the United States is dealing with in Nicaragua is a human-rights problem." They found it profoundly disturbing that "American policy toward that small and dependent country has come to be taken as symbolic of whether the administration is 'serious' about human rights." There were, the *Post* editors felt, more important questions that outweighed human rights considerations:

> What the United States is really dealing with in Nicaragua, or so we in-

creasingly suspect, is a revolution. It is comforting to think that the aging dictator Somoza* will somehow fade away and be replaced in the scheduled 1981 elections by moderate democrats friendly to the United States . . . [but] a 'second Cuba' . . . is not out of the question."

The danger, they concluded, required "an urgent diplomatic initiative."[57]

The *Post* editorial revealed much about strategic policy considerations, but it did little to help solve the problem of those who were trying to "steer" Nicaragua's "social and political change" away from revolutionary channels. The steerers could not agree on what kind of "urgent diplomatic initiative" to take, any more than they could agree on when to apply the carrot and when to apply the stick or how much of either might be needed at a given time. But events were about to force them to a consensus.

On August 22, 1978, a squad of FSLN combatants dressed in National Guard uniforms seized the National Palace in downtown Managua. Somoza's rubber stamp Congress was then in session, giving its approval to the economic aid package the Carter Administration had released in May. The guerrillas captured over 1,500 people, including forty-nine deputies and several of the dictator's close relatives. After riveting the attention of the world for the two days during which negotiations proceeded, the Sandinistas traded their hostages for the release of fifty-nine political prisoners (including the sole living founder of the FSLN, Tomás Borge), $500,000 in cash, and a plane to Panama. Thousands of cheering Managuans lined the road to the airport. In Panama, Edén Pastora, who led the raid, said, "We decided to strike when we saw the determination of the United States to keep Somoza in power until 1981."[58]

Sparked into action, opposition business and labor leaders declared a general strike the day after the phenomenally successful National Palace occupation ended. Spontaneous insurrections erupted in all major cities except Managua. Joined by FSLN guerrillas, the *muchachos* ("boys and girls") of the nation fought the Guardia for two weeks. *US News and World Report* asked, "Could the United States continue to support a government opposed by a nearly united people demanding an end to the dictatorship and what is called Latin America's 'biggest private ranch'?" US policymakers were agonizing over the question, reported the magazine: "What emerges from the debris 'could be worse than what we have now,' said one official." But outright intervention as in Guatemala or the Dominican Republic was not considered: "We no longer do that sort of thing," asserted another official interviewed by *US News.*[59]

US policy strategists finally did resolve upon an "urgent diplomatic initiative" as counseled by the *Post* editors, inducing Somoza to accept an

---

* Tachito was only in his early fifties.

offer of "friendly cooperation and conciliation" from the Organization of American States. "With the United States leading the way, the OAS is trying to manage the process of Nicaraguan political change," reported a *Post* editorial with apparent satisfaction.[60]

President Carter's special representative, William Bowdler, arrived in Managua on October 6, with token representatives of Guatemala and the Dominican Republic in tow. No one seemed to notice the curious (but apparently accidental) coincidence that both OAS mediators represented countries in which the United States had intervened to thwart revolutions in prior decades. The choice of Bowdler, however, was definitely not accidental—a former National Security Council member, he had helped set up the new government in the Dominican Republic during the intervention by US troops in 1965.[61]

The Carter Administration had now concluded that pressuring Somoza to resign was the only means to avert an eventual Sandinista victory. The plan, as reported by the Associated Press, was to have Somoza turn over power to a transitional government headed by some figure within the regime who was not a member of the Somoza family; Foreign Minister Julio Quintana was thought to be a good choice. The purpose of such a transitional regime would be "to keep reformist elements out of power." According to reporter Alan Riding, "Washington is gambling that, once General Somoza resigns, support for the guerrillas and pressures for reform will evaporate." At the same time the US launched a diplomatic offensive to pressure Venezuela, Panama, and Costa Rica to end their support for the Sandinistas.[62]

But Tachito refused to resign. The Carter Administration had influenced the International Monetary Fund to postpone a $20 million loan to Nicaragua to pressure Somoza, but it hesitated to take stronger action, reportedly for fear of alienating his friends in Congress. The politicans of the Nicaraguan opposition were told, meanwhile, that for the United States to remove Somoza would constitute intervention, which the US was now determined to avoid. "After so many years of intervention, you say, 'We don't intervene,' " remarked a Conservative Party leader close to the negotiations, "That's the most sophisticated intervention we have seen." The opposition felt that, having installed and supported Somocismo, the US had a responsibility to root it out; to Nicaraguans, Somoza was "the last Marine."[63]

Having failed to produce Somoza's resignation, the US mediation effort fell back to a "compromise" plan for a referendum on the dictator's future. A government of "national unity" would serve during the interim between a plebiscite, to be held within a few months, and elections in 1981; it would preserve the pro-Somoza Congress intact and divide the cabinet equally among the opposition, Somoza's Liberal Party, and "independents." If Tachito lost the plebiscite, an opposition leader approved by the Somozaists would become president but would have to govern through the cabinet. In no case would Somoza be required to leave the country, and the Guardia Nacional would remain in place. To most Nicaraguans it didn't even look like "Somoza-ism without Somoza but a good possibility of Somoza-ism with Somoza."[64]

Special Representative Bowdler found few, if any, takers for such a plan. Ten weeks of shuttle diplomacy between Somoza and the Broad Opposition Front (FAO) ended in failure. The Group of Twelve, who were allied with the Sandinistas, walked out of the talks as soon as it became clear that Somoza would not resign immediately; the reformists left soon afterward, and only right-wing elements remained. These stayed long enough to lose whatever credibility they still retained before the Nicaraguan public, but ultimately they too had to reject what looked like nothing more than a new version of the "deals" employed by the Somozas throughout their reign to keep themselves in power. A "moderate business leader" summed up their decision: "If the choice is between selling out to Somoza or a civil war, we'll reluctantly have to pick the latter." The hope of Nicaraguans for a solution that would avoid further bloodshed, found Alan Riding, "has given way to disappointment and anger." All but the most conservative were upset that the US thought Somoza could be replaced with "an equally conservative, though less brutal, successor," and bitter that

> Washington, fearing 'another Cuba,' is searching for stability rather than for social and economic change or even human rights—repeating, as they see it, American policy during its occupation of Nicaragua between 1912 and 1933, and its subsequent support for the Somoza family. Nicaraguans note that the Carter Administration was silent when the National Guard killed 3,000 people in crushing the September insurrection, but moved quickly to mediate when it recognized the popularity of the Sandinist guerrillas.

Evidently, the US was intent upon a political solution that "skims over social problems and ignores the guerrillas" so as to prevent them from gaining power or influence. All the while Somoza strung the mediators along, playing for time.[65]

As Somoza's National Guard gradually restored control over the country after the September insurrection, Washington's efforts to find a replacement for his regime lost their urgency. US intelligence analysts were predicting that the Guardia, through superior firepower, could defeat any new Sandinista military offensive. When talks between Somoza and conservative opposition figures broke off altogether in January 1979, the US showed its disapproval by canceling its remaining aid programs and cutting its embassy personnel in half. But with Somoza seeming to be securely in power once again, the Carter Administration lost interest in mediation. When members of The Twelve visited Washington in April they met with Senator Edward Kennedy, but the State Department made no effort to contact them. In May the US supported a $65.6 million IMF loan for Somoza.[66]

The FSLN's final offensive began on May 29. A series of coordinated attacks by Sandinista columns, strongly reinforced by the thousands of recruits gained in September, sparked new insurrections in the cities. Somoza and the Pentagon had underestimated both the Sandinistas' military capability and the depth of their popular support. The US government now began a Byzantine new series of efforts to keep those it considered "radicals" from gaining power.

The first plan called for intervention under the auspices of the OAS; it was reportedly formulated by Carter's national security advisor, Zbigniew Brzezinski, in consultation with Secretary of State Cyrus Vance, Defense Secretary Harold Brown, and CIA Director Stansfield Turner. The Brzezinski plan had three parts: to get a consensus among Latin American countries that Somoza had to go, to play up Cuban involvement in order to gain support for intervention, and to send an OAS "peacekeeping" force to halt fighting while a new government was set up.[67]

Secretary Vance addressed a special meeting of the OAS in Washington on June 21. He called for a change in government in Nicaragua, but did not mention either Somoza by name or the Junta of National Reconstruction, the five-member provisional government proclaimed by the FSLN a few days earlier. He also called for a peacekeeping force, citing "mounting evidence of involvement by Cuba and others." But Panama announced that it had already granted recognition to the Sandinist-led Junta. Mexico spoke against intervention: "It is not up to the OAS or anyone else to tell them how they should constitute their government once they knock down a dictator," said Mexican Foreign Minister Jorge Castaneda. The FSLN immediately rejected OAS intervention, and the proposal was withdrawn when it failed to get the support of a single OAS member.[68]

As a part of the campaign to generate support for OAS intervention, the US charged that Cuba was providing the Sandinistas with arms and instructors; stories even circulated that a Cuban army unit had arrived in Costa Rica. But the State Department could not produce convincing evidence to document its allegations, and when the campaign to alarm OAS members failed, the administration backed off from the charges of large-scale Cuban involvement.[69]

Testifying before a House Foreign Affairs subcommittee a few days later,

Assistant Secretary of State for Inter-American Affairs Viron Vaky said there was "cause for concern" over Cuban involvement and stressed the US objective of preventing a "second Cuba." But he downplayed the actual role of Cuba, admitting that it was "not the only or even the most important" of the Sandinista supporters. In fact, a US intelligence analysis quoted by the *New York Times* a few days later said, "Given the low-key approach Cuba has employed in Central America, Havana is likely to do its best to avoid a situation where it might be called upon to intervene directly with its own military units and thus risk a military confrontation with the United States." *Times* correspondent Riding wrote that Fidel Castro "had also urged the Sandinists to move cautiously and to do their utmost to maintain warm ties with Washington."[70]

As a substitute for the US-backed intervention plan, the OAS adopted a resolution that called for the complete replacement of the Somoza regime, but banned any outside intervention. Although the US voted for the measure, the Carter Administration immediately embarked on a new effort that appeared to violate the ban on interference. William Bowdler and the newly-appointed ambassador to Nicaragua, Lawrence Pezzullo, arrived in Central America on June 27 for what was described as another attempt to replace Somoza with a "broadly based provisional government." Pezzullo reportedly proposed to Somoza that he resign in favor of a "constitutional junta" appointed by the existing (Somozaist) Congress. Somoza, who had already lost control of most of the country outside Managua, indicated his willingness to resign in return for guarantees that the National Guard would be maintained intact and that his Nationalist Liberal Party would play a role in the transitional government. Pezzullo tried to persuade opposition figures to accept Somoza's terms "in the apparent hope of reducing the influence of the powerful Sandinist guerrillas over any new government." As the plan evolved over the next few days, the US negotiators proposed that Somoza be succeeded by a member of his own party to by chosen by the Congress; the new president would then name a five-member provisional government that would include representatives of the National Guard, Somoza's party, the conservative Broad Opposition Front, the Superior Council of Private Enterprise, and the Roman Catholic Church.[71]

Washington had concluded by this time that no new regime would be possible without some Sandinista representation. As soon as the new "national unity" government received diplomatic recognition from the US, therefore, it would invite the Junta of National Reconstruction to nominate two additional members. The US officials claimed their proposal was not intended to compete with the Sandinista-led Junta "but rather to bring together the widest possible coalition of democratic leaders."[72]

But within a few days this plan for a "moderate, more pro-U.S." provisional government had to be abandoned also. "Moderate political and business opponents" of Somoza had already endorsed the Junta of National Reconstruction, which included two conservatives—Alfonso Robelo, a wealthy cotton grower, and Violeta Barrios de Chamorro, the widow of Pedro Joaquin Chamorro.* Shunning the US plan, the "moderate" opposition groups issued a joint communiqué calling on Ambassador Pezzullo to conduct all future negotiations with the Junta.[73]

On July 6, Somoza said he was ready to leave without conditions, but that his departure was being delayed at the request of the US negotiators. Pezzullo and Bowdler had a new strategy, one aimed at "neutralizing" radical opposition elements in the Junta. "Three of the five are leftists," said State Department spokesmen, "We'd like to see a balance or preferably a majority of moderates." The US now tried to pressure Venezuela, Panama, and Costa Rica, all friendly to the Sandinistas, to cut off their support unless the Junta would agree to add two more "moderate" members. Pezzullo reportedly told opposition leaders that "the existence of a democratic regime in the future must be guaranteed in Nicaragua before General Somoza's departure." Another official said the US wanted to help Nicaragua "but can't be seen helping a bunch of radicals." The Junta had "to look moderate for us to be able to sell the package back home." Nicaraguans were bitter at the US stalling tactics. "No Nicaraguan sector is asking for expansion of the junta. They all feel properly represented. This request is a foreign one," declared Junta member Alfonso Robelo in Costa Rica.[74]

The future of the National Guard was another sticking point. As late as the Congressional hearings on June 26—after the murder of ABC newsman Bill Stewart, after the OAS human rights commission's documentation of Guardia atrocities committed the previous September, and in the face of universal repudiation—Assistant Secretary of State Viron Vaky refused to acknowledge that the US had been mistaken in aiding the Guardia. US officials now tried to persuade younger officers to maintain the force after Somoza's departure as insurance "against communist influence." All were talking about the need to replace Somoza's hated private army, but the United States had its own idea of what a new army would look like. According to *Washington Post* reporter Karen DeYoung, "U.S. policy calls for breaking up the Sandinista army after the war and integrating some 'moderate' guerrillas into a future armed force dominated by the National Guard."[75]

---

* The other Junta members were Daniel Ortega of the FSLN, Sergio Ramirez from the Group of Twelve, and Moisés Hassan, a leader of the United Peoples' Movement (MPU), a coalition of grass-roots organizations allied with the FSLN.

The Carter Administration's efforts to arrange things to its liking produced only widespread anger. "The United States has always intervened when we Nicaraguans have tried to define our own future," a "wealthy young businessman" told Alan Riding; "Now it is willing to see Nicaragua bombed back to the Stone Age in order to maintain its system of domination." Even conservative Managua Archbishop Obando y Bravo spoke out in a sermon against "the ambiguity of those governments who have thought or continue to think of their own political interests before the common good of the Nicaraguan people."[76]

The *New York Times* editors advised Carter to take a cue from Castro who reportedly said that the best thing Cuba could do for the Sandinistas was to do nothing. "America's moral credit in Nicaragua is slim," said the paper. "It is a little late in the day, after four decades of involvement with the Somoza dynasty, for the United States to insist that any successor to President Somoza's regime must now meet Washington's test of moderate democracy." They recommended instead that the US use the leverage of its economic aid to strengthen the "moderate center."[77]

On July 13, 1979, the provisional Government of National Reconstruction announced at a press conference in San José, Costa Rica, that the rebel armed forces were ready to "take Managua and annihilate the National Guard." Two days earlier, however, it had made public a peace plan that it had sent to the OAS. The plan called for Somoza to resign to his Congress, which in turn would hand over power to the Government of National Reconstruction. Civil rights of all Guardia members who immediately ceased hostilities would be respected. Those officers and enlisted men who wished to do so would be eligible to join a new national army, and Somozaist military or civilian personnel "who are not found to have been involved in serious crimes against the people" would be allowed to leave the country. In an accompanying letter to OAS Secretary General Alejandro Orfila, the Junta said it was "presenting to the community of nations in this hemisphere the purposes that have inspired our Government . . . as set forth in our documents and policy statements." Among these were the "firm intention to establish full respect for human rights" in accordance with the UN Universal Declaration of Human Rights and the Charter on Human Rights of the OAS, and to "call Nicaraguans to the first free elections that our country will have in this century."[78]

The option of a non-Somozaist "third force" strong enough to dominate the transition process and exclude radicals simply did not exist. Washington could accept the Sandinista peace plan and hope to use economic aid as leverage with the new government, or it could become totally isolated. It opted for the former. Ambassador Pezzullo arranged for Somoza's resignation and departure to Miami. In the early hours of July 17, the Somocista

Congress assembled in a salon of the Intercontinental Hotel to receive its last official communication from the dynasty. A few hours later Tachito was in Florida.

But the rest of the peace plan went awry. Instead of immediately turning over power to the Junta as he was supposed to do, Somoza's nominal successor, House of Deputies President Francisco Urcuyo, declared his intention to finish out Somoza's term, and ordered the Guardia to redouble its efforts to defeat the Sandinistas. Though Urcuyo's impromptu theatrics lasted only a day before he, too, fled, it was long enough to sabotage the OAS cease-fire arrangement. After another night of heavy fighting, Guard members lost all remaining semblance of discipline and panicked. Some commandeered planes out of the country or fled overland to Honduras; others hastily exchanged their uniforms for street clothes and tried to hide.[79]

Rebel fighters made their triumphal entry into Managua on the morning of July 19, 1979, carried on the shoulders of the people.

NATIONAL INTERESTS

*In school we learned about Redcoats,
the nasty British soldiers that tried to
stifle our freedom, and the tyranny of
George III . . . I began increasingly to
have the feeling that I was a Redcoat,
and I think it was one of the most
staggering realizations of my life.*

—*An ex-Marine, discussing his experiences in Vietnam.*

THE ACRIMONIOUS polemics that accompanied Reagan's election
in 1980 gave rise to an enduring myth—that the Carter Administration had in some way helped the Sandinistas to consolidate power.
As stated by Jeane Kirkpatrick, in Nicaragua and Iran Carter "actively col-
laborated" in the downfall of "moderate autocrats" friendly to the United States and their replacement with "less friendly autocrats of extremist
persuasion." In doing so, she said, he manifested a "predilection" for policies that contravened US strategic and economic interests. Liberals, also,
have lent credence to this fiction, apparently for the purpose of demonstrating Sandinista "ingratitude." For example, Theodore Sorensen, the
former White House counsel to President Kennedy, visited Nicaragua in
1985 as part of a congressional delegation. Engaging in some verbal spar-
ring with Nicaraguan President Daniel Ortega, Sorensen reportedly
"reminded" Ortega that when the Sandinistas came to power President
Carter had welcomed the revolution with "no hostility, no opposition of
any kind."[1]

The truth is that the Carter Administration's antagonism toward the
Sandinista revolution did not undergo any change after Somoza's fall. But
having failed in successive attempts to block the FSLN from coming to
power by replacing the dictator with a group of hand-picked "moderates,"
it had to make concessions to the new reality. The Carter strategy was sim-

ply adjusted to the terrain of post-Somoza Nicaragua. Economic aid would be used to help private enterprise recover. This would strengthen the "moderates" in a political context that Assistant Secretary of State Viron Vaky described as "very fluid, with heterogeneity, confusion, and flux in the power dynamics"—one in which "many outcomes or scenarios are still possible."[2]

The administration presented Congress with a $75 million assistance package, which Deputy Secretary of State Warren Christopher told the Senate Foreign Relations Committee was "carefully designed to provide direct support for the private sector." Use of the money would be restricted to purchases of "agricultural, industrial, medical, and transportation items that the U.S. has traditionally sold Nicaragua, thus helping to reconfirm our historically close trading ties"; loans would be administered and monitored by the US Agency for International Development.[3]

According to the Carter Administration plan, Nicaragua's desperate need for help in rebuilding its war-ravaged economy would give the US leverage in compelling the Sandinista government to adopt go-slow policies, in impeding the consolidation of its power, and in facilitating its early replacement with non-revolutionary elements. "There will be a number of ways to keep them aware of the fact that we have supplied this money," Ambassador Lawrence Pezzullo told members of Congress. Even before the funds were approved, Pezzullo felt, "that $75 million, in terms of the impact that we have had, in terms of the publicity . . . has been worth 10 times over that." The ambassador urged congressional approval of the loan because "the moderates need our support too badly for us to be sitting on the side of the road waiting for things to happen." Viron Vaky, quoting Hans Morgenthau, concluded that in Nicaragua "the real issue facing American foreign policy . . . is not how to preserve stability in the face of revolution, but how to create stability out of revolution."[4]

But the antagonism of the Right, which opposed any deviation from anticommunist orthodoxy, hobbled the attempt to stage manage events in revolutionary Nicaragua, just as it had thwarted earlier Carter efforts. The $75 million aid plan stalled in Congress.

Significantly, the early right-wing opposition was not based on considerations of Soviet or Cuban military presence, or on allegations that Nicaragua's revolution was being "exported" to El Salvador; the sticking point was the Sandinistas' economic and social policies.* The prevailing obsession was revealed by Representative Gus Yatron of Pennsylvania, chair-

---

* The situation in El Salvador did not attract wide attention until after the military coup there on October 15, 1979, whereas right-wing opposition to Carter policies was clearly established long before Somoza's fall. Jeane Kirkpatrick's theoretical formulation of this opposition in the November 1979 issue of *Commentary* (which won her a Reagan Administration

man of the House Subcommittee on Inter-American Affairs, when, during hearings on Carter's Central America policies, he queried Assistant Secretary Vaky about the meaning of statements by Humberto Ortega, "who said on September 3 that the Nicaraguan revolution aims at equal opportunity for all." In his oblique response, Vaky assured Yatron that "the whole economic planning sector of the Cabinet is in the hands of moderate, democratic, responsible bankers and professionals who are well known in international circles."[6]

The first suggestion of a "linkage" between El Salvador and Nicaragua came in February 1980, when the Carter Administration decided to reverse a previous policy and furnish military assistance to El Salvador. That decision prompted Salvadoran Archbishop Oscar Romero to write the famous protest letter to Carter that preceded by a month his assassination by a rightist death squad. Carter's resumption of arms shipments to El Salvador was reportedly motivated by the desire to prevent "another Nicaragua."[7]

Right-wingers in Congress lacked sufficient strength to defeat the $75 million Nicaragua aid package. Instead, as a delaying tactic, they hit upon the idea of tying approval to developments in El Salvador and Guatemala, and successfully passed an amendment requiring Carter to certify that Nicaragua was not aiding guerrilla movements in the region before the funds could be used. This tactic delayed release of the aid until September, and in so doing laid the groundwork for Carter's certification to become an issue in the 1980 presidential campaign. A few weeks later the Senate adopted two amendments by Jesse Helms to the fiscal 1981 foreign aid bill that made a different kind of linkage between Nicaragua and El Salvador—orienting US policy in both countries back to its traditional hostility to social change. The first of Helms' amendments eliminated an appropriation of $5.5 million for military assistance to Nicaragua; the second banned the use of US aid funds for land reform or bank nationalization in El Salvador.[8]

With the 1980 election drawing near, Carter showed signs of buckling under the Reaganite pressure, but he finally did assure Congress that Nicaragua was not supporting violence or terrorism. The $75 million in aid was released on September 12.[9]

By the end of the year, however, the deteriorating political and military situation in El Salvador had become acute. Holding up the tottering Central American dominoes became a more urgent priority than the problematic nurturing of the Sandinistas' conservative opposition. With just days

---

job) was firmly rooted in a view of Nicaragua and other Third World countries as pawns in an East-West chess game. But her implacable hostility to the Sandinistas did not draw upon any specific charges of Nicaraguan interference in other countries. It was based on the mere assumption that all revolutionaries and social reformers are dupes or agents of the Kremlin.[5]

remaining in office, Carter froze $15 million in undisbursed credits for Nicaragua, ostensibly pending an investigation of Nicaragua's role in the Salvadoran rebellion.[10]

THE REAGANITES' electoral platform deplored the "Marxist Sandinista takeover of Nicaragua"; it announced their opposition to Carter's aid program for that country, or "assistance to any Marxist government in this hemisphere."[11] When the new Republican administration proceeded to keep faith with its cold-warrior image it surprised only those pundits who had forecast that the responsibilities of state would exert a moderating influence.

Within a few months the Reagan State Department officially terminated the Nicaragua loans that Carter had suspended, and blocked an additional $9.6 million wheat sale as well. Both moves were linked to alleged Sandinista support for the Salvadoran guerrillas.[12]

The first attempt to document charges of Nicaraguan involvement in El Salvador's civil war came in a State Department "white paper" made public on February 23, 1981. The eight-page report, provocatively titled "Communist Interference in El Salvador," claimed to prove, on the basis of captured documents, the existence of a complicated plan by Soviet Bloc and other left-leaning countries to supply Salvadoran rebels with hundreds of tons of US and other Western-made arms. These were allegedly being transshipped through Nicaragua with the complicity of the Sandinista government. But despite the enormous quantities of weapons said to be flowing into El Salvador by air, land, and sea, the only hard evidence the authors of the "white paper" could produce was the discovery in Honduras of a single truck containing one hundred US-made rifles and the capture in El Salvador of a light plane with "numerous weapons" on board, which, though piloted by a Costa Rican, they said had come from Nicaragua.[13]

An analysis of the white paper a few months later by *Wall Street Journal* reporter Jonathan Kwitny revealed that the captured documents really contained little, if anything, to back up US charges. The State Department, he found, had "extrapolated" figures on arms shipments: it had simply presumed, for example, that increased air traffic between Cuba and Nicaragua, which could well have had several explanations, consisted of arms on their way to El Salvador. By the same token, its "proof" that weapons for the Salvadoran insurgency were being stored in Nicaragua rested on nothing more substantial than a single reference to a place called "Lagos." This, the paper's authors claimed, was a code word for Nicaragua.

In fact, Kwitny found, the guerrilla papers contained considerable evidence to support a contrary argument—that Nicaragua and the Soviet Bloc

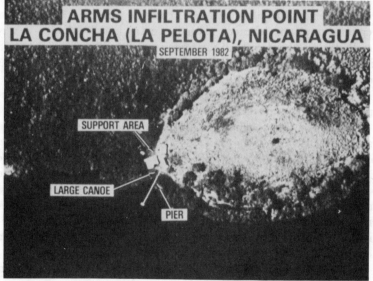

Two examples of ominous looking visual aids circulated by the Reagan Administration—in lieu of evidence—to convince the public that Nicaragua was "exporting" revolution. The map above, purporting to show arms infiltration routes, was circulated with the first white paper in 1981 and reproduced widely in the press. The aerial photo of a fishing cooperative (below) looks convincing, but has nothing other than its caption to link it with arms shipments (from Background Paper: Nicaragua's Military Build-Up and Support for Central American Subversion).

countries were doing little or nothing to help the Salvadorans. The authors of these mostly unsigned documents complained frequently of a lack of support from the Soviet Bloc. In one case they described a cool reception given to a Salvadoran rebel delegation in Managua.[14]

The authors of the white paper had made a "determined effort to create a 'selling' document, no matter how slim the background material," wrote Kwitny.[15] In this they succeeded: the mass media in the United States, with few exceptions, did buy the Reagan Administration's contention that Nicaragua was engaged in exporting revolution. In succeeding years the major information outlets continued to repeat and amplify the charges, ignoring the evidence of Kwitny and others that this pretext for US hostility toward Nicaragua was merely an attempt to make an uncooperative reality conform to the anti-Sandinista ideology enunciated in Reagan's 1980 electoral platform.

After the 1981 white paper, the Reagan Administration turned out new reports annually in an effort to strengthen its case against Nicaragua. But the sequels furnished no more convincing evidence than did the discredited first attempt. Despite the passage of several years, there was no interception of the arms shipments allegedly flowing into El Salvador—a very small country ringed with all the sophisticated military hardware at US disposal. A 1985 white paper attributed this failure to the delivery of arms in "canoes [that] are difficult to detect on radar because of their low profile and wooden construction." Yet the US Navy had no difficulty detecting and stopping such craft, with electric searchlights, in 1907.[16]

Indeed, the later policy statements made little pretense of supplying factual evidence. The *Background Paper: Nicaragua's Military Build-up and Support for Central American Subversion,* issued by the State and Defense Departments in 1984, tried to present itself as a scholarly effort, complete with footnoted sources. But these consisted largely of newspaper accounts, many from journals politically aligned with Reagan Administration positions such as the Rev. Sun Myung Moon's *Washington Times,* or publications of the American Enterprise Institute for Public Policy Research, a conservative think tank.

Apart from secondary sources, the *Background Paper* rested its case on the testimony of Miguel Bolaños Hunter, a Nicaraguan turncoat, and Alejandro Montenegro, a Salvadoran guerrilla who defected after his capture in Honduras. Both had been brought to the US during 1983-84 on publicity tours organized by the State Department and right-wing groups. But the star witnesses offered surprisingly little information, mainly confining themselves to general statements echoing administration charges. Where their testimony was specific, it was sometimes patently absurd, as when Bolaños Hunter asserted that Nicaraguan Vice Minister of Defense

Joaquin Cuadra (whose assistant he claimed to have been) had "five or six Soviet generals" as his advisors. The authors of the *Background Paper* tried to give substance to their flimsy evidence with a multitude of innocuous photographs, labeled and captioned in such a way as to make them appear sinister.[17]

Interdicting the alleged arms shipments to El Salvador was initially advanced as the reason for US support to the *contras* (short for *contrarevolucionarios,* or counterrevolutionaries), who made raids into Nicaragua from bases in Honduras and Costa Rica. These groups, whose core element was former Somoza National Guardsmen, received at least $70 million in assistance from the Reagan Administration before Congress voted to cut off their funding in 1984.* It became increasingly clear during 1983, however, that US support for the contras was out of proportion to the stated goal.[19] Accordingly, administration spokespersons began to articulate new justifications for covert actions against the Sandinistas.

In a 1985 radio speech in which Reagan called the contras "freedom fighters" and "our brothers," he asserted that Nicaragua's receipt of modern weapons "could even pose a strategic threat to the United States."[20] Both themes—the support for "freedom fighters" and the "strategic threat"— were reportedly developed to counter public and congressional opposition to further aid for the contras. Noting that both the United States and the Soviet Union "spend millions of dollars in covert efforts abroad to influence public opinion," *New York Times* Washington correspondent Philip Taubman cited administration officials as admitting that "presenting Nicaragua as a potential base for the projection of Soviet power in the hemisphere was part of an effort to persuade Congress and the public" that the US should continue funding the contras.[21]

The intensified anti-Sandinista rhetoric that followed Reagan's reelection in 1984 fleshed out suspicions that the real US goal was the overthrow of the Nicaraguan government. These suspicions were confirmed when Reagan told the first news conference of his second term that he sought to "remove it in the sense of its present structure, in which it is a Communist, totalitarian state and it is not a Government chosen by the people"—unless it "would turn around and . . . say uncle."[22]

A 1985 publication, jointly produced by the State and Defense Departments and titled *The Soviet-Cuban Connection in Central America and*

---

* Congress voted an additional $27 million in "humanitarian" assistance for the contras in 1985.

A report prepared for the congressional Arms Control and Foreign Policy Caucus in 1985 concluded that forty-six of the forty-eight military leaders of the FDN, the main contra group, were ex-National Guardsmen. Various reports have documented serious human rights abuses by the contras.[18]

the Caribbean, offered a multiplicity of arguments for Reagan Administration policy in Central America and the Caribbean. In this regard it was reminiscent of the varied justifications offered by the Coolidge Administration for sending US troops to Nicaragua in 1926-27, and of those employed by President Taft and Secretary Knox during the US interventions of 1909-10 and 1912. The scope had been broadened from earlier position papers to include Cuba's military capability and the alleged pre-US-invasion role of Grenada as a base for subversion. But the *Soviet-Cuban Connection* retreated even farther from making specific charges against Nicaragua than did its predecessors. The authors, perhaps reluctant to get bogged down in detailed allegations that could be refuted easily, largely confined themselves to insinuation and other propaganda techniques.

They presented pages of information on Cuba's military arsenal, complete with ominous-looking photographs. They informed the reader that Cuba has the capability to invade other Caribbean countries. Cuban MiG-23 aircraft, they asserted, "have the range to attack targets in the Caribbean and Gulf of Mexico, including key oil fields and refineries." They did not indicate, however, which oil fields or refineries the Cubans might bomb, or what countries Cuba could possibly invade without triggering immediate war with the United States. Likewise, the authors failed to mention the US-organized Bay of Pigs invasion or other early attempts to overthrow the Cuban government as a possible motive for Cuba's military buildup. They did not even suggest that Cuba's military preparedness would make any US invasion of the island extremely costly, and would entirely rule out an attack by other Western Hemisphere nations acting as proxies for the US.*[24]

The *Soviet-Cuban Connection* employed the same technique in discussing Nicaragua. Presenting evidence that the Sandinistas had acquired an amphibious armor capability, for example, the authors pointed out that this would be useful in crossing the rivers that form much of Nicaragua's borders with Honduras and Costa Rica. But they did not mention that such equipment is also necessary to defend Nicaragua, particularly its large Atlantic region, which has many rivers and few bridges. Nor did they refer to the large United States military presence in Central America, to US support for the contras, to the CIA mining of Nicaraguan harbors in 1984, or to the threat implied by earlier US interventions in Nicaragua and elsewhere in the region.

Perhaps the most significant omission from administration denuncia-

---

* During hearings on the 1968 foreign aid bill, General Robert W. Porter, chief of the US Southern Command, was asked if any suggestion had been made to the countries of Latin America that they "band together" to "eliminate the problem" of Cuba. Porter replied that Cuba's military strength excluded that option.[23]

tions of Nicaragua's military buildup, however, was what a classified Defense Department document called a "perception management" program, which the US has had in place since at least 1983. Revealed by the *New York Times,* the purpose of "perception management" is to keep the Nicaraguan government worried about an attack. A key component of the program has been the US military maneuvers in Honduras. A senior administration official quoted by the *Times* asserted, "One of the central purposes [of the maneuvers] is to create fear of an invasion." US troops, he said, "push very close to the border, deliberately, to set off all the alarms." Another aspect of the program was the creation of an uproar in November 1984 over the supposedly impending delivery of MiG aircraft to Nicaragua. During the MiG crisis, US SR-71 spy planes flew over Nicaraguan territory, deliberately causing sonic booms to heighten the atmosphere of tension. "Every time there's an invasion scare," said a State Department official explaining the program, "they make some concessions."[25] Another apparent benefit has been that Nicaragua's inevitable response—the sounding of invasion alarms—allowed the Reagan Administration to "manage" the "perceptions" of the North American news media and public, portraying Nicaraguan leaders as "paranoid." It also furnished new material for "white papers" on Nicaragua's military buildup.

A section of *The Soviet-Cuban Connection* titled "Nicaragua: A Betrayed Revolution" appended a list of other complaints to the assertion that the Sandinistas represent a threat to their neighbors. Included were the now-familiar charges of establishing a dictatorship, repressing the church, and censoring *La Prensa,* the right-wing Nicaraguan daily. Also added, however, were allegations of sponsorship of cocaine traffic and, of all things, having "demeaned the name of their patron, Cesar Augusto [sic] Sandino" (whom the United States labeled a "bandit" during his lifetime).[26]

In trying to make a case for the existence of a security threat to the United States, the *Soviet-Cuban Connection* became caught up in a curious contradiction. Explaining the reasons for alleged Soviet interest in Central America and the Caribbean, it stated:

> The Soviet Union sees in the region an excellent and low-cost opportunity to preoccupy the United States—the "main adversary" of Soviet strategy—thus gaining greater global freedom of action for the USSR . . . Working through its key proxy in the region, Cuba, the Soviet Union hopes to force the United States to divert attention and military resources to an area that has not been a serious security concern to the United States in the past.[27]

If the troubles in Central America were indeed a clever Soviet ploy to divert the attention of the United States, it would seem that the Reagan Administration fell for it hook, line, and sinker.

The publication also asserted, "The Soviets could decide in the future that it is to their advantage to fly long-range reconnaissance aircraft from Punta Huete [in Nicaragua] along the West Coast of the United States, just as they currently operate such flights along the East Coast of the United States by flying out of Cuba."[28] But Nicaragua is not conveniently located for surveillance of the US West Coast as Cuba is for the East Coast. In fact, it is not significantly closer to the West Coast than are existing Soviet air bases in eastern Siberia.

Reagan Administration arguments against Nicaragua were frequently shown to be based on outright falsehoods. Congressman Edward J. Markey tried unsuccessfully in 1983 to get the State Department to furnish the source of the phrase "revolution without frontiers" that administration officials, including Secretary of State Shultz, repeatedly attributed to the Sandinistas. Markey finally concluded that the phrase did not come from Nicaragua at all, but "originated inside the [Washington DC] Beltway."[29]

A similar case occurred when US officials, including President Reagan, quoted Nicaraguan Interior Minister Tomás Borge as saying that Costa Rica would be "the dessert" in Nicaragua's foreign conquests. Reporters traced the quote to a column by Huber Matos, Jr., an employee of a Miami-based Cuban exile organization. Matos admitted that while he had heard the phrase attributed to Borge in Costa Rica, he had never personally heard Borge use it, nor did he know anyone else who had.[30]

In April 1985, the Vatican was compelled to issue a formal denial when Reagan told a religious conference that the Pope had sent him a message expressing support for his Nicaragua policy. Eager to convict the Sandinistas of Marxism, meanwhile, Vice President Bush held up stamps issued by Nicaragua to commemorate the 100th anniversary of Karl Marx's death. But Nicaragua had also issued stamps honoring the 250th birthday of George Washington and the Pope's visit to Nicaragua.[31]

A more complex invention, but a widely-accepted one, involved the pledges supposedly made by the Sandinistas to the Organization of American States in 1979. In one form or another, this was repeated innumerable times by members of the Reagan Administration, the mass media, and even Reagan's Democratic Party opponents, to demonstrate that the Sandinistas had "betrayed" the Nicaragua revolution. The story, as told in *The Soviet-Cuban Connection*, runs as follows:

> In July 1979, a broad and popular coalition led militarily by the Sandinista National Liberation Front (FSLN) overthrew the government of General Anastasio Somoza and ended a family dynasty that had ruled Nicaragua for more than four decades. The new government owed much

of its success to international support for the anti-Somoza forces. The Organization of American States had even adopted a resolution calling for the "definitive replacement" of Somoza and free elections as soon as possible. In gaining this support, the Sandinistas had pledged to have free elections, political pluralism, a mixed economy, and a non-aligned foreign policy.[32]

Clearly implied in the statement is the idea that the Sandinistas made pledges to the OAS as a precondition for OAS support. In fact, the cited OAS resolution was adopted on June 23, 1979, while the frequently mentioned message of the provisional Junta of National Reconstruction (JRGN) was not telexed to the OAS secretary general until July 12, several weeks afterward. Nor did the JRGN communication take the form of a pledge, but of a "Plan to Achieve Peace." In a message introducing the plan, the members of the provisional government stated that they were "presenting to the community of nations in this hemisphere the purposes that have inspired our Government . . . some of which we would like to ratify here." Point 1 declared their intention to safeguard human rights in accord with the United Nations Universal Declaration of Human Rights and the Charter on Human Rights of the OAS. They invited the OAS Inter-American Commission on Human Rights to visit Nicaragua to monitor the human rights situation as soon as the new government was installed in power. Point 5 of the JRGN message announced

> The plan to call Nicaraguans to the first free elections that our country will have in this century, so that they may elect their representatives to the city councils and to a constitutional assembly, and the country's highest ranking authorities.[33]

The communication made no mention of a mixed economy, political pluralism, or a non-aligned foreign policy, although these points were contained in various programmatic statements of the Junta or the FSLN.

On the other hand, the first point of the June 23, 1979 OAS resolution referred to by the Reagan Administration declared "that the solution of the serious problem is exclusively within the jurisdiction of the people of Nicaragua."[34] That sentence alone would have prohibited the OAS from soliciting any formal commitment from the Nicaraguans regarding the character of the regime that was to replace Somoza, even if the OAS charter had allowed for the making of agreements with a provisional government that was then still in exile in San José, Costa Rica, and recognized by only one OAS member. If those obstacles had not existed, any express or implied "deal" would have been voided when Francisco Urcuyo, Somoza's nominal successor, failed to implement the terms of the Plan to Achieve Peace, which formed the basis of both the Junta's communication and the transition negotiations that followed.[35]

Nevertheless, both the FSLN and the governing Junta did view the statements to the OAS as moral commitments, and proceeded to act accordingly. In August 1980 the Council of State adopted a law that mandated the beginning of an electoral process in 1984, with elections to be held in 1985.[36]

The Inter-American Commission on Human Rights (IACHR) visited Nicaragua in October 1980 in response to the original JRGN invitation. It made its report to the OAS in June 1981. Its findings on the human rights situation in Nicaragua were generally favorable, especially when contrasted to its 1978 report on the Somoza regime or to those dealing with human rights in other countries of the region. The IACHR made a number of recommendations in areas where it saw the need for improvement; many of these were subsequently implemented by the Nicaraguan government.[37]

The IACHR report criticized Nicaragua's failure to adopt a law guaranteeing and regulating the functioning of political parties and the decision to postpone elections until 1985. Significantly, it did not condemn the Sandinistas for "betraying" a pledge, although it did cite these shortcomings as "having an effect on the existence of an authentically democratic system, to which the Government of National Reconstruction has committed itself." Nicaragua adopted a law on political parties in September 1983, after lengthy debate in the Council of State, and the elections were finally moved up to November 1984 by agreement of the seven parties participating.[38]

It was clear even before the ground rules were established for the Nicaraguan election or the candidates certified, however, that the United States government had determined to pursue an attitude of hostility, as it tried to influence opposition groups to abstain. The effort centered around Arturo Cruz, a conservative economist who served briefly as a member of the governing junta and then as Nicaragua's ambassador to the US. Cruz had since turned against the revolution, becoming the presidential candidate of a coalition of four small opposition groups called the Democratic Coordinator. Shortly before the election Cruz withdrew his candidacy and called on supporters to boycott the voting. According to New York Times reporter Philip Taubman, the CIA had worked with Cruz's associates to make sure they would block his participation, and the Wall Street Journal reported that Cruz himself had secretly received CIA funds. Asserted one US official interviewed by Taubman, "The Administration never contemplated letting Cruz stay in the race, because then the Sandinistas could justifiably claim that the elections were legitimate, making it much harder for the United States to oppose the Nicaraguan Govern-

Sergio Ramirez (center), FSLN candidate for vice president, during the 1984 election campaign (photo by Karl Bermann)

ment."[39] The bulk of the US mass media adopted a similarly antagonistic attitude toward the Nicaraguan election, apparently taking their cue that the election was a "sham" from the Reagan Administration.

The November 1984 Nicaraguan election was not perfect. "Perfectly" democratic elections probably have yet to be held anywhere. But it was far from being a "sham." Much was made of alleged harassment of opposition parties by Sandinista "mobs." Unquestionably, there were some instances where this occurred during early stages of campaigning. But, contrary to the US portrayals, these incidents were not orchestrated by the government; they resulted, rather, from the government's lack of control. Nicaraguan police did not at first act decisively to prevent clashes between supporters of competing political parties, evidently for fear that any large presence at political gatherings would be portrayed as "police state" intimidation. The FSLN—as a political party distinct from the government—deserved criticism for moving too slowly in exerting its authority with some of its youthful supporters. On the other hand, there is evidence that in at least some cases government opponents, especially Cruz partisans, deliberately provoked clashes with pro-Sandinista demonstrators.[40] The past record of the CIA and its close association with Cruz suggests the possible involvement of that agency in planning provocations.

But the instances of seeming intimidation, whatever their cause, were relatively minor. In the weeks before the election, the period when most activity by all parties took place, the incidences of violence had been brought under control so effectively that even the defacing of election posters and graffiti—a normal occurrence in most countries—was conspicuously absent. At the height of the campaign even minor opposition parties were able to hold street rallies and demonstrations with fewer impediments than such activity would encounter in the United States.*

There were instances when government vehicles, and perhaps other state resources, were used to bring party supporters to campaign rallies—a kind of practice by no means confined to Nicaragua. Such abuses appeared to be attributable mainly to Sandinista labor unions organized at public enterprises or government agencies. They were not, however, significant enough to affect the election's outcome.

Conservative Democratic Party spokesman denounces the government at an outdoor election rally in Managua, 1984 (photo by Karl Bermann)

The official FSLN newspaper, *Barricada*, gave almost no coverage to the opposition, a policy that did not help promote fair elections. As an avowedly

---

* Parties did not need a permit to hold an outdoor rally as they generally do in the United States, nor were they restricted in the use of sound equipment; they merely had to file a letter of intent with the Supreme Electoral Council stating the time and place of the intended activity. There were exceptions in some Atlantic Coast zones where fighting with the contras was underway and campaigning required special permission from the security forces.

partisan publication, it had no formal obligation to devote space to its opponents. But as one of only three dailies in a country with a severe shortage of newsprint, it should have seen this as a duty. Equally guilty, however, was *La Prensa,* the right-wing paper frequently portrayed as the innocent victim of government censorship. *La Prensa,* supporting the boycott position of Arturo Cruz, only printed articles attacking the electoral process as a whole. It even refused to give coverage to the opposition parties that were participating, portraying them as Sandinista puppets—something they clearly were not. Clemente Guido, presidential candidate of the Conservative Democratic Party, one of the most important opposition groups, charged that by this policy *La Prensa* itself was exercising censorship.[41] In refusing to cover the electoral process for political reasons, *La Prensa* demonstrated that it no longer exemplified independent or objective journalism. Only the independent pro-Sandinista paper *Nuevo Diario* made a serious effort to devote space to all parties.*

But the inadequacies of newspaper coverage were more than compensated by the equal and generous distribution of free television and radio time, and by equal allotments of government funds to all parties, regardless of size. In this, as in the easy registration for voters, the Nicaraguan electoral process was fairer than that of the United States.

Perhaps most deserving of praise, however, was the Supreme Electoral Council, an independent body in which opposition parties were well represented. The *Consejo Supremo* was remarkably efficient in ensuring that prospective voters were informed on the mechanics of the process, and in adopting measures to guarantee a secret ballot and safeguard against fraud in vote counting; in this it was aided by experts from France and Sweden. In the functioning of the Supreme Electoral Council and in its technical aspects, the 1984 Nicaraguan election could serve as a model for other countries.

What did not emerge from the election was a system dominated by more or less equally-balanced, supposedly middle-of-the-road parties á la the United States or Western Europe. Even if that were desirable, it could not be expected to come about in the polarized conditions of social revolution in post-Somoza Nicaragua. The FSLN won an overwhelming victory, not because the elections were a "sham," but because it continued to be the only well-organized, truly mass political party in the country. A majority of the population still adheres to its banner because it alone can take credit for ousting the dictatorship, and it alone has offered the workers, peasants, and marginalized poor any hope of reversing the country's severe under-

---

* The current *La Prensa* is not the same paper as the pre-1979 *La Prensa* of Pedro Joaquin Chamorro. In 1980, a majority of *La Prensa's* staff left in a dispute over editorial policy and formed *Nuevo Diario.* All three dailies are run by members of the Chamorro family.

development and improving their lot. Its competitors demonstrated their incapacity during the long decades of Somoza rule, when they alternated ineffectual forms of opposition—mainly efforts to appeal to the United States—with outright complicity with the dictatorship. These groups joined the Sandinista-led insurrection at the last minute, when the fall of Somoza was virtually an accomplished fact.

If a Western-style parliamentary or "representative" democracy does not emerge in Nicaragua, no one is more to blame than the United States. Any chance Nicaragua may have had of developing the necessary preconditions for such a system—a viable and independent economy on free market or "capitalist" lines—was destroyed when the US ousted the Zelaya government in 1909-1910. Zelaya's infrastructural improvements and democratization of education might have established the bases for a democracy of the type the United States always claims to be promoting. But the subsequent US political and military occupation, intentionally or not, inaugurated a seventy-year dark age, during which the country became a school not for democracy, but for dependency, sycophantism, corruption, and finally, tyranny.

Whatever its shortcomings, the Nicaraguan electoral experiment is of tremendous significance. It marked the first attempt in modern times to institutionalize a multi-party system in a country undergoing a profound social revolution. This is a radical departure from the practices in existing Socialist countries, where one-party, and usually one-candidate, elections are the general rule. The 33 percent of the vote garnered by opposition parties may have already exercised a significant influence on Sandinista policy.* Ultimately this could lead to the emergence of other viable, popularly-based parties within the framework of support for the revolution. Certainly the path toward development and social justice for the Third World is neither well-traveled nor clearly marked, and there is much room for honest disagreement.

Whether or not the experiment succeeds depends upon more than the will of the FSLN. If the United States continues to pursue a policy of escalating armed hostility it may reawaken a hope in opposition politicians, as in the past, that they will be placed in power by the military might of the US. This would deter them from seeking representation commensurate with their following through the development of the indigenous political process, now in its infancy. Instead they would be tempted to align themselves with the contras, engaging in provocation and confrontation in order to win the approval of the United States government and further its objectives.

---

* The FSLN received 67 percent of the vote (some of its leaders had predicted it would win 80 percent). Parties to the right of the FSLN polled 29.2 percent and far left groups 3.8 percent.[42]

I F, AS IS APPARENT, the official justifications for US actions against Nicaragua are mere pretexts, the question remains to be answered, what is the real motive for United States policy?

Almost from its beginning the United States has asserted the existence of a special relationship with Latin America. The nations of the New World were to form an "American system," a republican system distinct from the monarchical order of Europe with its closed colonial economies. The Monroe Doctrine was intended to secure for the United States the advantages of this American system—a hemisphere, as Secretary of State Henry Clay put it in 1825, "now open to the enterprize and commerce of all Americans."[43] If the influence of European nations could be excluded, or at least limited, the United States, with its enormous economic and geographic advantages, stood to be first among equals.

As the US grew larger and more powerful, the assertion of North American primacy became more aggressive, taking on strong racial overtones. Assaults on Mexico, Nicaragua, and Spain's Cuban colony served for a time to postpone the "irrepressible conflict" between slavery and free labor. The Monroe Doctrine became a shield for territorial expansion under the banner of "manifest destiny."

The growth of United States economic, political, and military power during the latter 19th century was closely bound up with the establishment of important commercial and transit routes through the Caribbean and Central America; the digging of the canal was key to Yankee ascendancy among the world's commercial empires. At the same time, the countries bordering the important trade channels offered fertile prospects for the investment of Yankee capital, then beginning to seek opportunities abroad. These interests carried with them the notion that the United States, for its own "self-protection," had a "right" to exercise superintendency in the region, that it formed a strategic "coastline" or "border" of the United States, vital to its well-being. Nowhere was this expressed more clearly than in the US relationship with Nicaragua in the era that began after the Civil War.

The United States was predominant because it had no real competition in the Western Hemisphere. "To-day the United States is practically sovereign on this continent," wrote Secretary of State Olney in 1895, "because, in addition to all other grounds, its infinite resources combined with its isolated position render it master of the situation and practically invulnerable as against any or all other powers." All of this would be jeopardized, he said, if competitors gained a foothold:

The disastrous consequences to the United States of such a condition of things are obvious. The loss of prestige, of authority, and of weight in the councils of the family of nations, would be among the least of them. Our only real rivals in peace as well as enemies in war would be found located at our very doors.[44]

The fear that powerful European rivals might establish themselves in the Caribbean, crippling the economic and military power of the United States, led Theodore Roosevelt to declare his "corollary" to the Monroe Doctrine, which was really nothing more than an articulation of the policy that had been developing over several decades. Under this American version of the White Man's Burden, the Yankee government arrogated to itself the right—the "duty"—to intervene in the affairs of the small states of the Caribbean and the Middle American isthmus, ostensibly to forestall intervention by others.

President Taft and Secretary Knox sought to institutionalize the preventive superintendence embodied in the Roosevelt Corollary by establishing protectorates. Under the rubric of Dollar Diplomacy they promoted loans by US bankers as a means of gaining customs receiverships and other mortgages on sovereignty. These arrangements appeared to offer the best of all possible worlds, giving the United States maximum control with minimum responsibility. They also served to displace European financiers and promote investment by Yankee enterprise. Though the policy of US overlordship was openly proclaimed by Theodore Roosevelt and William Howard Taft, it was consummated behind the moralizing hypocrisy of Woodrow Wilson.

To Puerto Rico, annexed after the Spanish-American War, and Cuba, made a protectorate with the Platt Amendment, were added formal or de facto protectorates in Panama, Haiti, and the Dominican Republic. But Nicaragua gave the United States a severe case of indigestion.

The ouster of President Zelaya and the suppression of Nicaraguan Liberalism by the Taft Administration in 1909-10 marked the first instance in Latin America—perhaps anywhere—in which the United States intervened to remove an established government. Now not only European rivals were to be barred, but indigenous nationalists as well—those whose pursuit of the interests of their own nation might lead them to make arrangements with US competitors or take other actions counter to US interests (as interpreted by the State Department).

The long intervention in Nicaragua that followed produced one of the clearest formulations of United States policy toward the region. Early in 1927, Undersecretary of State Robert Olds wrote a "Confidential Memorandum on the Nicaraguan Situation" for Secretary Kellogg and President Coolidge outlining the considerations that required the US to maintain Adolfo Diaz in power during the Constitutionalist War. "This Government indisputably has what may be designated a Caribbean policy which has never been definitely formulated and openly avowed," Olds began. The whole of Central America and the Isthmus of Panama, he continued, constituted "a legitimate sphere of influence for the United States, if we are to have due regard for our own safety and protection"; he saw it as "equally vital" that the United States control both the Panama Canal and the potential canal route through Nicaragua.[45]

Up to that time, Olds said, "the world at large" had "at least tacitly conceded" the existence of this "special interest":

> International practice over a long period of time has enforced the idea of a dominant influence by this country in Central American affairs. Our ministers accredited to the five little republics stretching from the Mexican border to Panama have always been more than mere diplomatic representatives. They have been advisers whose advice has been accepted virtually as law in the capitals where they respectively reside . . . Call it a sphere of influence, or what you will, we do control the destinies of Central America, and we do so for the simple reason that the national interest absolutely dictates such a course.

Olds' perception of the threat to the United States in the 1926-27 Nicaraguan civil war bore an uncanny resemblance to Reagan Administration pronouncements on Sandinista Nicaragua: "At this moment," he said, "a deliberate attempt to undermine our position and set aside our special relationship to Central America is being made." The bogeyman of Olds' day was not Cuba or the Soviet Union, however, but Mexico, with whom the United States was engaged in "the most insidious type of international struggle imaginable." Referring to Mexico's projected nationalization of its oil and other mineral wealth, Olds asserted that its policy "for many years has been progressively anti-American. Mexico has consistently attacked us by confiscation of the rights of our nationals on her own soil and is now delivering this flank attack upon us through Central America." If Mexico's alleged "maneuver" were allowed to succeed through the victory of the Nicaraguan Liberals,

> the tangible evidence of our influence will have disappeared and notice will have been conveyed to all Central America, and to the rest of the world, that recognition and support by this Government means nothing. Until now Central America has always understood that governments which we recognize and support stay in power, while those which we do not recognize and support fall. Nicaragua has become a test case. It is difficult to see how we can afford to be defeated . . . The main thing we have at stake in this controversy is our prestige. If we permit the issue to be resolved against us we shall, at least for a time, take rank as a second-rate power so far as influence in Central America is concerned.

Previously, Olds explained, it had been enough for the United States "to intervene on the sole pretext of furnishing protection to American lives and property." But under the circumstances he described, it seemed that measures consonant with that pretext would not be sufficient. He recommended, therefore, consideration of "whether the time has not arrived for a definite pronouncement" by the United States of its "special and paramount interest" and its intention to "not tolerate interference by any outside power in that area." He believed that, despite the risks, "sooner or later it may be highly advantageous to clear the atmosphere by an open avowal."

Most of the considerations outlined by Undersecretary Olds were—in a suitably expurgated form—incorporated by the Coolidge Administration in public justifications of its Nicaragua intervention. But it was not deemed advisable to make explicit the danger posed by the spread of Mexican nationalism. To make the "threat" plausible to public opinion, therefore, State Department spokesmen sought to depict Mexico as a conduit for Bolshevism, just as Cuba and Nicaragua would later be pictured as Soviet "proxies."

The difficulty in imposing on Nicaragua the kind of stability that harmonized with US interests did more than give gas pains to several successive Yankee presidents and secretaries of state. The decades-long North American occupation, culminating with the embarrassment of Sandino's six-year guerrilla war, proved to be counterproductive. It became a focal point for Latin nationalism—"anti-Americanism" in the lexicon of the State Department. Instead of adopting Olds' suggestion of an "open avowal" that the Caribbean area constituted an exclusive sphere of influence, the US government became ever more reticent about publicly explaining the nature of this supposed national interest.

In 1930, during the war against Sandino, Secretary of State Stimson suggested to President Hoover the project of a major policy statement, an "amendment" of the Monroe Doctrine that would answer criticism of US actions in Latin America. In it, Stimson proposed to outline the special interest in Central America "arising out of its propinquity to the Panama Canal." Hoover interrupted him "to say that he thought that we had better be careful about making too elaborate discussion of our own interest on that point." Stimson explained that he "didn't intend to prod that idea forward but to show that it was in line with the preservation of the independence of the countries themselves."[46]

The failures and liabilities inherent in open intervention—made manifest largely by the negative experience of Nicaragua—led to a search for less direct methods. The rhetoric of the Monroe Doctrine was exchanged for that of the "Good Neighbor." But the underlying policy remained the same.

The hegemonic considerations spelled out by Secretary Olney in 1895 proved their value to the US as never before during World War II. The United States' unchallenged dominance of the Western Hemisphere allowed it to establish a chain of bases in Central and South America well in advance of its own entry into the war. The "inter-American system"—providing the United States with secure supplies of strategic raw materials at the prices it dictated—proved to be more dependable than the colonial arrangements of the great powers of Europe.

But this "national security" justification for US Caribbean policy, if it was ever valid, is obsolete in the nuclear age. Any military showdown between the United States and the USSR, or any other nation conceivably capable of seizing the canal, would be over in a matter of hours, if not minutes. The important strategic concerns of an earlier era—the capture of territory, the supply of raw materials, the severing of trade routes, or slow strangulation by naval blockade—would be irrelevant.

Nonetheless, it seems there is still a great deal of political mileage left in the argument that the Panama Canal and Caribbean sea lanes are vital to US security. It has been unquestioned for so long that it has a strong emotional attachment—the population of the United States, the most powerful nation in the world, has been conditioned to feel more insecure than any other people. No doubt, too, part of the argument's appeal lies in the dependence upon it of so many military programs and jobs. But the national security justification for US control in the Caribbean region is today a red herring.

AT ONE TIME, Central America was thought to offer great potential for Yankee enterprise. The promise went largely unfulfilled, however, due to changing investment patterns after the two world wars, retrenchment caused by the Great Depression, the lack of necessary infrastructure in the Central American countries themselves, and other factors. Investments in Nicaragua grew to a significant size in the period 1880-1920, but later declined to the extent that by the 1930s only Paraguay in all Latin America had less US investment than Nicaragua.[47]

Direct investments by US companies have never been of paramount importance in determining United States policy toward Nicaragua, at least not in an immediate sense. The interests of North American investors on the Miskito Coast clashed with State Department policy vis-a-vis Britain in 1894. Government and business joined in ousting Zelaya fifteen years later, but the influence of the latter was secondary to larger policy considerations.

"Few underdeveloped countries have so great a physical potential for growth as does Nicaragua," concluded a lengthy study by the Internation-

al Bank for Reconstruction and Development in 1953. Direct US investment did increase during the Alliance for Progress/Central American Common Market period in the 1960s and '70s, but in 1978, the year before
Somoza's fall, it totaled only $90 million, a comparatively insignificant
figure.[48] The Reagan Administration's pressure on US companies to pull
out of Nicaragua (along with its economic boycott) would in any case seem
to argue powerfully that direct economic interests in Nicaragua itself are
not a determining factor in current policy.

What is at stake for the United States today, in the view of the policymakers, is the "big picture." Nicaragua, though small and poor, is part of an
intricate web of economic and political relationships. As with other Third
World countries, the commodities it produces are marketed and refined
by large multinational corporations that take a lion's share of the profits.*
Unable to control prices or quotas for their products, Third World countries suffer from long-term deterioration in the terms of trade: income from
their exports continually declines, while the costs of imported machinery,
manufactured goods, and other items continue to rise. The increasingly
large deficits that result must be financed through increased borrowing
at ever higher interest rates, such that for two-thirds of the Latin countries, interest payments alone on external debts represent from 20 to 50
percent of the value of their exports, while total debt service payments
reach as high as 70 percent. As they fall farther into debt they are compelled to seek new loans merely to service the existing debts. All thought
of development is abandoned. Spending for health care, education, housing, and other basic social services, already woefully inadequate, is cut even
further to pay off bankers in gleaming skyscrapers in New York or Western
Europe. Today each child in Latin America is born with a debt of $650.[50]

But while the unending cycle of indebtedness has become an important factor in the decapitalization of the Third World, it has been a boon
to the advanced market economy nations, particularly the United States.
Loans now account for the greater part of foreign investment in underdeveloped countries, contributing 90 percent of the foreign capital earnings
derived from the energy importing nations of the Third World in 1981.[51]

Two-thirds of all direct investment by US-based multinational corporations in the Third World is in Latin America. Direct investment by multinationals (such as building factories) is often pictured as beneficial to these
countries. But US multinationals typically invest very little outside capital
in underdeveloped nations. Instead, they borrow from lending institutions
(often branches of US banks) in the host countries themselves, and there-

---

* For example, one of Nicaragua's chief export commodities is cotton. It is estimated that
the cotton producer receives only 6.4 percent of the final retail price for a pair of denim
jeans.[49]

fore simply divert capital from locally-generated development projects. Much of this investment in recent years has gone into the creation of "export platforms"—manufacturing enclaves established to take advantage of abundant sources of cheap, unorganized labor in countries where going wage rates are frequently one-tenth, or less, of those prevailing in the United States. Despite the claims of the multinationals' publicists, such operations do not as a whole contribute to lessening unemployment or to improving these countries' balance of payments. In most cases they perform simple, partial processes like the assembly of electronic components or garments, whose final destination is not the host country, but the consumer societies of the United States and Western Europe. They do not, therefore, substitute for imports. Moreover, by absorbing scarce local investment capital, buying out local companies, or introducing labor-saving technology, they often contribute to greater, not lesser, unemployment. And as a result of intra-corporate price manipulation ("transfer pricing"), profit repatriation, and other practices they actually contribute to a worsening of the balance of payments. US multinationals reap annual profits of 40 to 400 percent from these operations, four-fifths of which they repatriate to the United States, helping to offset a large part of the US balance of trade deficit with Western Europe and Japan.[52]

But these exploitative relationships are very fragile. Studies indicate that merely by enacting tougher tax laws on foreign investments, the countries of Latin America could generate considerable capital for their own development. A UN study of ten Third World commodities has shown that if the exporting countries had been able to perform just the first stages of processing, their earnings on these products would have increased nearly two-and-one-half times. Besides cutting into the profits of the multinationals, such measures would create new competitors in the production of manufactured goods and in the bidding for raw materials. Underdeveloped countries do not usually take such steps, despite the enormous potential advantages. One reason is that the elites that govern most of them see a smoother path for themselves in joining, not fighting, the multinationals; direct bribery of government officials also plays a part. In any case, the Third World countries' enormous debts have put them at the mercy of international lending agencies, like the largely US-controlled International Monetary Fund, which block nationalist economic policies through restrictive loan conditions.[53]

The government inaugurated in Nicaragua in July 1979 is an entirely different matter, however. From the outset the Sandinistas enacted a series of measures aimed at breaking out of the dependency model: nationalization of the financial system and foreign trade, creation of a public sector in the economy, launching an ambitious agrarian reform, and passing new tax laws.⁵⁴ In doing so they declared their intention to cease playing by the established rules for economic relations between the Third World and the developed metropolises.

Nicaragua's challenge to the United States involves much more than the immediate economic interests represented by its small economy. What matters most is its threat to the workings of the system as a whole. If a nationalist experiment in Nicaragua is allowed to succeed it will furnish an alternative development model with enormous attractive power for the rest of the Third World. The loss of United States "prestige" and "influence" is therefore just as much a consideration today as when Under-secretary Olds worried about it in 1927. Reagan's concern that "the greatest power in the world" not appear "unwilling and incapable of stopping communist aggression in our own backyard" can be understood in the same sense as Olds' fear that a victory by the Mexican-backed Constitutionalists in Nicaragua would relegate the US to the status of "a second-rate power so far as influence in Central America is concerned."⁵⁵

Just as a successful strike in a very small workshop can have enormous repercussions in an area where low wages are endemic, so Nicaragua's success could cause the economic dominoes to fall rapidly, particularly in Latin America—most of which shares with Nicaragua not only common problems but a common language and culture. Just as employers attempting to mobilize public opinion against strikers routinely accuse them of being communists, radicals, or mobsters, attacking the Sandinistas as "Marxist-Leninists" or charging them with planning to establish Russian bases is more likely to achieve results than denouncing them for wanting to cease being hewers of wood and drawers of water.

I F MILITARY security were a real concern, it could be addressed easily enough. In 1983, Nicaragua offered to sign a treaty with the United States guaranteeing, among other things, that it would not allow its territory "to be utilized to affect or to threaten the security of the United States or to attack any other state."⁵⁶ The Reagan Administration chose not to pursue the offer, even though it included a proposal to allow on-site inspections.

Many expert analyses have appeared showing that, contrary to Reagan Administration claims, the Soviet Union has been reluctant to become involved in Nicaragua, while the Sandinistas have demonstrated their independence from Moscow on such issues as Afghanistan or attendance at the 1984 Los Angeles Olympics.⁵⁷ Unlike the United States, the Soviet Union has traditionally shunned security commitments far from its own borders. In the one notable exception, the 1962 Cuban Missile Crisis, the USSR ultimately withdrew its missiles, giving the appearance of having backed down before the US. The experience, with its consequent loss of prestige, is one the Soviets are not likely to repeat.

But the litany of unsubstantiated charges against Nicaragua is not intended to withstand close scrutiny. It is designed to play on the image, cultivated through many years of cold war, of a monolithic international communist conspiracy bent on world domination. To a population thoroughly imbued with cold war ideology, it is thought to be enough to make a case that some Nicaraguan leaders are "Marxist-Leninists" in order to convince the public that they are, as Reagan put it, planning to "destroy the fragile flower of democracy and force communism on our small Central American neighbors."[58]

Individual Sandinistas may or may not call themselves "Marxist-Leninists" or "Communists." It is very likely that those that do would be unable to agree on the definition of the terms, at least as they apply to concrete policies. But even if the FSLN as a whole were to describe itself as "Marxist-Leninist" (which it does not) and agree on what that meant, it would tell little about what it was actually going to do. Those countries presently governed by parties claiming to be Marxist-Leninist pursue very different domestic and foreign policies; at least two of them—China and Yugoslavia—have friendly relationships with the United States.

On the other hand, there has grown up in Latin America in the decades following the Cuban Revolution and the failure of the Alliance for Progress, what might be called an "historic program" that transcends ideology or party labels. It is based on the experience of a century of failed reforms and on both the positive and negative experiences of the Cuban and other Third World revolutions. Broadly outlined, the principal features of this program include:

• **A thoroughgoing land reform.** The concentration of land in underutilized latifundia while large masses of the rural population subsist on tiny inadequate plots or have no land at all is characteristic of most, if not all, of Latin America. Land redistribution is necessary as a measure of elementary social justice, as well as to increase productivity, reduce or eliminate reliance on imported foodstuffs, eradicate hunger, and reverse patterns of migration into urban slums. There need not be maximum limits on land ownership, and former owners may be compensated; what is key is that fundamental restructuring of land tenancy take place. Best results will be achieved not by applying a dogmatic model, but by establishing a mix of private ownership, cooperatives, and publicly-owned agricultural enterprises, adapted to specific circumstances.

• **Nationalization of the financial system** is necessary to reorient lending policy to the needs of national development, rather than immediate profitability. Without it, land reform is doomed to failure. Investment must also be channeled into rational industrialization, particularly the elaboration of the country's own raw materials. Nationalization of the banking system is important also to minimize the effects of the inevitable resistance that will be organized by at least some sectors of the old economic elite and, as in the case of Nicaragua, externally-directed destabilization efforts.

• **The nationalization of foreign trade** is essential for controlling and ultimately reducing the country's level of indebtedness through reduction or elimination of unnecessary imports, and for assuring that products are exported on the most favorable terms.

• **The creation of a public sector in the economy** is needed to carry out infrastructural improvements, provide needed services like housing construction, and create new branches of the economy needed for national development. The extent to which private capitalists have failed to invest in industrialization is proof that they are unwilling or unable to do so. This and other measures require some degree of central economic planning.

• **Fundamental restructuring of notoriously lax tax systems** to assure that those who can afford it, including foreign corporations, pay their fair share. Along with the creation of a public sector, tax law overhaul is necessary to generate investment funds and to pay for improvements in social services.

• **Nationalization of natural resources** to guard against continued depletion of mineral wealth, and to eliminate catastrophic practices like wholesale deforestation.

• **Preservation of private enterprise in a mixed economy.** The vast majority of productive units in the underdeveloped world are very small. Philosophical considerations aside, these thousands of small, dispersed producers provide vital goods and services, and cannot be efficiently absorbed or replaced by the state, as some Socialist countries have tried to do with disastrous results. It is also desirable from an economic standpoint that efficiently operated larger enterprises remain in private hands, provided they are willing to adapt to the new political and social reality and subordinate the quest for profit to the needs of the nation.

• **Basic restructuring of consumption patterns and radical reform of the educational and health systems** are needed to alleviate the critical conditions of the poor and to create the cultural foundation necessary for real development.

• **Democratization of society.** Of all necessary measures, this is perhaps the most important and the one in which there has been the least positive experience anywhere. It does not mean the mere holding of formal elections while the basic structures of oligarchic/military control remain intact, or the declaration by a single "proletarian" party that it represents the will of the masses. Ultimately it may or may not involve traditional parliamentary methods, some form of industrial democracy, or specialized vehicles for the expression of public will such as trade unions, consumer groups, or farmers' and womens' associations. Probably it will need to incorporate elements of all three. Democracy, in the original meaning of the word—"the rule of the people," is necessary to ensure that development is equitable, to prevent the public sector from becoming a breeding ground for a new privileged elite, to control bureaucratism, and to guarantee the public participation that is necessary if the entire experiment is not to wither and die.

• **Nonalignment.** In order to develop, Third World nations need both the technology of the West and the flexibility offered by trade relations with the planned economies of the Socialist countries. They cannot solve their problems by imitating the economic or political models of either, or by becoming cold war pawns.

THE KISSINGER Commission report on Central America stated:

There is room in the hemisphere for differing forms of governance and different political economies. Authentically indigenous changes, and even indigenous revolutions, are not incompatible with international harmony in the Americas.[59]

All the evidence, however, shows that the attitude of the United States is exactly the opposite. The US intervened overtly or covertly to overthrow elected governments in Guatemala, the Dominican Republic, and Chile (and there are strong indications it was involved in the military coup that ousted President Goulart of Brazil in 1964), just to cite examples from the second half of the 20th century. It tried and failed to oust the revolutionary government in Cuba, and is now embarked on the same course in Nicaragua. Assuming that the term "revolution" is not used in the Madison Avenue sense of an old product in new packaging (the Reagan Administration termed its effort to legitimatize the Duarte government in El Salvador a "democratic revolution"), not a single example can be offered of a country in the Americas where the United States has willingly tolerated a government, revolutionary or not, that seeks basic alterations in the status quo.[60]

In 1979 Nicaragua regained the independence it lost with the signing of the Dawson Pact in 1910. Embarking on a serious attempt to overcome its enormous problems, its leaders and people have registered notable achievements in education, health, and other fields. They have also made mistakes, and many problems remain to be solved. But given the legacy of the past, the paucity of resources, and the brutal—not to say medieval—political tradition of the region, they have done remarkably well.

Nicaragua's resumed pursuit of its own national interests is, however, once again seen as a challenge to the "prestige" and "influence" of the United States. Once more, therefore, as Undersecretary Olds said in 1927, it has become a "test case." And once more, disproportionate power is being brought to bear to make it return to the fold of the "inter-American system" that has served the United States so well for so long.

The effort to make Nicaragua again conform to Washington's prescriptions clearly does not rest on international law, which the United States has told the world does not apply to Central America. Does it rest on Manifest Destiny, on some new corollary of the Monroe Doctrine, or merely on the doctrine of the highwayman—that might makes right? As the denizens of consumer society are summoned to hold back the strivings of the Third World, in the jungles of Nicaragua or elsewhere, these will be unavoidable questions.

SOURCE NOTES

CHAPTER I. TWO AMERICAS

1. Francisco Pérez Estrada, *Historia Precolonial de Nicaragua: Sintesis* (Managua: Editorial Nueva Nicaragua, 1980), passim.
2. As quoted in ibid., p. 10.
3. José Dolores Gámez, *Historia de Nicaragua* (Madrid: Escuela Profesional de Artes Gráficas, 1955, repr. of 1888 ed.), p. 59.
4. Ibid., p. 252.
5. Ibid., p. 337.
6. Ibid., p. 267.
7. Jaime Wheelock Román, *Imperialismo y Dictadura: Crisis de una Formación Social* (Mexico, DF: Siglo Veintiuno Editores, quinta ed., 1980), p. 52, passim.
8. Sergio Ramírez, "El Muchacho de Niquinohomo," intro. to Sergio Ramírez, ed., *El Pensamiento Vivo de Sandino* (Managua: Editorial Nueva Nicaragua, 1981), p. ix.
9. Dexter Perkins, *A History of the Monroe Doctrine* (Boston: Little Brown & Co., 1963), p. 99.
10. James D. Richardson, comp., *A Compilation of the Messages and Papers of the Presidents, 1789-1904* (Washington, DC: Bureau of National Literature and Art, 1904), II:218-219.
11. Dexter Perkins, "John Quincy Adams," in Samuel Flagg Bemis, ed., *The American Secretaries of State and Their Diplomacy* (New York: Alfred A. Knopf, 1928), IV:78.
12. R.B. Cunninghame Graham, José Antonio Páez (New York: Cooper Square, 1970. repr. of 1929 ed.), p. 239n; Michel Vaucaire, *Bolivar the Liberator* (Boston: Houghton Mifflin, 1929), p. 172.
13. Perkins, "John Quincy Adams," pp. 79, 82-85.
14. S.M. Harrison, ed., *The Writings of James Monroe* (New York: G.P. Putnam's Sons, 1898-1903), VI:324-325.
15. Andrew A. Lipscomb, ed., *The Writings of Thomas Jefferson* (Washington, DC: US Thomas Jefferson Memorial Association, 1903), XV:478-479.
16. From Adams' *Memoirs*, in Walter LaFeber, ed., *John Quincy Adams and the American Continental Empire* (Chicago: Quadrangle Books, 1965), p. 101.
17. Harrison, *Writings of Monroe*, VI:344.
18. Richardson, *Messages and Papers*, II:334.
19. Dexter Perkins, *The Monroe Doctrine, 1823-1826* (Gloucester, MA: Peter Smith, 1965, repr. of 1927 ed.), p. 166.
20. "Morning Edition," *National Public Radio*, April 6, 1984.
21. V.G. Kiernan, *America: The New Imperialism* (London: Zed Press, 1978), p. 6.
22. *The United States Magazine and Democratic Review*, XVII:85 (July 1845), p. 5.
23. New York *Herald*, January 10, 1846, as quoted in John Douglas Pitts Fuller, *The Movement for the Acquisition of All Mexico* (Baltimore: Johns Hopkins Press, 1936), p. 30.
24. Allen Johnson and Dumas Malone, eds., *The Dictionary of American Biography* (New York: Charles Scribner's Sons, 1931), XV:519.
25. Quoted in Fuller, *Movement for . . . All Mexico*, p. 29.
26. New York *Herald*, January 1, 1846, as quoted in ibid., p. 26.
27. Ibid.
28. Ibid., p. 34; George Lockhart Rives, *The United States and Mexico* (New York: Charles Scribner & Sons, 1913), II:135.
29. See Fuller, *Movement for . . . All Mexico*, pp. 39ff.

30. Kiernan, *America,* p. 20.

CHAPTER II. THE PATH OF DESTINY

1. Quoted in Samuel Eliot Morison, *"Old Bruin": Commodore Matthew C. Perry 1794-1858* (Boston: Little Brown and Co., 1967), p. 228.
2. J.D.B. DeBow, "The South American States," *DeBow's Review* (New Orleans), July 1848, pp. 8-9.
3. Gámez, *Historia de Nicaragua,* pp. 90-91.
4. Ibid., p. 102.
5. Ibid., p. 124.
6. David I. Folkman, Jr., *The Nicaragua Route* (Salt Lake City: U. of Utah Press, 1972), pp. x, xii; material on the history of the canal plans, unless otherwise noted, is from Ephraim G. Squier, *Nicaragua; Its People, Scenery, Monuments, Resources, Condition, and Proposed Canal* (New York: Harper and Brothers, rev. ed., 1860), pp. 657-679.
7. William R. Manning, ed., *The Diplomatic Correspondence of the United States Concerning the Independence of the Latin-American Nations* (New York: Oxford U. Press, 1925), I:881.
8. Louis Napoleon is quoted in Harold Norman Denny, *Dollars for Bullets: The Story of American Rule in Nicaragua* (New York: Dial Press, 1929), p. 22.
9. Quoted in Dexter Perkins, *The Monroe Doctrine 1826-1867* (Gloucester, MA: Peter Smith, 1965, repr. of 1933 ed.), pp. 18-19n.
10. Judy Tazewell, ed., *The Miskito Question and the Revolution in Nicaragua* (Hampton, VA: Compita Publishing, 1984), passim.
11. William R. Manning, ed., *Diplomatic Correspondence of the United States, Inter-American Affairs, 1831-1860* (Washington, DC: Carnegie Endowment for International Peace, 1933), III:254-258.
12. Ibid., pp. 259-260.
13. Ibid., pp. 265-266n.
14. Ibid., p. 273.
15. Ibid., pp. 286, 291.
16. Perkins, *Monroe Doctrine 1826-1867,* p. 170.
17. A good example is W.S. Murphy to Daniel Webster, June 1842, in Manning, *Diplomatic Correspondence, Inter-American Affairs,* III:183-186.
18. Richardson, *Messages and Papers,* IV:398.
19. See Perkins, *Monroe Doctrine 1826-1867,* pp. 64-83. The quote is from p. 83.
20. Robert G. Cleland, *One Hundred Years of the Monroe Doctrine* (Los Angeles: Times Mirror Press, 1923), pp. 59-60.
21. Manning, *Diplomatic Correspondence, Inter-American Affairs,* III:31.
22. Ibid., pp. 35, 32-33.
23. Ibid., pp. 288-289.
24. Ibid., pp. 289-290.
25. Ibid., p. 347.
26. The text of the Hise-Selva Treaty is in ibid., pp. 376-377.
27. Ibid., p. 347n.
28. Ibid., pp. 379-386.
29. Ibid., p. 38.
30. Folkman, *Nicaragua Route,* p. 13.
31. Ibid., p. 5.
32. Squier, *Nicaragua,* p. 75.
33. Ibid., p. 388.

34. Ibid., p. 327.
35. As quoted in ibid., pp. 387-388.
36. Manning, *Diplomatic Correspondence, Inter-American Affairs*, III:40-41.
37. As quoted in Albert Z. Carr, *The World and William Walker* (New York: Harper & Row, 1963), p. 66.
38. Perkins, *Monroe Doctrine 1826-1867*, p. 203.
39. See Henry Clay to William Miller, April 22, 1825, in Manning, *Diplomatic Correspondence Concerning the Independence of the Latin-American Nations*, I:239-240.
40. As quoted in Mary Wilhelmine Williams, "John Middleton Clayton," in Bemis, *American Secretaries of State*, VI:57.
41. Charles I. Bevans, comp., *Treaties and Other International Agreements of the United States of America 1776-1949* (Washington, DC: US Department of State, 1974), XII:105-106.
42. Manning, *Diplomatic Correspondence, Inter-American Affairs*, III:60.
43. Ibid., p. 52.
44. Perkins, *Monroe Doctrine 1826-1867*, p. 204.
45. Ibid., p. 212n.
46. Manning, *Diplomatic Correspondence, Inter-American Affairs*, III:60.
47. Folkman, *Nicaragua Route*, pp. 23-28; *New York Times*, January 14, 1854, p. 2.
48. Carr, *The World and William Walker*, pp. 33, 70; Folkman, *Nicaragua Route*, p. 43.
49. Manning, *Diplomatic Correspondence, Inter-American Affairs*, IV:236.
50. Ibid., pp. 235-237.
51. Ibid., p. 247; Pedro Joaquin Chamorro Z., *Fruto Chamorro* (Managua: Editorial Unión, 1960), pp. 177-184.
52. Carr, *The World and William Walker*, pp. 70-71.
53. Manning, *Diplomatic Correspondence, Inter-American Affairs*, IV:11.
54. Ibid., pp. 293-294n.
55. The text of the Webster-Crampton Agreement is in ibid., pp. 18-19n.
56. Ibid., p. 314.
57. Ibid., p. 315.
58. Ibid., pp. 297, 299.
59. Ibid., p. 279.
60. Ibid., p. 298n.

CHAPTER III. ADVENTURES ON THE MISKITO COAST

1. The account of events at San Juan/Greytown leading up to the Marine landing is taken from William M. Hillsman, *The British Diplomatic Response to the Central American Policies of the Franklin Pierce Administration, 1853-1856* (Norfolk, VA: masters thesis, Old Dominion University, 1978), p. 18, and *New York Times*, April 2, 1853, p. 3.
2. *New York Times*, April 5, 1853, p. 4.
3. The protest is reprinted in ibid., April 2, 1853, p. 3.
4. Ibid., February 6, 1852, p. 2.
5. Manning, *Diplomatic Correspondence, Inter-American Affairs*, IV:45.
6. Ibid., pp. 364-366n.
7. Ibid., p. 359.
8. Ibid., p. 352n.
9. Ibid., p. 354.
10. Unless otherwise noted, material on the murder of Paladino and subsequent events is from Andrés Vega Bolaños, ed. and comp., *1854: Bombardeo y Destrucción del Puerto de San Juan del Norte de Nicaragua* (Managua: Editorial Unión, 1970), passim (a col-

lection of some 300 pages of documents), Folkman, *Nicaragua Route*, pp. 63-68, United States, Senate, "Message of the President . . . Respecting the Bombardment of San Juan de Nicaragua," S. Ex. Doc. 85, 33 Cong., 1 Sess. (serial 702), pp. 6-7, and Henri Weidemann to R. Schleiden, January 20, 1855, in United States, Senate, "Message of the President . . . on the Subject of Claims for Losses . . . by Subjects of the Hanse Towns," S. Ex. Doc. 10, 35 Cong., 1 Sess. (serial 918), pp. 8-9.

11. Squier, *Nicaragua*, pp. 42-44.
12. Letter of Don Leopoldo Augusto de Cueto to the First Secretary of State of Spain, August 10, 1854, in Vega B., *1854*, p. 41.
13. Squier, *Nicaragua*, pp. 43-44.
14. Manning, *Diplomatic Correspondence*, IV:453n.
15. Second Annual Message to Congress, December 4, 1854, in Richardson, *Messages and Papers*, V:282, 284.
16. Reprinted in Folkman, *Nicaragua Route*, pp. 65-66.
17. Manning, *Diplomatic Correspondence*, IV:59-60; See also Marcoleta to Marcy, July 28, 1854, in ibid., pp. 413-414.
18. Ibid., pp. 415-416.
19. *New York Times*, December 15, 1854, p. 3.
20. Robert E. May, *The Southern Dream of Caribbean Empire* (Baton Rouge: Louisiana State U. Press, 1973), p. 95; Carr, *The World and William Walker*, p. 157; William O. Scroggs, *Filibusters and Financiers: The Story of William Walker and His Associates* (New York: Russell & Russell, 1969, repr. of 1916 ed.), p. 100.
21. Edward T. James, ed., *Notable American Women, 1607-1950* (Cambridge, MA: Belknap Press, 1971), I:316; Edward S. Wallace, *Destiny and Glory* (New York: Coward McCann, 1957), p. 266.
22. Manning, *Diplomatic Correspondence*, IV:447n.
23. Ibid., p. 65.
24. See for example the letter of Cooper to Hopkins, May 30, 1855, in ibid., p. 465n.
25. Scroggs, *Filibusters and Financiers*, p. 102.
26. Manning, *Diplomatic Correspondence*, IV:463.
27. For Kinney history see Scroggs, *Filibusters and Financiers*, pp. 93-107 and the letters of Marcoleta to Marcy from May 4, 1854 to September 15, 1855, in Manning, *Diplomatic Correspondence*, IV:404ff.

Chapter IV. Slavery, War, and William Walker

1. The item on Walker from a 1942 edition of *Ripley's Believe It or Not* is reprinted in facsimile in Frederic Rosengarten, Jr., *Freebooters Must Die!* (Wayne, PA: Haverford House, 1976), p. vi.
2. The four editions of the *Times* were February 23, March 21, March 30, and August 19, 1857.
3. The account of Walker's life before going to Nicaragua is based on Scroggs, *Filibusters and Financiers*, pp. 9-17, 31-70, and Carr, *The World and William Walker*, pp. 3-111.
4. *Alta California*, December 8, 1853, quoted in Scroggs, *Filibusters and Financiers*, p. 38.
5. United States, House, "Correspondence Between the Late Secretary of War and General Wool," H. Ex. Doc. 88, 35 Cong., 1 Sess. (serial 956), p. 52.
6. Herbert Wender, *Southern Commercial Conventions, 1837-1859* (Baltimore, Johns Hopkins Press, 1930), p. 123. Biographical information on James Gadsden is from Johnson and Malone, *Dictionary of American Biography*, VII:84. For a discussion of the anticipated application of slave labor to Southwestern mining, see Eugene D. Genovese, *The Political Economy of Slavery* (New York: Pantheon, 1966), pp. 256-258.

7. Unless otherwise noted, the account of the filibusters in Nicaragua is from Francisco Ortega Arancibia, *Cuarenta Años (1838-1878) de Historia de Nicaragua* (Managua: Colección Cultural Banco de America, 1975, repr. of 1911 ed.) and William Walker, *The War in Nicaragua* (Mobile, AL: S.H. Goetzel & Co., 1860), passim. Ortega was an officer in the Legitimist army that fought Walker.

8. Rosengarten, *Freebooters Must Die!*, p. 102; Gámez, *Historia de Nicaragua*, p. 513.

9. Quoted in Ortega A., *Cuarenta Años*, p. 161.

10. Gámez, *Historia de Nicaragua*, pp. 519-520.

11. Johnson and Malone, *Dictionary of American Biography*, VII:168; Frederick Engels, "The Concentration of Capital in the United States," in *Marx and Engels on the United States* (Moscow: Progress Publishers, 1979), p. 257.

12. Scroggs, *Filibusters and Financiers*, p. 89; Carr, *The World and William Walker*, p. 104.

13. Scroggs, *Filibusters and Financiers*, p. 125.

14. Folkman, *Nicaragua Route*, pp. 73, 75, 83, 163.

15. Ibid., p. 77.

16. Ibid., pp. 78, 161.

17. Ibid., pp. 49-50.

18. Manning, *Diplomatic Correspondence, Inter-American Affairs*, IV:501.

19. The standard English-language histories of Walker (Scroggs' *Filibusters and Financiers* and Carr's *The World and William Walker*) portray him, to one extent or another, as a misunderstood reformer whose downfall was brought about by a combination of British intrigue, the hostility of Vanderbilt, and the stupidity or treachery of ungrateful natives.

20. *El Nicaraguense*, February 12, 1856, quoted in James T. Wall, *Manifest Destiny Denied* (Washington, DC: University Press of America, 1981), p. 139.

21. *El Nicaraguense*, March 15, 1856, as quoted in ibid., p. 144. Biographical information on Schlessinger is from May, *Southern Dream*, p. 29.

22. Wall, *Manifest Destiny Denied*, p. 145.

23. Walker, *War in Nicaragua*, p. 184.

24. Folkman, *The Nicaragua Route*, pp. 84, 86.

25. Walker, *War in Nicaragua*, pp. 253-254.

26. The *Richmond Enquirer*, November 18, 1856, p. 1. See also May, *Southern Dream*, pp. 107-108.

27. Gámez, *Historia de Nicaragua*, pp. 540-541, 541-542n; Laurence Greene, *The Filibuster* (New York: Bobbs Merrill, 1937), pp. 235-236.

28. Ramirez, "El Muchacho de Niquinohomo," p. xii.

29. Scroggs, *Filibusters and Financiers*, p. 258.

30. Reproduced in Rosengarten, *Freebooters Must Die!*, p. 131.

31. Walker, *War in Nicaragua*, p. 310.

32. Gámez, *Historia de Nicaragua*, p. 559; Ortega A., *Cuarenta Años*, pp. 333, 339.

33. Walker, *War in Nicaragua*, p. 340.

34. Greene, *The Filibuster*, p. 264.

35. Quoted in ibid., p. 278.

36. Folkman, *The Nicaragua Route*, p. 91.

37. Gámez, *Historia de Nicaragua*, pp. 573-574n.

38. Scroggs, *Filibusters and Financiers*, pp. 301, 304-305.

39. *New York Times*, March 17, 1857, p. 1.

40. Rosengarten, *Freebooters Must Die!*, pp. 211-212.

CHAPTER V. IRREPRESSIBLE CONFLICT

1. Carr, for example, in *The World and William Walker*, depicts Walker as a slavery oppo-

nent forced to adopt a proslavery position as an expedient, when maintaining his "anti-slavery stand" would have caused him to "go down with his men to sure disaster" (p. 202). Though less sympathetic to Walker, *The Nation Thief,* Robert Houston's 1984 novel about the filibuster, is largely based on Carr's interpretation.

2. Walker, *War in Nicaragua,* p. 264.
3. *DeBow's Review,* XX (June 1856): 670.
4. See Scroggs, *Filibusters and Financiers,* p. 67.
5. As quoted in Greene, *The Filibuster,* p. 300.
6. Charles W. Doubleday, *Reminiscences of the "Filibuster" War in Nicaragua* (New York: G.P. Putnam's Sons, 1886), pp. 166-167.
7. Walker, *War in Nicaragua,* pp. 213-214.
8. *Blackwood's Magazine,* March 1856, p. 314.
9. *New York Times,* December 22, 1856, p. 2.
10. Rosengarten, *Freebooters Must Die!,* p. 145.
11. Karl Marx, "The North American Civil War," in *Marx and Engels on the United States,* pp. 89-90.
12. *Congressional Globe,* 34 Cong., 1 Sess. (April 1, 1856), App., pp. 299-300.
13. Reprinted in *DeBow's Review,* XVII (September 1854): 281-282.
14. Walker, *War in Nicaragua,* pp. 364-365.
15. March 1856, as quoted in Greene, *The Filibuster,* p. 223.
16. See May, *Southern Dream,* p. 48, for a discussion of this question in relation to Cuba.
17. Marx, "The North American Civil War," p. 91.
18. *Encyclopaedia Britannica,* 1981 edition, 18:967-968.
19. From the Miscellaneous Papers in the Louisiana State U. Archives, as quoted in May, *Southern Dream,* pp. 92-93.
20. On the ties between the slaveholders and Northern merchants see Herbert Wender, *The Southern Commercial Conventions, 1837-1859* (Baltimore: Johns Hopkins Press, 1930), passim. Philip S. Foner's *Business and Slavery* (Chapel Hill: U. of North Carolina Press, 1941) deals with the political ties of New York merchants with the slave power. For an analytical treatment see Elizabeth Fox-Genovese and Eugene Genovese, *Fruits of Merchant Capital* (New York: Oxford U. Press, 1983). Vanderbilt amassed a fortune of $10 million from the Nicaragua transit, using the capital to build up the New York Central Railroad empire, which later linked his fortunes with those of Northern industrialists and small farmers.
21. Richardson, *Messages and Papers,* V:202.
22. Ibid., pp. 198-200.
23. May, *Southern Dream,* p. 55.

Chapter VI. The Doctrine of the Highwayman

1. May, *Southern Dream,* p. 107; the Wheeler quote is from Rosengarten, *Freebooters Must Die!,* p. 141.
2. Ortega A., *Cuarenta Años,* p. 322; Scroggs, *Filibusters and Financiers,* pp. 86-87.
3. As quoted in Greene, *The Filibuster,* p. 170.
4. Manning, *Diplomatic Correspondence, Inter-American Affairs,* IV:491.
5. Hillsman, *British Diplomatic Response,* p. 137n.
6. See, for example, *New York Times,* December 25, 1855, p. 1.
7. Richardson, *Messages and Papers,* V:371.
8. Thomas Hudson McKee, ed., *The National Conventions and Platforms of All Political Parties* (Baltimore: Friedenwald Co., 1906), p. 92. The Montgomery *Advertiser* is quoted in May, *Southern Dream,* p. 72.

9. Ibid., p. 101.
10. McKee, *Conventions and Platforms,* p. 93.
11. May, *Southern Dream,* pp. 106-107; Gámez, *Historia de Nicaragua,* p. 546.
12. May, *Southern Dream,* pp. 104-105.
13. See Richardson, *Messages and Papers,* V:388-389.
14. Walker, *War in Nicaragua,* p. 28.
15. *New York Times,* June 15, 1857, p. 4; Carr, *The World and William Walker,* p. 227.
16. *New York Times,* May 24, 1856, p. 1.
17. Ibid., December 31, 1857, p. 4.
18. *Congressional Globe,* 35 Cong., 1 Sess. (January 14, 1858), p. 293.
19. Scroggs, *Filibusters and Financiers,* p. 369.
20. Richardson, *Messages and Papers,* V:466-467.
21. The speech is in Rebecca Paulding Meade, *The Life of Hiram Paulding* (New York: Baker & Taylor, 1910), pp. 281-283.
22. Scroggs, *Filibusters and Financiers,* p. 372; the Clarendon quote is from Hillsman, *British Diplomatic Response,* p. 22n.
23. *New York Times,* July 17, 1857, p. 4.
24. Ibid., December 31, 1857, p. 4.
25. Richardson, *Messages and Papers,* V:468.
26. See Buchanan's message to Congress, December 2, 1858, in ibid., V:471-481.
27. Ibid., p. 514.
28. Doubleday, *Reminiscences,* p. 166.
29. *The National Cyclopaedia of American Biography* (New York: James T. White & Co., 1902), IV:223-224.
30. *Congressional Globe,* 35 Cong., 1 Sess. (January 14, 1858), p. 293.
31. Reprinted in the *New York Times,* December 31, 1857, p. 2.
32. Buchanan's letter is in the *American Historical Review,* V:100-101.
33. Philip S. Klein, *President James Buchanan* (University Park, PA: Penn. State U. Press, 1962), p. 319.
34. Richardson, *Messages and Papers,* V:469.
35. *Congressional Globe,* 35 Cong., 1 Sess. (January 13, 1858), pp. 277-278.
36. Manning, *Diplomatic Correspondence,* IV:590.
37. Ibid., IV:650-651.
38. See ibid., pp. 629-630n.
39. A translation of the "Rivas Manifesto" is in ibid., pp. 692-693n.
40. Ibid., p. 695.
41. Ibid., p. 696.
42. Ibid., p. 728n.
43. Ibid., p. 133.
44. Ibid., pp. 702-703n.
45. Ibid., pp. 136, 135.
46. Ibid., pp. 685, 127.
47. Ibid., p. 686.
48. Ibid., p. 689.
49. Second Annual Message to Congress, December 6, 1858, in Richardson, *Messages and Papers,* V:515-517.
50. James Buchanan, *Mr. Buchanan's Administration on the Eve of the Rebellion* (New York: Books for Libraries, 1970, repr. of 1865 ed.), pp. 274-275.
51. Manning, *Diplomatic Correspondence,* IV:947.
52. Karl Marx, "The North American Civil War," p. 84.
53. McKee, *Conventions and Platforms,* p. 99.
54. *New York Times,* July 22, 1856, p. 1.
55. Manning, *Diplomatic Correspondence,* IV:929-933.

Chapter VII. From Sea to Shining Sea

1. *Congressional Globe,* 41 Cong. 2 Sess. (July 7, 1870), p. 5316.
2. "Report to the Senate on the Condition of Commercial Relations Between the United States and the Spanish American States," in Richardson, *Messages and Papers,* VII:75.
3. *New York Times,* April 26, 1870, p. 1.
4. Ibid., May 14, 1870, p. 4.
5. Johnson and Malone, *Dictionary of American Biography,* XVIII:338; I:399-400.
6. *New York Times,* May 13, 1870, p. 1.
7. *Congressional Globe,* 41 Cong., 2 Sess. (May 28, 1870), App., p. 408.
8. Richardson, *Messages and Papers,* VII:62.
9. *New York Star* editorial, May 7, 1870, repr. in *New York Times,* May 8, 1870, p. 3.
10. Johnson and Malone, *Dictionary of American Biography,* XVIII:209-212; XVI:466-468.
11. *Congressional Globe,* 41 Cong., 3 Sess. (December 21, 1870), pp. 228-231.
12. This and other incidental information on the Dominican Republican annexation scheme, not otherwise noted, is from William S. McFeely, *Grant: A Biography* (New York: W.W. Norton & Co., 1981), pp. 336-352.
13. *Congressional Globe,* 41 Cong., 3 Sess. (December 21, 1870), p. 225.
14. The texts of the draft treaties and related correspondence appear in United States, Senate, "The Interoceanic Canal," S. Ex. Doc. 112, 46 Cong., 2 Sess. (serial 1885), pp. 25-83. See also Joseph V. Fuller, "Hamilton Fish," in Bemis, *American Secretaries of State,* VII:206-207.
15. *New York Times,* February 2, 1874, p. 2.
16. United States, Senate, "Report of the Interoceanic Canal Commission," S. Ex. Doc. 15, 46 Cong., 1 Sess. (serial 1869), pp. 1-2.
17. See "Treaty of June 21, 1867" (Dickinson-Ayón Treaty), Article XIV, in Bevans, *Treaties,* X:343.
18. United States, Senate, "The Interoceanic Canal," pp. 144-149.
19. Ibid., pp. 137, 138, 140.
20. Ibid., pp. 141, 143.
21. Fish to Riotte, Instruction no. 43, February 1, 1871, National Archives (hereinafter abbreviated NA), Department of State (hereinafter abbreviated DS), microfilm series M77, roll 29.
22. Riotte to DS, January 26, 1872, NA, DS, microfilm series M219, roll 17.
23. Riotte to A.H. Rivas, January 30, 1872, on ibid.
24. *New York Times,* May 30, 1879, p. 1; July 30, 1879, p. 1.
25. Richardson, *Messages and Papers,* VII:585-586.
26. United States, House, "The Clayton-Bulwer Treaty," H. Rep. 1121, 46 Cong., 2 Sess. (serial 1937), p. 7.
27. United States, House, "The Interoceanic Canal and the Monroe Doctrine," H. Rep. 224, 46 Cong., 3 Sess. (serial 1982), p. xi.
28. Instructions of James G. Blaine to J.R. Lowell, US minister to Britain, June 24, 1881, sent as circular to other US ministers in Europe, in United States, DS, *Documents Pertaining to the Foreign Relations of the United States, 1881* (hereinafter cited as FR with year), pp. 537-540.
29. *FR, 1881,* pp. 554-559.
30. Quoted in A.L.P. Dennis, "John Hay," in Bemis, *American Secretaries of State,* IX:155.
31. John Bassett Moore, "The Interoceanic Canal and the Hay-Pauncefote Treaty," in *New York Times,* March 4, 1900, p. 23.
32. London *Times,* December 17, 1881, p. 9.
33. The text of the treaty appears in United States, Senate, "The Nicaragua Canal," S. Doc. 291, 55 Cong., 2 Sess. (serial 3615), pp. 4-11.
34. *New York Times,* December 15, 1884, p. 1.

35. See Richardson, *Messages and Papers,* VIII:256-260.
36. *New York Times,* December 16, 1884, p. 1.
37. New Orleans *Daily Picayune,* December 26, 1884, p. 4.
38. Richardson, *Messages and Papers,* VIII:327.
39. Except as otherwise noted, the account of the Maritime Canal Company of Nicaragua is from Gerstle Mack, *The Land Divided: A History of the Panama Canal and Other Isthmian Canal Projects* (New York: Alfred A. Knopf, 1944), pp. 213-223.
40. *New York Times,* December 10, 1879, p. 3; Letter to Daniel Ammen, June 22, 1880, reprinted in ibid., February 15, 1888, p. 5.
41. U.S. Grant, "The Nicaragua Canal," in *North American Review,* CXXXII (February, 1881): 107-116.
42. See especially, United States, House, "The Nicaragua Canal," H. Rep. 1698, 47 Cong., 1 Sess. (serial 2070).
43. Mary Wilhelmine Williams, *Anglo-American Isthmian Diplomacy, 1815-1915* (Washington, DC: American Historical Association, 1916), pp. 302-306.
44. Bevans, *Treaties,* XII:258-260.
45. *Congressional Record,* XXXIII, 56 Cong., 1 Sess. (May 1, 1900), App., p. 393.
46. Ibid., p. 4945.
47. Ibid., p. 4924.
48. United States, Isthmian Canal Commission, *Report of the Isthmian Canal Commission 1899-1901* (Washington, DC: USGPO, 1901), p. 251.
49. Ibid., p. 261.
50. United States, Senate, "Report of the Isthmian Canal Commission on the Proposal of the New Panama Canal Company," S. Doc. 123, 57 Cong., 1 Sess. (serial 4230).
51. *Congressional Record,* XXXV, 57 Cong., 1 Sess. (June 18, 1902), p. 7008; ibid. (June 26, 1902), p. 7428; ibid. (June 30, 1902), p. 7704.

Chapter VIII. The Rise and Fall

of José Santos Zelaya

1. Ortega A., *Cuarenta Años,* p. 416. The author gives a good insider's view of the evolution of the Conservative Party during this period.
2. Ibid., p. 405.
3. Gámez, *Historia de Nicaragua,* p. 442; Wheelock R., *Imperialismo y Dictadura,* p. 25.
4. Ortega A., *Cuarenta Años,* pp. 392-407.
5. *New York Times,* July 31, 1868, p. 5.
6. Published in ibid., December 24, 1878, p. 2.
7. Wheelock R., *Imperialismo y Dictadura,* p. 77n.
8. Ibid., p. 77.
9. Ibid., p. 14; the data on coffee exports is from the *New York Times,* December 24, 1878, p. 2 and *FR, 1894,* p. 449.
10. Enrique Aquino, *La Personalidad Politica del General José Santos Zelaya* (Managua: Talleres Gráficos Pérez, 1944), pp. 34-37; José Joaquin Morales, *De la Historia de Nicaragua de 1889-1913* (Granada: Editorial Magys, 1963), I:31.
11. Charles L. Stansifer, "José Santos Zelaya: A New Look at Nicaragua's 'Liberal' Dictator," *Revista/Review Interamericana,* VII:3 (Fall 1977), p. 468.
12. The text of the Treaty of Managua is in *Correspondence in Relation to the Proposed Interoceanic Canal Between the Atlantic and Pacific Oceans, the Clayton-Bulwer Treaty, and the Monroe Doctrine* (Washington, DC: USGPO, 1885), pp. 299-302.
13. *FR, 1888,* Pt. 1, p. 763.

14. *FR, 1894,* App. I, p. 278; the Russell quote is from *FR, 1888,* Pt. 1, p. 760.
15. Ibid., p. 759.
16. Robert N. Keely, "Nicaragua and the Mosquito Coast," *Popular Science Monthly,* XLV (June 1894): 162, 165, 167.
17. *FR, 1894,* App. I, pp. 290, 243.
18. Ibid., p. 243.
19. Ibid., p. 236.
20. See ibid., p. 242.
21. *FR, 1893,* pp. 165-166.
22. *FR, 1888,* Pt. 1, p. 124.
23. *FR, 1894,* pp. 469, 472.
24. Ibid., p. 474.
25. *FR, 1888,* Pt. 1, p. 765.
26. *FR, 1894,* App. I, pp. 234, 257.
27. See ibid., pp. 272-273.
28. Ibid., p. 331.
29. O'Neil's reports are in United States, Senate, "Affairs at Bluefields," S. Ex. Doc. 20, 53 Cong., 3 Sess. (serial 3275), pp. 135-149, 158-167; see also report of Captain J.C. Watson, Commander of *USS San Francisco,* in ibid., pp. 52-67.
30. Ibid., p. 137.
31. Ibid., pp. 142, 159.
32. Ibid., p. 159.
33. Ibid., pp. 64, 140, 159.
34. Ibid., pp. 159-160.
35. Ibid., pp. 136, 149.
36. Ibid., p. 163.
37. *FR, 1894,* App. I, pp. 344-345.
38. The document is reprinted in ibid., pp. 361-362.
39. Ibid., p. 355.
40. *FR, 1895,* Pt. 1, p. 558.
41. *FR, 1899,* p. 570.
42. Ibid., pp. 549-550.
43. Ibid., p. 584.
44. Ibid., p. 575.
45. Ibid., pp. 554, 557.
46. Sánchez to Corea, April 8, 1903 (telegram), in Morales, *De la Historia,* I:226.
47. Translations of telegrams exchanged between Zelaya and Bonilla are in *FR, 1907,* Pt. 2, pp. 609-612.
48. Morales, *De la Historia,* I:256-258; *New York Times,* February 20, 1907, p. 4.
49. The text of the accord is in Morales, *De la Historia,* I:268-270.
50. Ibid., pp. 271-272.
51. Ibid., p. 272.
52. The documents from the conference, and a report by the US representative, are in *FR, 1907,* Pt. 2, pp. 665-727.
53. Ibid., p. 721.
54. The charges and the decision in the first case brought before the Central American Court of Justice are in the *American Journal of International Law,* II:835-841 and III:434-436.
55. Coolidge to DS, November 12, 1908, in NA, DS, Despatches from the American Legation, Nicaragua, 1908-1909, Vol. 5.
56. Coolidge to DS, November 5, 1908, in ibid.
57. Coolidge to DS, November 12, 1908, in ibid.

58. Coolidge to DS, November 18, 1908 (telegram), in ibid.
59. Coolidge to DS, November 19, 1908 (telegram), in ibid.
60. See Coolidge to DS, September 9, 1908 and October 27, 1908, in ibid.
61. Gregory to DS, March 9, 1909, in ibid.
62. De Olivares to DS, April 9, 1909, in ibid.
63. *New York Times,* January 3, 1898, p. 5, January 17, 1901, p. 2; *FR, 1900,* p. 814; Message of Roosevelt to Zelaya, June 10, 1908, in NA, DS, Instructions to American Legation, Nicaragua, 1908-1909.
64. United States, Senate, *Foreign Loans,* hearings before the Senate Committee on Foreign Relations pursuant to S. Con. Res. 15, 69 Cong., 2 Sess. (Washington, DC: USGPO, 1927), p. 43; see Denny, *Dollars for Bullets,* p. 72, regarding ex-minister Coolidge's influence.
65. *New York Times,* May 18, 1909, p. 2; a denial by Pio Bolaños, Nicaragua's Consul General in New York, is reported in ibid., May 19, 1909, p. 5; an example of an article by Frederick Palmer is in ibid., March 2, 1909, p. 8; a letter from DS commending Palmer to Coolidge is in NA, DS, Instructions to the American Legation, Nicaragua, 1908-1909. Coolidge acknowledged Palmer's arrival in Despatches from American Legation, Nicaragua, 1908-1909, Vol. 5.
66. See *FR, 1907,* Pt. 2, p. 697.
67. *New York Times,* March 19, 1909, p. 6.
68. See, for example, "Zelaya: the Menace of Central America," *Review of Reviews,* Vol. 37 (April 1908): 496-497, or article by Frederick Palmer, cited in note 65, above.
69. See *New York Times,* January 5, 1907, p. 1; *FR, 1909,* p. 465; United States, Senate, *Foreign Loans,* p. 26.
70. *FR, 1909,* p. 452.
71. Ibid.; Morales, *De la Historia,* I:281; Castrillo was the attorney for one of the US companies with a claim against Zelaya; United States, Senate, *Foreign Loans,* p. 33.
72. Data on Diaz's loan is in Gunther to DS, January 11, 1912 (Confidential Dispatch No. 169), copy in NA, Legislative Section, File 63B-B28; United States, Senate, *Foreign Loans,* p. 36.
73. Gunther to DS, January 11, 1912; Muñoz (Nicaraguan minister to Honduras) to Zelaya, October 20-November 10, 1909, in José Santos Zelaya, *La Revolución de Nicaragua y los Estados Unidos* (Madrid: Imprenta de Bernardo Rodriguez, 1910), pp. 24-42.
74. Altschul (Nicaraguan consul in New Orleans) to Zelaya, October 13-November 29, 1909, in ibid., pp. 45-49; Morales, *De la Historia,* I:319; Denny, *Dollars for Bullets,* p. 79.
75. *New York Times,* December 24, 1909, p. 2; Leslie R. Hahn, "What the War in Nicaragua Means to the United States," *Cosmopolitan,* XLIX:1 (June 1910), pp. 48-50; Morales, *De la Historia,* I:319, 382, 389.
76. The quote is from Muñoz to Zelaya, November 20, 1909, in Zelaya, *Revolución de Nicaragua,* p. 42. Biographical material on Cannon and Groce is from ibid., testimony given at the court martial, in ibid., pp. 138-152, and Morales, *De la Historia,* I:309, 312-313, 326-327.
77. "Manifesto of J.S. Zelaya to the Nicaraguan People," December 22, 1909, in Zelaya, *Revolución de Nicaragua,* p. 126.
78. The Knox Note is in *FR, 1909,* pp. 455-457.
79. For a discussion of the treatment given Zelaya in the history books, see Stansifer, "José Santos Zelaya," pp. 468-485.
80. Zelaya, *Revolución de Nicaragua,* p. 25.
81. The work in question is Morales' *De la Historia.*
82. On the execution of Ambrister and Arbuthnot, see *American State Papers, Military Affairs,* Vol. I: No. 164, pp. 721ff; also, Herbert Bruce Fuller, *The Purchase of Florida: Its History and Diplomacy,* (Gainsville: U. of Florida, 1964), pp. 250ff; President Taylor's proclamation of August 11, 1849 is in Richardson, *Messages and Papers,* V:7-8;

Fillmore's proclamation of April 25, 1851 is in ibid., pp. 111-112.

83. *New York Times,* December 20, 1909, III:2.

84. *FR, 1910,* pp. 750-751; Denny, *Dollars for Bullets,* pp. 86-87.

85. Zelaya, *Revolución de Nicaragua,* p. 7.

86. Correspondence regarding the Sánchez-Merry Agreement, including a copy of the draft treaty and signed protocol are in Hay to Merry, December 5, 1901, NA, DS, Instructions to American Legation, Costa Rica, Vol. 4715, and Merry to DS, November 29, December 1, and December 6, 1901, in NA, DS, Despatches from the American Legation, Costa Rica, Vol. 4694. The draft treaty contained the Suez-type neutrality guarantees, presumably as the Hay-Pauncefote Treaty had not yet been ratified. If Nicaragua had been chosen as the site for the canal, the US would undoubtedly have insisted that these be removed from the final treaty.

87. See Walter Scholes and Marie V. Scholes, *The Foreign Policies of the Taft Administration* (Columbia, MO: U. of Missouri Press, 1970), p. 50.

88. Castrillo's evaluation of Zelaya is published in Aquino, *La Personalidad Política,* pp. 113-115. No date is given, but it was apparently written in 1930, at the time Zelaya's remains were returned to Nicaragua.

CHAPTER IX. THE BEST LAID PLANS

1. See Benjamin Harrison Williams, *The Economic Foreign Policy of the United States* (New York: McGraw Hill, 1929), pp. 142-143.

2. Biographical data on Dawson is from Johnson and Malone, *Dictionary of American Biography,* III:153-154.

3. The text of the Dawson agreements is in *FR, 1911,* pp. 652-653.

4. John Parke Young, *Central American Currency and Finance* (Princeton, NJ: Princeton U. Press, 1925), p. 135.

5. The statement quoted, issued in May 1904, is in Dexter Perkins, *The United States and the Caribbean,* (Cambridge, MA: Harvard U. Press, 1966), pp. 102-104; a later version, with slightly different wording, was included in Roosevelt's annual message to Congress, December 1904.

6. The Taft statement is in *FR, 1912,* p. xii; information on Zelaya's debt record is from Archibald R. Colquhoun, *Greater America,* (New York: Harper & Bros., 1904), p. 420 (table comparing the records of fourteen Latin American countries for the period 1883-1903), and from Coolidge to DS, September 12, 1908, in NA, DS, Despatches from the American Legation, Nicaragua, 1908-1909, Vol. 5. On Taft's attitude toward Nicaragua, see also Perkins, *United States and the Caribbean,* pp. 107-108.

7. *FR, 1912,* p. xii.

8. Both quotes are from *FR, 1911,* p. 650.

9. Ibid., p. 37; *FR, 1912,* p. 1015.

10. *FR, 1911,* pp. 655-656.

11. Ibid., pp. 657-658.

12. Ibid., pp. 660-661; *FR, 1912,* p. 1014.

13. *FR, 1911,* pp. 661-662.

14. United States, Senate, *Foreign Loans,* p. 35; *FR, 1911,* p. 666.

15. Ibid., p. 667.

16. An English translation of the constitution is in *FR, 1912,* pp. 997-1011. The quote is from p. 997.

17. Ibid., pp. 993, 997.

18. Pio Bolaños, *Génesis de la Intervención Norteamericana en Nicaragua* (Managua: Editorial Nueva Nicaragua, 1984, repr. of 1915 ed.), p. 22; the agreement is published in Richard

W. Dunn, *American Foreign Investments* (New York: Heubsch and Viking, 1926), pp. 337-372.

19. Carlos Quijano, *Nicaragua: Un Pueblo, Una Revolución* (Mexico, DF: Editorial Pueblo Nuevo, 1978, repr. of 1927 ed.), pp. 27-28; Bolaños, *Génesis,* pp. 22-25; Young, *Central American Currency,* pp. 135-136, 146, 160; United States, Senate, *Foreign Loans,* pp. 4-5.

20. Confidential memorandum from F.M. Gunther to DS, January 11, 1912 and appended copies of Nicaraguan treasury records, in NA, Legislative Section, File 63B-B28. The latter constitute a partial list of payments totaling more than 21 million pesos—nearly $2 million. These reflected the unadjudicated claims paid by the Estrada-Diaz government in 1910-1911; see also United States, Senate, *Foreign Loans,* pp. 43, 57-60; Bolaños, *Génesis,* pp. 25-26; Quijano, *Nicaragua,* p. 39. The mixed claims commission ultimately processed more than $13 million in claims, recognizing about $5.5 million.

21. Article 7 of the loan agreement, as published in Dunn, *American Foreign Investments,* pp. 348-350.

22. *FR, 1912,* p. 1096; see also ibid., p. 1094.

23. Quijano, *Nicaragua,* pp. 24-25.

24. Bolaños, *Génesis,* pp. 27-31.

25. Denny, *Dollars For Bullets,* p. 109.

26. Dunn, *American Foreign Investments,* pp. 342, 350, 351; Bolaños, *Génesis,* pp. 33-34.

27. United States, Senate, *Foreign Loans,* p. 23; William Alden Smith in *Congressional Record,* 63 Cong., 2 Sess., Vol. 51, pt. 2 (June 16, 1914), p. 10514; Rafael De Nogales, *The Looting of Nicaragua* (New York: Arno Press, 1970, repr. of 1928 ed.), p. 15.

28. *FR, 1912,* pp. 1027-1028, 1034.

29. Ibid., pp. 1031-1032; United States, Senate, *Foreign Loans,* pp. 69-70; Quijano, *Nicaragua,* pp. 53-54.

30. *New York Times,* August 15, 1912, p. 4; United States, House, "Annual Report of the Navy Department of 1912," H. Doc. 952, 62 Cong., 3 Sess. (serial 6405), pp. 12-13; United States, House, "Annual Report of the Secretary of the Navy, 1913," H. Doc. 681, 63 Cong., 2 Sess. (serial 6630), p. 38; *FR, 1912,* p. 1033.

31. The Araujo quotes are from ibid., pp. 1042, 1049; Taft is from ibid., p. 1043; reports on the hostile demonstrations are in NA, Navy and Old Army Branch, Correspondence of the Secretary of the Navy, file 27475.

32. *FR, 1912,* pp. 1043-1044.

33. Zeledón to Southerland, September 19, 1912, original in NA, Navy and Old Army Branch, Correspondence of the Secretary of the Navy, file 27475-95.

34. United States, House, "Annual Report of the Secretary of the Navy, 1913," p. 38.

35. Butler to Southerland, October 4, 1912 (telegram), in Major General Joseph Pendleton Papers at the Marine Corps Historical Center, Washington Navy Yard; *New York Times,* October 6, 1912, III:1; Ramirez, "El Muchacho de Niquinohomo," p. xviii.

36. Dana G. Munro, *The Five Republics of Central America* (New York: Oxford U. Press, 1918), p. 245; United States, Senate, *Foreign Loans,* p. 42; De Nogales, *Looting,* p. 20; *FR, 1912,* pp. 1063-1064.

37. Ibid., p. 1069.

38. Bolaños, *Génesis,* p. 59; Raymond Leslie Buell, "Reconstruction in Nicaragua," *Foreign Policy Association Information Service,* Vol. VI (November 12, 1930), p. 316n.

39. Bolaños, *Génesis,* pp. 49-50; 41-43.

40. Ibid., pp. 43-44.

41. Ibid., pp. 40, 63-64, 90.

42. Ibid., pp. 67-68; Memorias del Recaudador General de Aduanas, 1917, quoted in Quinjano, *Nicaragua,* pp. 73-74.

43. Bolaños, *Génesis,* pp. 65-66, 68, 76; United States, Senate, *Foreign Loans,* p. 24.

44. *FR, 1913,* pp. 1035, 1036.

45. Wilson's statement is in *FR, 1913*, p. 7; the Bryan quote is from Ray Stannard Baker, *Woodrow Wilson, Life and Letters* (New York: Greenwood Press, 1968, repr. of 1931 ed.), IV:431.
46. Ibid., pp. 433-434, 438; Joseph Vincent Fuller, "William Jennings Bryan," in Bemis, *American Secretaries of State*, X:11.
47. *New York Times*, July 21, 1913, p. 6.
48. Memorandum of Bryan to the Senate Foreign Relations Committee, undated (probably June 1913), carbon copy in NA, Legislative Section, file 63B-B28; *New York Times*, July 21, 1913, p. 1.
49. Ibid., p. 6, July 22, 1913, p. 2.
50. Bryan to Wilson, June 12, 1914, quoted in W. Stull Holt, *Treaties Defeated by the Senate* (Baltimore: Johns Hopkins Press, 1933), p. 241.
51. Wilson to Diaz (telegram, undated), text in NA, Legislative Section, file 63B-B28.
52. Cole is quoted in John Kenneth Turner, "Nicaragua," *The Nation*, 114:2969 (May 31, 1922), p. 648; on Emiliano Chamorro, see Wheelock R., *Imperialismo y Dictadura*, p. 111n.
53. The story on the Canadian investors is in *New York Times*, November 21, 1915, p. 1, November 23, 1915, p. 12, and November 24, 1915, p. 12; the Bryan memorandum is in NA, Legislative Section, file 63B-B28.
54. Wilson to Bryan, January 20, 1914, quoted in Baker, *Woodrow Wilson*, IV:440; Bevans, *Treaties*, X:379n; De Nogales, *Looting*, pp. 11-12.
55. Quijano, *Nicaragua*, pp. 69-70.
56. Ibid., pp. 110-113, 115-116; *FR, 1921*, I:143-164.
57. See United States, Senate, "American Policy in Nicaragua," S. Doc. 334, 64 Cong., 1 Sess. (serial 6952), pp. 8-10.
58. Bryan to Senate Foreign Relations Committee (see note 48).
59. Quijano, *Nicaragua*, pp. 80-81.
60. Turner, "Nicaragua," p. 648.
61. Bolaños, *Génesis*, pp. 53, 57-58; Quijano, *Nicaragua*, p. 84; De Nogales, *Looting*, pp. 21-22; United States, Senate, *Foreign Loans*, p. 4.
62. As quoted in David Healy, *US Expansionism: The Imperialist Urge in the 1890s* (Madison, WI: U. of Wisconsin Press, 1970), pp. 197-198. Healy devotes an entire chapter (pp. 194-209) to Conant.
63. Quijano, *Nicaragua*, pp. 26-43; Turner, "Nicaragua," p. 647; Bolaños, *Génesis*, pp. 65-66, 76.
64. Quijano, *Nicaragua*, pp. 81-84; Dunn, *American Foreign Investments*, pp. 381-382; United States, Senate, *Foreign Loans*, p. 25.
65. Clifford Ham, "Americanizing Nicaragua," *Review of Reviews*, Vol. 53 (February 1916), p. 188.
66. Wright to Polk, July 28, 1916, DS 817.00/2546, on NA microfilm M632, roll 16; Jefferson to DS, September 21, 1916 (telegram), DS 817.00/2493, and Jefferson to DS, October 10, 1916, DS 817.00/2526, on ibid.
67. Quijano, *Nicaragua*, p. 96.
68. United States, Senate, *Foreign Loans*, pp. 10-11; Bolaños, *Génesis*, pp. 75-76, 86-88; Quijano, *Nicaragua*, pp. 94-95; Dunn, *American Foreign Investments*, p. 377; De Nogales, *Looting*, p. 22; Aquino, *La Personalidad Política*, p. 119; author's interview with José Valdivia, Director General of Nicaraguan Railroads, October 26, 1984.
69. Roscoe H. Hill, "Los Marinos en Nicaragua 1912-1925," *Revista Conservadora del Pensamiento Centroamericano*, Vol. 27, No. 135 (December 1971), p. 10. Hill was a US appointee to the High Commission for Nicaragua.
70. Details of these incidents are in United States, Senate, "Payment of Indemnity to Nicaragua . . . Property of Salvador Buitrago Diaz," S. Rep. 355, 68 Cong., 1 Sess. (serial 8220), and United States, Senate, "Payment of Indemnity to Nicaragua . . . Killing

and Wounding of Nicaraguans," S. Rep. 354, 68 Cong., 1 Sess. (serial 8220). Some of the Marines received prison sentences; small indemnities were paid to the victims or their families.

71. Carlos Pérez Bermúdez and Onofre Guevara López, *El Movimiento Obrero en Nicaragua* (Managua: Editorial El Amanecer, 1984), 1ra Pte., pp. 25-27.

72. Wheelock R., *Imperialismo y Dictadura,* p. 113; De Nogales, *Looting,* pp. 25-26.

73. *FR, 1923,* II:607.

74. Ibid.

75. Major Jesse I. Miller, "Final Report on the 1920 Nicaraguan Presidential Elections," DS 817.00/2760, on NA microfilm M632, roll 18; the quote is from p. 146. Other documents on the election begin with DS 817.00/2671.

76. *FR, 1923,* II:605, 606.

77. *FR, 1924,* II:487-502 passim.

78. Quijano, *Nicaragua,* p. 125.

79. *FR, 1924,* II:502-506.

80. *FR, 1925,* II:621-634.

81. Dunn, *American Foreign Investments,* p. 55.

82. De Nogales, *Looting,* pp. 24-25; Quijano, *Nicaragua,* pp. 97-98; United States, Senate, *Foreign Loans,* p. 7.

83. Ibid., pp. 9, 17, 49; Quijano, *Nicaragua,* pp. 98-100. For another attempt by the bank's North American employees to create panic, see the *New York Times,* March 29, 1925, p. 19.

84. United States, Senate, *Foreign Loans,* pp. 16-20; Quijano, *Nicaragua,* p. 101; *New York Times,* March 27, 1925, p. 31; Thurston to DS, January 1, 1925, DS 817.001/So4, on NA microfilm M632, roll 57.

85. United States, Senate, *Foreign Loans,* pp. 12-14, 50-51.

86. For the sequence of events in Chamorro's return to power see *FR, 1925,* II:639-640, 644; *FR, 1926,* II:784-785, 805; Eberhardt to DS, March 26, 1926 (telegram), 817.001/So4/5, on NA microfilm M632, roll 57.

CHAPTER X. ALL BUT ONE

1. *FR, 1925,* II:619; Eberhardt to DS, March 26, 1926 (telegram), DS 817.001/So4/5, on NA microfilm M632, roll 57. Eberhardt asserted in this telegram that Chamorro received $85,000 from the Vaccaro and Zemurray banana interests, presumably for overthrowing the *Transacción* government. See also William Kamman, *Search for Stability: United States Diplomacy Toward Nicaragua, 1925-1933* (Notre Dame, IN: U. of Notre Dame Press, 1968), pp. 23n, 27, 37.

2. Denny, *Dollars for Bullets,* pp. 201-202.

3. *FR, 1925,* II:646; see also Kamman, *Search for Stability,* p. 49n.

4. *FR, 1925,* II:641, 643; the Chamorro quote is from Denny, *Dollars for Bullets,* p. 218; Sacasa is quoted in Humberto Ortega Saavedra, *50 Años de Lucha Sandinista,* (Havana: Editorial de Ciencias Sociales, 1980), p. 83; Eberhardt is from Eberhardt to DS, April 26, 1926, DS 817.00/3570, NA microfilm M632, roll 26.

5. *FR, 1926,* II:786, 788-789, 790, 793; *New York Times,* September 26, 1926, p. 1.

6. *FR, 1926,* II:795-801; the Dennis quote is from p. 799. Formal international arbitration of a question of internal constitutional law was indeed novel, but it would have been quite consistent with the 1923 Washington agreements, which established criteria for determining whether a government was "constitutional," and therefore entitled to recognition.

7. *FR, 1926,* II:797.

8. Ibid., pp. 803-804.
9. Ibid., pp. 805-807, 811.
10. See ibid., p. 812.
11. United States, House, *Conditions in Nicaragua and Mexico,* hearings before the House Committee on Foreign Affairs pursuant to H. Res. 373, 69 Cong., 2 Sess. (Washington, DC: USGPO, 1927), p. 7; *FR, 1926,* II:812; *New York Times,* January 10, 1927, p. 1. The *Times* has the Sacasa quote.
12. The Eberhardt quote is from *FR, 1927,* III:299; see also *FR, 1926,* II:794, 808, 812-816, 818; *New York Times,* January 10, 1927, p. 1, January 16, 1927, p. 2, January 6, 1927, p. 1, January 27, 1927, p. 1; Denny, *Dollars for Bullets,* p. 265.
13. See *New York Times,* January 1, 1927, p. 1.
14. Ibid., January 4, 1927, p. 1; January 9, 1927, p. 1; the text of Wheeler's speech is in ibid., January 31, 1927, pp. 1-2.
15. Ibid., December 26, 1926, p. 2; the AP dispatch is quoted in Denny, *Dollars for Bullets,* p. 243; Diaz is quoted in the *New York Times,* December 12, 1926, pp. 1-2; see also *Literary Digest,* December 4, 1926, p. 14.
16. *New York Times,* January 6, 1927, p. 1, January 7, 1927, p. 18.
17. United States, House, *Conditions in Nicaragua and Mexico,* pp. 4, 7, 8, 9.
18. *New York Times,* January 13, 1927, p. 1; the text of Kellogg's statement is in ibid., p. 2.
19. For more on the Mexico war scare see Bryce Wood, *The Making of the Good Neighbor Policy* (New York: Columbia U. Press, 1961), pp. 18-23; see also Denny, *Dollars for Bullets,* pp. 244-249, and *Literary Digest,* December 4, 1926, p. 14.
20. See Denny, *Dollars for Bullets,* pp. 281-285.
21. *New York Times,* March 2, 1927, p. 2; United States, Senate, *Use of United States Naval Forces in Nicaragua,* hearings before the Senate Foreign Relations Committee pursuant to S. Res. 137, 70 Cong., 1 Sess. (Washington, DC: USGPO, 1928), pp. 43-44.
22. According to Bryce Wood, there were "no less than nine distinct and chronologically separate" policy justifications during the first two weeks of 1927 alone. He doesn't list them, however. See Wood, *Making of the Good Neighbor Policy,* p. 18.
23. *FR, 1927,* III:471-475; see also Kamman, *Search for Stability,* pp. 94-96.
24. *New York Times,* March 10, 1927, p. 24.
25. Denny, *Dollars for Bullets,* p. 164; *FR, 1927,* III:426.
26. United States, Senate, "Report of the Collector General of Customs of Nicaragua for the Year 1927," S. Doc. 164, 70 Cong., 1 Sess. (serial 8871), p. 7.
27. The account of the war is assembled from documents in *FR, 1927,* III, the *New York Times,* the writings of Sandino in Ramirez, *Pensamiento Vivo de Sandino,* and Ortega S., *50 Años,* pp. 99-103. The bombing of Chinandega gave rise to atrocity stories. Intervention opponents circulated photos purportedly showing the destruction caused by the bombing, including charred bodies. Others have disputed the charges, claiming the destruction resulted from the battle for the town, not the bombing.
28. Biographical information on Moncada is from Morales, *De la Historia,* I:255, Denny, *Dollars for Bullets,* p. 95, de Nogales, *Looting,* pp. 89, 134-135, and Moncada to Huntington Wilson, November 21, 1912, DS 817.00/2155, NA microfilm M632, roll 13.
29. See Ramirez, "El Muchacho de Niquinohomo," p. xxx.
30. Biographical information on Sandino is from ibid., pp. xxvi-xxviii, xxx, also chronology, pp. lxi-lxiii, and Joseph O. Baylen, "Sandino: Patriot or Bandit?" *Hispanic American Historical Review,* XXX (August 1951): 394.
31. Ramirez, *Pensamiento Vivo,* p. 91.
32. Baylen, "Sandino: Patriot or Bandit?" p. 395; Neill Macaulay, *The Sandino Affair* (Chicago: Quadrangle Books, 1967), p. 53; the quote is from Ramirez, *Pensamiento Vivo,* p. 97.
33. Ibid., p. 98.
34. Ibid.
35. Ibid., pp. 425-426.

36. Ibid., pp. 102-110, 119; Major Berry is quoted in Macaulay, *Sandino Affair*, p. 29.
37. Ramirez, *Pensamiento Vivo*, pp. 104-115, 133.
38. As quoted in Denny, *Dollars for Bullets*, p. 244.
39. *FR, 1927*, III:331; for Stimson's mandate see ibid., pp. 327-329.
40. The quotes are from Henry L. Stimson, *American Policy in Nicaragua* (New York: Charles Scribner's Sons, 1927), p. 72, and the Henry L. Stimson Diaries, VI:99-100 (microfilm edition, reel 1), Manuscripts and Archives, Yale University Library, New Haven, Connecticut.
41. Moncada to DS, October 8, 1912, DS 817.00/2078, on NA microfilm M632, roll 13; Moncada to DS, November 21, 1912, DS 817.00/2155, on ibid. See also Moncada to DS, December 9, 1912, DS 817.00/2174, NA microfilm M632, roll 14, and Jefferson to DS, September 21, 1916 (telegram), DS 817.00/2493, on M632, roll 16.
42. Stimson, *American Policy*, pp. 63-64; Robert H. Ferrell, "Frank B. Kellogg," in Robert H. Ferrell, ed., *The American Secretaries of State and their Diplomacy* (new series) (New York: Cooper Square Publishers, 1963), XI:54.
43. Stimson, *American Policy*, pp. 76-78, 80; United States, Senate, *Use of United States Naval Forces*, p. 38; *FR, 1927*, III:340-341; Ramirez, *Pensamiento Vivo*, p. 124; Kamman, *Search for Stability*, p. 110. The Stimson quotes are from *American Policy*, p. 76, and the Stimson Diaries, VI:106 (microfilm reel 1).
44. Stimson, "American Policy in Nicaragua," *Saturday Evening Post*, 200:15 (October 8, 1927), p. 212. Stimson's articles in nos. 14-16 of the magazine were later reprinted as the book of the same name (see note 40 above).
45. Ramirez, *Pensamiento Vivo*, pp. 121-122.
46. Ibid., pp. 123-124.
47. Ibid., pp. 122, 125.
48. Ibid., p. 126.
49. Ibid., p. 140.
50. Ibid., pp. 142-143.
51. Ibid., p. 143; Kamman, *Search for Stability*, p. 125.
52. *New York Times*, July 2, 1927, p. 10; Denny, *Dollars for Bullets*, p. 314.
53. Ramirez, *Pensamiento Vivo*, pp. 148-149.
54. Ibid., p. 305.
55. Macaulay, *Sandino Affair*, p. 81.
56. United States, Senate, "Operation of the Naval Service in Nicaragua," S. Doc. 86, 70 Cong., 1 Sess. (serial 8871), p. 5.
57. *New York Times*, July 19, 1927, p. 1, November 20, 1927, p. 4, January 22, 1928, p. 2; United States, Senate, *Use of United States Naval Forces*, pp. 48-49; Ramirez, *Pensamiento Vivo*, pp. 150-151; Carleton Beals, "With Sandino in Nicaragua," *The Nation*, 126:3273 (March 28, 1928), p. 340.
58. See *New York Times*, July 19, 1927, p. 10.
59. Ramirez, *Pensamiento Vivo*, p. 306.
60. Eberhardt is from *FR, 1927*, III:444-445; the Marine intelligence report is quoted in Kamman, *Search for Stability*, p. 129; Feland is in the *New York Times*, August 28, 1927, VIII:14.
61. Ramirez, *Pensamiento Vivo*, p. 152; the Marine report is quoted in Macaulay, *Sandino Affair*, p. 85.
62. Ramirez, *Pensamiento Vivo*, p. 307.
63. Ibid., pp. 172-173; Macaulay, *Sandino Affair*, p. 92; *New York Times*, October 14, 1927, p. 31.
64. Ibid., October 22, 1927, p. 3, December 10, 1927, p. 16.
65. *FR, 1928*, III:560-561.
66. *New York Times*, November 26, 1927, p. 5; Macaulay, *Sandino Affair*, p. 68; Ramirez, *Pensamiento Vivo*, p. 265.

67. *New York Times,* January 2, 1928, p. 1.
68. Ibid., January 2, 1928, p. 20, January 4, 1928, p. 1.
69. Ibid., January 4, 1928, pp. 1, 3, January 10, 1928, p. 33, January 19, 1928, p. 1, January 28, 1928, p. 17.
70. Ramirez, *Pensamiento Vivo,* p. 310; *New York Times,* January 19, 1928, p. 1, January 30, 1928, p. 3.
71. Ibid., February 4, 1928, p. 5, February 6, 1928, p. 2, February 10, 1928, p. 4.
72. Ibid., February 12, 1928, p. 2; United States, Senate, *Use of United States Naval Forces,* pp. 1-2.
73. Feland is quoted in Carleton Beals, *Banana Gold* (Philadelphia: J.B. Lippincott, 1932), p. 306; *New York Times,* March 2, 1928, p. 2, March 15, 1928, p. 9, March 17, 1928, p. 1; Bernard C. Nalty, *The United States Marines in Nicaragua* (Washington, DC: Historical Branch, US Marine Corps, 1962), p. 25.
74. *FR, 1928,* III:575-576.
75. Carleton Beals, "With Sandino in Nicaragua," p. 341.
76. *New York Times,* January 30, 1928, p. 2, January 31, 1928, p. 6. Senator Dill is quoted in ibid., p. 3.
77. Captain P.C. Geyer Jr., "Report on the Coco River Expedition," 12 October, 1928, NA, Navy and Old Army Branch, RG 127, B-2 File, Box 6, file no. 855.
78. On the deserters, see Macaulay, *Sandino Affair,* pp. 75, 146.
79. Harold N. Denny in *New York Times,* January 21, 1928, p. 3.
80. See Eugene L. Hasluck, *Foreign Affairs 1919-1937* (New York: Macmillan and Co., 1938), p. 281.
81. United States, Senate, "Operation of the Naval Service," p. 3; Kamman, *Search for Stability,* pp. 133-134; the Munro quote is from ibid., p. 134.
82. Ramirez, *Pensamiento Vivo,* pp. 310-311.
83. *FR, 1928,* III:588; the manifesto is in Ramirez, *Pensamiento Vivo,* pp. 225-228.
84. *FR, 1927,* III:363-364, 367-368.
85. *FR, 1928,* III:418-420, 476-485; Raymond Leslie Buell, "American Supervision of Elections in Nicaragua," *Foreign Policy Association Information Service,* VI (December 24, 1930): 399. Buell, in ibid., pp. 385-402, provides probably the best and most balanced general account available in English of US involvement in Nicaraguan elections.
86. *FR, 1928,* III:502; Buell, "American Supervision of Elections," p. 387; Beals, *Banana Gold,* pp. 293-294.
87. See ibid., p. 389 and Kamman, *Search for Stability,* pp. 150-151.
88. See *New York Times,* October 26, 1928, p. 8, October 27, 1928, p. 17; *FR, 1927,* III:373-374; Moncada is quoted in George T. Weitzel, "The United States and Central America," *Annals of the American Academy of Political and Social Science,* CXXXII (July 1927): 124. The Stimson quotes are from Kamman, *Search for Stability,* pp. 151, 152.
89. Buell takes up most of these questions, based on first-hand observation, in "American Supervision of Elections."
90. Ramirez, *Pensamiento Vivo,* pp. 146, 147-148.
91. Ibid., pp. 228-231.
92. Ibid., pp. 238-239.
93. Ibid., pp. 273-275.
94. Ibid., pp. 276-293.
95. Ibid., pp. xiv, 323-324, 334-338; Macaulay, *Sandino Affair,* pp. 148-149, 159-160.
96. Ramirez, *Pensamiento Vivo,* pp. 255-263, 320, 357.
97. Ortega S., *50 Años,* p. 112; Kamman, *Search for Stability,* p. 208.
98. See Raymond Leslie Buell, "Reconstruction in Nicaragua," *Foreign Policy Association Information Service,* VI (November 12, 1930): 328-330.
99. *FR, 1929,* III:565, 568, 574; Kamman, *Search for Stability,* p. 185; Macaulay, *Sandino Affair,* pp. 139-144; Buell, "Reconstruction in Nicaragua," p. 338n.

100. Ibid., pp. 337-338; Kamman, *Search for Stability*, pp. 187-188.
101. Ortega S., *50 Años*, pp. 110-111, 113-117, 122, 130-131; *FR, 1931*, II:826, 828, 829.
102. *FR, 1929*, III:564, 577-578.
103. Buell, "Reconstruction in Nicaragua," pp. 340, 341-342; Stimson is quoted in Kamman, *Search for Stability*, p. 203.
104. United States, Senate, "United States Marines in Nicaragua," S. Doc. 288, 71 Cong., 3 Sess. (serial 9347), p. 2; *New York Times*, January 2, 1931, p. 1, January 3, 1931, p. 5, January 6, 1931, p. 12, February 7, 1931, p. 8, February 14, 1931, p. 1.
105. Nalty, *United States Marines in Nicaragua*, pp. 32, 33; Kamman, *Search for Stability*, pp. 174-180; Richard Millett, *Guardians of the Dynasty* (Maryknoll, NY: Orbis Books, 1977), p. 74.
106. Baylen, "Sandino: Patriot or Bandit," pp. 416-417.
107. *FR, 1932*, V:877-878.
108. William Krehm, *Democracia y Tiranias en el Caribe* (Buenos Aires: Editorial Parnaso, 1957), p. 170. This book is now available in English as *Democracies and Tyrannies of the Caribbean* (Westport, CT: Lawrence Hill & Co., 1984).
109. Ibid., p. 169.
110. As quoted in Kamman, *Search for Stability*, p. 210.
111. Ramirez, *Pensamiento Vivo*, pp. l-li; Baylen, "Sandino: Patriot or Bandit," pp. 418-419.
112. Dana G. Munro, "The Establishment of Peace in Nicaragua," *Foreign Affairs*, XI (July 1933): 704-705.
113. Munro to Robert H. Ferrell, quoted in Ferrell, "Frank B. Kellogg," pp. 298-299, note 48.
114. See Joseph O. Baylen, "Sandino: Death and Aftermath," *Mid America*, 36 (April 1954): 116-128 and Macaulay, *Sandino Affair*, pp. 254-256.

CHAPTER XI. GOOD NEIGHBORS

1. Biographical material on Somoza is from Bernard Diederich, *Somoza and the Legacy of U.S. Involvement in Central America* (New York: E.P. Dutton, 1981), pp. 6, 10-12, Ramirez, "El Muchacho de Niquinohomo," pp. xxvi-xxvii, and Millett, *Guardians*, p. 49.
2. Diederich, *Somoza*, p. 13; Kamman, *Search for Stability*, p. 107; Eduardo Crawley, *Nicaragua in Perspective* (New York: St. Martin's Press, 1984), p. 70; the Stimson quote is from the Stimson Diaries, VI:101 (microfilm edition, reel 1).
3. Kamman, *Search for Stability*, p. 179; United States, Senate, *Use of United States Naval Forces*, pp. 39-40; Diederich, *Somoza*, p. 13.
4. See for example the *New York Times*, September 2, 1934, IV:8.
5. Ibid., April 14, 1934, p. 10, June 27, 1934, p. 10; Diederich, *Somoza*, p. 19; *FR, 1934*, V:530-531, 535, 540-541, 556-558; the Lane quote is from ibid., p. 535.
6. See for example *FR, 1934*, V:534, 536; also *FR, 1935*, IV:845, 877.
7. See Alexander DeConde, *Herbert Hoover's Latin American Policy* (Stanford, CA: Stanford U. Press, 1951), p. 18.
8. Baylen, "Sandino: Death and Aftermath," pp. 133, 135, 139; Crawley, *Nicaragua in Perspective*, p. 92; the Lane quote is from *FR, 1934*, V:531.
9. *FR, 1935*, IV:845, 861, 865; the quote is from Lane to Willard Beaulac, July 27, 1935, Arthur Bliss Lane Papers, Box 61, Folder 1102, Manuscripts and Archives, Yale University Library.
10. *FR, 1935*, IV:872; *FR, 1936*, V:816; Millett, *Guardians*, pp. 159, 171, 177, 178, 181; Pérez B. and Guevara L., *El Movimiento Obrero*, p. 71; Crawley, *Nicaragua in Perspective*, p. 92.
11. *FR, 1933*, V:850.
12. *FR, 1935*, IV:873, 874.

13. *FR, 1936,* V:829-830.
14. See ibid., pp. 136-148.
15. *FR, 1936,* V:840, 841-842.
16. Ibid., p. 844; Crawley, *Nicaragua in Perspective,* p. 95.
17. *FR, 1936,* V:844-847.
18. *Harpers,* 185 (September 1942): 424. For examples of other articles favorable to Somoza see *New York Times,* July 19, 1937, p. 7, and *Christian Science Monitor Sunday Magazine,* February 21, 1942, p. 5.
19. Krehm, *Democracia y Tiranias,* p. 183. According to Krehm, a *Time* reporter, Somoza had portraits of Mussolini and Franco on his wall that he replaced with Roosevelt's picture (ibid., p. 185); see also Millett, *Guardians,* p. 190; the quotes are from *New York Times,* February 11, 1938, p. 15.
20. The Nicholson quotes are from Nicholson to DS, April 11, 1939, DS 817.001/Somoza, NA microfilm M1273, roll 17; the Somoza quote is from *Time,* February 10, 1947, p. 39.
21. *New York Times,* December 31, 1939, III:4.
22. Ibid., July 19, 1937, p. 7; *FR, 1938,* V:798-799; on Somoza's buying properties near the canal route, see Nicholson to DS, April 26, 1939, DS 817.001/Somoza/74, NA microfilm M1273, roll 17.
23. The Somoza quotes are from *New York Times,* November 20, 1938, p. 31; the State Department quote is from *FR, 1939,* V:721.
24. Pérez B. and Guevara L., *El Movimiento Obrero,* pp. 72-73.
25. *New York Times,* March 25, 1939, p. 7.
26. *New York Times,* May 6, 1939, pp. 1, 3, IV:8; the FDR quote is from *Time,* November 15, 1948, p. 43.
27. United States, Senate, "Address of Anastasio Somoza, President of Nicaragua, before the Senate, Washington, D.C., May 8, 1939," S. Doc. 73, 76 Cong., 1 Sess. (serial 10316), pp. 2-3; *New York Times,* May 8, 1939, p. 5.
28. Ibid., May 13, 1939, p. 5, May 19, 1939, p. 2.
29. The quote is from ibid., May 7, 1939, p. 1; for the text of the loan agreement and related correspondence, see *FR, 1939,* V:728-731, 736.
30. *New York Times,* May 26, 1939, p. 22.
31. *FR, 1939,* V:735.
32. *New York Times,* November 23, 1939, p. 20.
33. Ibid., January 17, 1942, p. 5, February 28, 1942, p. 6, May 26, 1943, p. 10.
34. The quotes regarding the canal are from Stimson to Welles, January 31, 1941, DS 817.812/993, NA, Diplomatic Section, and *FR, 1939,* V:747n; the Somoza quote is from *FR, 1942,* VI:569.
35. On the Rama road project, see *FR, 1942,* VI:568-576; the Eisenhower letter is in ibid., p. 570.
36. Millett, *Guardians,* p. 197.
37. The quote is from Dr. Paul L. Guest, "Nicaraguan Agriculture Looks Ahead," *Agriculture in the Americas,* X (October 1943): 187. The author was in charge of horticulture at the El Recreo station. See also Dr. Ross E. Moore, "What Shall the Americas Grow," in ibid., III (May 1943): 83, and Philip Green, "Nicaragua—Lake Country of Central America," in ibid., III (July 1943): 130.
38. Inter-American Development Commission, *Comparative Outline of the Recommendations Adopted at the Conference of Commissions of Inter-American Development and of the Resolutions on Economic and Social Matters Adopted at the Inter-American Conference on Problems of War and Peace* (Washington, DC: Inter-American Development Commission, 1945, mimeograph), passim; Frederick C. Adams, *Economic Diplomacy: The Export-Import Bank and Inter-American Foreign Policy 1934-1939* (Columbia MO: U. of Missouri Press, 1976), pp. 215-216.
39. *New York Times,* December 10, 1941, p. 13, October 26, 1941, p. 27; *FR, 1941,*

VII:410-413; Diederich, *Somoza,* p. 22; Millett, *Guardians,* pp. 200, 252.

40. Krehm, *Democracia y Tiranias,* pp. 175-176; Diederich, *Somoza,* p. 22.

41. Ovidio Gondi, "All Nicaragua is His Hacienda," *UN World,* March 1948, pp. 30-31; Krehm, *Democracia y Tiranias,* pp. 173-175; Millett, *Guardians,* pp. 197-198; United States, House, *Rethinking United States Foreign Policy Toward the Developing World: Nicaragua,* hearings before the Subcommittee on International Development, 95 Cong., 1 Sess. (Washington, DC: USGPO, 1978), p. 8; *Time,* July 17, 1944, p. 43, June 9, 1947, p. 36; Nicholson to DS, April 11, 1939, DS 817.001/Somoza, and Nicholson to DS, April 26, 1939, DS 817.001/Somoza/74, NA microfilm M1273, roll 17; the quote is from the latter.

42. Moncada is quoted in Gondi, "All Nicaragua is His Hacienda," p. 30; Somoza quote is from *Time,* July 17, 1944, p. 43.

43. Ibid., July 10, 1944, p. 43.

44. *FR, 1944,* VII:1392-1393.

45. *Time,* July 17, 1944, p. 43; Krehm, *Democracia y Tiranias,* p. 184.

46. *FR, 1944,* VII:1396, 1400-1401, 1409, 1418-1424.

47. Ibid., pp. 1403-1404.

48. *FR, 1945,* IX:1213-1230.

49. The Warren quote is from ibid., p. 1204; *New York Times,* June 19, 1945, p. 8; Millett, *Guardians,* p. 206.

50. *New York Times,* February 2, 1947, p. 16, February 3, 1947, p. 1, February 4, 1947, p. 11; Crawley, *Nicaragua in Perspective,* pp. 105-106.

51. Krehm, *Democracia y Tiranias,* pp. 190-191; *Newsweek,* June 30, 1947, p. 40.

52. *Time,* June 30, 1947, p. 43.

53. Krehm, *Democracia y Tiranias,* p. 191; *Time,* February 2, 1948, p. 26, November 15, 1948, p. 43; Crawley, *Nicaragua in Perspective,* p. 108.

54. *Time,* May 17, 1948, p. 34.

55. See Jack Anderson's column in the *Washington Post,* September 30, 1977, p. D17.

56. *New York Times,* May 26, 1952, p. 12.

57. *Envio,* 4:38 (August 1984), pp. 2b-4b; Ortega S., *50 Años,* pp. 153.

58. Diederich, *Somoza,* p. 33.

59. Wheelock R., *Imperialismo y Dictadura,* pp. 126-127; *Time,* November 15, 1948, p. 39; Diederich, *Somoza,* p. 71. For an example of the "benevolent" Somoza image, see Sidney Gruson in *New York Times,* November 17, 1953, p. 14.

60. James L. Busey, "Foundations of Political Contrast: Costa Rica and Nicaragua," *Western Political Science Quarterly,* 11 (Summer 1958): 639-642; *New York Times,* May 7, 1950, p. 106, May 8, 1950, p. 11, May 9, 1950, p. 28, May 23, 1950, p. 24, November 2, 1950, p. 6, May 2, 1951, p. 29.

61. *Time,* January 29, 1951, p. 17.

62. *New York Times,* May 9, 1950, p. 28.

63. Acheson is in *FR, 1952-1954,* IV:1370; the Somoza quotes are from the *New York Times,* May 2, 1952, p. 2 and June 21, 1952, p. 6; see also ibid., May 3, 1952, p. 2.

64. The memorandum is in *FR, 1952-1954,* IV:1376; see also p. 1043; Millett, *Guardians,* p. 213; Susanne Jonas and David Tobis, eds., *Guatemala* (New York: NACLA, 1974), pp. 57, 69-70; Diederich, *Somoza,* p. 45; Crawley, *Nicaragua in Perspective,* p. 111.

65. On repayment of the Ethelburga loan, see the *New York Times,* April 17, 1953, p. 35; for Lindberg see *Time,* January 30, 1950, p. 32.

66. Ibid., October 1, 1956, p. 36; the quote is from ibid., October 8, 1956, p. 43; Diederich, *Somoza,* p. 48; López Pérez's last letter to his mother is in Crawley, *Nicaragua in Perspective,* p. 115.

67. *New York Times,* October 1, 1956, p. 6; the Dulles quote is from ibid., September 30, 1956, p. 3.

68. Ibid., September 24, 1956, p. 26.

69. Diederich, *Somoza*, pp. 67-68; *Time*, November 8, 1956, p. 43; Millett, *Guardians*, pp. 223-224.
70. Marvin Alisky, "Our Man in Managua," *The Reporter*, December 22, 1960, pp. 26-27. Alisky was a professor at the journalism school.

CHAPTER XII. THE LAST MARINE

1. See *New York Times*, December 8, 1957, p. 21; Diederich, *Somoza*, p. 57; Milton S. Eisenhower, *The Wine is Bitter* (Garden City, NY: Doubleday & Co., 1963), pp. 218-219.
2. Wheelock R., *Imperialismo y Dictadura*, pp. 127, 202; *New York Times*, December 8, 1957, p. 21.
3. The text of Kennedy's March 13, 1961 speech is in *Department of State Bulletin*, April 3, 1961, pp. 471-474.
4. The quotes are from Beatrice Bishop Berle and Travis Beal Jacobs, eds, *Navigating the Rapids: from the Papers of Adolf A. Berle* (New York: Harcourt Brace Jovanovitch, 1973), pp. 725, 726; see also p. 695.
5. Ibid., pp. 768-769; on Tio Luz see Thomas W. Walker, *Nicaragua: The Land of Sandino* (Boulder, CO: Westview Press, 1981), p. 89, and United States, House, *Rethinking United States Foreign Policy Toward the Developing World: Nicaragua*, p. 8; see ibid. for US aid funds being used to build roads to Somoza properties.
6. Millett, *Guardians*, p. 226; Diederich, *Somoza*, pp. 68, 74.
7. Berle and Jacobs, *Navigating the Rapids*, pp. 745, 819.
8. Wheelock R., *Imperialismo y Dictadura*, p. 128; United States, House, *Rethinking United States Foreign Policy*, p. 17; Henri Weber, *Nicaragua: The Sandinist Revolution* (London: Verso Editions and NLB, 1981), pp. 28-29.
9. For the history and functioning of the Central American Common Market, see Susanne Jonas, "Masterminding the Mini-Market: U.S. Aid to the Central American Common Market," *NACLA's Latin America and Empire Report*, 7:6 (July-August 1973), pp. 3-18; see also Wheelock R., *Imperialismo y Dictadura*, p. 128.
10. David Tobis, "The U.S. Investment Bubble in Central America," *NACLA's Latin America and Empire Report*, 7:6 (July-August 1973), pp. 27, 35; Susanne Jonas, "Nicaragua," ibid., 10:2 (February 1976), app., pp. 36-38.
11. Jonas, "Masterminding the Mini-Market," p. 13; Wheelock R., *Imperialismo y Dictadura*, pp. 128n, 129n; Diederich, *Somoza*, p. 76.
12. World Bank, *Nicaragua: The Challenge of Reconstruction* (Washington, DC: The World Bank, 1981), p. 86; Wheelock R., *Imperialismo y Dictadura*, p. 129; Weber, *Nicaragua*, p. 26.
13. Wheelock R., *Imperialismo y Dictadura*, p. 126n; United States, House, *Rethinking United States Foreign Policy*, pp. 16, 17; ECLA table repr. in Weber, *Nicaragua*, p. 27; Jerome Levinson and Juan de Onis, *The Alliance That Lost Its Way: A Critical Report on the Alliance for Progress* (Chicago: Quadrangle Books, 1970), passim.
14. Ibid., p. 219.
15. Ibid., p. 308.
16. Ibid., pp. 137 (chart), 139, 134.
17. *Miami Herald*, September 30, 1967, p. 6A; the section on CONDECA and counterinsurgency is based on "Integrating the Big Guns," *NACLA's Latin America and Empire Report*, VII:6 (July-August 1973), pp. 22-26, United States, House, *Human Rights in Nicaragua, Guatemala and El Salvador: Implications for U.S. Policy*, hearings before the Committee on International Relations, 94 Cong., 2 Sess. (Washington, DC: USGPO, 1976), statement of Don L. Etchison, pp. 124-131, and Millett, *Guardians*, pp. 227, 229-230.

18. United States, House, *Foreign Assistance Act of 1967,* hearings before the Committee on Foreign Affairs, 90 Cong., 1 Sess. (Washington DC: USGPO, 1967), pt. III, p. 536.

19. Millett, *Guardians,* p. 228.

20. Ibid.; Diederich, *Somoza,* p. 75.

21. Ibid., p. 78; Millett, *Guardians,* pp. 229-230.

22. Diederich, *Somoza,* p. 81; see also pp. 79-80, and Millett, *Guardians,* p. 229.

23. Ibid., pp. 230, 232, 234.

24. Except as otherwise noted, material on the earthquake is from Diederich, *Somoza,* pp. 93-96, 100, 102, *New York Times,* January 2, 1973, p. 1, March 23, 1977, p. 10, Jack Anderson's columns in the *Washington Post,* August 2, 1975, p. D15, July 6, 1976, p. C17, and R.W. Kates, et al, "Human Impact of the Managua Earthquake," *Science,* 182 (December 7, 1973): 981-990.

25. *Time,* January 15, 1973, p. 29; Jack Anderson in the *Washington Post,* March 20, 1975, p. F25, March 31, 1975, p. D11; Diederich, *Somoza,* p. 105.

26. Shelton is quoted by Alan Riding in the *New York Times,* August 11, 1975, p. 3; see also Diederich, *Somoza,* p. 88; a photo of the 20 córdoba note is in EPICA Task Force, *Nicaragua: A People's Revolution* (Washington, DC: EPICA, 1980), p. 6.

27. Jonas, "Nicaragua," pp. 17, 19; Diederich, *Somoza,* pp. 90, 116; Millett, *Guardians,* p. 237.

28. *New York Times,* April 30, 1973, p. 12.

29. Diederich, *Somoza,* p. 104.

30. Alan Riding in the *New York Times,* January 3, 1975, p. 4. See Diederich, *Somoza,* pp. 106-114, for a good account of the Christmas party raid.

31. Ortega S., *50 Años,* p. 148.

32. Ibid., pp. 142-143.

33. Material on Fonseca and the formation of the FSLN is from ibid., pp. 17, 148-154, 187, and Diederich, *Somoza,* pp. 68-69, 85.

34. See Macaulay, *Sandino Affair,* pp. 262-263. Macaulay, a former US Army officer, had fought with the 26th of July Movement in Cuba, but later turned against the Cuban Revolution.

35. Ortega S., *50 Años,* pp. 165-166.

36. The Capuchins' letter is in United States, House, *Human Rights in Nicaragua,* app. 7, pp. 238-244; the pastoral letter is quoted by Alan Riding in the *New York Times,* March 2, 1977, pp. 1, 9; see also the *Washington Post,* August 16, 1977, p. A12, and *Time,* March 14, 1977, pp. 29-30.

37. Diederich, *Somoza,* p. 122.

38. Ibid., p. 120; see also Alan Riding's analysis in the *New York Times,* March 2, 1977, pp. 1, 9.

39. The quote on the replacement of Shelton is from ibid., August 11, 1975, p. 3; see also Diederich, *Somoza,* p. 116.

40. *New York Times,* August 11, 1975, p. 3; see also Jonas, "Nicaragua," p. 19, and Ortega S., *50 Años,* p. 101.

41. Interview with Marta Harnecker, published as an introduction to ibid., pp. 21-22.

42. Jack Anderson in the *Washington Post,* July 6, 1976, p. C17; Theberge letter in ibid., October 22, 1977, p. A20.

43. *New York Times,* July 29, 1977, p. A5; the Theberge quote is from *Time,* March 14, 1977, p. 30.

44. *Washington Post,* August 31, 1977, p. A20, June 22, 1977, p. A22, September 20, 1977, p. A15, September 29, 1977, p. A3.

45. Karen DeYoung in ibid., October 5, 1977, p. A10. The Christopher quote is from ibid., October 24, 1977, p. A8.

46. Diederich, *Somoza,* p. 149.

47. Material on the Sandinista offensive is from Marta Harnecker interview with Humberto

Ortega, in Ortega S., *50 Años,* pp. 19, 21-22, 27-28.

48. Diederich, *Somoza,* pp. 148-150.
49. Ibid., pp. 157-158.
50. The State Department report on Nicaragua is in United States, House, *Foreign Assistance Legislation for Fiscal Year 1979,* hearings before the Subcommittee on International Organizations, 95 Cong., 2 Sess. (Washington, DC: USGPO, 1978), p. 85; Shelton's testimony is from ibid., pp. 126-127.
51. Ibid., pp. 128, 130-131.
52. *New York Times,* February 7, 1978, p. A3, March 5, 1978, p. A14.
53. New York Times News Service dispatches, September 21, 1978 and October 15, 1978. The *Times* was then on strike, but the News Service copy is on *Times* microfilm for dates indicated; Diederich, *Somoza,* p. 216.
54. *Washington Post,* May 16, 1978, p. A1; *New York Times,* May 12, 1978, p. 10; the editorial quoted is in ibid., June 22, 1978, p. 22.
55. A DeYoung interview (apparently unpublished) of February 1978 is quoted in Diederich, *Somoza,* p. 165; Alan Riding is in *New York Times,* March 5, 1978, p. A14.
56. *Washington Post,* August 1, 1978, pp. A1, A9.
57. Ibid., August 3, 1978, p. A22.
58. Diederich, *Somoza,* pp. 176-188, has a good account of the National Palace action; the Pastora quote is from an interview with Tad Szulc in the *Washington Post,* September 3, 1978, p. C4.
59. Carl J. Migdail, "Nicaragua: Cuba All Over Again," *US News and World Report,* September 11, 1978, p. 37.
60. *Washington Post,* September 27, 1978, p. A22.
61. Diederich, *Somoza,* p. 207.
62. The plan and the quote are from the New York Times News Service, October 15, 1978, p. 9 (see note 53 above). Riding is in the *New York Times,* December 17, 1978, IV:3; see also ibid., November 16, 1978, p. A3., December 11, 1978, p. A3.
63. Ibid., November 16, 1978, p. A3; June 19, 1979, p. A13; the Conservative leader is quoted by Diederich, *Somoza,* p. 196; the "last Marine" quote is from *Time,* September 25, 1978, p. 32.
64. *New York Times,* December 17, 1978, IV:3; the quote is from Diederich, *Somoza,* p. 221.
65. The quotes are from Alan Riding in *New York Times,* December 17, 1978, IV:3; see also Diederich, *Somoza,* pp. 211-213.
66. *New York Times,* June 27, 1979, p. A3, July 1, 1979, IV:3; William M. LeoGrande, "The Revolution in Nicaragua: Another Cuba?" *Foreign Affairs,* 58:1 (Fall 1979), p. 35; *Washington Post,* July 7, 1979, p. A1.
67. *New York Times,* June 22, 1979, pp. A1, A8.
68. Ibid.; ibid., June 23, 1979, pp. A1, A3.
69. Ibid.
70. The Vaky quote is from United States, House, *United States Policy Toward Nicaragua,* hearings before the Subcommittee on Inter-American Affairs, 96 Cong., 1 Sess. (Washington, DC: USGPO, 1979), pp. 33, 34; the intelligence report is quoted in the *New York Times,* July 4, 1979, p. A3; Riding is in ibid., June 27, 1979, p. A3.
71. Ibid., June 29, 1979, pp. A1, A6.
72. Ibid.; the officials are quoted in ibid., June 28, 1979, p. A3.
73. Alan Riding in ibid., July 2, 1979, p. A3; Stephen Kinzer in the *Washington Post,* July 1, 1979, p. A27.
74. The quotes are from ibid., and from Riding in the *New York Times,* July 2, 1979, p. A3 and July 6, 1979, p. A3, and Warren Hoge in ibid., July 14, 1979, p. A4; see also ibid., July 10, 1979, p. A3, and the *Washington Post,* July 7, 1979, p. A1.
75. United States, House, *United States Policy Toward Nicaragua,* p. 44; Karen DeYoung in the *Washington Post,* July 10, 1979, p. A2.

76. Alan Riding in the *New York Times*, July 10, 1979, p. A3. Obando y Bravo is quoted in Diederich, *Somoza*, p. 298.
77. *New York Times*, July 11, 1979, p. A20.
78. *Washington Post*, July 12, 1979, p. A21; Organization of American States, *Report on the Situation of Human Rights in the Republic of Nicaragua* (Washington, DC: OAS, 1981), pp. 3-7.
79. For the final days of the regime and the failure of the peace plan see ibid., pp. 7-9, and Diederich, *Somoza*, pp. 318-321.

CHAPTER XIII. NATIONAL INTERESTS

1. See Jeane Kirkpatrick, "Dictatorships and Double Standards," *Commentary*, 68:5 (November 1979), pp. 34, 42; Sorensen is quoted by Mary McGrory in *Washington Post*, April 14, 1985, p. B5.
2. The Vaky quotes are from Viron Vaky, "Central America at the Crossroads," *Department of State Bulletin*, January 1980, p. 60.
3. Ibid., p. 69; see also United States, House, *Assessment of Conditions in Central America*, hearings before the Committee on Foreign Affairs, 96 Cong., 2 Sess. (Washington, DC: USGPO, 1980), pp. 64-65.
4. Pezzullo is in ibid., pp. 66, 65, 70; Vaky is from Vaky, "Central America at the Crossroads," p. 65.
5. See Kirkpatrick, "Dictatorships and Double Standards," passim.
6. United States, House, *Central America at the Crossroads*, hearings before the Subcommittee on Inter-American Affairs, 96 Cong., 1 Sess. (Washington, DC: USGPO, 1979), pp. 24-25.
7. *New York Times*, February 23, 1980, p. A2.
8. Ibid., September 4, 1980, p. A6, September 13, 1980, p. 2, June 18, 1980, p. A7.
9. On Carter's certification, see United States, House, *Review of the Presidential Certification of Nicaragua's Connection to Terrorism*, hearings before the Subcommittee on Inter-American Affairs, 96 Cong., 2 Sess. (Washington, DC: USGPO, 1980), pp. 1, 25; *New York Times*, September 13, 1980, p. 2.
10. Ibid., January 23, 1981, p. A3; February 11, 1981, p. A4.
11. The 1980 Republican platform is excerpted in ibid., July 13, 1980, p. 14.
12. *Department of State Bulletin*, May 1981, p. 71; *New York Times*, February 11, 1981, p. A4.
13. See "Communist Interference in El Salvador," *Department of State Bulletin*, March 1981, pp. 1-7.
14. See Jonathan Kwitny in *Wall Street Journal*, June 8, 1981, p. 1.
15. Ibid.
16. United States, Department of State and Department of Defense, *The Soviet-Cuban Connection in Central America and the Caribbean* (Washington, DC: Departments of State and Defense, 1985), p. 34.
17. United States, Department of State and Department of Defense, *Background Paper: Nicaragua's Military Build-up and Support for Central American Subversion* (Washington, DC: Departments of State and Defense, 1984); the Bolaños Hunter quote is from p. 26.
18. See United States, Congress, Arms Control and Foreign Policy Caucus, "Who are the Contras," repr. as App. 2 of Reed Brody, *Contra Terror in Nicaragua* (Boston: South End Press, 1985). On the role of former National Guardsmen in the formation of the contras, see "A Secret War for Nicaragua," *Newsweek*, November 8, 1982, pp. 42ff. On human rights violations, see Brody, *Contra Terror*, and Americas Watch Committee, *Violations of the Laws of War by Both Sides in Nicaragua 1981-1985* (New York: Americas Watch, 1985).

19. See, for example, the *Washington Post,* October 21, 1983, p. A27; the figure on contra aid is from "Honduras: U.S. Military Activities," *Congressional Research Service Issue Brief* (Washington, DC: CRS, 1985), p. 3.
20. The speech is quoted in the *New York Times,* February 17, 1985, p. 1.
21. Philip Taubman in the *New York Times,* November 14, 1984, p. A10.
22. The text of Reagan's February 21, 1985 news conference is in ibid., February 22, 1985, p. A14.
23. United States, House, *Foreign Assistance Act of 1968,* hearings before the Committee on Foreign Affairs, 90 Cong., 2 Sess. (Washington, DC: USGPO, 1968), Pt. V, pp. 844-845.
24. United States, Departments of State and Defense, *The Soviet-Cuban Connection,* passim; the quote is from p. 6.
25. *New York Times,* March 30, 1985, p. 5.
26. United States, Departments of State and Defense, *The Soviet-Cuban Connection,* p. 20.
27. Ibid., p. 2.
28. Ibid., p. 28.
29. *Washington Post,* October 4, 1983, p. A10.
30. *New York Times,* March 30, 1985, p. 5.
31. *Washington Post,* April 19, 1985, p. A28; *New York Times,* March 30, 1985, p. 5.
32. United States, Departments of State and Defense, *The Soviet-Cuban Connection,* p. 19.
33. The text of the Plan to Achieve Peace as well as the message transmitting it are in OAS, *Report on the Situation of Human Rights in the Republic of Nicaragua,* pp. 4-7.
34. Ibid., p. 2.
35. See Chapter XII.
36. OAS, *Report on the Situation of Human Rights,* pp. 135-136.
37. See ibid., pp. 1, 168-171. For comparision see Organization of American States, *Report on the Situation of Human Rights in the Republic of Guatemala* (Washington, DC: OAS, 1981).
38. OAS, *Report on the Situation of Human Rights in Nicaragua,* p. 139; Consejo Supremo Electoral, *Republic of Nicaragua Electoral Law, Law of Political Parties, Regulations of Political Parties* (Managua: Consejo Supremo Electoral, English ed., 1984).
39. The quote is from Philip Taubman in the *New York Times,* October 21, 1984, p. 12; on the CIA payments to Cruz, see *Wall Street Journal,* April 23, 1985, p. 64.
40. Material on the elections is based on the author's interviews and first-hand observations during the election campaign. Many of these are published in Karl Bermann and Glen Fiscella, *Nicaragua Votes: A Special Report by the Tidewater Nicaragua Project Foundation* (Hampton, VA: Tidewater Nicaragua Project Foundation, 1984). A longer and more detailed report, containing extensive documentation on the sources and nature of the early disruptions of campaign activities and other complaints, and reaching similar conclusions, is Latin American Studies Association, *The Electoral Process in Nicaragua: Domestic and International Influences,* (Austin, TX: LASA, 1984).
41. Author's interview with Clemente Guido, October 1984.
42. Bermann and Fiscella, *Nicaragua Votes,* p. 4.
43. Letter to the US minister to Mexico, in J. Reuben Clark, *Memorandum on the Monroe Doctrine* (Washington DC: USGPO, 1930), p. 106.
44. Instruction to the US minister to Britain, July 20, 1895, in *FR, 1895,* I:558.
45. Robert Olds, "Memorandum on the Nicaraguan Situation," DS 817.00/5854, NA microfilm M632, Roll 41.
46. Henry L. Stimson Diaries, X:145, 244 (microfilm edition, reel 2).
47. W.W. Cumberland, *Nicaragua, An Economic and Financial Survey* (Washington DC: USGPO, 1928), p. 15.
48. International Bank for Reconstruction and Development, *The Economic Development of Nicaragua* (Baltimore: Johns Hopkins Press, 1953), p. 3; *Business Week,* February

27, 1978, p. 44.

49. From a UN survey cited in Fidel Castro, *The World Economic and Social Crisis: Report to the Seventh Summit of Non-Aligned Countries* (Havana: Publishing Office of the Council of State, 1983), p. 64.

50. United Nations, *World Economic Survey, 1984* (New York: UN, 1985), p. 14; United Nations, *World Economic Survey, 1983* (New York: UN, 1984), p. 51; the per capita debt figure is based on data in Organisation for Economic Co-operation and Development, *External Debt of Developing Countries, 1983 Survey* (Paris: OECD, 1984), p. 83.

51. Based on data in United Nations, *World Economic Survey, 1981-1982* (New York: UN, 1983), p. 66.

52. Richard J. Barnet and Ronald E. Muller, *Global Reach: The Power of the Multinational Corporations* (New York: Simon and Schuster, 1974), pp. 127, 132, 138, 152-153, 155, 157, 158-159, 162; Peggy B. Musgrave, *Direct Investment Abroad and the Multinationals: Effects on the United States Economy,* a committee print of the Senate Committee on Foreign Relations, 94 Cong., 1 Sess. (Washington, DC: USGPO, 1975), p. 12 (table).

53. Barnet and Muller, *Global Reach,* p. 156; Castro, *World Economic and Social Crisis,* p. 61; for an analysis of how the IMF is used to maintain the economic status quo, see Cheryl Payer, *The Debt Trap: The International Monetary Fund and the Third World* (New York: Monthly Review Press, 1974), especially pp. 22-49.

54. See Bayardo Arce, *Romper La Dependencia, Tarea Estratégica de la Revolución* (Managua: FSLN, 1980), passim.

55. The Reagan quote is from a radio address of March 30, 1985. The text is in *Department of State Bulletin,* June 1985, pp. 11-12.

56. *Washington Post,* October 21, 1983, p. 1.

57. See *Wall Street Journal,* April 3, 1985, p. 1, the *Washington Post,* March 24, 1985, p. A1, and *New York Times,* August 7, 1983, p. E1.

58. Reagan radio address, March 30, 1985.

59. *Report of the National Bipartisan Commission on Central America* (Washington, DC: USGPO, 1984), p. 12.

60. The *Washington Post,* January 17, 1984, p. A11, for example, reported that the US was withholding rice and wheat from Bolivia, where people were starving, until the government agreed to eliminate domestic price subsidies. The "democratic revolution" phrase is from United States, Departments of State and Defense, *The Soviet-Cuban Connection,* p. 31.

INDEX